RESPONSIBILITY, LAW AND THE FAMILY

Responsibility, Law and the Family

Edited by

JO BRIDGEMAN, HEATHER KEATING and CRAIG LIND
University of Sussex, UK

Routledge
Taylor & Francis Group
LONDON AND NEW YORK

First published 2008 by Ashgate Publishing

Published 2016 by Routledge
2 Park Square, Milton Park, Abingdon, Oxfordshire OX14 4RN
711 Third Avenue, New York, NY 10017, USA

First issued in paperback 2016

Routledge is an imprint of the Taylor & Francis Group, an informa business

British Library Cataloguing in Publication Data
Responsibility, law and the family
1. Parent and child (Law) - England 2. Parent and child
(Law) - Wales 3. Responsibility 4. Parenting - Government
policy - England 5. Parenting - Government policy - Wales
I. Bridgeman, Jo II. Lind, Craig III. Keating, Heather M.
346.4'2017

Library of Congress Cataloging in Publication Data
Responsibility, law, and the family / [edited] by Jo Bridgeman, Craig Lind, and Heather Keating.
p. cm.
Includes index.
ISBN 978-0-7546-7109-1
1. Parent and child (Law)--England. 2. Parent and child (Law)--Wales. 3. Responsibility. 4. Parenting--Government policy--England. 5. Parenting--Government policy--Wales. I. Bridgeman, Jo. II. Lind, Craig. III. Keating, Heather M.

KD772.R47 2008
346.4201'7--dc22

2008010606

ISBN 13: 978-1-138-27052-7 (pbk)
ISBN 13: 978-0-7546-7109-1 (hbk)

Contents

List of Contributors

Jo Bridgeman is a senior lecturer in the Sussex Law School, University of Sussex. She is a founder member of the child and family research group and the Centre for Responsibilities, Rights and the Law. Jo has researched and published in books and journals in the field of healthcare law and the law regulating the care of children. This includes work on the healthcare of teenagers, a range of publications analysing the issues arising from the Bristol Royal Infirmary Inquiry and a monograph which offers a critical analysis of moral, social and legal responsibilities for the healthcare of babies, infants and young children, *Parental Responsibility, Young Children and Healthcare Law* (2007). It is in this latest work that she has commenced analysis, adopting a critical feminist perspective informed by, and developing, the feminist ethic of care, of the moral, social and legal responsibilities of parents, professionals and the state to children. Her current research in relation to the legal regulation of care, draws upon the feminist ethic of care in order to develop a conceptual framework of relational responsibility.

Harriet Churchill is a lecturer in public and social policy at the University of Manchester and is an associate lecturer with the Open University. Previously, she has worked as a research fellow with the ESRC Care, Values and the Future of Welfare Research Group at the University of Leeds (2003-2005) and gained her PhD on *Lone Motherhood, Paid Work and Welfare Reform* in 2004 from Oxford Brookes University. Harriet's research includes cultural materialist theories of social change, contemporary family practices and parent/child relations, families and social exclusion, family policy, programme evaluation and qualitative research methods. She has published book chapters and articles on lone mothers' agency and identity as paid workers and mothers; including service users in social policy making; and, reflecting on the PhD research process, Harriet is also co-author of *Getting Your PhD: A Practical Insider's Guide* (with T. Sanders 2007). Harriet is currently undertaking a pilot evaluation of parent education programmes for parents with adolescents (with Karen Clarke, University of Manchester) and is the author of two forthcoming books with Policy Press – *Active Citizenship, Families and Welfare Reform* and *Governance and the Welfare State* (with Kirstein Rummery, University of Stirling).

Richard Collier is Professor of Law at the University of Newcastle. His primary research interests concern questions around law and gender, with a particular focus on issues surrounding men and masculinities, ranging from family law and social change to legal education, crime and criminology. He has published widely in these and other fields and Richard has recently been the recipient of the British Academy

'Thank-offering to Britain' Fellowship (January 2007-January 2008) for a project entitled 'The Fathers' Rights Movement and Law Reform: The UK Experience'. His books include *Masculinity, Law and the Family* (1995), *Masculinities, Crime and Criminology: Men, Corporeality and the Criminal(ised) Body* (1998), *Fathers' Rights Activism and Law Reform in Comparative Perspective* (edited with Sally Sheldon 2007) and *Fragmenting Fatherhood: A Socio-Legal Study* (with Sally Sheldon 2008). He is presently completing the book, *Learned Friends, Gentlemen Scholars: Essays on Law, Men and Gender*. Richard has presented a wide range of international plenary and keynote addresses and has most recently been a visiting fellow at Emory University Law School, the University of Florida and the Socio-Legal Research Centre, Griffith University. Richard is an editorial board member of *Social and Legal Studies.*

Alison Diduck teaches law at UCL. Her research interests are in the fields of child and family law, legal theory, gender issues and feminist perspectives in law, and legal history. Alison has published work on the legal treatment of motherhood, families and children, on the legal regulation of family forms, family property issues, and family care responsibilities, on feminist approaches to understanding legal personality and legal obligation and on socio-legal and historical perspectives on family and gender issues. She is the author of *Law's Families* (2003), is co-author, with Felicity Kaganas, of *Family Law, Gender and the State* (1st ed., 1999 and 2nd ed., 2006), and is co-editor, with Katherine O'Donovan, of *Feminist Perspectives on Family Law* (2006). Alison is currently doing research on feminist perspectives on law's treatment of personal and social relationships.

Michael Freeman is Professor of English Law and Fellow at UCL, where he has taught since 1969. His books include *The Rights and Wrongs of Children*; *Children, Their Families and the Law*; *The Moral Status of Children*; *Understanding Family Law*; and several editions of Lloyd's *Introduction to Jurisprudence*. He is the editor of the *International Journal of Law in Context* (with Carrie Menkel-Meadow) and of the *International Journal of Children's Rights*. He edited *Current Legal Problems* for 12 years. He is also the General Editor of *Medicine, Ethics and the Law* and of *Family, Society and Law* (his volume on *Domestic Violence* is forthcoming). He teaches Family Law, Medicine, Ethics and Law, Jurisprudence, Conflict of Laws and Children and their Rights. He has published on subjects as diverse as immigration control, police powers, statutory construction, cultural pluralism, and the jury.

Jonathan Herring is a Fellow at Exeter College, Oxford and Lecturer in Law at Oxford University. He is the author of *Family Law* (Pearson), currently in its third edition. He has also written *Criminal Law* (5th ed., 2007); *Criminal Law: Text Cases and Materials* (3rd ed., 2008); and *Medical Law and Ethics* (2006). He has written a large number of articles covering issues including children's rights; intersex conditions; domestic violence; ownership of the body; and sexual offence. He is currently working on a book on law and older people.

Adrian James qualified as a social worker in 1970 and worked in the probation service for eight years. He joined the University of Hull in 1978 where he developed his research interests in the field of socio-legal studies, incorporating family law and criminal justice policy. He has researched and published widely in both of these areas, including the completion of two major ESRC-funded projects on aspects of child welfare in family proceedings, as well as various projects funded by the Home Office, the Prison Department and the Legal Services Commission. He was a Special Adviser to the House of Commons Select Committee that examined the work of the Lord Chancellor's Department and CAFCASS in 2003.

He was appointed as Professor of Applied Social Sciences at the University of Bradford in 1998 and Professor of Social Work at the University of Sheffield in 2004. In 2005, he was also appointed as Professor II at the Norwegian Centre for Child Research, University of Trondheim. His latest major publications are *Constructing Childhood: Theory, Policy and Social Practice*, written jointly with Allison James (2004); *The Politics of Childhood: International Perspectives, Contemporary Developments*, edited with J. Goddard, A. James and S. McNamee (2004); and the third edition of *The Child Protection Handbook*, edited with Kate Wilson (2007). Forthcoming books include *European Childhoods: Cultures, Politics and Participation*, edited with A. James and *Key Concepts in Childhood Studies*, with A. James.

Heather Keating is Senior Lecturer in Law at the Sussex Law School, University of Sussex. She is co-author (with Chris Clarkson and Sally Cunningham) of *Criminal Law: Text and Materials* (6th ed., 2007). She has also written widely on issues relating to criminal law and child law and her research now focuses upon children and the criminal law. She was co-editor (with Craig Lind) of a special issue of the *Journal of Law and Society*, *Children, Family Responsibilities and the State*, published in March 2008 which was simultaneously published by Blackwell as a book. Her next project is a monograph on children and the criminal law.

Craig Lind holds law degrees from the University of the Witwatersrand (in Johannesburg) and the London School of Economics. He has taught at the University of the Witwatersrand, the University of Wales in Aberystwyth and is now a senior lecturer in law at the University of Sussex in Brighton. He teaches (amongst other subjects) Family Law and Constitutional Law. He also teaches courses in Family and Child Law on a Masters programme aimed at exploring the legal regulation of family responsibility. His major research interests lie in the areas of family law and sexuality and have a strong cultural focus and a comparative slant. He is currently completing a book, *A Global Family Law?*, in which he explores the relationship between culture, sexuality and the legal regulation of the family.

Virginia Morrow is Reader in Childhood Studies at the Institute of Education, University of London where she is course organiser of the MA Childhood Studies, based on the sociology of childhood and children's rights. Children and young people have been the focus of her research activities since 1988. Her main research interests are methods and ethics of social research with children; sociology of childhood and children's rights; social capital in relation to children and young people; child labour and children's work; and children's understandings of family and other social environments. She is the author of numerous papers and reports including *Networks and neighbourhoods: Children's and Young People's Perspectives* (2002), and she is an editor of *Childhood: A Global Journal of Child Research.*

Amanda Wade's interests are in the field of exploratory qualitative social research, particularly that involving memory, biography and narrative, and dealing with family life and childhood. She has undertaken research (with colleagues at the former Centre for Research on Family, Kinship and Childhood at the University of Leeds) on children's experiences of parental separation and divorce, and is now teaching in the Department of Sociological Studies at the University of Sheffield.

John Williams is Professor of Law in the Department of Law and Criminology at Aberystwyth University. His teaching interests are Family and Child Law, Medicine, Ethics and the Law, Crime and Psychology, and Welfare Law. For a number of years he has been researching on the impact of the law on vulnerable adults, with particular reference to older people. Currently, he is working in the area of older people within the prison system. A central theme of his research is that ageism is endemic and that at present the law does very little to protect the interests of older people. In 2002, he presented written and oral evidence to the House of Lords/House of Commons Joint Committee on the Draft Mental Incapacity Bill. In addition to academic teaching and research, he provides legal professional training for social care workers, health professionals and the voluntary sector. John is a member of the Welsh Consumer Council, CAFCASS Cymru, the Standing Committee on Legal Wales and Citizens Advice Cymru. Since 2006, he has been a trustee for Help the Aged UK. John has also worked with the British Psychological Society in drafting their new Code of Professional Conduct.

Preface

The idea for this book arose from a symposium, organised by the Law School's Child and Family Research Group, held at the University of Sussex one beautiful September day in 2005, which brought together philosophers, sociologists and lawyers to explore *Responsibility and the Family*. The interesting and lively discussion which occurred amongst the participants confirmed our view that there is a lot of thinking to be done and much that is interesting to be said about responsibility in family life and family law. Many of the papers delivered then are published in this book which commences the process of exploring the distinctive nature of family responsibility. Our second symposium, the following September, focused upon *State Responsibility for the Family*, the papers from which were published in a special issue of the *Journal of Law and Society* (co-edited by Heather Keating and Craig Lind), *Children, Family Responsibilities and the State* (simultaneously published as an edited collection by Blackwell, 2008).

At Sussex we have developed this research project further with an international, interdisciplinary conference on *Gender, Family Responsibility and Legal Change*, held under the auspices of the Centre for Responsibility, Rights and the Law, in July 2008. It is our aim that this book contributes to the development of understanding of, and encourages wider debate and discussion about the nature of, family responsibility.

Jo Bridgeman, Heather Keating, Craig Lind
Centre for Responsibility, Rights and the Law
Sussex Law School
University of Sussex

30 January 2008

Chapter 1

Introduction: Conceptualising Family Responsibility

Jo Bridgeman and Heather Keating

Introduction

Responsibility, like rights, duties, obligations, justice and fairness, is a concept employed by the law in the ordering, regulation and resolution of conflicts in human life. This book contributes to analysis of responsibility, in which there is currently a renewed interest amongst politicians, in law and in academic research. At the same time, as a term employed by family members to describe the nature of their relationships with one another, responsibility is a concept employed in the ordering and negotiation of family relationships. Yet, it is only recently that its application to family law has begun to be examined. The aim of this book is to advance a process of conceptualising responsibility in family life, law and practice from sociological, legal and socio-legal perspectives.

Responsibility is a concept with many different meanings ranging across accountability, answerability, responsibility for, responsible behaviour, being made to take responsibility or as a corollary to rights. This introductory chapter examines the development of the discourse on family responsibility by exploring the moral, social and legal theorisation of the concept of responsibility. We start by considering 'traditional' approaches to responsibility (within liberal theory) that centre upon capacity and conduct (especially in relation to criminal behaviour) and then examine post-liberal conceptualisations of responsibility found in communitarian thought. Our introduction concludes by exploring some of the themes which emerge from the rich variety of material on responsibility in the chapters which follow. But, first, a few words about the family.

Conceptualising Family

In this book we have chosen to use the commonplace label, 'family', to identify the boundaries of our undertaking. The vast majority of us have experienced 'family' life and continue to live within our families. We know what this concept means to us. However, as many writers have commented, as a concept it is far from simple. What it encapsulates has varied over time and differs between, and within, cultures. As Douglas has commented,

> the family may be constructed from a variety of perspectives including the genetic, focusing upon the blood-tie; social, emphasizing the functions carried out by those standing in a family relationship to each other; psychological, exploring the ties of affect and emotion between individuals; legal, defining the family for the purposes of legally binding decisions and rules; and ideological, promoting a particular form of family structure and behaviour as the desirable norms. … It can follow that differing notions of what is meant by the family may be masked by an assumption that we are all talking about the same thing and from the same perspective. (Douglas 2004, 2)

We take this warning seriously (for example, Diduck in this book); each interpretation of the family does, indeed, come with 'a baggage of competing values' (Douglas 2004, 1). And, if the concept of 'family' is dynamic, contested and capable of being misunderstood or manipulated, the concept of 'family law' is likewise problematic. What is family law about? And is 'family law' the best label to employ?

Douglas has rightly stated that 'the essence of family law is that part of the law which is concerned with the recognition [and non-recognition] and regulation of certain family relationships and the implications of such recognition' (Douglas 2004, 3). As such, 'the boundaries of family law are no more static than those of the family' (Probert 2004, 903). Politicians (and the advertising industry) may still hold dear the 'cornflake packet' ideal of the family (of married, heterosexual parents with children) but there has been acknowledgment, and increasing recognition, of the diversity of forms families may take. The interrelationship between 'family law' and the 'family' or 'families' is itself problematic. One view is that

> family law itself really hasn't changed; it has simply extended its remit to permit a wider range of people and relationships within it. Another view, however, is that family law has not so much responded to social change as it has participated in it. Expanding family law may have helped to facilitate changing family practices and new "personal familiarities". (Diduck in this book, 252)

It is beyond the remit of this introductory chapter to explore fully the changing shape of family law – many of the chapters in this book contribute to that endeavour – but before leaving the question of what is family law, three further inter-related points should be noted. First, the extent to which and the ways in which governments choose to recognise and regulate family life are political decisions based on ideological and pragmatic considerations. Such decisions are made as part of a rich – but non-uniform and indeed chaotic (Dewar 1998) – tapestry woven together from threads of intervention and privacy. Secondly, securing the appropriate balance between state intervention and respect for the privacy of the family (and individuals within families) is at the heart of family law – and is a recurring theme in this book. Finally, when it comes to the mode of intervention, the pattern shifts (over time and over issues) between a welfare (and thus, typically, discretion) based approach and a rights (and thus more typically rule) based approach. Into what has arguably become once again[1] a more rights based family law (Dewar 1998; Diduck in this book; Parker 1992), this book wishes to add a further strand: responsibility.

1 Parker has argued that early 'classical' family law was justified in terms of rights and duties and that this was replaced during the twentieth century by a concern to weigh

Before beginning to explore that concept a final word needs to be said about whether, in the face of the difficulties attaching to family and family law, some other phrase should be employed to convey the subject of this book. Eekelaar has suggested the phrase 'personal law' (Eekelaar 2006, ix) and Probert has commented that 'we should even consider re-adopting the term "the law of domestic relations"' (Probert 2004, 905). Other possibilities include 'dependency', 'caring' or 'intimate' relations or, more modestly, 'families' law'. Each of these has its merits but potential pitfalls as well. To say that our subject is 'personal law' might risk losing the essence of family life: interdependency (Diduck in this book); to use 'domestic relations' might be as much as a mixed blessing as it has been with 'domestic violence'. Have we really come so far as to free understandings of 'the domestic' from the association with the private and unregulated realm that it patently is not? 'Families' law' or 'the law of families' may come the closest to encapsulating the range of relations within what we understand and experience as families. However, it is not our endeavour to identify a concept which achieves this more successfully than 'family' and 'family law'. Like Alison Diduck, we believe that 'embedded within the pluralism and the tensions is the glimmer of a thread of normative consistency' (Diduck in this book, 254) based on interdependence, intimacy and care that a study of responsibility may help to draw out.

Conceptualising Responsibility

'Traditional' approaches to responsibility (within liberal theory)

Liberal theories of responsibility were developed predominantly within the framework of discussions about wrongful behaviour. At face value it seems more than a little strange to discuss 'responsibility' in the context of criminal or other wrongful behaviour: such actions are more likely (at least in media accounts) to be perceived as 'irresponsible' or 'out of control'. A 'responsible' person: 'one who is disposed to take his duties seriously' (Hart 1967, 348) would not, one could imagine, willingly behave in a wrongful manner. However, perhaps one of the most important of all features ascribed to the criminal law, at least, is that it is concerned with the actions of 'responsible' agents. So, 'responsible' agents do things that we might condemn as irresponsible. What, then, does it mean to be described as 'responsible' in this context and how does this relate to responsibility and the family?

This is a question that has long occupied the writings of criminal scholars and philosophers of such eminence as H.L.A. Hart, Anthony Honoré and, more recently, John Gardner. For theorists who adopt the agency model a common starting point is causation: 'the most basic element of responsibility' is that the actor *caused* the result (Hart 1967, 348; Tadros 2005, 22). But, of course, although the phrases 'to cause' and 'be responsible for' a result may be used interchangeably, they are not the same: we are not responsible for every result we cause. Thus, very young children

---

competing interests (by, for example, discretionary mechanisms such as the welfare principle) (Parker 1992). Dewar has argued that family law is now moving away from discretion (Dewar 1998).

or the legally insane may cause harm but not be held responsible. To be so held involves, according to Tadros, 'attribution-responsibility' (Tadros 2005, 22). The basis on which the harm caused by an actor can be 'attributed' to him or her derives from the meaning of the word responsibility itself. For example, Gardner has argued that responsibility in its 'basic' sense is an ability to respond (Gardner 2003, 161, and discussed in Keating's chapter); Duff expresses it in terms of 'being answerable' (Duff 2001, 184; see also Hart 1967, 363[2]); whilst for Tadros it is the ability to give an account of oneself (Tadros 2005, 25). The common thread here is that in order to be described as responsible, the agent must have rational reasons for acting. Gardner describes these as 'explanatory reasons' (which the agent is able to communicate) while Tadros prefers 'motivating reasons' (Gardner 1996; Tadros 2005, 28):

> Why should explanation in terms of motivating reasons ground the idea of responsibility? The obvious answer is that motivating reasons are constituents of agency. Insofar as an action is performed under the guidance of a motivating reason of the agent, it might be thought, that action is performed under the guidance of the agent. And that grounds the agent's responsibility for the action. … An agent is responsible for an action … insofar as that action reflects on the agent *qua* … agent. (Tadros 2005, 31, 44)

However, according to Tadros, an ability to provide reasons is insufficient for a 'full account of responsibility', which also includes being an appropriate target for the 'reactive attitudes'[3] (such as condemnation or approval, leading to blame or praise) of others (2005, 25). Both are central elements of a theory of responsibility. It should be noted that even if one is 'responsible' in this sense it does not follow that the agent is at fault or is subject to legal liability for what he or she has done (he or she may have, for example, a justification or excuse; Tadros 2005, 25; see further Gardner 1998); instead we are 'put on notice' (Tadros 2005, 25) that some kind of reactive attitude may be appropriate.

Beyond (broad) acceptance of the etymological significance of the word 'responsibility', theorists have proceeded to offer very different theories of criminal responsibility. Classical liberal accounts are underpinned by an acceptance of the value of autonomy: 'in a liberal society where political freedom is valued people must be free from criminal liability and punishment unless they "voluntarily" break the law in the sense of doing something that they can properly acknowledge as wrongdoing' (Clarkson and Keating 2007, 108 citing Williams 1997; Duff and von Hirsch 1997). This led Hart to develop the 'capacity' theory of responsibility:

> What is crucial is that those whom we punish should have had, when they acted, the normal capacities, physical and mental, for doing what the law requires and abstaining from what it forbids, and a fair opportunity to exercise those capacities. Where these capacities and opportunities are absent … the moral protest is that it is morally wrong to punish because "he could not have helped it" or "he could not have done otherwise" or "he had no real choice". (Hart 1968, 152)

---

2 Although for Hart this is not the 'primary' sense of responsibility, which is 'liability-responsibility' (Hart 1967, 368).

3 Drawing upon the work of Strawson (2003).

This theory has been of profound significance to generations of criminal lawyers (see, for example, Horder 2004) and is drawn upon by Heather Keating in her critique of government policy in relation to the criminal responsibility of children. However, this theory has also been subject to sustained criticism by, for example, those who (in varying degrees) challenge the idea of humans as freely choosing and acting beings.[4] More recently, Tadros, for example, has argued that 'neither capacity nor choice is central to the *attribution* of responsibility' (Tadros 2005, 46) although he does acknowledge that capacity is relevant to determining status-responsibility (so it is relevant to ask if a child has capacity for the purposes of criminal responsibility). Tadros and a number of other theorists prefer a 'character theory of responsibility'. An agent can only be criminally responsible for his or her behaviour if it is properly related to his or her character and is not 'out-of-character'. This involves introducing a temporal aspect to responsibility: 'When we are punished, we are punished as agents who persist over time. The character theory encourages criminal responsibility to consider the agent more broadly than at the moment of action, and thus is considered more likely to lead to just punishment' (Tadros 2005, 47; see also Gardner 1998; Lacey 1988). Character theorists also uphold the value of autonomy in the criminal law but do not accept that it is inextricably linked to choice as is the case with capacity theorists. Just as capacity theory has been challenged, so too has character theory: it has been argued that it amounts to punishing a person for what he *is* rather than what he *does* (although that is to over-simplify the theory). While it is probably true to say that character theory is growing in importance, capacity theory is far from being eclipsed.

The basis of much of the above work has been challenged by Cane on several levels, not all of which can be explored here but some of which should be noted for their implications for family law. First, Cane has argued that accounts of legal responsibility have tended to focus upon 'historic responsibility' at the expense of 'prospective responsibility'.[5] His view is that the law is just as much concerned with establishing prospective responsibilities ('what our responsibilities are') as with holding us to account for what we have done, or failed to do (2002, 31).[6] Secondly, Cane argues that while the agency-focused analysis of responsibility 'fits the contours of criminal responsibility reasonably well ... when we turn from criminal law to civil law – contract and tort [and, we would add, family law], for instance – the picture looks very different. ... Responsibility in civil law is always *to* someone as well as *for* something' (2002, 49-50). Cane offers an alternative perspective that focuses not upon human agency, but sees responsibility as a 'heterogeneous, context-specific practice and concept' (Cane 2002, 25).[7] For Cane, responsibility in

4 Cane argues that worries about whether our actions are determined need not stop us holding people responsible because, even if it were proved that our actions are not determined, our responsibility *practices* would remain 'more or less intact' (2002, 24).

5 Drawing on but not the same as Hart's 'role responsibility' (1967, 347).

6 Cane distinguishes between two types of prospective responsibilities; those that are directed at the *production* of good outcomes and those aimed at the *prevention* of bad outcomes (2002, 31).

7 Cane does not reject the modern, 'naturalistic' account of responsibility but claims 'that in the absence of agreement as to what the truth about responsibility is, social practice

law is a relational concept and practice, 'in the sense that it concerns the three-way relationship between agents, "victims" and the wider community' (2002, 56). Cane's *Responsibility in Law and Morality* extends beyond criminal law and tort to explore his taxonomy of responsibility in a range of areas of law but does not venture into family law. Clearly, there is much for the family lawyer to consider in an approach that sees responsibility as prospective, contextual and relational.

Post-liberal conceptualisations of responsibility: Communitarian thought

Alongside traditional ideas about responsibility, policies of the New Labour government on the family have been influenced by communitarian approaches to responsibility. In general terms, communitarianism responds to critiques of the individualism and universalism of liberal political theory. Communitarians, such as Amitai Etzioni, argue that the focus upon the dichotomy of the market (private sector) and the state (public sector) has been at the expense of consideration of the role of society. He argues that 'much of social conduct is, and that more ought to be, sustained and guided by an informal web of social bonds and by moral voices of the community' (Etzioni 1998, xii). In brief, communitarian thought recognises both the individuality and social connectedness of human beings; considers that protection of individual liberty requires recognition of both the self and of others (respect for self and others; personal and social responsibilities; individual rights and those of others; governance of self and others) and that the obligation of communities and the state is 'to be responsive to their members and to foster participation and deliberation in social and political life' (Etzioni 1998, xxv).

A fundamental tenet of communitarian thought is that individual rights need to be balanced with social responsibilities in order to create the conditions in which individuals can enjoy rights: 'ordered liberty requires communitarian foundations' (Etzioni 1995, 24). Importantly, communitarians do not advocate the erosion of individual liberty nor the replacement of rights with responsibilities, rather that the latter (community and responsibility) are necessary to support and sustain the former (freedom and rights):

> The exclusive pursuit of private interest erodes the network of social environments on which we all depend, and is destructive to our shared experiment in democratic self-government. For these reasons, we hold that the rights of individuals cannot long be preserved without a communitarian perspective. (Etzioni 1998, xxv)

Individuals are understood to be distinct entities but are also seen as members of communities (Etzioni 1995, 18). Each individual may belong to a number of communities – neighbourhood, religious, ethnic, workplace, professional or, importantly in our context, families. Thus, communities may link or overlap but will also be 'nested' within bigger communities (Etzioni 1995, 24-25).

One of the characteristics of a community is 'shared moral and social values' according to which individuals within communities are expected to behave (Etzioni

---

provides us with an extensive and extremely rich data set about responsibility'. Thus, his account is contextualised and concrete rather than abstract (2002, 279).

1995, 17; Etzioni 1998, 41-45). Values are not imposed upon individuals but are 'generated' by the community itself: they are passed down through generations and updated through a dialogue amongst community members to reflect changed conditions, circumstances and issues (Etzioni 1995, 17). Etzioni is of the view that there exist basic overarching values to which the values of each community must conform and that the bigger communities, within which the smaller communities are 'nested', offer the widely shared moral values (Etzioni 1995, 24-25, 28). Departure from community norms is censured by other members of the community in a process which reinforces shared community values and means that communities are self-regulating, limiting the need for intervention such as legal regulation (Etzioni 1996, 5).

Amitai Etzioni identifies how the very existence of individuals depends upon their communities, as does their liberty, but argues that the communities that sustain individuals need to be maintained by their members (Etzioni 1998, xxv):

> At the heart of the communitarian understanding of social justice is the idea of reciprocity: each member of the community owes something to all the rest, and the community owes something to each of its members. Justice requires responsible individuals in a responsive society. (Etzioni 1998, xxxiv)

The community is responsible for protecting all, meeting the basic needs of those who cannot provide for themselves, recognising the contributions of all, and providing opportunities for all. And individuals have a responsibility to work, to provide for themselves and their families, and for the well-being of others.

For communitarians, the family is an important community in which moral education and the nurturing of responsible individuals does, and should to an even greater extent, occur. Thus communitarian arguments, based on the view that children are best raised by two parents supported by the wider family, have been made for family policies which re-structure working arrangements so that both parents can contribute to the moral education of their children. And, whilst moral education should principally be the role of parents, they should be supported by institutions such as schools in the teaching of shared moral values (Etzioni 1998, xxvii-xxx).

There has been interesting analysis of the New Labour government's approach to youth justice and anti-social behaviour, influenced by the ideas of communitarian thought: in particular, the importance of parents in the moral education of their children and making parents take responsibility for their children's behaviour (Keating, in this book, and, for example, James and James 2001). However, as Laurence Koffman has argued,

> it seems that the numerous statements made by New Labour about parental responsibility are little more than an assertion of some generic moral responsibility to the community. This, in turn, is used to justify an onerous and far-reaching legal responsibility, and the imposition of punitive measures in the event of parental "failure". (Koffman 2008, 130)

Policies informed by a more considered reading of communitarian approaches to social responsibility, the moral education of children and the law would, we suggest, hesitate before using the law to impose coercive, punitive, remedial 'support' upon parents.

Helen Reece has developed this analysis beyond legislative developments in the criminal justice field to post-separation contact, applying the approach to the legal regulation of the parent/child relationship she earlier used to analyse Part II of the Family Law Act 1996 (Reece 2003; Reece 2006). Reece's argument is that, in contrast to liberal approaches to responsibility framed in terms of capacity, freely chosen actions and causation, post-liberal responsibility is conceived of in terms of responsible process (that of seeking advice) and responsible attitude (a willingness to learn). As such, she identifies a shift from parental authority to parental accountability. Likewise, Val Gillies has analysed family policies of the New Labour government directed at supporting parents which, she demonstrates, are aimed at securing their compliance with norms of 'good', 'successful' or 'responsible' parenting (Churchill in this book; Gillies 2005, 75). More recently, as Jo Bridgeman argues in her chapter, family policies for 'supporting' families have focused upon supporting parents to meet their responsibilities (Bridgeman in this book). Beyond the indisputable aim of improving universal services for children and families, there is an explicit view that some parents need to be supported to be responsible parents all of the time and all need support to be responsible parents some of the time. Yet, she argues, surely responsible parenting is an experience tried and learned within the specific context of a particular relationship and set of circumstances. A similar conclusion is reached by Harriet Churchill who contrasts maternal accounts of parental responsibility as a 'situated process of interpreting and responding to children's needs on a daily basis' with the family policy of the Labour government across welfare, work and income and children's education, health and behaviour (Churchill in this book, 63). It is to responsibility in family life and law that we now turn.

Conceptualising family responsibilities

There is remarkably little literature on responsibility in family life, or law. A recent exception which begins to explore responsibility as a value in family life, alongside power, friendship, truth, respect and rights, is offered by John Eekelaar in *Family Law and Personal Life* (Eekelaar 2006). Eekelaar draws upon Cane's analysis of historic and prospective responsibility to consider the allocation and exercise of responsibility in the two examples of divorce and adult responsibilities to children. He argues that 'Responsible people will exercise restraint within their legal rights. They will also act beyond their legal duties' (Eekelaar 2006, 128). He cautions against the attempt to convert the practice, within personal life, of this 'fuller' concept of responsibility into legally enforceable responsibilities.

The reasoning for Eekelaar's caution is grounded in the understanding that there is a difference between the concepts of rights and responsibilities. Communitarian approaches understand responsibilities as the corollary of rights whilst responsibilities may also be understood as having developed out of the discourse on rights as, for example, in the shift from perceiving the parent/child relationship in terms of rights to responsibilities. Our enterprise thus occurs against the backdrop of the more established discourse of rights, including those which parents may continue to enjoy with respect to their children and the issue of whether children can be said to possess rights (see, for example, the philosophical writing of Archard 1993).[8] In his chapter in this book, Michael Freeman very clearly makes the point that to focus upon the responsibilities of parenthood is not to 'resile' from a commitment to children's rights. This, we submit, is a centrally important aspect of theorising the contribution of moral, social and legal responsibilities in family life and law. Where responsibility is merely understood as that which is owed as a consequence of another's entitlements, it serves no purpose of its own: rather, it merely offers a mirror image to a rights perspective. Michael Freeman's discussion of whether children have a right to a minimum standard of parenting care, or the right to responsible parents, very nicely illustrates how responsibilities sit alongside, rather than replace, rights.

As Michael Freeman identifies, to focus upon responsibilities is to concentrate upon agents rather than recipients and he challenges Onora O'Neill's assertion that children's rights will be better secured through consideration of obligations to them – what is owed to them – rather than their rights. The question which this book sets out to explore is whether family responsibilities are more than merely the correlative of rights or any different from obligations. Joan Tronto, for example, has argued for a focus upon responsibilities rather than upon obligations, suggesting that the question which needs to be asked is not 'What, if anything, do I (we) owe to others? But rather – How can I (we) best meet my (our) caring responsibilities?' (Tronto 1993, 137). The chapters in this book contribute to the process of examining the distinctions between rights, obligations and responsibilities in their moral, social and legal guises. It is notable, and important for our understanding of responsibility, that there is no single approach adopted. Jonathan Herring, having noted the differences that could be considered to exist between responsibilities and obligations, uses the terms interchangeably. In their chapters, Amanda Wade, Heather Keating and Adrian James employ responsibility in the sense of accountability. Amanda Wade explores parental understandings of how they ought to raise their children and thus responsibility in the sense of moral accountability. Heather Keating examines the extent to which developments in the field of youth criminal justice can be understood to hold children to account and thus as 'being responsible', see children as 'becoming responsible' and extend to making parents take responsibility for their children. Similarly, Adrian James considers children exercising responsibility in the sense of moral and behavioural competence. In a chapter which is also focused upon the responsibilities of children, Ginny Morrow explores ways in which children take responsibility and behave responsibly in their work and childcare contributions.

In his chapter in this book, Adrian James directly addresses the position of children within the communitarian conceptualisation of responsibility. He identifies the enduring dominance of developmentalism, and hence the view of children as incompetent and dependent upon their parents, upon social and legal constructions of childhood. This he traces through developments in law and policy in relation to children and crime (where one of the constructions is of children as irresponsible and under the control of their parents who must be made to 'take responsibility' for them), in relation to family law (where children are understood and, in turn,

---

8 That discourse now includes the significance and impact of European and international conventions on children's rights (see, for example, Fortin 2003).

treated as in need of protection rather than as active participants in major decisions affecting their lives) and education (where the focus is upon teaching children about citizenship rather than permitting them to practise it). These dominant, and conflicting, constructions have an impact, James argues, upon the way that parents treat their children, reinforced by the approach of professionals to children (learned in their training), and affect children's own understandings of what is expected of them and what they can do. Importantly, he questions the implications for the communitarian coupling of individual rights with social responsibilities for children: the mantra 'no rights without responsibilities' holds a chilling resonance for children.

If this needs to be countered by recognition of children's responsibilities as well as their rights, Ginny Morrow's chapter unveils children as responsible actors. Commencing from the same constructionist position as Adrian James, Ginny Morrow highlights the way in which social and legal constructions of childhood as a period of dependency and incompetence and the preferred view that childhood is a time of freedom, play and fun, render children's responsibilities and work contributions invisible. She reflects upon the nature, and extent, of children's responsibilities through the findings of three studies which revealed children's participation in work and childcare. Babysitting and childminding involve taking responsibility for the life of a younger sibling, relative or unrelated child which means that it is a responsible occupation. Parents who rely upon children to take sole responsibility for childcare trust them to manage the risks involved in fulfilling this responsibility. This example, Ginny Morrow suggests, points to interdependency within families and, by acknowledging children's being responsible and taking responsibility, of reciprocal relationships. Seeing children taking responsibility and the trust placed in them by parents who rely upon them to care for other children highlights adult dependence upon children such that, Ginny Morrow suggests, rather than the dichotomy of independent adult/dependent child, interdependence may be a more useful concept in theorising responsibility within families.

Social and legal constructions of childhood, that is, understandings of what children are allowed and expected to do, are historically and culturally specific, changing over time and place. Shifting conceptions of family responsibility are the subject of analysis in the chapters of Amanda Wade, Craig Lind and Richard Collier. Whilst Amanda Wade explores changing understandings of parental responsibility across the generations, Richard Collier examines the extent to which and ways in which the responsibilities of fathers have altered and Craig Lind considers how assisted reproductive technology offers the potential to locate family responsibility in social relationships rather than genetic. Amanda Wade explores practices of family responsibility amongst the participants in her study of parent/child relationships across three generations. She identifies how ideas about responsible parenting, that is, 'parents' beliefs about the ways in which they "should" raise their children' and, hence, parental responsibility in the sense of moral accountability, shift over time (Wade in this book, 214). She observes how one accepted role of parenting is to enable children to become responsible for themselves but that understandings of responsible parenting with respect to children's autonomy shifted over the course of the three generations in her study: from responsibility through material provision necessitating long adult working days and, consequently, children's independence and contribution to domestic work; through parental responsibility for helping children to seize opportunities; to responsibility for developing children as choosers and rational decision-makers. Whilst the common thread across the generations was the promotion of children's autonomy, what this involved shifted over time from self-reliant, productive autonomy through freedom, and self-directive autonomy to participative autonomy.

The focus of Richard Collier's chapter is the shifting responsibilities of the father as 'family man'. Whilst this involves a shift from the father as financial provider for the household economy and authority figure to caring, nurturing, emotionally involved fathering, he argues 'that unpacking the conceptual basis of these changes around fathers' responsibilities in law ... reveals diverse, and frequently contradictory beliefs about the gendered nature of divisions of labour, paid employment, sexualities, class and masculinities' (Collier in this book, 171). His view is that the 'father as breadwinner' model has not been supplanted in law but exists 'alongside, and in tension with, the new ideology of the "father as carer"' and that a focus upon the latter runs the risks of 'obfuscating as much as it reveals about the complexities of men's parenting' (Collier in this book, 182).

Craig Lind explores the implications of methods of assisted reproduction for the allocation of family responsibility, lamenting the judicial reluctance to take the opportunity presented in recent cases to focus upon social responsibilities rather than genetic contributions. It is, he argues, the relationship between parent and child in which responsibilities arise and are met: 'What matters most to us are the relationships which serve to meet our (emotional and material) needs. What matters to children must be the relationships that result in adults exercising beneficial responsibility for them' (Lind in this book, 204). In the light of this argument, the proposed reforms to the Human Fertilisation and Embryology Act 1990 are criticised as conservative and backward-looking; whilst the rules on the allocation of paternity will be clarified it will not mean that better decisions are made:

> It does not attempt to come to terms with what the status of parent – and in particular, father – should be. Nor is there a principled view on the relationship between that status and the responsibility which fathers ought to have for their children. (Lind in this book, 208)

Lind argues that if the law were better able to negotiate the link between parental status and family responsibility, better decisions could be made and, given the failure of the proposed reforms to do so, this 'may require a clearer mapping out of that relationship in future legislation' (Lind in this book, 206).

If the relationship between parental status and family or parental responsibility requires further clarification, it is also true, as has been commented upon before, that the Children Act 1989 defines parental responsibility in very broad terms and with reference back to parental rights, duties and powers. As Jo Bridgeman explains in her chapter, parental responsibility has been defined in the case law as responsibility for the major decisions affecting the child's upbringing, whilst it is clear that it is so much more. The chapters in this book contribute to understanding of the concept of parental responsibility: its legal definition; social practices; descriptively and normatively; in relation to liberal theory or the influence of communitarian approaches upon its content; and the responsibilities of parents prior to the birth of their child.

Michael Freeman, in agreement with John Eekelaar, suggests that, as a normative standard by which to judge parenting, parental responsibility could be grounded in Finnis's theory of human flourishing (Eekelaar 1991 drawing upon Finnis, 1980 and 1983). There is, Michael Freeman suggests, 'an irreducible minimum content to a child's well-being' which responsible parents will secure. Theoretical reflection upon the minimum owed by parents to their children is a useful starting point for thinking about family responsibilities, as is research that reveals experiences of responsibility, what we might refer to as 'responsibility practices'. Mary Urban Walker encourages us to explore social practices of responsibility which, she argues, 'follow the trails of people's diverse responsibilities through different domains. ... Being held responsible in certain ways, or being exempted or excluded from responsibility of certain types or for certain people, forms individuals' own senses, as well as other's expectations, of to whom and for what they have to account' (Urban Walker 1998, 78). Janet Finch, in her work on family responsibility, observed that we should not assume that conclusions can be drawn about what people ought to do from findings about what people do; in other words that we cannot derive 'ought' from 'is' or moral understandings from social. But, as she acknowledges, people's sense of what they ought to do is in part formed by experiences of what is done, in this context with respect to responsibilities to care for other, adult, family members (Finch 1994, 68). Tracing social practices of responsibility in the way Mary Urban Walker has suggested, Harriet Churchill contrasts the understanding of responsibility within current government policy with that of single mothers for whom 'responsibilities for children are sustained, negotiated and contested through everyday maternal beliefs and practices' (Churchill in this book, 68). 'Following the trails of people's diverse responsibilities', Amanda Wade traces shifting concepts of parental responsibility in relation to prevailing social and cultural conditions and Ginny Morrow examines the ways in which children take responsibility for the care of others.

Jonathan Herring explores the extent to which responsibilities of parents continue once children reach the age of majority and the extent to which adult children have moral, or legal, obligations to their parents. He examines whether the moral basis for such an obligation could be based in reciprocity, relationship, the parent/child bond, or the rights of older people. In his chapter, Jonathan Herring considers the arguments of a number of authors who have suggested that family obligations are based in reciprocity. As he explains, these authors propose that reciprocal *duties* may be owed by adult children to their parents as recompense for the debt incurred from earlier provision and care by the parent. Ginny Morrow concludes, from analysis of the findings of her studies, that reciprocity is at the heart of the parent/child relationship, arising from contemporaneous interdependency rather than in payment of a debt previously accrued. Likewise, there are differences between Ginny Morrow's advocacy of responsibility in reciprocal relationships, Jo Bridgeman's conceptualisation of relational responsibilities and Jane English's obligations arising from the quality of the relationship which Jonathan Herring also considers as a possible moral grounding for obligations (Herring in this book). Jonathan Herring outlines his reservations with the argument that the extent of the obligation owed depends upon the quality of prior or current relationships noting that, in practice, obligation is not limited in this way. Rather than the quality of the relationship, Ginny Morrow's conceptualisation of reciprocal relationships is based on recognition of the extent to which parents rely upon their children to take responsibility for childcare and hence a relationship of interdependency. Giving relationships a central position in her conceptualisation of relational responsibility, Jo Bridgeman argues that parental responsibilities arise from the relationship of dependency, intimacy and care between parent and child in which the parent is concerned to achieve the best for the child in the present and future. Making a similar point, Craig Lind argues that responsibility should be allocated according to the adult/child relationship which will secure the best for the child. Jonathan Herring finds more convincing the argument made by Kellet that the parent/child relationship itself and not the quality of the relationship gives rise to responsibilities (Kellet 2006), something with which Jo Bridgeman would agree although, as her focus is the responsibility of parents to children rather than vice versa, she does not base this, as Kellet does, on a lifetime of shared experience and history. There does appear to be common ground, in conceptualising the responsibilities of adults to children and adult children to parents, arising from Jonathan Herring's observation that this basis – that there is something special shared – has less force with regard to those obligations the law is able to enforce, such as financial obligations. Although perhaps we might choose to draw the conclusion that the moral basis of responsibilities of parents to their children is different from that of adult children to their parents?

Jonathan Herring notes the work of Janet Finch and Jennifer Mason on the negotiation of family responsibilities in which they observe that, in relation to the care of family members, individual obligations are determined in part by 'normative guidelines' applicable to certain types of relationship and in part upon 'negotiated commitments' conditional upon the quality of the relationship (Herring in this book, discussing Finch and Mason 1993). Negotiated commitments are not confined to working out the extent of responsibility to care for adults; rather, within families, parents and children are in a continual process of negotiating and re-negotiating responsibilities. Indeed, as Heather Keating considers, a fundamental feature of parenting is reflecting on and responding to the capacity of one's child to be 'responsible' for his or her behaviour. Her consideration of criminal law and justice shows how the law has also struggled to determine the point at which children should be responsible for their decisions and behaviour or the extent to which parents should bear responsibility instead of, or as well as, their children.

The responsibilities of parents for their children, for example, include financial responsibility, care, nurturing, protection, guiding and, the focus of Amanda Wade's chapter, fostering the ability to live independently. Both Amanda Wade and Richard Collier explore the shifting balance between financial and caring responsibility over time, of parents and fathers respectively; from what could be considered to be 'traditional' ideas of family responsibility where there is a clear division between paternal responsibility as financial responsibility and the responsibility of mothers to care. Financial responsibility is, as Joan Tronto has observed, a step removed from care giving; money does not itself meet needs, it has to be converted into care (Tronto

1993, 107). As Mavis Maclean and John Eekelaar have observed, historically the law has not intruded far into the care provided by parents of their children in the privacy of the home: 'when members of a family are living together, the law is strangely reticent in articulating and enforcing the obligations they may owe to one another. That does not mean that they do not have duties to each other. But these duties may be only indirectly recognized or enforced by the law. Indeed, they may not be legal duties at all.' (Maclean and Eekelaar 1997, 1). Responsibilities of parents thus come to be played out in the public realm of the law once their relationships have broken down and there are disputes over who should have primary care for children or the extent of financial obligations.

Jonathan Herring considers the responsibilities of children and their adult parents in terms of financial responsibility, decision-making responsibility or caring responsibility. But his chapter, like those of Alison Diduck and Harriet Churchill, gives emphasis to the extent to which thinking about responsibilities within families focuses attention upon caring. What matters most, Jonathan Herring suggests, in the adult child/parent relationship is care and contact, not cash. Harriet Churchill's analysis of the accounts of the single mothers in her study reflects the disposition in the caring work captured in the title of Eva Kittay's book, *Love's Labor*: 'the active, attentive and reflective process of needs interpretation that many of the mothers detailed … constitutes a fundamental aspect of a caring orientation' (Kittay 1999) (see Churchill in this book, 77). Alison Diduck identifies 'the thread of coherence' in family law 'in its role as shaper of responsibility to care' within families, whether it is for children, for parents, by children or spouses for each other. Reflecting debates about the recognition of, and exploitation of, caring, her chapter highlights the way in which family law has reinforced the privatisation of caring work within the family so that social and public responsibility to care can be avoided. Further, she argues, responsibility for social problems has increasingly been placed within the family, enabling governments to individualise culpability and avoid their responsibility. And Alison Diduck observes that, despite the democratisation of the family and 'gender convergence', responsibilities within the family are still allocated to women as the primary providers of care. Giving focus to caring responsibilities means that questions about who provides care, for whom, cannot be ignored; neither can questions of dependency, vulnerability and need which, as Martha Fineman has demonstrated, have been hidden behind 'the autonomy myth' (Fineman 2004).

The law, Alison Diduck suggests, 'is about allocating responsibility for responsibility' (Diduck in this book, 258) and increasingly she suggests, public responsibility has been reallocated to the family. Taking up the issue of public responsibility, John Williams explores the responsibilities of the state to vulnerable older people; that is, older people with disabilities, who lack capacity, are frail or dependent. Exploring state responsibility through human rights, John Williams examines the balance which has to be achieved between the conflicting rights invoked in cases of the abuse of vulnerable older people, between their right to respect for private and family life (ECHR Article 8) and right to protection from inhuman or degrading treatment (ECHR Article 3). In analysing the responsibility of the state to respond, John Williams argues that the current welfare based measures, found in a bewildering array of statutes, are inadequate and unlikely to satisfy the positive obligation of the state to protect vulnerable adults from abuse under Article 3. This is so despite the recent addition of guidance that aims to provide a framework for action to protect vulnerable adults, which he condemns as 'soft-law, without the backing of legislation' (Williams in this book, 99). However, he also cautions about seeking to draw parallels from child protection measures, policies and services to the protection of older people if there is to be respect for the autonomy and experience of older people. He concludes that, while identifying the appropriate point of intervention is the challenge for any new legislation (99), it is possible and desirable to devise a public law requiring intervention in a way that would allow a sensitive response to be made to individual cases of abuse (99). A statutory duty to investigate concerns about abuse of vulnerable adults, for example, would not only extend protection to individuals at risk of, or suffering abuse, but would also seek to change attitudes towards such abuse and send out a message that the state takes its responsibilities seriously.

Responsibility, Law and the Family

How responsibility is understood has implications for the role of the law, which may be holding to account, enforcing or supporting responsibilities. Those familiar with liberal theories in the work, for example, of Tony Honoré and H.L.A. Hart (Hart 1968; Honoré 1999), will be comfortable with the use of the law to enforce responsibilities. For example, as noted above, H.L.A. Hart (Hart 1967, 363) expressed the view that 'liability responsibility' is responsibility in the primary sense (drawing upon causal, capacity and role responsibility). In this approach, the law has a central place in holding individuals to account for their freely chosen acts. The tension between a liberal and a communitarian approach to responsibility, as it has developed in relation to the criminal or anti-social behaviour of children, is discussed by Heather Keating in her chapter. She argues that although there are instances where the government appears to endorse the liberal understanding of capacity responsibility (controversially arguing that even children of ten are responsible in this sense), increasingly this has been sidelined in favour of communitarian based policies that seek to *make* children responsible and make their parents *take* responsibility. This employs the law in ever-widening areas of children's behaviour, irrespective of the child's capacity to have understood the law's commands.

Thus, different understandings of responsibility will lead to different conclusions about the role of the law. Jonathan Herring concludes that many may feel comfortable with the view that adult children should have responsibilities to their parents, but that there are practical difficulties and personal consequences which mean that there should not be a legally enforceable obligation (indeed, he concludes that it is only financial responsibility which could be enforced by the law, not caring responsibility). However, he suggests that the law can be used to encourage and support adult children's responsibilities to care for their parents. Jo Bridgeman, drawing distinctions between rights, duties, obligations and responsibilities, likewise concludes that responsibilities cannot be legally enforced; rather that responsibilities to children arising from relationships with them should be fostered and supported.

Likewise, Harriet Churchill's conclusion, that the best interests of the child depend upon meeting their changing needs in the face of external constraints and internalised expectations of 'good' mothering, suggests a complexity to family responsibility which is beyond the scope of legislation.

The four parts in this book consider, in turn, the nature of family responsibility, constructions of children's responsibilities, shifting conceptions of family responsibilities and family, responsibility and the law. This book brings together researchers from the disciplines of sociology, socio-legal studies and law to explore moral, social and legal responsibilities prior to birth, to children, of children, and of the state towards family members. The chapters which follow make significant strides to inform, and challenge, the developing conceptualisation of responsibilities which arise in interdependent, intimate and caring relationships and their legal regulation.

References

Archard, D. (1993), *Children: Rights and Childhood* (London: Routledge).

Cane, P. (2002), *Responsibility in Law and Morality* (Oxford: Hart).

Clarkson, C. and Keating, H. (2007), *Criminal Law: Text and Materials* (London: Sweet and Maxwell).

Dewar, J. (1998), 'The Normal Chaos of Family Law', *Modern Law Review* 61, 467.

Douglas, G. (2004), *An Introduction to Family Law* (Oxford: Oxford University Press).

Duff, A. (2001), *Punishment, Communication and Community* (Oxford: Oxford University Press).

Duff, A. and von Hirsch, A. (1997), 'Responsibility, Retribution and the "Voluntary": A Response to Williams', *Cambridge Law Journal* 56, 103.

Eekelaar, J. (1991), 'Are Parents Morally Obliged to Care for their Children?', *Oxford Journal of Legal Studies* 11, 340.

Eekelaar, J. (2006), *Family Law and Personal Life* (Oxford: Oxford University Press).

English, J. (1993), 'What Do Grown Children Owe Their Parents' in Sommers, C. and Sommers, F. (eds), *Vice and Virtue in Everyday Life* (Fort Worth: Harcourt).

Etzioni, A. (1995), *New Communitarian Thinking: Persons, Virtues, Institutions, and Communities* (Charlottesville: University Press of Virginia).

Etzioni, A. (1996), 'The Responsive Community: A Communitarian Perspective', *American Sociological Review* 61, 1-11.

Etzioni, A. (ed.) (1998), *The Essential Communitarian Reader* (Lanham: Rowman & Littlefield Publisher, Inc).

Finch, J. (1994), 'The Proper Thing to Do' in Eekelaar, J. and Maclean, M. (eds), *A Reader on Family Law* (Oxford: Oxford University Press).

Finch, J. and Mason, J. (1993), *Negotiating Family Responsibilities* (London: Routledge).

Fineman, M.A. (2004), *The Autonomy Myth: A Theory of Dependency* (New York: The New Press).

Finnis, J. (1980), *Natural Law and Natural Rights* (Oxford: Oxford University Press).
Finnis, J. (1983), *Fundamentals of Ethics* (Oxford: Oxford University Press).
Fortin, J. (2003), *Children's Rights and the Developing Law* (London: Butterworths).
Gardner, J. (1996), 'Justifications and Reasons' in Simester, A. and Smith, A.T.H. (eds), *Harm and Culpability* (Oxford: Oxford University Press).
Gardner, J. (1998), 'The Gist of Excuses', *Buffalo Criminal Law Review* 1, 575.
Gardner, J. (2003), 'The Mark of Responsibility', *Oxford Journal of Legal Studies* 23, 157.
Gillies, V. (2005), 'Meeting Parents' Needs? Discourses of "Support" and "Inclusion" in Family Policy', *Critical Social Policy* 25, 70-90.
Hart, H.L.A. (1967), 'Varieties of Responsibility', *Law Quarterly Review* 83, 346.
Hart, H.L.A. (1968), *Punishment and Responsibility: Essays in the Philosophy of Law* (Oxford: Clarendon Press).
Hart, H.L.A. (1984), 'Are There Any Natural Rights?' reproduced in Waldron, J., *Theories of Rights* (Oxford: Oxford University Press).
Honoré, A. (1999), *Responsibility and Fault* (Oxford: Hart).
Horder, J. (2004), *Excusing Crime* (Oxford: Oxford University Press).
James, A.L. and James, A. (2001), 'Tightening the Net: Children, Community and Control', *British Journal of Sociology* 52, 211.
Kellet, S. (2006), 'Four Theories of Filial Duty', *The Philosophical Quarterly* 56, 233.
Kittay, E. (1999), *Love's Labor: Essays on Women, Equality and Dependency* (New York: Routledge).
Koffman, L (2008), 'Holding Parents to Account: Tough on Children, Tough on the Causes of Children', *Journal of Law and Society* 35, 113.
Lacey, N. (1988), *State Punishment: Political Principles and Community Values* (London: Routledge).
Maclean, M. and Eekelaar, J. (1997), *The Parental Obligation: A Study of Parenthood Across Households* (Oxford: Hart).
Parker, S. (1992), 'Rights and Utility in Anglo-Australian Law', *Modern Law Review* 55, 311.
Probert, R. (2004), 'Family Law – a Modern Concept', *Family Law* 34, 901.
Reece, H. (2003), *Divorcing Responsibly* (Hart: Oxford).
Reece, H. (2006), 'From Parental Responsibility to Parenting Responsibly' in Freeman, M. (ed.), *Law and Sociology, Current Legal Issues 2005* (Oxford: Oxford University Press).
Strawson, P. (2003), 'Freedom and Resentment' in Watson, G. (ed.), *Freewill* (Oxford: Oxford University Press).
Tadros, V. (2005), *Criminal Responsibility* (Oxford: Oxford University Press).
Tronto, J. (1993), *Moral Boundaries: The Political Argument for an Ethic of Care* (New York: Routledge).
Urban Walker, M. (1998), *Moral Understandings: A Feminist Study in Ethics* (New York: Routledge).
Williams, B. (1997), 'Moral Responsibility and Political Freedom', *Cambridge Law Journal* 56, 96.

PART 1
The Nature of Family Responsibility

Chapter 2

The Right to Responsible Parents

Michael Freeman

Introduction

Sitting on a *Justice* committee more than 30 years ago I urged the members to think about parental responsibilities rather than, as was then the currency, parental rights (*Justice* 1975). There were precedents, in Norway and West Germany.[1] The Committee was persuaded and so recommended. This was not, I hasten to add, why the Children Act in 1989 adopted the language of responsibilities rather than rights.[2] But it is the beginning of my association with the concept of parental responsibility. In 1993 I gave a public lecture at the University of Essex entitled 'Do Children Have the Right Not To Be Born?' (Freeman 1997). This explored the concept of parental responsibility further. This chapter builds on some of the ideas formulated there.

Thinking about responsibility has shifted from the liberal paradigm that was dominant at the time of the *Justice* committee and even at the time of the Essex lecture. Post-liberalism, manifested in communitarianism[3] and the feminist ethics of care,[4] has called for a re-evaluation of what responsibility involves. Tronto argues that the moral question central to an ethic of care is not what we owe others but 'rather – How can we best meet our caring responsibilities?' (Tronto 1993, 137). Reece explains

> Post-liberal responsibility is no longer about discrete decisions; responsible behaviour has become a way of being, a mode of thought; the focus has shifted from the content of the decision to the process of making the decision. (Reece 2003, 232)

What is required, Gillies has argued in a recent paper, is

> ethical self-management within the moral parameters of normative definitions of "successful parenting". Reasonable, rational moral citizens … seek to do the best for their children. (Gillies 2005, 75)

---

1 On West Germany see Frank 1990.

2 This was the recommendation of the Law Commission, 1988, Law Com. 172.

3 A good discussion of which (in the context of family law) is Eekelaar 2001a. See also Eekelaar 2000 (an article I only discovered after I wrote this chapter but wish I had seen earlier).

4 Which is usually traced to Carol Gilligan (1982), and see Smart and Neale 1999.

At the same time parental responsibility has expanded, and has been redefined. The introduction of the parenting order by the Crime and Disorder Act 1998,[5] and its subsequent extension by the Anti-social Behaviour Act 2003,[6] imposes on parents responsibility for the anti-social behaviour of their children. This can be looked at simplistically as taking the rap. But it is more than this. The 'good' parent is constructed as resourceful and ethically responsible 'able to recognize or learn what is best for their children and tailor their behaviour accordingly' (Gillies 2005, 85). 'Good' parenting, as Reece interprets it is 'an attitude, and an important part of that attitude is being prepared to learn' (Reece 2006, 470). From being about authority – as it certainly became with the passage of the Children Act 1989 (Eekelaar 1991a) – current governmental initiatives identify parental responsibility with accountability.

English law does not define parental responsibility very fully. The formulation in section 3 of the Children Act 1989 is clumsy and inchoate.[7] Of course, a non-definition allows the policy-maker to mould it to meet changing imperatives: no one was thinking of the parenting order in 1989. The Scottish formulation is, by contrast, fuller.[8] Does the absence of a definition make it more difficult for a child to bring a parent to account? It has certainly not prevented the state from so doing. Does it deprive a parent of fair opportunity (see further, Hart 1968) to know what standards are expected of him or her (Lyon 2000)? This is particularly important where there is an allegation of child abuse or neglect.[9] But could it be defined? Of course, some content can clearly be poured into it. However, this does little more than reaffirm jurisprudence which has emerged from isolated pieces of litigation.[10] Acting responsibly is to act ethically. Benhabib puts this well:

> To be a family member, a parent, a spouse or a brother means to know how to reason from the standpoint of the concrete other. One cannot act within these ethical relationships … without being able to think from the standpoint of our child, our spouse, our sister or brother, mother or father. (Benhabib 1992, 10)

And this requires, as Reece acknowledges, 'far more than the simple assertion of rights and duties in the face of the other's needs' (Reece 2003, 231). It is not enough to 'be' family: it is necessary also to 'do' family. This was recognised by the judiciary when it formulated the test for the granting of a parental responsibility order in 1991.[11]

---

5 See s. 8.

6 See s. 18.

7 This states that parental responsibility comprises 'the rights, duties, powers, responsibilities and authority which by law a parent has in relation to the child and his property'. Lord Meston (Hansard, H.L. vol. 502, col. 1172) described this as a 'non-definition'.

8 It is in the Children (Scotland) Act 1995 s. 1(1) (responsibilities); s. 2(1) (rights).

9 And particularly so in the less-than-obvious case. These include (unfortunately) cases of 'excessive' physical chastisement (*Re R (Care: Rehabilitation in Context of Domestic Violence)* [2007] 1 FLR 1830) and excessive feeding (see *The Guardian*, 13 July 2007).

10 This does not necessarily offer a coherent theory. Whether 'parental responsibility' as such does is debatable. One thoughtful view is John Eekelaar's that it creates a new legal status of 'social parenthood' (2001b).

11 *Re H* [1991] 1 FLR 214. See also *D v Hereford and Worcester CC* [1991] 1 FLR 205.

Parental Rights

We didn't always think this way. Throughout most of our history children were treated as the property of their fathers (unless illegitimate – such children were the 'children of no one').[12] Parental rights vested in him. In the *Gillick* decision in 1985 the concept of the child as property of the father was deemed 'a historical curiosity'.[13] The Lords acknowledged that parental rights (we were no longer talking of paternal rights) existed but not for the benefit of the parent. Lord Fraser said:

> They exist for the benefit of the child and they are justified only in so far as they enable the parent to perform his duties towards the child, and towards other children in the family. (at 170)

There are similar, if more overtly Dworkinian, sentiments in Lord Scarman's speech.

> The principle of the law … is that parental rights are derived from parental duty and exist only so long as they are needed for the protection of the person and property of the child. (at 184)

The father's powers – he was the natural guardian of a legitimate child – limped on until this status was finally abolished in 1989.[14] Few will even have noticed this, and its passing was not mourned. Parents still have parental rights, but these are subsumed in parental responsibilities.

Is there a Right to Have Children?

One right which is still aired is the right to have children. Parenting is an activity which is 'potentially very harmful to children' (LaFollette 1980, 182). We are not allowed to drive a car unless we pass a driving test. We do not license parenthood. Do we depreciate parenting because it is not regarded as having economic value (Westman 1994, 3), or is it because it is largely done by women? A society's children are its future citizens. The public, therefore, has 'a legitimate concern with the selection of child rearers' (Blustein 1982, 119). Should parenting be a privilege? Rather than criticising the welfare norm that governs fertility treatment[15] (Jackson 2002), should we be urging its adoption across the board? Is this to urge a utopian solution or to envisage a ghastly dystopia?[16]

---

12 A good account (in the US context) is found in Mason 1994.

13 *Gillick v West Norfolk and Wisbech A.H.A* [1986] AC 112.

14 Children Act 1989 s. 2(4).

15 Human Fertilisation and Embryology Act 1990 s. 13(5), on which see Jackson 2002. For differing views contrast HC Science and Technology Committee, 2005 (it 'discriminates against the infertile and some sections of society'), and the Joint Committee on the Human Tissue and Embryos (Draft) Bill Report, 2007, 65.

16 See Gray 2007.

There is a school of thought that urges the licensing of parenthood (Covell and Howe 1998; Eisenberg 1994; LaFollette 1980; Mangel 1988; Westman 1994). Is this to think the unthinkable? For Covell and Howe parents must demonstrate that they can be responsible for their own lives 'before being allowed to assume responsibility for a child's life' (1998, 34). The questions are at the very least worth asking. Should there be a minimum age requirement – there is for marriage,[17] for voting, even for purchasing tobacco products. And, if a minimum, why not a maximum age too?[18] Is it responsible to bring children into the world when it is unlikely that you will see them into adulthood? Or when you don't have adequate income to provide for a child's basic necessities? Should those who have abused a child previously be allowed to parent further children? If we could identify potential child abusers in advance should we deny them the freedom to procreate? Predictive screening questionnaires have been developed (see Schneider et al. 1972, discussed in Freeman 1979, 108-111). But it has been shown that false positive errors could potentially be as high as 85 per cent, with the result that many would-be parents would be mistakenly labelled (Light 1973). There would also be false negatives, so that abusers would fall through the net. Together this suggests low practical ability for an unacceptably high social cost (Daniel et al. 1978). But not only do we not know what causes abuse – if the cultural explanation of child abuse is accepted we are all potential child abusers (Gil 1978) – but there is no consensus on what constitutes child abuse. We can list categories, certainly. We can agree on the worst cases. But what of the 'penumbral' case (see further, Hart 1958)? Is 'vulgar but inappropriate horseplay' sexual abuse?[19] Is feeding a child inappropriately so that he becomes obese neglect?[20] Is causing a male child to be circumcised physical abuse (Fox and Thomson 2005)?[21] How relevant is the cultural and religious context? Should those who put serious barriers in the way of the child's capacity for autonomous decision-making (for example, Christian fundamentalists, Hasiddim, racists, etc., etc.) forfeit their freedom to create another generation? And what then about those who would deny their children immunisations (the MMR vaccine, for example[22]), or blood transfusions because

17 Marriage Act 1949 s. 2.

18 On fertility treatment for post-menopausal women see Cutas 2007. On 30 December 2006, a 67-year-old Spanish woman gave birth to twins. I believe this is the record, but I do not expect it to stand.

19 See *C v C (Child Abuse: Access)* [1988] 1 FLR 462.

20 See Jenkins, 'Obese girl taken into care because of her weight', *The Times*, July 13 2007 and Templeton, 'Fat boy may be put into care', *Sunday Times*, 25 February 2007.

21 The English courts have said 'no': *Re J (A Minor) (Prohibited Steps Order: Circumcision)* [2000] 1 FLR 571, though in this case they did hold that ritual circumcision of a five-year-old child was not in his best interests. He was being brought up by a nominally Christian mother and had a Muslim father who barely practised his religion. Viens (2004, 246) is surely right to stress the need 'to differentiate between rituals and practices that are in fact grievously harmful and those which relate to the enhancement of a child's religious and cultural identity'.

22 *Re B (A Child) (Immunisation)* [2003] 3 FCR 156.

they are Jehovah's Witnesses,[23] or the celebration of Christmas because they are Plymouth Brethren[24] or, worse, Jews!

Eisenberg calls his proposal 'modest'. He argues

> It is time to say aloud what many people are saying privately: society must be much more proactive in assuring that only people who can properly raise children are allowed to become and remain parents. (Eisenberg 1994, 1416)

Eisenberg's is a detailed blueprint. Earlier proposals by LaFollette (1980) and Mangel (1988) had tried to identify and screen out 'bad parents'. And critics like Frisch (1981), commenting upon LaFollette, had attacked this proposal as being inconsistent with usual licensing requirements, for example to drive a car, which focuses on the knowledge and skills of the applicant, not his or her lack of suitability. Earlier proposals have also been criticised because they rely on the assumption that 'bad parents' can be identified in advance. Adoption panels and clinics offering assisted reproduction services already screen out certain applicants:[25] would-be foster parents, child-minders and teachers are carefully scrutinised before they are permitted to care for (or educate) children.[26] In the United Kingdom some 30 years ago, a parliamentary select committee endorsed screening, though, unsurprisingly, it gave little attention to the concept or its implications (Select Committee 1977). I suspect few remember this.

Eisenberg's model is different. It makes no effort to evaluate subjectively who will be a 'good parent' (1994, 1440). Rather it puts a premium on providing prospective parents with knowledge and skills relevant to parenting. But it is, I think, equally flawed. As he concedes, one of the principal problems is what to do with the children of unlicensed parents. He puts his faith in adoption and in communal institutions (the Israeli Kibbutz model appeals to him), but, even if practical problems could be surmounted, ethical ones would remain. Any proposal that would have a disproportionate impact on those already disadvantaged by low income, poor education, race or disability would be very difficult to defend.

Whether there is 'a right' to have children remains contentious. John Robertson (1983; 1994) is one who argues that we do have such a right. Although he concedes that the desire to reproduce is in part socially constructed, he sees personal identity, meaning and dignity as at the root of the right. But as Purdy (1996, 218) points out, 'is it really such a good idea to conceptualise the relationship between childbearing

---

23 *Wright v Wright* (1981), 2 FLR 276; *Re T (Minors) (Custody: Religious Upbringing)* [1981] 2 FLR 239.

24 *Hewison v Hewison* (1977), 7 Fam Law 207; *Re S (A Minor) (Medical Treatment)* [1993] 1 FLR 377. A striking contrast is the Illinois case of *Re Brown* 689 NE 2d 397 (Ill, 1997) (court refused to order a blood transfusion for a pregnant woman to save the life of her foetus).

25 See Adoption Agency Regulations 2005 on adoption panels and above, n. 14 in relation to fertility clinics (see also *R v Ethical Committee of St Mary's Manchester ex parte Harriott* [1998] 1 FLR 512).

26 See Fostering Services Regulations 2002 and Care Standards Act 2000 s. 79 (and Day Care and Child Minding (National Standards) (England) Regulations 2001, SI 2001/1818).

status and one's core self the way Robertson does?' And she argues that 'it encourages people to care too much about their ability to have children'. If, she adds, 'a person's whole self-concept depends on having them, they are set up for devastating disappointment' (1996, 219). This is especially so for women who 'because of their socialization – as well as continuing sexist and pronatalist pressure – will more likely adopt this understanding of the meaning of life without seriously questioning it' (ibid.). Another to argue the case for a right to have children is Dan Brock (1996). He appeals to self-determination and individual well-being. His argument is couched within the question of access to the new reproductive technologies, but what he says can be generalised. But neither Robertson nor Brock claims that the right to have children is an absolute right. Thus, Robertson requires the capacity to appreciate the meaning of parenthood (which may be absent in people with severe learning disabilities), and the absence of what he calls 'manifest unfitness' (1994, 127). This would certainly be manifested where there was a real risk of harm to the child. The argument against the natural right to have children was put – before either Robertson or Brock presented their case – by Floyd and Pomerantz (1981). They criticise both the self-determination argument (now associated with Brock), and the bodily autonomy argument. They reject the self-determination argument: 'one can have a relational right based on self-determination only if all the parties to the relation consent, and no one consents to be introduced into the world by someone else'. From this it follows that while there might be a right to marry, provided the potential partner consents, there is 'no relational right to be parent'. And they find it even easier to dispose of their bodily autonomy argument. It treats the child as a 'mere appendage', but a child is, of course, a distinct person, a rights-bearing individual. A different argument for the right to have children is the 'desire' argument. There is a thorough examination of this by Ruth Chadwick (1987). She shows that the desire for a child may be one of a number of different desires, or even a combination of them: a desire to rear, a desire to bear, a desire to beget (used more commonly of men than women), a desire to have a child with someone, a desire to be (or appear to be) a 'normal' family, a desire for an heir. There are questions as to whether the desire is socially induced, and is natural or artificial. But do any of these desires generate a right to have a child? Chadwick does not think so. And why should she or we? That something is desired does not turn this into a right in other contexts. Those who desire wealth or an honour (a knighthood, for example) do not thereby acquire a right to it.

These debates in the recent past took place in the context of sterilisation.[27] A book on sterilisation policies was even entitled *The Right to Reproduce* (Trombley 1988). Indeed, my own critique of the notorious case of 'Jeanette' (*Re B*)[28] argues, naively perhaps, for her right to reproduce (Freeman 1988). Most discussion of the 'right to reproduce' today focuses on the infertile and the obligation to provide fertility treatment at state expense. As we have seen, Robertson and Chadwick situate their discussion in this context, and come to different conclusions. That the state assists

27 The Brock report of 1934, which now has a discreet veil placed on it, planned the sterilisation of 3.5 million people – in Britain, I hasten to add, not Nazi Germany (Brock 1934).

28 *Re B (A Minor) (Wardship: Sterilisation)* [1988] 1 AC 199.

people to have children in a myriad of other ways does not mean that it ought to assist with IVF treatment (Uniacke 1987). Nor does it mean that the government rejection of the recommendation of NICE that three cycles of IVF should be available on the NHS – it substituted one – was right. There is a difference between arguing for a right to reproduction when the issue is whether this should be taken away from someone on grounds of lesser intelligence or parenting abilities and where what is being argued for is a positive right. The latter falls outside the remit of this chapter: the former firmly within it.

But this is about the right to responsible parents and so we must question whether talking about the right to reproduce is ever an appropriate way of thinking. Should we not reject the rights framework when the issue is about having children, and substitute instead the language of responsibility?[29]

Procreation as a Responsibility

To see procreation as a huge responsibility rather than as a right or a privilege is, I believe, relatively uncontentious – and surely less so if we accept the norm of 'ethical self-management' to which reference was made at the beginning of this chapter. We may differ over the implications of this, but not, I suggest, over the characterisation of procreation as a serious responsibility.

This responsibility will increase in the future when it becomes possible to choose the characteristics of our children. We are moving – I use this relatively neutral language, but others might say advancing, which I think begs the question – into a future shaped by assisted reproduction, cloning and other reprogenetic opportunities (Knowles and Kaebnick 2007). Parents will increasingly be accorded the opportunity to select embryos according to their characteristics. It is already possible to screen out genetic disease by using the technique of preimplantation genetic diagnosis (PGD).[30] We have the ability to use this technique (and others) to enable prospective parents to choose the sex of their children. Some fear that this could lead to gendercide, particularly amongst Asian populations.[31] It is also already possible to combine PGD with tissue matching technologies (HLA – human leukocyte antigen) to provide a 'saviour sibling' (Freeman 2006; McLean 2006, Ch. 3) for an existing seriously ill child.[32] PGD is not as yet used commonly: about 100 babies have been born in the UK after the use of PGD and some 1,000 worldwide (Human Genetics Commission 2006, para. 4.1).

It may be that eugenics is 'inescapable' (Kitcher 1996). It is a real concern. One suggestion (by Kitcher) is for what he calls 'utopian eugenics', offering prenatal testing to all, and educating people about the decisions they may take and the implications of those decisions. It should not be forgotten that these private decisions

---

29 In line with the emphasis on responsibility elsewhere (see e.g. Reece 2003 and 2006).

30 The fullest discussion of this is Franklin and Roberts 2006.

31 It is allowed in Israel: see Siegel-Itzkovich 2005.

32 This was challenged by a pro-life pressure group in the 'Hashmi' case. The challenge was unsuccessful, see *R (Quintavalle) v Human Fertilisation and Embryology Authority (Secretary of State for Health Intervening)* [2005] 2 AC 561.

affect the population as a whole. There are also concerns that parents may select embryos for non-medical reasons beyond the sex of the child: intelligence, height, athletic potential, eye colour, perhaps even sexual orientation. And what if – in the future – we could select not just the characteristics of our children but, by altering genetic make-up, also effect a change in the human germ line (Stock and Campbell 2000). The private would become not just public, but also 'future'. Fukuyama (2002) is not alone in being concerned about the possibility of altering 'human nature' (but compare Stock 2002).

But, of course, it has altered already. We have eliminated diseases which in previous generations decimated populations. Life expectancy is now considerably greater than it was only a generation ago. Infertile women can now have children. We can live with someone else's heart, kidney, even face.[33] Kurzweil asks: 'If we regard a human modified with technology as no longer human, where would we draw the defining line? Is a human with a bionic heart still human? How about someone with a neurological implant?' (Kurzweil 2005, 374).

The questions raised – the implications for dignity, for example (and see Bostrom 2005) – go beyond the remit of this chapter. Our concern is with what, if any, are the implications for parental obligation.

Savulescu coined the expression 'procreative beneficence' (Savulescu 2001). Under this principle

> couples or single reproducers should select the child, of the possible children they could have, who is expected to have the best life, or at least as good a life as the others, based on the relevant, reliable information. (Savulescu 2001, 415)

This implies that 'couples should employ genetic tests for non-disease traits in selecting which child to bring into existence and that we should allow selection for non-disease genes in some cases even if this maintains or increases social inequality' (ibid.). There can be little doubt that there will be an increase in social inequality. But it will not necessarily lead to greater discrimination against those with disabilities. Savulescu believes we can distinguish between disability and persons who have disabilities: 'selection reduces the former, but is silent on the value of the latter' (ibid., 423). And there are, he believes, better ways to make statements about the equality of people with disabilities. There will be always be people with disabilities even if procreative beneficence becomes the norm and it is interpreted so that disability is screened 'out' (and not 'in' as some disabled people would apparently prefer). Not all disability has a genetic cause – most does not; accidents will always occur; people will become disabled as a result of, for example, strokes.

Nevertheless, there are question marks over procreative beneficence. Should one be able to select for disability? If you are deaf and belong to the community of the deaf, is there anything wrong in wanting to bring a child into the world who can glory in this deaf culture? Is the fact that you use assisted techniques of reproduction to achieve this – destroying embryos with the capability of hearing in the process – deliberately selecting a deaf embryo – unethical? Many do not think so (for example,

33 See Swindell 2007; Hartman, 2005; Freeman and Abou-Daudé 2007.

Holm 1998). They (for example, Häyry 2004) distinguish deliberately selecting a deaf embryo from deafening a hearing child. We all accept that the latter is child abuse. I think we would all accept it would be child abuse if a pregnant woman deliberately ingested a liquid that she knew would have the effect of causing her child to be born without hearing.[34] That the alternative to being selected is not to become a person at all – the standard defence – is not a satisfactory answer to anyone who is concerned with parental responsibility. The intention (in the ingestion example it is recklessness) in all three cases is the same: to produce a deaf child, and this is to act irresponsibly. More difficult is the case of the deaf couple (or couple where one of them is deaf) who know (because of the genetic tests) that if they have a child he/she will be deaf. Should they refrain from reproducing? Use the new reproductive techniques and have a child who is not genetically related to them? Counselling may assist them to come to an informed decision. And it must be their decision, freely reached without coercion or inducement. Too many of those sterilised in the name of eugenics allegedly consented (Kevles 1985; Trombley 1988).

A second problem with 'the perfect baby ideal' (McGee 2000) is what this does to the children. Robertson captures this concern well.

> The very concept of selection of offspring characteristics or "quality control" reveals a major discomfort – the idea that children are objects or products chosen on the basis of their qualities, like products in a shop window, valued not for themselves but for the pleasure or satisfaction they will give parents. (Robertson 1994, 150)

Children are persons, not property; individuals with rights, not commodities (Freeman 2007). A major – I have suggested *the* major – objection to the institution of surrogacy is that it commodifies children (Freeman 1989; Radin 1987). If a child is chosen to be 'intelligent' and turns out to be dull, or is selected to have athletic prowess and is instead slow and clumsy, if in other words parental expectations are thwarted, how will disappointment be expressed. In the worst case scenario the child may be rejected. There is a real danger that children may be damaged as a result.

In the future, as already indicated, it may be possible not merely to choose characteristics but to change them: to manipulate the genetic make-up of the embryo to programme in the desired characteristic. And we may transcend somatic gene therapy to embrace human germ-line therapy, enabling us to enhance the characteristics not just of our children, but of their children and grandchildren. This has caused alarm: George Annas and his colleagues have indicted this as a crime against humanity (Annas, Andrews and Isasi 2002), and such gene therapy has been outlawed in Australia and Canada.[35] The European Convention on Human Rights and Biomedicine also does not permit human germ-line therapy. Article 13 of this states:

---

34 The question has not been considered by any court. The pregnant woman who uses heroin has been considered, in the controversial case of *Re D (A Minor)* [1987] 1 AC 317.

35 See Australian Act 2005, Canadian Act of 2006.

> An intervention seeking to modify the human genome may only be undertaken for preventative, diagnostic or therapeutic purposes and only if its aim is not to produce any modification in the genome of any descendants.

UNESCO's Universal Declaration on Bioethics and Human Rights purports to offer a justification for such a ban. In Article 3 it states 'human dignity' is to be 'fully respected'. But it also acknowledges that 'the impact of the life sciences on future generations, including in their genetic constitution, should be given due regard'. There is a concern that we may lose our sense of what is human. But do we know what being 'human' is? As already indicated in this essay, there have been shifts in our understanding of this.

A Right not to Be Born?

What of the couple who discover that the foetus being carried is so damaged that the child who will be born will have a life of no quality at all? Of course, it is difficult to judge quality. A child who knows no difference may tolerate more than we might objectively suppose. The substituted judgement test, sometimes employed,[36] is not helpful. But let us say that the child's life, to quote an early English case, is going to be 'demonstrably so awful'.[37] The law permits the pregnancy to be terminated (Abortion Act 1967, s. 1(1) (d)). Should we also say that there is a responsibility to do so? Abortion is a rights issue: does it also translate into a matter of responsibility?[38]

Feinberg (1984) argues that biological parents 'do not harm' a child even if the child comes into existence in a state that makes 'life worth living' impossible. But it is still possible, he argues, to talk of a right not to be born. He refers to the 'plausible moral requirement' that

> no child be brought into the world unless certain very minimal conditions of well-being are assured, and certain basic "future interests" are protected in advance, at least in the sense that the possibility of his fulfilling those interests is kept open. When a child is brought into existence even though these requirements have not been observed, he has been wronged thereby. (Feinberg 1984, 101)

Feinberg concedes that not all interests should qualify for prenatal legal protection, but only the very basic ones whose satisfaction is indispensable. But he lists a large number of these including blindness, deafness and even 'economic deprivation so far below a reasonable minimum as to be inescapably degrading and sordid' (ibid., 99). Harris, rightly, finds the list 'astonishing' (Harris 1992, 91).

Are there people who would have been 'better off unborn'? And does this mean that there is a responsibility to abort them? It may be best to start by asking whether it can be better to be 'better off dead'. For Steinbock this phrase suggests that 'life is so terrible that it is no longer a benefit or a good to the one who lives'

36 *Re J (A Minor) (Wardship: Medical Treatment)* [1991] 1 FLR 366, 383-384 per Taylor LJ.

37 *Re B (A Minor) (Wardship: Medical Treatment)* [1981] 1 WLR 1421, 1424 per Templeman LJ.

38 See Hursthouse 1991.

(Steinbock 1992, 120). Feinberg offers a thought experiment in which we are given the opportunity after death to be reincarnated 'but only as a Tay-Sachs baby with a painful life expectancy of four years to be followed by permanent extinction or [we] can opt for permanent extinction to begin immediately' (Feinberg 1986, 164). He is of the opinion that we would have to be 'crazy' to select the first option, and that if required to make the choice for a loved one we would also opt for immediate non-existence. However, non-existence is rationally preferable only if all interests, present and future, are 'doomed to defeat'. Such a test works optimally where there is chronic pain combined with such severe mental retardation that the child will not be able to develop any compensating interests.

There are actually two different questions. One asks whether we might be acting wrongly to bring children into existence because of what is wrong with those children; the other whether it is wrong to bring children into the world when we cannot adequately parent them. Mill, writing in 1859, (1972, 239) saw this latter question long before anyone was considering either of the two questions – the former for obvious reasons. For Mill, to bring a child into the world 'without a fair prospect of being able, not only to provide food for its body, but instruction and training for its mind, [was] a moral crime', one against the child and society. It is politically incorrect to ponder the implications of Mill's concern today. It takes us back to the question, considered earlier in this essay, of the licensing of parenthood.

I will concentrate here on the first question. The complexity of this is well brought out by comparing two examples given by Derek Parfit. He invites us to consider the dilemmas faced by two women.

> The first is one month pregnant and is told by her doctor that, unless she takes a simple treatment, the child she is carrying will develop a certain handicap ... Life with this handicap would probably be worth living, but less so than normal life. It could obviously be wrong for the mother not to take the treatment, for this will handicap her child. (Parfit 1976, 76)

One can pause and ask: what if the 'treatment' alters the genetic composition of the child, changing its identity into that of a different person? This has teased philosophers (Agar 1995; DeGrazia 2005; Holtug 1993; Persson 1995; Zohar 1991) but need not detain us. Has a healthy B lost anything of value in being an unhealthy A? Parfit's second woman

> is about to stop taking contraceptive pills so that she can have another child. She is told that she has a temporary condition such that any child she conceives now will have the same handicap, but that if she waits three months she will then conceive a normal child. (Parfit 1976, 76)

In Parfit's view it would be as wrong for the second woman not to take her doctor's advice as for the first woman.

The first case is relatively uncontentious, but the second is far from straightforward, as Parfit himself acknowledges. In his *Reasons and Persons* (Parfit 1984, 358-359) he uses the example of the 14-year-old girl who wants a child. He notes we might say to her: 'You should think not only of yourself, but also of your child. It will be worse for him if you have him now'. But, of course, it will not be 'worse for him', for clearly if she has a child later it will not be the same child. Similarly, if the woman takes the advice she deprives a potential person, albeit one with a handicap, of the chance of having a life. It is his/her only chance: he/she may be glad to have the opportunity. Locke (1987), using a similar example to Parfit's second case, invokes what he calls the 'Possible Persons Principle' – 'in judging the rightness or wrongness of an action or decision we need to take account not merely of those who actually do, or will, exist, but also of those who would have existed if there had been a different action or decision'. However, acceptance of this principle would have enormous repercussions, not least for abortion. If, therefore, the second case can be explained by a more limited (or at any rate different) principle, it would be better to invoke this.

In seeking this, it is well to remember Richard Brandt's observation that 'no person is frustrated or made unhappy or miserable by not coming to exist' (Brandt 1974). Appealing to the concept of deprivation may assist us to understand the differences between being born with a handicap and not being conceived. Steinbock (1992, 74) puts it thus: 'the point of morality is to make people…happy, not to make more happy people'. We may thus be able to conclude that the woman in Parfit's second example also does the right thing if she postpones conception and avoids having a handicapped child. But suppose the second woman is told that any child she bears, now or in the future, will be handicapped, should she avoid conception? Unlike the woman in the second case, she will be depriving herself of the interest in being a mother (though the value of this interest may be diminished in those circumstances), but again it cannot be said that she is depriving anyone else of life.

But if failing to have a child is not wrong, having a child may, in certain circumstances, be wrong. Indeed, the belief that a child may be wronged by being brought into existence in certain circumstances has given rise to so-called 'wrongful life' actions.

The first case is *Zepeda v Zepeda.*[39] The injury claimed here, by a healthy child, was having been born illegitimately. The case was brought in 1963, when considerably greater stigma attached to illegitimacy (in Illinois, where the case was brought, as well as in the United Kingdom). Recovery was denied by courts which, unsurprisingly, feared the floodgates would open if it were permitted. The American courts have since distinguished between being born under adverse conditions and being born with a severe handicap or fatal disease. A clear statement of this distinction can be found in Justice Jefferson's judgment in *Curlender v Bio-Science Laboratories*,[40] a case where a child was born suffering from Tay-Sachs disease:

> A cause of action based upon impairment of status – illegitimacy contrasted with legitimacy – should not be recognizable at law because a necessary element for the establishment of any cause of action in tort is missing, *injury* and damages consequential to that injury. A child born with severe impairment, however, presents an entirely different situation because the necessary element of *injury* is present.

---

39 190 N.E. 2d 849 (1963). See also *Williams v State of New York* 223 N.E. 2d 343 (1966).
40 106 (al. App (3d) 811, 165 Cal Repts. 477 (1980)).

But what constitutes an injury? Is it an 'injury' to be born a girl? Does the answer to this depend on culture and community? Is it an injury to be born gay rather than heterosexual? Or to be born with criminal propensities?[41]

The courts have not been very receptive to wrongful life claims, though they have succeeded in a number of American states.[42] The English courts have rejected the concept. In *McKay v Essex Area Health Authority*,[43] the Court of Appeal expressed the view that 'the difference between existence and non-existence was incapable of measurement by a court'.[44] Ackner LJ said that he could not accept that 'the common law duty of care to a person can involve, without specific legislation to achieve this end, the legal obligation to that person, whether or not *in utero*, to terminate his existence.'[45] Such a proposition, he thought, ran wholly contrary to the concept of the sanctity of human life.

It is not surprising that courts should have had problems with the concept of wrongful life. Their concern are concrete and do not involve 'meditation on the mysteries of life' (as one court put it).[46] But we can delve into more abstract questions. It may be that if one can sustain a reasoned argument for a moral right not to be born that this will provide the foundation for a legal action in tort. My concern, though, is with moral entitlement, and the moral duties of potential parents.

Since we now regard parental responsibility as integral to an understanding of parent/child relations, what are the implications of this before the child is born? Does it cast any light on the constraints, if any, on having children? The law draws the line between parental autonomy and parental responsibility at 'significant harm'. It is at this level that intervention is pitched. Does this offer clues as to what may be expected of those endowed with parental responsibility?

Parental responsibility is a normative standard by which to judge the decisions and actions of parents or of those who wish to become parents. What it will look like will depend upon how it is justified. John Eekelaar, writing of parents' moral obligation to care for their children, has demonstrated that contractarian theories, motivated at least in part by self-interest, cannot really account for the obligation to care (Eekelaar 1991b). He found the true basis for these moral obligations in Finnis's

---

41 This was highlighted in the *Mobley* case in Georgia, USA in 1995.

42 California: see above, n. 40; New Jersey: *Berman v Allen* 404 A 2d 8; Washington: *Harbeson v Parke-Davis Inc*. 656 P 2d 483 (1983).

43 [1982] 2 All ER 771.

44 Ibid., 790.

45 Ibid., 787. 'Wrongful life' has also been rejected in Canada: *Cherry v Borsman* (1992), 94 DLR (4th) 487 and South Africa: *Friedman v Glickson* 1996 (1) SA 1134. Israel has allowed it: *Zeitsov v Katz* (1986), 40(2) P.D. 85, and so has France: *X v Mutuelle d'Assurance du Corps Sanitaire Francais et al.* (2000), JCP 2293 (the *Perruche* case). This case encountered criticism in France from the medical profession, as well as the anti-abortion lobby and disabled support groups, and the government was forced into initiating emergency legislation. The Dutch courts have also now recognised the wrongful life action in the *Molenaar* case (see *X v Y*, Court of Appeal in The Hague 26 March 2003, discussed by Nys and Date 2004, and since upheld by the Supreme Court). The literature on wrongful life is vast: although quite old. I would single out Morreim (1988) as offering particularly interesting insights.

46 In *Curlender v Bio-Science Laboratories*, above, n. 40.

theory of human flourishing (see Finnis 1980, 80-99). Finnis sees the procreation and education of children as 'an indistinguishable cluster of moral responsibilities' (ibid., 83). Eekelaar's arguments have equal force in our context.

To exercise parental responsibility is to put the interests and welfare of children (or future children) above one's own needs, desires or well-being. There may be disputes as to what is in a child's best interests, but there is an irreducible minimum content to a child's well-being, and this must be satisfied by anyone carrying out the role of, or purporting to become, a parent.

This means that the very young should not become parents. Whether it also means that older people should also consider not having children is debatable. The debate has focused on the post-menopausal woman, but applies equally to older men. With more time on their hands, more experience and perhaps more money such people may be excellent parents. Our intuition (or is it our prejudice?) sets its face against them, but the arguments against fertility treatment for post-menopausal women do not stand up to critical examination (Cutas 2007; Fisher and Sommerville 1998). Are couples in their sixties who have children acting irresponsibly? If they can more than meet their child's needs for the 'basic goods' of human flourishing, and if their parenting reaches or excels minimum standards ('the significant harm' test), why should we place obstacles in their way?

Conclusion

To view the problem through the lens of parental responsibility is to focus on the decision-making process. It is to recognise the commitment involved in bringing a child into the world. It is to acknowledge that having children is an exercise of commitment to love, nurture and care. It is to accept that parents should want the best for their children. To exercise parental responsibility – I use the concept normatively, not descriptively – is to plan parenthood sensibly, and with empathy for the needs and future of the child. It is thus not an exercise of parental responsibility to bring a child into the world whose life will be demonstrably awful. Nor is it an exercise of parental responsibility to bring a child into the world when that child will be cruelly deprived of all, or most, of the basic goods of human flourishing.

I have in the past been critical of those (Onora O'Neill is a good example) who have argued that adults' duties are more important than children's rights (Freeman 1992). O'Neill (1988) believes that taking rights as fundamental in ethical deliberation about children has neither theoretical nor political advantages. In emphasising responsible parenthood, in focusing on obligations, on agents rather than recipients, I do not resile from a commitment to the importance of taking children's rights seriously. Rather I begin to formulate a right overlooked by legislation, international[47] and national – the right to have responsible parents. Once a child is born, responsibility is more recognisable. This chapter has focused on decisions pre-birth. An article in preparation, for publication elsewhere, will examine the right to responsible parents

47 It is not in the United Nations Convention on the Rights of the Child of 1989.

as it is tested in important day-to-day decisions on such matters as education, medical treatment, punishment and religious upbringing.

References

Agar, N. (1995), 'Designing Babies: Morally Permissible Ways to Modify the Human Genome', *Bioethics* 9:1.

Annas, G., Andrews, L. and Isasi, R.M. (2002), 'Protecting the Endangered Human: Toward an International Treaty Prohibiting Cloning and Inheritable Alterations', *American Journal of Law and Medicine* 28:151.

Baker, H. (2004), 'MMR: Medicine, Mothers and Rights', *Cambridge Law Journal* 49.

Benhabib, S. (1992), *Situating the Self* (Cambridge: Polity Press).

Blustein, J. (1982), *Parents and Children* (New York: Oxford University Press).

Bostrom, N. (2005), 'In Defence of Posthuman Dignity', *Bioethics* 19:32.

Brandt, R. (1974), 'The Morality of Abortion' in Perkins, R. (ed.), *Abortion: Pro and Con* (Cambridge, MA.: Schenkman).

Bridgeman, J. (2007), *Parental Responsibility, Young Children and Healthcare Law* (Cambridge: Cambridge University Press).

Brock, D. (1996), 'Funding New Reproductive Technologies' in Cohen, C.B. (ed.), *New Ways of Making Babies: The Case of Egg Donation* (Bloomington: Indiana University Press).

Brock, Sir L. (chair) (1934), *Report of the Departmental Committee on Sterilization* (London: HMSO).

Chadwick, R.F. (1987), *Ethics, Reproduction and Genetic Control* (London: Croom Helm).

Covell, K. and Howe, R.B. (1998), 'A Policy of Parent Licensing' in Institute for Research on Public Policy, *Policy Options* (London: Institute for Research on Public Policy).

Cutas, D. (2007), 'Postmenopausal Motherhood: Immoral, Illegal? A Case Study', *Bioethics* 21:458.

Daniel, J. (1978), 'Child Abuse Screening: Implications of the Limited Predictive Power of Abuse Discriminants from a Controlled Family Study of Pediatric Social Illness', *Child Abuse and Neglect* 2:247.

DeGrazia, D. (2005), *Human Identity and Bioethics* (New York: Cambridge University Press).

Eekelaar, J. (1991a), 'Parental Responsibility: State of Nature or Nature of the State?', *Journal of Social Welfare and Family Law* 13:37.

Eekelaar, J. (1991b), 'Are Parents Morally Obliged to Care for their Children?', *Oxford Journal of Legal Studies* 11:340.

Eekelaar, J. (2000), 'Uncovering Social Obligations: Family Law and the Responsible Citizen' in Maclean, M. (ed.), *Making Law for Families* (Oxford: Hart).

Eekelaar, J. (2001a), 'Family Law: The Communication Message', *Oxford Journal of Legal Studies* 21:181.

Eekelaar, J. (2001b), 'Parental Responsibility – A New Legal Status: Social Parenthood', *Law Quarterly Review* 117:233.

Eisenberg, H.B. (1994), 'A "Modest" Proposal: State Licensing of Parents', *Connecticut Law Review* 26:1415.
Feinberg, J. (1984), *Harm to Others* (New York: Oxford University Press).
Feinberg, J. (1986), 'Wrongful Life and the Counterfactual Element in Harming', *Social Philosophy and Policy* 4:145.
Finnis, J. (1980), *Natural Law and Natural Rights* (Oxford: Clarendon Press).
Fisher, F. and Sommerville, A. (1998), 'To Everything There is a Season? Are There Medical Grounds for Refusing Fertility Treatment to Older Women?' in Harris, J. and Holm, S. (eds), *The Future of Human Reproduction* (Oxford: Oxford University Press).
Floyd, S.L. and Pomerantz, D. (1981), 'Is There a Natural Right to Have Children?' in Arthur, J. (ed.), *Morality and Moral Controversies* (Englewood Cliffs, NJ: Prentice Hall).
Fox, M. and Thomson, M. (2005), 'Short-Changed? The Law and Ethics of Male Circumcision', *International Journal of Children's Rights* 13:161.
Frank, R. (1990), 'Family Law and the Federal Republic of Germany', *International Journal of Law, Policy and the Family* 4:214.
Franklin, S. and Roberts, C. (2006), *Born and Made – An Ethnography of Preimplantation Genetic Diagnosis* (Princeton, NJ.: Princeton University Press).
Freeman, M. (1979), *Violence in the Home: A Socio-Legal Study* (Aldershot: Saxon House).
Freeman, M. (1988), 'Sterilising the Mentally Handicapped' in Freeman, M. (ed.), *Medicine, Ethics and Law* (London: Stevens).
Freeman, M. (1989), 'Is Surrogacy Exploitative?' in McLean, S., *Legal Issues in Human Reproduction* (Aldershot: Gower), Ch. 7.
Freeman, M. (1992), 'Taking Children's Rights More Seriously' in Alston, P., Parker, S. and Seymour, J. (eds), *Children, Rights and the Law* (Oxford: Clarendon Press), 52-71.
Freeman, M. (1997), 'Do Children Have the Right Not to Be Born' in Freeman, M., *The Moral Status of Children* (The Hague: Martinus Nijhoff), Ch. 9.
Freeman, M. (2006), 'Saviour Siblings' in McLean, S. (ed.), *First Do No Harm* (Aldershot: Ashgate).
Freeman, M. (2007), 'Why It Remains Important to Take Children's Rights Seriously', *International Journal of Children's Rights* 15:5.
Freeman, M. and Abou-Doudé, P. (2007), *Journal of Medical Ethics.*
Frisch, L.E. (1981), 'On Licentious Licensing: A Reply to Hugh LaFollette', *Philosophy and Public Affairs* 11:173.
Fukujama, F. (2002), *Our Posthuman Future* (New York: Farrar, Straus and Giroux).
Gil, D. (1978), 'Societal Violence and Violence in Families' in Eekelaar, J. and Katz, S. (eds), *Family Violence* (Toronto: Butterworths), Ch. 1.
Gillies, V. (2005), 'Meeting Parents' Needs? Discourses of "Support" and "Inclusion" in Family Policy', *Critical Social Policy* 25:70.
Gilligan, C. (1982), *In a Different Voice: Psychological Theory and Women's Development* (Cambridge, MA: Harvard University Press).
Gray, J. (2007), *Black Mass: Apocalyptic Religion and the Death of Utopia* (London: Allen Lane).

Harris, J. (1992), *Wonderwoman and Superman* (Oxford: Oxford University Press).
Hart, H.L.A. (1958), 'Positivism and the Separation of Law and Morals', *Harvard Law Review* 71:593.
Hart, H.L.A. (1968), *Punishment and Responsibility* (Oxford: Clarendon Press).
Hartman, R.G. (2005), 'Face Value: Challenges of Transplant Technology', *American Journal of Law and Medicine* 31:7.
Häyry, M. (2004), 'There is a Difference between Selecting a Deaf Embryo and Deafening a Hearing Child', *Journal of Medical Ethics* 30:510.
Holm, S. (1998), 'Ethical Issues in Pre-implantation Diagnosis' in Harris, J. and Holm, S. (eds), *The Future of Human Reproduction* (Oxford: Oxford University Press), Ch. 10.
Holtug, N. (1993), 'Human Gene Therapy: Down the Slippery Slope?', *Bioethics* 7:402.
House of Commons Science and Technology Committee (2005), *Human Reproductive Technologies and the Law* (5th Report), HC 7-1 (London: TSO).
House of Commons Select Committee on Violence in the Family (1977), *Violence in the Family. Volume 1: Report* (First report from the Select Committee on Violence in the Family), HC 329 (London: HMSO).
Human Genetics Commission (2006), *Making Babies: Reproductive Decisions and Genetic Technologies* (London: Human Genetics Commission).
Hursthouse, R. (1991), 'Virtue Theory and Abortion', *Philosophy and Public Affairs* 20:223.
Huxtable, R. (2004), 'Re C (A Child) Immunisation: Parental Rights', *Journal of Social Welfare and Family Law* 26:69.
Jackson, E. (2002), 'Conception and the Irrelevance of The Welfare Principle', *Modern Law Review* 65:176.
Joint Committee on the Human Tissue and Embryos Draft Bill (2007), *Human Tissue and Embryos (Draft) Bill Volume I: Report* (London: The Stationery Office).
Justice (1975), *Parental Rights and Duties and Custody Suits* (London: Stevens).
Kevles, D. (1985), *In the Name of Eugenics: Genetics and the Uses of Human Heredity* (Cambridge, MA: Harvard University Press).
Kitcher, P. (1996), *The Lives to Come* (New York: Simon and Schuster).
Knowles, L. and Kaebnick, G.E. (2007), *Reprogenetics: Law, Policy and Ethical Issues* (Baltimore: Johns Hopkins University Press).
Kurzweil, R. (2005), *The Singularity Is Near: When Humans Transcend Biology* (New York: Viking).
LaFollette, H. (1980), 'Licensing Parents', *Philosophy and Public Affairs* 9:182.
Light, R. (1973), 'Abused and Neglected Children in America: A Study of Alternative Policies', *Harvard Educational Review* 43: 455.
Locke, D. (1987), 'The Parfit Population Problem', *Philosophy* 62:131.
Lyon, C.M. (2000), 'The Definition of, and Legal and Management Responses to, the Problem of Child Abuse in England and Wales' in Freeman, M. (ed.), *Overcoming Child Abuse: A Window on a World Problem* (Aldershot: Ashgate), Ch. 6.
Mangel, C.P. (1988), 'Licensing Parents: How Feasible?', *Family Law Quarterly* 22: 17.
Mason, M.A. (1994), *From Father's Property to Children's Rights* (New York: Columbia University Press).

McGee, G. (2000), *The Perfect Baby* (Lanham: Rowman and Littlefield).
McLean, S. (2006), *Modern Dilemmas – Choosing Children* (Edinburgh: Capercaillie Books).
Mill, J.S. (1972), *On Liberty* (Warnock, M. (ed.)) (London: Fontana).
Morreim, E.H. (1988), 'The Concept of Harm Reconceived: A New Look at Wrongful Life', *Law amd Philosophy* 7:3.
Morris, A. and Saintier, S. (2003), 'To Be or Not to Be: Is That the Question? Wrongful Life and Misconceptions', *Medical Law Review* 11:167.
Nys, H.F.L. and Date J.C.J (2004), 'A Wrongful Existence in the Netherlands', *Journal of Medical Ethics* 30:393.
O'Neill, O. (1988), 'Children's Rights and Children's Lives', *Ethics* 98:445.
Parfit, D. (1976), 'Rights, Interests and Possible People' in Gorovitz, S. (ed.), *Moral Problems in Medicine* (Englewood Cliffs, NJ: Prentice Hall).
Parfit, D. (1984), *Reasons and Persons* (Oxford: Oxford University Press).
Persson, I. (1995), 'Genetic Therapy, Identity and Person-regarding Reasons', *Bioethics* 9:16.
Purdy, L. (1996), *Reproducing Persons: Issues in Feminist Bioethics* (Ithaca, NY: Cornell University Press).
Radin, M. (1987), 'Market-inalienability', *Harvard Law Review* 100:1849.
Reece, H. (2003), *Divorcing Responsibly* (Oxford: Hart).
Reece, H. (2006), 'From Parental Responsibility to Parenting Responsibly' in Freeman, M. (ed.), *Law and Sociology* (Oxford: Oxford University Press), 459.
Robertson, J. (1983), 'Procreative Liberty and the Control of Conception, Pregnancy and Childbirth', *Virginia Law Review* 69:405.
Robertson, J. (1994), *Children of Choice: Freedom and the New Reproductive Technologies* (Princeton, NJ: Princeton University Press).
Savulescu, J. (2001), 'Procreative Beneficence: Why We Should Select the Best Children', *Bioethics* 15:413.
Schneider, C., Hoffmeister, M. and Helfer, R. (1972), 'The Predictive Questionnaire: A Preliminary Report' in Kempe, C.H. and Helfer, R. (eds), *Helping the Battered Child and his Family* (Philadelphia: Lippincott).
Select Committee (1977).
Siegel-Itzkovich, J. (2005), 'Israel Allows Sex Selection of Embryos for Non-Medical Reasons', *British Medical Journal* 330:1228.
Smart, C. and Neale, B. (1999), *Family Fragments*? (Cambridge: Policy Press).
Steinbock, B. (1992), *Life Before Birth* (New York: Oxford University Press).
Stock, G. (2002), *Redesigning Humans: Our Inevitable Genetic Future* (Boston: Houghton, Mifflin).
Stock, G. and Campbell, J. (2000), *Engineering the Human Germline* (New York: Oxford University Press).
Swindell, J.S. (2007), 'Facial Allograft Transplantation: Personal Identity and Subjectivity', *Journal of Medical Ethics* 33:449.
Trombley, S. (1988), *The Right to Reproduce* (London: Weidenfeld and Nicolson).
Tronto, J. (1993), *Moral Boundaries: The Political Argument for an Ethic of Care* (New York: Routledge).

Uniacke, S. (1987), 'In Vitro Fertilization and the Right to Reproduce', *Bioethics* 1:241.

Viens, A.M. (2004), 'Value Judgment, Harm and Religious Liberty', *Journal of Medical Ethics* 30:241.

Westman, J.C. (1994), *Licensing Parents: Can We Prevent Child Abuse and Neglect?* (Cambridge, MA: Perseus Books).

Wilson, J. (2007), 'Transhumanism and Moral Equality', *Bioethics* 21:419.

Zohar, N.J. (1991), 'Prospects for "Genetic Therapy" – Can a Person Benefit from Being Altered?', *Bioethics* 5:275.

Chapter 3

Together Forever? The Rights and Responsibilities of Adult Children and their Parents

Jonathan Herring

Introduction

> How sharper than a serpent's tooth it is
> To have a thankless child.
>
> (Shakespeare, 2002, Act 1, Sc. 4, ln. 286-87)

That was King Lear, and I suppose he should know. There is widespread agreement that parent/child relationships are very important. The relationship between older people and their children is of enormous social and personal value (Grundy and Murphy 2006); people regard their relationships with their parents and/or children as of central importance to their sense of self, whether or not these relationships are good. The death of a parent or child is universally regarded as a significant loss, even where there has been a protracted period without communication between them.

But the parent/adult child relationship is significant for more than just personal reasons. In the United Kingdom, as in the rest of Europe, society is ageing rapidly (European Commission 2005). The care of older people has become a major social issue. The financial costs of long-term health and social care, concerns over the quality of care in nursing homes, the debate about pensions, and the widespread perception that older people provide a huge resource which our society has barely begun to exploit, are all 'hot topics'. The parent/child relationship can be implicated in all of these. The weaker the child/parent bond, the greater the likelihood that there will be a financial or social cost to society. These relationships are becoming strained in response to social changes. Delayed motherhood, greater levels of paid work among women, increased levels of divorce, and more movement of people (both domestically and internationally) could all be said to put pressure on adult child/parent relationships (Gans and Silverstein 2006; Peek et al. 1998). On the other hand there is the increasing number of adult children living with their parents because they are unable to enter the housing market; 23 per cent of the over twenties in a recent survey (Wicks and Asato 2003, 3).

Despite its significance the relationship between adult children and parents is a difficult one to regulate. The law has plenty to say about the rights and responsibilities parents owe their minor children, but once the child reaches the age of majority the law generally falls silent (Oldham 2001). It would be wrong, as we shall see, to suggest that the law imposes *no* rights or obligations between adults and their parents. But they are few and of a limited nature. Indeed they are shockingly few and limited. As Mika Oldham has pointed out:

> We are free to refuse to render any form of assistance to our parents or grandparents, regardless of their, or our own, circumstances. Support for the elderly is considered to fall within the realm of public rather than private intergenerational transfer. (Oldham 2006, 223)

Before perusing these ideas, a brief discussion of terminology is necessary. The concepts 'responsibility' and 'obligation' are used interchangeably in most of the writings on this topic. However, the concepts could be said to have important differences. One argument would be that responsibility carries with it an element of causality. A parent owes their child responsibilities because they are 'responsible for' the child coming into existence. By contrast an obligation carries no causal connotation. Hence if a person came across an abandoned baby in a field, to say she owed the baby a responsibility would, from this view, be incorrect; to say she owed the baby an obligation would be preferable. This view may, however, confuse the distinction between being 'responsible for' something and owing responsibilities to do something. These terms are not synonymous. Another possible distinction between obligations and responsibilities is their source. One might say that responsibilities are imposed upon people, by the state, because of another's rights. But an obligation might arise with no corresponding right of another. You may owe an obligation not to harm the environment, but not a responsibility not to harm the environment (if you take the view that no one has a right to have the environment protected). By contrast Gilligan's writing on the ethic of care sees responsibilities as arising not out of rights, but out of relationships (Gilligan 1982; see also Bridgeman, in this book). For the purposes of this chapter the terms obligation and responsibility will be used interchangeably, but clearly there is more discussion to be had (see Eekelaar 2006) about the distinction between them, if any.

This chapter will start by considering the legal rights and duties that govern the adult children/parent relationship. Then, it will consider how the law should respond to the relationship.

Financial Responsibility

Financial responsibility owed by adult children for their parents

In English and Welsh law people are not financially responsible for the care of their parents. Some countries have filial support legislation, under which an adult can be required to contribute to the costs of their parents' care (see Blair 1996; Fennell 2004; Kline 1992; Moskowitz 2001; Wise 2002). England and Wales have no such equivalent. There is no basis, apart from a formal contract drawn up between the parties, under which parents can sue their children for financial or any other form of support. Under the social security system children are not 'liable relatives' and so their wealth is not taken into account when considering a parent's claim for benefits. Nor is there even any claim on the death of a child from the parent against the child's estate, unless the parent can claim that he or she falls into the category of those being maintained by the deceased (*Bouette v Rose*[1]).

It would, of course, be quite wrong to think that because there is no legal duty to provide financial or other support it is not done. Many older people are receiving and giving support to their children. In the recent OASIS survey 75 per cent of older people in the United Kingdom had face to face contact at least weekly; 61 per cent received instrumental help; and 76 per cent felt very close to their children (Lowenstein and Daatland 2006).

Financial liabilities of parents towards adult children

The law is a little, but only a little, more willing to accept financial responsibilities owed by parents towards their adult children. Normally a parent is only required to support a child until their 18th birthday. This is all that is required under the Child Support Act 1991. The fact that liability lasts until majority is dramatically shown in several recent cases of extremely wealthy fathers who have been required to pay substantial sums to house appropriately children born out of marriage; in one case to the tune of £1.2 million (*P v T*[2]). But the courts have accepted that the father is only obliged to support the child until his or her 18th birthday and hence in these cases the order has been in terms of a trust, so that the property reverts to the father on the child's 18th birthday (*J v C*[3]). So, the child will live in luxury, in a style appropriate for the child of a millionaire, but only until their 18th birthday. Then nothing. It is the same where a married father is required to pay child support under the Child Support Act: ordinarily this will cease on the child's 18th birthday.

However, there are some exceptional circumstances in which a parent can be required to support an adult child. Under the Children Act 1989, schedule 1, paragraph 2, if a child is a student or trainee and the parents are living apart, the child can apply to the court for a lump sum or periodical payments order. This is true even beyond the age of 18. In relation to married couples who are divorcing, an application can be made under the Matrimonial Causes Act 1973. Section 29 makes it clear that financial support for a child cannot be ordered beyond a child's 18th birthday, unless he or she 'is, or will be or [if provision extending beyond 18 years of age were made] would be, receiving instruction at an educational establishment, or undergoing training for a trade, profession or vocation, whether or not he is also or will also be in gainful employment' or there are 'special circumstances which justify' the making of a different order (*B v B (Adult Student: Liability to Support)*[4]; see further Letts 2001).

So then, children beyond the age of 18 can seek orders against their parents under the Children Act 1989 or, where the parents are divorcing, a court can make

1 [2000] 1 FCR 185.
2 [2003] *Fam Law* 303.
3 [1998] 3 FCR 79.
4 [1998] 1 FCR 49.

an order under the Matrimonial Causes Act 1973. But this is subject to two important restrictions. First, they must show that they are receiving full-time education or training; or are suffering a disability (*T v S (Financial Provision for Children)*[5]). Second, and more significantly, the liability arises only where the children's parents are divorcing or, if unmarried, have separated.

These provisions are problematic. First, if the children have justifiable claims against their parents in these circumstances, why are they limited to where the parents have separated?. Children's needs do not necessarily increase or diminish just because their parents have separated. The explanation for this restriction which is commonly given is that there would be too great an intrusion into family privacy if a claim could be brought by the child against parents who are still together. It may be that the better explanation is that these provisions are not actually about giving an adult child a claim against a parent. Rather what the courts are doing here is, in effect, requiring one parent to meet a financial burden which would otherwise unfairly fall on another parent. In other words it is about ensuring that the financial burden of supporting the adult child is shared equally between the parents, rather than giving a child a claim against their parents.

The second oddness about these provisions is that the claim can only be met if the child can show that she or he falls into the circumstances mentioned. In the cases of disability and further education it is true that a person can be in serious financial need. However, why should this be restricted to those two situations? An adult child may be in great need through no fault of his or her own in other scenarios. They may, for example, suffer a burglary while uninsured; or suffer unexpected redundancy; or suffer an injury or illness or mental illness short of disability. Why are adult children suffering a disability or in full-time education more worthy than other such needy adults?

There is a further way in which the courts can protect the interests of an adult child. Under the Matrimonial Causes Act 1973 the courts have wide powers to redistribute the property of divorcing couples. One popular form of order in relation to the house is that the mother and children be permitted to live in the family home until she dies, remarries, cohabits or the children reach the age of 18 or finish their full-time education. When one of those events occurs the house must be sold and the proceeds divided between the parties. This has become known as a *Mesher* order. It reflects the statutory provisions mentioned earlier about an individual's obligations to their children ceasing upon the child's 18th birthday unless the the child is receiving further education. However, the case law has taken an interesting twist in the recent decision of the Court of Appeal, *Sawden v Sawden.*[6] Here the Court made a version of the *Mesher* order with the 'child triggering event' being, not the children finishing education but rather 'that the charge be realised in the event that both children leave home and settle independently in homes of their own'. This could be seen as a recognition of ongoing parental responsibility beyond minority. Further orders can be made to support a carer of children into majority.

---

5 [1994] 1 FCR 743.

6 [2004] EWCA Civ 339.

If a person dies leaving a will his or her property will be distributed in accordance with the instructions set out in the will. If the person dies without a will then the rules of intestacy will determine inheritance. However, in either case it is open to an individual to challenge the provision he or she received (if any) under the Inheritance (Provision for Family and Dependants) Act 1975. For our purposes it is of interest that children of the deceased are included within the list of those who can claim under the Act. The courts have, in fact, not been particularly sympathetic to such claims. The basic approach has been that an adult child will need to show some special circumstance in order to justify a claim (*Re Hancock (decd)*[7]). Successful claims from adult children tend to rely either on some special need of the child or on some special obligation owed to them by their parents (*Re Peace (decd)*[8]). There does appear here, then, to be a recognition that a parent can owe an adult child an obligation, if the child is in need or there has been some special undertaking to provide for the child. Notably these obligations are not ones that are enforceable during the life of the parent, but appear to become so on death (Oldham 2001). This is not entirely unjustifiable. To enforce an obligation during life, as we shall discuss later, may strain a relationship, which may be of greater value than the benefits of the enforcement of financial orders. Further, such enforcement requires a difficult balance to be struck between the interests of the parties. However, on death there is no fear about pressurising the relationship and the balance is between the adult child and other relatives or friends who may have a claim on the estate.

Responsibility under the Criminal Law

An adult child who commits an assault against an older parent (or vice versa) will, of course, be criminally liable. But are there any special responsibilities under the criminal law concerning parents and adult children? The issue comes to the fore in relation to the criminal law on omissions.

The starting point is that, generally, people are not normally criminally liable for failing to act unless they were under a duty to act. Hence, criminal lawyers, repeatedly point out that you can walk past someone drowning in a pond and do nothing to save her without fear of criminal prosecution, unless you owe her a duty of care. The issue for this chapter is whether persons owe a duty of care in this sense towards their parents or adult children.

It appears well established that parents owe their minor children a duty of care and spouses and cohabitants owe each other a duty of care (e.g. *R v Hood*[9]). But does this extend when children are older? The Smith and Hogan textbook states 'As a matter of principle, it can be argued that the important issue is not one of blood or formal legal relationship, but of interdependence' (Ormerod 2005, 81). This might indicate that an older child who is no longer living with their parents does not owe them a duty of care. Simester and Sullivan (2003, 76) argue that the key issue is whether there is a commitment to take responsibility for another's welfare. Although

7 [1998] 2 FLR 346.
8 [1999] 2 FCR 179.
9 [2004] 1 CAR (S) 431.

this might be true in the context of a particular relationship (for example, where an infirm adult has been taken into the home of an adult child who cares for him or her), it is not automatically so in the case of parents and adult children or adult children and parents.

So the law is not completely clear, but it appears that unless an adult child has specifically undertaken an obligation to care for their parent there is no duty to rescue. The fact that an adult child can walk past his or her drowning parent and offer no assistance is a dramatic demonstration of the law's reluctance to impose obligations on adults in respect of their parents.

Protecting the Adult Child/Parent Relationship in a Caring Context

When a local authority wishes to take a child into care, a protective order can only be made if the 'threshold criteria' in section 31 of the Children Act 1989 are met, which include a requirement that the child is suffering or likely to suffer significant harm and that this is attributable to the care of the parents. But if a local authority wishes to remove an incompetent adult from the care of his or her parents or adult child there are no such hurdles to overcome, if it does so under the inherent jurisdiction.

In *A Local Authority v Mr BS*[10] (2003) Ms S, aged 33, suffered from a moderate/severe learning disability and atypical autism and epilepsy. She lacked capacity to decide where she should live and who should provide care for her. Since the death of her mother, her father (Mr S) had been her sole carer, assisted by some privately arranged support workers. There had been an allegation that Mr S struck S and this led the local authority to institute proceedings to protect her. Under the inherent jurisdiction S was placed in a residential placement and contact between S and Mr S was limited to supervised contact.

What is most notable is that in deciding whether such orders should continue Wall J distinguished cases such as the present with that of a child being removed into care. Remarkably, Wall J did not even think there was a presumption that an incapable person was best cared for by the person who had been caring for them (in this case) for the past 33 years. The question was simply one of applying the best interests principle. The contrast between the protection offered parents whose minor children cannot be removed without the strongest justification and parents whose adult children can be removed if it is assessed to be in their best interests is striking.

A slightly different issue arose in *Re D-R (Adult: Contact)*[11] where a father sought contact with his 19-year-old daughter who was suffering from cerebral palsy. He had had no contact with her since his relationship with the child's mother had ended several years previously. The court made it clear that there was no presumption of a right to contact between a parent and an adult child. The issue was solely whether or not contact was in the best interests of the adult child. The judge, considering all the factors, had decided it was not and the Court of Appeal did not want to interfere with

10 [2003] EWHC 1909.
11 [1999] 2 FCR 49.

that decision. Again the contrast between this approach with that in cases involving parents and minor children, where the courts are very willing to assume that parental contact is in the child's interests, is remarkable.

Adult Child and Parents and Decision Making

It is possible to find some statutory recognition of the adult child/parent relationship. For example, the 'nearest relative' of a person detained under the Mental Health Act 1983 has a special place in the legislation to ensure the rights of detained people are respected. It is not appropriate to list here all the roles of the nearest relative under the legislative regime, but they include, for example, that the nearest relative must be consulted before an application is made to admit a patient under section 3. The definition of 'nearest relative' is the person highest up the list of relations found in section 26. Son or daughter is second on the list (after spouse or civil partner) and parent is third. Similarly under the Human Tissue Act 2004, in the absence of other 'qualifying consent' in relation to certain activities undertaken on the body (or to material from a corpse), consent can be provided by the person who is highest on the following list of 'qualifying relationships'. The list is similar to that in the Mental Health Act 1983, although the 2004 Act lists parents and children on an equal footing.[12] It is far from clear why there is recognition of the parental/adult child relationship in these cases, where one of the parties has died or is suffering from a mental condition, but not in others.

Adult Children's Moral Responsibilities towards their Parents

The debate over legal enforcement of filial responsibility can raise strong feelings. Judge Wald, an American judge, expressed well the ambiguous feelings some people have over this issue:

> On the one hand, the dependency of frail or ill elderly people is viewed as "not their fault" and as part of the "natural progression of life". Younger people can picture themselves in the same unenviable spot down the road and feel strong filial responsibilities to the parents who cared for them as children. Nonetheless, negative feelings toward the elderly run strong in our society. ... Many Americans feel that the care of the elderly should be paid for by their families or from their own savings, rather than by the government – they resent subsidizing other people's failure to plan ahead. Conversely, younger working Americans resent the notion that in their peak years, they must bear the burden of supporting older relatives. (Wald 1997, 1091)

There is also at the heart of the debate a clash between the wish of older people to be independent, while at the same time treasuring relationships of care and dependency. Many infirm older parents want children to help; but not too much. This tension is apparent in government policy too. The *National Service Framework for Older People* (Department of Health 2001) promotes independence and person-centred

12 Section 27.

care among older people (Harper and Leeson 2002; 2003; Leeson 2004); while at the same time the *National Strategy for Carers* (Department of Health 1999) seeks to enable, encourage and support those with caring roles.

In deciding how the law should govern the adult child/parent relationship one starting point is to consider whether there is a moral obligation for children to care for their older relatives (Collingridge and Miller 1997). There is a widespread feeling that there is, but its exact basis and what is required is much debated (Ganong et al. 1998). Four possible bases for such an obligation will be outlined below:

Reciprocated duty

This view is based on the argument that in the same way parents are financially responsible for the care of young children (when those children are vulnerable) so children should reciprocate with the care of their parents (when the parents are vulnerable) (see, for example, Blustein 1983). It was recently announced that raising a child costs parents an average of £180,137 (BBC 2006). Given the amount of money and care expended by a parent on a child, it is the least a child can do to reciprocate when their parent becomes needy. Blackstone wrote in 1765:

> The duties of children to their parents arise from a principle of natural justice and retribution. For to those, who gave us existence, we naturally owe subjection and obedience during our minority, and honour and reverence ever after; they who protected the weakness of our infancy, are entitled to our protection in the infirmity of their age; they who by sustenance and education have enabled their offspring to prosper, ought in return to be supported by that offspring, in case they stand in need of assistance. Upon this principle proceed all the duties of children to their parents which are enjoined by positive law. (Blackstone 1976, Book 1, Chapter 16)

This argument can also be put in terms of children being unjustly enriched at the hands of their parents unless the children can provide financial support when needed (see Laslett 1992 for discussion of whether there is a contract between the generations). Margaret Brinig (1994) has even argued that parents are less willing to make sacrifices for their children because they are not guaranteed their children's support in old age.

There are problems with this approach. One is that many deny the alleged symmetry between the kinds of claim (for example, Daniels 1988, 29). It could be said that the financial responsibility of parents is justified by the fact they have caused the child to be born (inevitably in a state of dependency) and because they can be said, implicitly, to have consented to undertake the financial obligation. However, there is no causal responsibility from a child to their parent's dependency, nor can there be an implied consent to be responsible from the child (Feinberg 1966, 139; Locke 1988, 141).

A further difficulty with an approach based on reciprocity is that it would appear to imply a child owes more to their parents if they have spent large sums of money or expended a substantial amount of effort on the child than where the parents have spent little money on the child, or expended less effort. This is especially so in a version of the approach which emphasises the notion that children owe their parents a 'debt'. But it is by no means obvious that wealthy parents who lavished many gifts on their children are 'owed' more than the impoverished parents who were able to provide their children with little more than necessities. Indeed it is not hard to imagine that the impoverished parents may be owed more by their children than wealthy parents.

This last criticism may lead to the argument being put in a different way: after all that parents have done for their children, their children owe them honour and respect (Blidstein 1975). This should be manifested in appropriate assistance to their needy parents as a reflection of their respect (see further, Wise 2002). The benefit of this argument is that is does not so directly tie in the level of assistance expected of the child and the level of assistance provided by the parent. The difficulty with it is that it is not clear that the payment of money or the performance of a duty is an expression of gratitude or honour (Kellet 2006). The giving of it is not valued or intended to be valued for its 'thank you value'. So if a child assisted in a way that was effective as an expression of gratitude but did not resolve the need of the ageing parent it is not apparent that that would meet the obligation owed by the child. Nor is it clear that an adult child who grudgingly met the needs of their parents would be said not to have met their obligations even if the assistance could not be said to have expressed respect.

An attractive form of the reciprocity argument has been put by the Lindemann Nelsons:

> The parental giving and filial receiving characteristic of early childhood is a major theme of the very beginning of the child's story, and one cannot yet tell what moral significance the child will make of it. But when that child grows into full moral agency, he is able retrospectively to make that giving and receiving mean a variety of things, depending on how he treats his parents now. If his parents now come to him in need and he spurns them, he is declaring that the relationship he had with them as a child was largely instrumental: he was using them only as a means to his own ends, and they are no more to him than that. Alternatively, if he now responds to their needs, he is redeeming that childhood relationship of its instrumentality, and declares by his actions that he was not merely using his parents to provide goods and services for him. (Lindemann Nelsons 1992, 757)

The benefit of putting the argument this way is that it is sensitive to the long-term nature of the relationship. An adult child who is legitimately unable to assist their parents due to their own financial difficulties may not be showing that they have declared they were being used instrumentally, especially if they offer whatever assistance they can. Similarly what is required of the adult child depends on the parties' currents needs and relationship, rather than simply upon how much was given during childhood.

Relational support

Jane English (1993) has argued that the parent/child link on its own does not generate obligations. However, the quality of the current relationship might create obligations, just as the relationship between two friends might. In other words, parents and children owe obligations in the same way that any two people in a relationship might. This would mean that a child who was currently in a hostile relationship (or indeed a non-existent one) would owe nothing (Dixon 1995).

This is, with respect, not a wholly convincing argument. Many children do feel obligations towards parents, even where the relationship is a bad one. Further, even where a relationship with parents is positive it has a stronger element than that with a friend. There must be few people who if required at the same time to be both at the bedside of a sick parent with whom they got on well and a friend with whom they got on equally well, would not feel the obligation towards a parent to be the stronger.

The strength of English's point lies in the fact that the obligation felt between children and parents is not a monolithic concept and will vary over time and can vary from one relationship to another. Her insistence that the obligation depends on the relationship between the parties seems hard to deny. Indeed the research of 'felt filial obligation' indicates that respondents do feel that the quality of the current relationship with the parent can affect what is expected of them (Gilleard and Higgs 2000). Some studies have suggested low levels of felt obligation where the parent has abandoned, neglected or mistreated a child (Storm et al. 1985). Nevertheless, it is submitted that it would be wrong to suggest that obligations are only dependent on the current relationship.

The parent/child bond

By contrast with English's approach there are those who argue that obligations flow automatically from the nature of the child/parent relationship itself (Brannen 2006). Stephen Kellet (2006), for example, has argued that the child/parent relationship is 'like nothing else'. He points out that to many people their relationship with their parents and/or their children are of great value and cannot be readily replaced. He argues that a child of an older parent is in a position to provide to their parent a good which no one else can provide; and similarly a parent towards an adult child. A parent can provide to an adult child advice and support based on bonds formed over a lifetime together, and a shared history which no one else can provide. He argues:

> There are important goods that you can provide only to your parents, and that your parents can receive from no one but you. My suggestion is that the reason why you have special duties to your parents is that you are uniquely placed to provide them with these goods and find yourself in a relationship in which they have provided (and perhaps continue to provide) special goods to you. And the duties themselves are duties to provide the special goods to your parents, within the context of the reciprocal relationship that you and your parents share. (Kellet 2006, 254)

There is much to this argument (see also Wicclair 1993). It is, however, weaker when it comes to the kind of duties that the law is most likely to enforce: duties to pay money. The payment of money is not a need that a child is in a unique position to meet.

The rights of older parents

So far, the approaches under consideration have focused on the adult child and sought to find a way of imposing an obligation on them. This approach starts with the rights of the older parent. It claims that an older person has a right to be provided with a reasonable level of support and assistance. Indeed, Article 25 of the European Charter of Fundamental Rights recognises the rights of the elderly 'to lead a life of dignity and independence and to participate in social and cultural life'. An older person is in a state of dependency and needs financial assistance from someone (Goodin 1985). Any proper moral system will place an obligation to meet those needs on someone and the adult child is uniquely well placed to provide the emotional comfort and financial support needed (Garrison, 1998). Further such responsibility would reflect a strong cultural tradition that children care for their aged parents (Teitelbaum 1992; Wang 1999).

So at the heart of this argument is the claim that the older person in need has a right to receive support and the question is who should provide it: the state or the adult child? Of course this is not necessarily an 'either/or' issue. It would be possible to share the burden between the state and the children.

It is also sometimes argued that the majority of older people would prefer to receive care and support from their children, rather than the 'impersonal, unfeeling' care provided at an institutional or state level. This, however, is not the correct question in this context. The right question to ask is whether an older person would prefer to receive care from an adult child who has been compelled to offer this care or to receive care from the state and the answer is far from clear. There is, for example, evidence that each familial generation seeks to promote the economic well-being of the following generation, even at their own expense (Todorova 2005). Further, there is a danger of developing a 'romanticised' vision of how family care is offered (Wise 2002). It overlooks the growing evidence of elder abuse, which certainly occurs in both domestic and institutional settings, but is perhaps easier to combat in the latter (see Payne and Fletcher 2005; Williams, in this book).

Considering the arguments on filial responsibility

Many of those who have considered the moral basis of filial responsibility have struggled to find a single model upon which to justify it. This naturally leads to the conclusion that filial responsibility is based on a combination of these theories. Indeed this appears to reflect the findings from research conducted with members of the public about feelings of filial responsibility. It is clear that there is a general sense that adult children owe their parents some limited obligations. In the OASIS survey only 47 per cent of people in the UK questioned thought children should make sacrifices for parents and only 31 per cent thought that children should live close to their aged parents, but 76 per cent thought that children should give emotional or practical help to parents (Lowenstein and Daatland 2006). In a leading work on the experience of filial obligation, Janet Finch and Jennifer Mason (1993) have distinguished how people's perceptions of filial obligations in practice depend on what they call 'normative guidelines' and 'negotiated commitment'. Normative guidelines apply across the board to certain relationships. Negotiated commitments are negotiated over time. They depend on the quality of the relationship between the particular individuals concerned. Thus the obligations people feel towards their parents are a mixture of those that flow from the fact of the parent/child relationship and those that flow from the quality of the actual relationship itself. Hence some studies have suggested low levels of felt obligation where the parent has abandoned, neglected or mistreated a child (Storm et al. 1985). It may be best to regard the obligation as a guideline, from which there may be good reasons to depart (Finch and Mason 1990, 1993). The above evidence suggests that the normative limits in filial obligation can, essentially, be defined as lying where 'providing support to aged parents begins to exceed adult children's *capacity* to do so without jeopardising their conjugal family's present needs or their ability to service their welfare in the future' (Aboderin 2005).

It should not, then, be surprising that something as sensitive and complex as moral obligations owed by parents to children cannot be captured in a single model. That, however, causes a problem for a lawyers. If the moral obligation cannot be neatly summarised or formulated, this generates uncertainty over the basis on which the legal obligation should be based.

Before moving on to discuss the appropriate legal response to this issue I want to raise three concerns about much of the writing on filial responsibility. First, there is a danger of the arguments assuming that the older person is passive. The focus of much of the writing is on what parents did in the past, generating an obligation. This overlooks the positive role that even a very infirm person can play in an adult child's life, not least the ever increasing role that grandparents play in providing child care (Douglas and Ferguson 2003; Hunt 2006).

Second, there is a concern that by emphasising filial responsibility, especially when it is contrasted with the 'opposite' – care of the state – the responsibility of local communities and wider families towards older people can be overlooked.

Third, it should not be thought that a person undertaking care is necessarily acting out of any kind of obligation to the person being cared for; instead, they may be acting out of concern for the person who would be the carer but for their intervention (Dellmann-Jenkins 2003). So an individual may assist her aunt, not out of a particular obligation to the aunt, but out of a realisation that the caring burden would fall on her mother if she did not undertake it.

Parental responsibility beyond minority

Much of the philosophical debate over the adult child/parent relationship has focused on filial responsibility. There is very little that can be found on the responsibilities a parent owes to their adult child. This may be because the basis of providing a satisfactory explanation for why parents are said to owe their young children obligations has proved so intractable (see Herring, 2007b, 379-81 for a summary of these). John Eekelaar's (1991) careful analysis suggests that the obligation flows from the fact that children are born vulnerable and must be cared for by someone in any decent society. Our society (for understandable reasons) places that burden on parents. Eekelaar's view is, therefore, that parental obligations flow from societal norms. If this is accepted, then we could readily say that by the time a child's minority is over the child's vulnerability has been largely overcome and society no longer places the burden for dealing with any disadvantage the adult may suffer on their parents. Whether, however, this is true in the case of a child who suffers a disability or other form of vulnerability is unclear. Society may not have developed a clear allocation of moral responsibility in such a case. A similar problem arises where the obligation upon parents is based on the responsibility they are said to voluntarily agree to when having a child. Does this include taking on responsibility only for the child's minority or beyond? These are questions our society has not yet adequately addressed.

From Moral to Legal Obligation

Let us accept for the moment that a case is made out for there being a moral obligation that is owed by some adult children to their parents and some parents to their adult children. How should the law respond? An obvious point to make initially is that the law does not directly enforce every moral obligation. There are plenty of immoral behaviours which are not subject to legal sanctions.

The law traditionally imposes obligations that are, at least in theory, enforceable. Hence, even if there is a moral obligation to love your parent a legal duty to do so will not be imposed. So what might influence the decision of whether to render a child's moral obligation to care for their parents into a legal one?

(1) Whether the legal obligation is imposed on the state or on adult children, it is important to realise that either system is liable to have loopholes. There is the inevitable concern that family members may seek to take steps to avoid potential liability for older people. This is always true of any means tested obligation. There may be concerns that avoidance measures would mean that enforcement would fall disproportionately on women (Korzec 1997). As Mika Oldham points out:

> The advantages of public provision include safeguarding the independence of elderly people, who are not made to feel they have become a burden on their families, and the redistribution of wealth, via the state, to those in greatest need. But when public provision fails or is inadequate, its tendency to isolate different generations is accompanied by other adverse consequences. Chief among these is the fact that insufficient funding means that the system depends hugely on informal carers who are unrecognised, uncompensated and inadequately supported. (Oldham 2001, 163)

One point here, then, is that accepting that the legal burden is on the state to protect the rights of older people is all well and good if the state provides that function. However, where the state fails to fulfil its obligation individuals take up that crucial role. But they are seen then as 'informal carers' offering 'gratuitous' services. In such a case, at least from the carers' point of view, it would almost be better if it was recognised that they were obliged to meet the needs of the older people and then could be officially recognised as the people providing the services to which an older person has a right.

There is another point to which Oldham alludes and that is that if the obligation is in a straightforward way placed on the state then this may be seen as weakening the link between children and parents. If in that case the state fails and children feel that the inadequate care their parent is receiving is the 'state's fault' and not their responsibility; then again older people may suffer. Whether Oldham is correct to think that state support for older people weakens the bonds of obligation between generations is open to debate, but these things are hard to measure. Janet Finch has suggested that:

> If anything it has been the state's assuming some responsibility for individuals – such as the granting of old age pensions – which has freed people to develop closer and more supportive relationships with their kin. (Finch 1984, 243)

Further, an important point is that those without children or whose children were unable to support them or could not be found would need to be cared for. There would, in this regard, be concerns that a system that was based primarily on enforcement of filial responsibility would work against the interests of gay and lesbian people or infertile heterosexual couples who may be less likely to have children (Boushka 2006).

(2) Any system of filial support legislation that sought to enforce financial liability for parents on adult children would face difficulties of enforcement (Edelstone 2002; Moskowitz 2001). As the problems facing the Child Support Agency demonstrate, there can be huge problems concerned with enforcement which may render such a scheme highly inefficient (Walters 2000).

(3) A further difficulty would be in drafting any filial responsibility legislation. It would need to address the following issues:

a. At what degree of need for the older person does the obligation to support 'kick in'?
b. What level of income does the child have to have before the obligation is imposed?
c. How are the obligations of an individual towards their parents and their children to be balanced?
d. Which relatives would be covered? For example, would it cover the spouses of children?
e. How can the obligations be shared between different children who could be liable?
f. Will there be exceptions, for example, in respect of abandoned or abused children? If so, how will such 'defences' be assessed (see Day 2000; Kline 1992).

It is not suggested that any of these are insurmountable. It is simply that they are likely to lead to a complex and cumbersome law. Another message from the Child Support Agency's problems is the difficulty in developing a scheme that is able to take account of each individual's circumstances, without being administratively unworkable. Any kind of formula for parental support is likely to be even more complex than that used for child support.

The kind of problems that can arise with a filial responsibility statute can be demonstrated by a consideration of those countries that do have such legislation. This is not the place to provide an extensive discussion of the detailed provisions of jurisdictions that have enacted filial responsibility legislation. Examples of countries that currently have filial support legislation are some states in the United States, Canada, France and Japan. In the United States, where filial responsibility statutes exist in a surprising number of states (around 30) they are rarely enforced (Oldham 2006; Wise 2002). In fact, in nearly half of those which have them they have never been used. That said, in Singapore, Canada and Malaysia these have been enforced with more vigour (Bracci 2000). But even there enforcement is hardly a regular occurrence. Filial responsibility legislation takes on the role of setting out a moral ideal, rather than being a set of enforced regulations.

(4) A final practical concern is that older people may be deterred from seeking state aid for fear of thereby bringing about proceedings under the statute against their children (Kline 1992). The flip side of this is the argument that one of the benefits of filial responsibility statutes to the state is that family members may as a result be encouraged to prevent and ameliorate dependency. It gives them a clear financial stake in promoting independence (Fennell 2004). This, however, is not always a benefit. It may lead to unwanted family intervention into the life of an older person. It may also lead to unrealistic expectations or demands of the family on the older people. Although family members may be said in some cases to have the 'expert' knowledge to assess the level of dependency of an older person and the extent to which their needs may best be met, there may also be cases where family members lack the emotional detachment to assess effectively the welfare of the older person. Denial of the impact of age can lead relatives to be overly optimistic as to the capabilities of their parent (Fennell 2004). There are also the wider costs to be considered of placing the burden of care on family members. For adult children this may involve the loss of their employment; the postponement or abandonment of a plan to have children; the giving up of other caring roles they have been performing. These are costs that will be felt by the individual, but also the wider society. One might also want to be confident that the effect of any filial responsibility statute would be felt fairly across society (Edelstone 2002). There are particular concerns that the 'felt obligations' appear to be shaped along lines of gender and cultural background (Harper and Levin 2003). It has been suggested, for example that in the context of the United Kingdom in white families the obligation runs first to a spouse, then to daughter and then to other close relations (Harper and Levin 2003). There is evidence that care for older people falls primarily on women (e.g. Abel 1991; Korzec 1997). Finch and Mason (1991) found that adult sons felt expected to provide financial support and adult daughters personal care and housing.

(5) Overriding all of these concerns is the fear that any potential financial liability will affect other aspects of the parent/child relationship (van Houtte and Breda

2005). For many older people it is the emotional aspects of the relationship with their children that are of far more value than any financial aspect. If assistance is wanted it is likely to be of most value in terms of hands-on care rather than by cash payments. Legally enforced payment is likely to foster feelings of guilt among older parents and feelings of resentment among the adult children. The same would be true if parents were compelled to support their adult children. The fear that potential liability will pollute such an important relationship, combined with the practical problems mentioned above, provide a strong case for not creating a legally enforceable obligation on adult children to support their parents.

A Preferable Response

It must not be thought, however, that where there is a moral obligation the legal response is either to enforce it or ignore it. The law is capable of being far more subtle than that. It can uphold, bolster or reinforce the obligation in other ways, free of direct enforcement. For example, the law can leave an obligation not legally enforceable but offer benefits or advantages to those who fulfil their obligations. The law could be used to provide encouragements for family members to undertake practical or financial aid for aged dependant members (Wise 2002). This could take a number of forms, for example:

1. Tax advantages. A tax credit similar to that available to those caring for children could be offered to those caring for relatives in need. Tax benefits could be available to those spending on the care of relatives of the kind that is available to those donating money to charity.
2. Employment protection could be provided for those seeking to provide care for dependants (Smith 2004).
3. Grants and benefits to those caring for dependent people (Shaver Bryant 2002). It is true that the Carers (Recognition and Services) Act 1995, the Carers and Disabled Children Act 2000, and the Carers (Equal Opportunities) Act 2004 provide some assistance to those caring for dependent people, although it is widely accepted that these are still at an inadequate level (see further Herring 2007a).
4. It would be possible to change the law on inheritance whereby a carer could receive a privileged position on inheritance (Oldham 2001). At least a relative who had provided material support could claim a return of the money given. Germany, France and China have legislation in this vein (Moskowitz 2002).
5. State support for children wishing to move close to their dependent parents to take care of them. Singapore has legislation of this kind (Collingridge and Miller 1997).

All of these would be ways in which the broader parent/child relationship could be encouraged, and given social recognition and value.

It is suggested that this is the preferable way to proceed. As emphasised already the adult child/parent relationship can provide enormous benefits to society and the individuals themselves. Enforcement of obligations between adults and their parents and children would probably be unworkable and counterproductive, for the many reasons outlined above. However, that does not mean the law should not encourage and enable the provision of financial and practical help for a vulnerable person. This can be done in the several ways outlined above.

Conclusion

We have seen that there are virtually no legal responsibilities that are imposed directly on the adult/child relationship. Be the adult child or the parent in the most dire of need, there is generally no obligation to offer assistance. That, however, is as it should be. Realistically the law cannot enforce the obligations that matter most in the parent/adult child relationship: the obligations to care, to keep in contact, to love (Bridgeman, in this book). The only obligation that could realistically be enforced is the payment of money to the child or parent in need. However, such a legally enforceable obligation faces all kinds of practical difficulties and runs the risk of disrupting an important relationship. It has been suggested that a preferable legal response is to support and encourage those who fulfil their obligations under the parent/adult child relationship. Love, care and support may not be legally enforceable, but that does not mean they cannot be recognised, treasured and supported by the law.

References

Abel, E. (1991), *Who Cares for the Elderly?* (Temple University Press: Philadelphia).

Aboderin, I. (2005), *'Conditionality' and 'Limits' of Filial Obligation* (Oxford Institute of Ageing: Oxford).

BBC Newsonline (2006), 'Raising a Child Costs £180,137' (published online 10 November 2006), http://news.bbc.co.uk/1/hi/business/6134926.stm, accessed 10 November 2006.

Blackstone, W. (1976), *Commentaries on the Laws of England* (Clarendon Press: Oxford).

Blair, J. (1996), '"Honour Thy Father and Thy Mother" – but for How Long?', *Journal of Family Law* 35:4, 765-82.

Blidstein, G. (1975), *Honor Thy Father and Mother* (KTAV: New York).

Blustein, J. (1983), *Parents and Children* (Oxford University Press: New York).

Boushka, B. (2006), 'Editorial: Filial Responsibility Laws: The Next Iceberg for GLBT People', http://www.doaskdotell.com/controv/filial.htm, accessed 6 May 2007.

Bracci, C. (2000), 'Ties That Bind: Ontario's Filial Responsibility Act', *Canadian Journal of Family Law* 17:2, 455-500.

Brannen, J. (2006), 'Cultures of Intergenerational Transmission in Four-generation Families', *The Sociological Review* 54:1, 133-154.

Brinig, M. (1994), 'Finite Horizons – The American Family', *International Journal of Children's Rights* 2, 293-315.
Collingridge, M. and Miller, S. (1997), 'Filial Responsibility and Care of the Aged', *Journal of Applied Philosophy* 14:2, 119-128.
Daniels, N. (1988), *Am I My Parents Keeper?: An Essay on Justice Between the Young and the Old* (Oxford University Press, New York).
Day, S. (2000), 'The Abandonment Defense to a Claim for Parental Support', *Journal of Contemporary Legal Issues* 11, 380-7.
Dellmann-Jenkins, M. (2003), 'Young Adults' Attitudes towards Filial Responsibility and Actual Assistance to Elderly Family Members', *Journal of Applied Gerontology* 22:2, 214-29.
Department of Health (1999), *Caring about Carers: A National Strategy for Carers* (Department of Health: London).
Department of Health (2001), *National Service Framework for Older People* (Department of Health: London).
Dixon, N. (1995), 'The Friendship Model of Filial Obligations', *Journal of Applied Philosophy* 12:1, 77-87.
Douglas, G. and Ferguson, N. (2003), 'The Role of Grandparents in Divorced Families', *International Journal of Law Policy and the Family* 17, 41.
Edelstone, S. (2002), 'Filial Responsibility: Can the Legal Duty to Support Our Parents Be Effectively Enforced?', *Family Law Quarterly* 36, 501-14.
Eekelaar, J. (1991), 'Are Parents Morally Obliged to Care for their Children?', *Oxford Journal of Legal Studies* 11:3, 340-53.
Eekelaar, J. (2006), *Family Life and Personal Life* (Oxford University Press: Oxford).
English, J. (1993), 'What Do Grown Children Owe their Parents' in Sommers, C. and Sommers, F. (eds), *Vice and Virtue in Everyday Life* (Harcourt: Forth Worth).
European Commission (2005), *Green Paper: Confronting Demographic Change* (European Commission: Brussels).
Feinberg, J. (1966), 'Duties, Rights, and Claims', *American Philosophical Quarterly* 3:2, 137-44.
Fennell, L. (2004), 'Relative Burdens: Family Ties and the Safety Net', *William and Mary Law Review* 45, 1453-1523.
Finch, J. (1984), *Education as Social Policy* (Longman: London).
Finch, J. (1989), *Family Obligations and Social Change* (Polity Press: Oxford).
Finch, J. and Mason, J. (1990), 'Filial Obligations and Kin Support for Older People', *Ageing and Society* 10, 151-75.
—— (1991), 'Obligations of Kinship in Contemporary Britain: is there a Normative Consensus?', *British Journal of Sociology* 42:3, 345-67.
—— (1993), *Negotiating Family Responsibilities* (Routledge: London).
Ganong, L., Coleman, M., McDaniel, A. and Killian, T. (1998), 'Attitudes Regarding Obligations to Assist an Older Parent or Stepparent Following Later Life Remarriage', *Journal of Marriage and the Family* 60, 595-610.
Gans, D. and Silverstein, M. (2006), 'Norms of Filial Responsibility for Aging Parents Across Time and Generations', *Journal of Marriage and Family* 68:4, 961-76.

Garrison, M. (1998), 'An Evaluation of Two Models of Parental Obligation', *California Law Review* 86, 41-117.

Gilleard, C. and Higgs, P. (2000), *Cultures of Ageing: Self, Citizen and the Body* (Prentice Hall: New York).

Gilligan, C. (1982), *In a Different Voice: Psychological Theory and Women's Development* (Harvard University Press: Cambridge, MA).

Goodin, R. (1985), *Protecting the Vulnerable* (University of Chicago Press: Chicago).

Grundy, E. and Murphy, M. (2006), 'Kin Availability, Contact and Support Exchange' in Ebtehaj, F., Lindley, B. and Richards, M. (eds), *Kinship Matters* (Hart: Oxford).

Harper, S. and Leeson, G.W. (2002), *Active Ageing, Social Inclusion and Independence: UK, UN and European Policy Development* (Oxford Institute of Ageing: Oxford).

— (2003), *Independent Living: Literature Review* (Department of Work and Pensions: London).

Harper, S. and Levin, S. (2003), *Changing Families as Societies Age; Care Independence and Ethnicity* (Oxford Institute of Ageing: Oxford).

Herring, J. (2007a), 'Where are the Carers in Healthcare Law and Ethics', *Legal Studies* 27:1, 51-73.

— (2007b), *Family Law* (3rd ed.) (Pearson: Harlow).

Houtte, J. van and Breda, F. (2005), 'Maintenance of the Aged by their Adult Children: an Adequate Legal Institution?' in Maclean, M. (ed.), *Family Law and Family Values* (Hart: Oxford).

Hunt, J. (2006), 'Substitute Care of Children by Members of their Extended Families and Social Networks' in Ebtehaj, F., Lindley, B. and Richards, M. (eds), *Kinship Matters* (Hart: Oxford).

Kellet, S. (2006), 'Four Theories of Filial Duty', *The Philosophical Quarterly* 56:233, 254-74.

Kline, T. (1992), 'A Rational Role for Filial Responsibility Laws in Modern Society', *Family Law Quarterly* 26:3, 195-210.

Korzec, R. (1997), 'A Feminist View of American Elder Law', *University of Toledo Law Review* 28, 547-61.

Laslett, P. (1992), 'Is there a Generational Contract?' in Laslett, P. and Fishkin, J. (eds), *Justice between Age Groups and Generations* (Yale University Press: New Haven).

Leeson, G. (2004), *The Demographics and Economics of UK Health and Social Care for Older Adults* (Oxford Institute of Ageing: Oxford).

Letts, M. (2001), 'Children – The Continuing Duty to Maintain', *Family Law* 31:839-41.

Lindemann Nelson, H. and Lindemann Nelson, J. (1992), 'Frail Parents, Robust Duties', *Utah Law Review* 3, 747-63.

Locke, J. (1988), *Second Treatise on Government* (Laslett, P. (ed.)) (Cambridge University Press: Cambridge).

Lowenstein, A. and Daatland, S.O. (2006), 'Filial Norms and Family Support in a Comparative Cross-national Context: Evidence from the OASIS Study', *Ageing and Society* 26, 203-23.

Moskowitz, S. (2001), 'Filial Responsibility Statutes: Legal and Policy Considerations', *Journal of Law and Policy* 9, 709-33.

—— (2002), 'Adult Children and Indigent Parents: Intergenerational Responsibilities in International Perspective', *Marquette Law Review* 9, 401-55.

Oldham, M. (2001), 'Financial Obligations within the Family – Aspects of Intergenerational Maintenance and Succession in England and France', *Cambridge Law Journal* 60:1, 128-77.

—— (2006), 'Maintenance of the Elderly and Legal Signalling – Kinship and State' in Ebtehaj, F., Lindley, B. and Richards, M. (eds), *Kinship Matters* (Hart: Oxford).

Ormerod, D. (2005), *Smith and Hogan Criminal Law* (Oxford University Press: Oxford).

Payne, B. and Fletcher, L. (2005), 'Elder Abuse in Nursing Homes: Prevention and Resolution Strategies and Barriers', *Journal of Criminal Justice* 33:2, 119-25.

Peek, M., Coward, R., Peek, C. and Lee, G. (1998), 'Are Expectations for Care Related to the Receipt of Care?', *Journals of Gerontology, Psychology Sciences and Social Sciences* 53:3, ss. 127-36.

Shakespeare, W. (2002), *King Lear* (Oxford University Press: Oxford).

Shaver Bryant, H. (2002), 'Funding Kinship Care: A Policy-Based Argument for Keeping the Elderly in the Family', *William and Mary Journal of Women and the Law* 8:3, 459-88.

Simester, A. and Sullivan, G. (2003), *Criminal Law: Theory and Doctrine* (Hart: Oxford).

Smith, P. (2004), 'Elder Care, Gender, and Work: The Work–Family Issue of the 21st Century', *Berkley Journal of Employment and Labour Law* 25:2, 351-99.

Sparato, A. (2000), '"Prodigal Parent" as a Defense to Proceedings Brought to Require Support from a Child', *Journal of Contemporary Legal Issues* 11, 385-8.

Storm, C., Storm, T. and Strike-Schurman, J. (1985), 'Obligations for Care: Beliefs in a Small Canadian Town', *Canadian Journal on Aging* 4:1, 75-84.

Teitelbaum, L. (1992), 'Intergenerational Responsibility and Family Obligation', *Utah Law Review* 765-802.

Todorova, V. (2005), 'Obligations of Grown-up Children to their Elderly Parents: Bulgarian Legislation and Practice' in Maclean, M. (ed.), *Family Law and Family Values* (Hart: Oxford).

Wald, P. (1997), 'Looking Forward to the Next Millennium: Social Previews to Legal Change', *Temple Law Review* 70, 1085-96.

Walters, J. (2000), 'Pay Unto Others as They Have Paid Unto You: An Economic Analysis of the Adult Child's Duty to Support an Indigent Parent', *Journal of Contemporary Legal Issues* 11, 376-9.

Wang, J. (1999), 'The Confucian Filial Obligation and Care for Aged Parents' in Fan, R. (ed.), *Confucian Bioethics* (Kluwer Academic: Dordrecht).

Wicclair, M. (1993), *Ethics and the Elderly* (Oxford University Press: Oxford).

Wicks, R. and Asato, J. (2003), *Lifelong Parenting: the Shape of British Life* (Social Market Foundation: London).

Wise, K. (2002), 'Caring for our Parents in an Aging World: Sharing Public and Private Responsibility for the Elderly', *New York University Journal of Legislation and Public Policy* 5, 563-98.

Chapter 4

Being a Responsible Mother: New Labour Policy Discourses versus Lone Mothers' Contextualised Accounts

Harriet Churchill

Political Discourses and Maternal Accounts of Responsibility

Since 1997, New Labour has extended both public support for, and regulation of, families and parenting. The extension of state intervention in family lives has been justified as necessary in tackling welfare dependency, child poverty, problematic youth behaviour and health/educational problems. Lone parents, of whom around 92 per cent were lone mothers and 8 per cent were lone fathers in the last census (ONS 2006), have figured highly in these policy shifts as a group at risk and contributing to contemporary social problems (Williams 2004). In more pessimistic terms, higher rates of lone mother headed households are associated with a problem of 'dwindling social responsibility' (Cameron 2007); and the generation of new risks for children, parents and society (Lewis 2006; Williams 2004). For New Labour, responding to these concerns demanded the establishment of a new 'citizen–government contract' and a reorientation of the role of the state in relation to children, families and parents (DfES 2003; DSS 1998).

In light of these debates, this chapter contrasts policy with lone mothers' accounts of contemporary family responsibilities for children. The analysis draws on the findings of an empirical study of New Labour policy discourses and maternal accounts of lived experiences. The findings of this study highlighted many similarities and differences between New Labour's and lone mothers' accounts of parental responsibility. Both viewed families as primarily responsible for providing for, and raising, children. However, responsible parenting in New Labour policy discourses tends to focus on responsibilities for income maintenance, paid work involvement and child development; whereas maternal accounts of responsible parenting tend to focus on responding to perceptions of their children's needs. Policy discourses are also inclined to downplay how social location, family circumstances and personal experiences inform everyday parental practices and perceptions of maternal responsibility. Maternal understandings of children's needs, shaped by personal/social contexts suggest a conceptualisation of parental responsibility as an active socially situated process of interpreting and responding to children's needs on a daily basis. This process can involve conflict and uncertainty as mothers negotiate children's changing needs or conflicts between their perceptions of children's particular needs and normative social expectations or policy prescriptions. Using this more grounded, and perhaps arguably gendered, notion of parental responsibility, 'irresponsibility' becomes a lack of attentiveness and concern for children's needs. For some this kind of irresponsibility was implied by some of New Labour's parenting prescriptions. For example, the appropriate relationship between paid work involvement and good mothering was morally disputed; as was the appropriate type and level of parental involvement in children's development. These differences between policy and maternal accounts of parenting bring into view the socially contested nature of contemporary parenting responsibilities and children's needs, the complexity of defining parental responsibilities at the level of national policy making and the politics of regulating parenting. The discussion first turns to examine New Labour policy discourses and maternal perspectives in more detail and then returns to a critical analysis of the policy implications of more grounded perspectives of parental responsibility.

New Labour, Parental Responsibilities and Lone Parents

In the last ten years, parental responsibilities for income maintenance, paid work involvement and child development outcomes have at different times dominated family orientated policy discussions. From the outset, New Labour was concerned to reduce welfare dependency and labour market exclusion among lone parent families. However, more recently a number of policy initiatives have been primarily concerned with parents as parents. These spheres of concern arguably express conflicting policy agendas, analysed in turn below. A discourse analysis is offered of policy speeches, statements and documents over the course of New Labour's three terms in office. The analysis focuses on identifying definitions of normative and problematic parental responsibilities within New Labour policy agendas and reforms; and the politically strategic use of language and responsibility discourses (see Churchill 2007 for further details of methodology).

Parental responsibilities, income maintenance and paid work

New Labour was elected in 1997 on a platform of Third Way welfare reform. Supporting 'ordinary hard-working' families, tackling the injustices of welfare dependency, reducing child poverty, enabling opportunity and retaining 'prudent' welfare expenditure were all prominent phrases used to portray policy agendas (Blair 1998). New Labour's platform of centre-left welfare reform drew on influential critiques of both the traditional post-war welfare state and New Right alternatives. Characterised as a passive rights-based approach to welfare provision, the expansion of welfare rights, expenditure and taxation in the post-war era was criticised for encouraging lone motherhood and absent fatherhood (by providing entitlements to and choices of welfare provision), penalising higher earners and enterprising predispositions, and creating long-term welfare dependency (Blair 1998). From the outset lone parent families were considered disproportionately at risk of poverty but it was their higher rates of welfare reliance (rather than the financial level of welfare benefits or levels of child maintenance) that were defined as the main cause of their poverty (DSS 1998). Early policy statements stressed citizen responsibilities for income maintenance:

> Parents are expected to take up the opportunity to be:
> Independent if they are able to do so;
> Give support, financial or otherwise, to their children and other family members;
> [And] Save for retirement when possible. (DSS 1998, 80)

Welfare reliance, however, was not only a problem of poverty and welfare dependency, but was also constructed as a problem of worklessness, social exclusion and rising welfare expenditure. Recipients of out of work benefits have been positioned as undeserving of public support, as economically unproductive and as 'getting something for nothing' (Blair 1998; DWP 2006). Drawing on social research, long-term welfare reliance was associated with poor health, social stigma, child poverty and low aspirations (DWP 2006). While this is consistent with much social research, New Labour policy discourses identify the primary solution as 'empowering people to take up paid work' and have been criticised for not fully recognising the difficulties many experience in moving from welfare into paid work, the significance of unpaid caring work within the lives of welfare recipients or the creation of poverty traps via low welfare benefit rates (Hills and Stewart 2005). For New Labour, paid work not only offers the best route out of poverty, it enhances self-respect and social inclusion (DWP 2006).

With 57 per cent of lone parent families reliant on welfare benefits in 1997, lone parents became a priority target group for welfare to work reforms. In 1998 the lone parent premium on Income Support was abolished, causing much disquiet (on the backbenches and amongst lobby groups) about the implementation of Conservative inspired social security proposals (Bochel and Defty 2007). The introduction of Work Focused Interviews and the voluntary New Deal for Lone Parents scheme put the onus on lone parents, receiving out of work welfare benefits, to demonstrate their intentions and plans for returning to paid work. Recent DWP proposals have discussed extending the requirement that welfare reliant lone parents should take up training or paid work once their youngest child is 12 years old (DWP 2006; Freud 2007). Policy measures have also sought to reduce the barriers to taking up employment which generate 'poverty and welfare reliance traps' (DWP 2006). Reforms have endorsed ideas that low-paid part-time work, a lack of childcare, a lack of personalised employment advice, employability and rights to flexible working hours are the primary barriers that lone parents face (DWP 2006). The target is to raise lone parent's employment rates to 70 per cent by 2010.

However, while lone parents' special welfare rights have been reduced under New Labour and expectations have increased in terms of their responsibilities for income maintenance and paid work involvement, children have been constructed as the deserving poor. Albeit following the backbench rebellion after the abolition of the lone parent premium on Income Support, New Labour announced increases in child benefit and a pledge to 'end child poverty in 20 years' (Bochel and Defty 2007). Welfare benefit and welfare to work reforms have arguably collectively contributed to an estimated reduction in the proportion of children in poverty by 12 per cent, from 35 per cent of all children in 1997 to 23 per cent in 2004; and an increase in lone parent employment rates of 11 per cent from 46 per cent in 1997 to 57 per cent in 2007 (ONS 2008). However, there are worrying continuities in the higher rates of labour market exit, lower rates of pay and long-term welfare reliance among lone parent families in the UK (Evans et al. 2004). Furthermore, policy discourses have recently emphasised individualistic explanations for these continuities. The DWP recently announced that lone parents are not 'making serious efforts' to return to paid work as they 'lack independence' and possess a 'fear of the unknown [paid work]' and 'fear losing benefit' (DWP 2006). These orientations are presented as irrational and deviant as the government asserts that there is 'no excuse not to try and obtain a job if additional subsidies are available to "make work pay"' and 'there are enough paid work opportunities' (Bennett 2006, 117; DWP 2006; SEU 2006). Further, New Labour is concerned that these deviant dispositions are transmitted to children when they grow up in a household where their parent(s) are not engaged in the formal labour market (SEU 2006). The second wave of welfare reform seeks to address these problems of welfare dependency and to tackle the other main cause of lone parent poverty – low employability (Freud 2007). Similar concerns inform the policy proposals set out by the opposition political parties (Cameron 2007).

Parental responsibilities and children's outcomes

Another major strand of New Labour's family orientated policies can be identified as those policies more explicitly aimed at intervening in parenting (Bridgeman, in this book). Concerns about educational, health and behavioural standards among children and young people have led to a number of policy initiatives that are underpinned by notions of parental and public responsibilities for children's outcomes. A major turning point in policy occurred with the publication of *Every Child Matters* (DfES 2004a) which set out a major reform of children's services.

One policy objective has been to increase parental involvement in children's formal education. Prominent research had concluded that parental involvement in children's early education and school education was 'more influential than professional practices' in determining children's attitudes to their education and educational attainment (SEU 2006). Home–school contracts have been introduced that encourage parents to monitor their child's homework and schools are expected to encourage parent/school partnerships, informing parents of their children's progress and encouraging parental involvement. Parents are expected to ensure that their children attend school, with LEAs having new powers to penalise parents for children's poor attendance (DfES 2004).

The development of Sure Start and the recent reform of children's services have provided further scope for analysing New Labour's understandings of parental responsibilities. These reforms were introduced to improve children's outcomes, particularly in relation to cognitive development, health and welfare. Sure Start and *Every Child Matters* drew on US and Canadian programmes and sought an interventionist approach to supporting parents at the 'earliest possible stage' to prevent the 'escalation of behaviour and health problems' in children (DofH 2006;

Home Office 2006; SEU 2006). So although Sure Start, Children's Centres and Extended Schools have sought to expand childcare, family support and children's health services for families with children (focused upon neighbourhoods classed as economically deprived), improving parenting has been a focal concern.

In this endeavour, the definition, reward and punishment of responsible parenting has become the terrain of welfare policies and professionals. Health reforms have sought to encourage responsible parenting in relation to health choices (DofH 2006). Additional financial support is available for low income parents, but in the example of the new maternity payment this is conditional upon parents having contact with a health official (Bennett 2006). The Home Office-led 'Respect' campaign claimed that it is through improved parenting that the problems of truancy, anti-social behaviour and offending will in part be addressed (Home Office 2006; Keating, in this book). The Home Office has subsequently invested in local 'supernanny' figures and intensive health-led parenting programmes within wards with high levels of 'problem families with multi-faceted problems' in order to instil 'commonly held values', support parents to overcome health and addiction problems, and provide parent education (Home Office 2006, 21). Anti-social behaviour legislation has brought in powers to 'order' parents to restrict their child's social mobility and to attend a parenting programme if their children are subject to a behaviour or truancy order (DfES 2004; Home Office 2003). Policy initiatives have also demonstrated a punitive approach. Families can be evicted from social housing, have welfare benefits reduced or be fined on account of children's anti-social behaviour or truancy from school (Bennett 2006). Professionals have been encouraged to monitor children's health, educational attainment and personal safety to a greater extent; and parent education programmes have recently undergone substantial investment and professionalisation with a new National Academy for Parenting Practitioners (SEU 2006).

Overall, therefore, New Labour has sought to clarify the nature of contemporary parenting responsibilities as well as enhance support for, and extend regulation of, responsible parenting. Responsibilities for income maintenance and paid work involvement; and the role of parents in determining children's outcomes have dominated policy debates. While the beneficial outcomes for parents of these reforms need to be acknowledged and empirically derived, there are concerns that New Labour's policy discourses and reforms present tensions for lone mother headed households. For Bennett the focus on paid work involvement and engaged parenting portrays conflicting messages to lone mothers as the 'responsibilities expected of parents come into conflict, placing strains on lone mothers in particular' (Bennett 2006, 61). There is also concern about the detrimental outcomes of these policy initiatives for lone mothers. Given lone mothers' higher rates of poverty, labour market insecurity and disproportionate care demands, paid work involvement could increase their levels of work/family conflict. The regulatory gazes and punitive consequences of enhanced professional monitoring of child development, parenting orders or truancy fines disproportionately affect the resident parent in the case of a lone parent household. Further, lone parents have been identified as a group at risk of parenting problems and aligned with a problematic, irresponsible minority. Policy rhetoric has perhaps drawn on these stereotypes to a greater extent than enacted policy; but for many the tone of recent policy debates has preceded moves to withdraw essential welfare support in order to punish irresponsible parenting. According to some this is a 'step too far' and 'erodes both parents and children's rights' (Bennett 2006, 129; Henricson and Bainham 2005, 86). The following analysis of lone mothers' accounts of their responsibilities highlights the socially contested and socially situated nature of maternal conceptions of parental responsibility.

Lone Mothers' Accounts of Parental Responsibility

The following analysis of lone mothers' accounts reports findings from a qualitative study of lone motherhood that ran for five years from 1999 to 2004 (Churchill 2007). Informed by an interpretive approach, interview methods and grounded thematic analysis of the interview data, the research aimed to give voice to maternal perspectives and concerns, and to generate grounded conceptualisations of maternal responsibility in light of an increasingly prescriptive policy environment. Forty-three lone mothers were interviewed, all living within the same city in central England. Many of the mothers had one child (22), worked part-time (17), received welfare benefits (25 Income Support; 8 Working Tax Credit; 4 disability benefits) and were separated (23). There was a low representation of minority ethnic groups in the study (37 were from White British; 4 Afro-Caribbean and 2 British Asian backgrounds). Twenty-seven of the mothers were in paid employment while 11 of those not in paid work were undertaking some form of voluntary or informal community work. The sample reflected higher rates of maintenance receipt, larger families and more full-time employed mothers compared to national estimates among all lone parent families.

The discussion focuses on in-depth analysis of maternal perspectives to illuminate the way family responsibilities for children are sustained, negotiated and contested through everyday maternal beliefs and practices. Notions of maternal responsibilities for care and child development and maternal perceptions of responsibilities for paid work and economic self-sufficiency are explored in turn, before consideration is given to the significance of narratives of capability and capacity in the mothers' accounts of fulfilling these maternal responsibilities.

Situated interpretations of maternal responsibilities: Care and child development

The mothers presented powerful images of active and everyday responsibility for their children's welfare which in turn reflected normative perspectives on childhood, motherhood and family responsibilities as well as the particular circumstances within which they were raising children. Across the range of accounts, the mothers set out their responsibilities for meeting children's everyday basic care needs, attachment and emotional needs, and developmental needs. However, these responsibilities were defined and practised in a variety of ways.

Everyday basic care responsibilities

Lucinda, one of the single mothers interviewed in the study, provided a stark image of maternal care for young children when she described becoming a mother as 'having someone to look after constantly':

> I think the biggest change [when you have a baby] is that you are not on your own, and you have got someone to look after constantly. It is not just you, you have got someone that is your responsibility and it is all the time. (Lucinda, 28, one child)

Lucinda cohabited with her daughter's father until her daughter was five years old and she contrasted her own experiences of becoming a parent with that of her ex-partner's where 'he continued to do all the things he did before'. Lauren, another mother in the study, emphasised her children's dependency on her as the sole resident parent providing for their basic daily needs:

> When you are ill ... [t]hey go all quiet. You have stopped working. If you stop doing everything at home, everything stops. If you can't function, their world stops. That is when it is a bit scary for them. They are fretting, am I going to be alright? (Lauren, 37, five children)

When asked about their typical day, the mothers detailed routines for meeting children's everyday needs for food, warmth and shelter, and the domestic labour involved. For many, providing such care personally was an important part of being a good mother. Hence Sue stated that she preferred not to use formal childcare provision as it was 'her job' and 'she did not see the point of giving them to someone else to look after'. Other mothers felt that childcare could be delegated to formal childcare services and sought to monitor this.

Attachment and relational responsibilities

Many of the mothers also discussed children's relational and attachment needs. Being with their children (in out-of-school hours for school age children) was important for facilitating maternal/child attachment. Being absent from children or using formal childcare services could, therefore, be viewed negatively. For Charlotte the significance of maternal presence for children resonated with her own childhood experiences:

> I think it is nice to be there when they come home from school. My Mum was always there for me. It is nice to see your mum at the end of the day. (Charlotte, 42, three children)

For others, setting time aside to spend with their children was an important way of expressing their attachment, and giving their attention, to children. Mandy acknowledged the significance of spending time with children (and encouraging their literacy skills) when she criticised her own practices in this respect:

> I read all these books that you sit down and you paint with your children. I did read to them and with them. I taught them how to read. But I still think I did not spend enough time with them. (Mandy, 36, two children)

Many of the mothers also actively sought to sustain their child's relationships with their father, other family members and other children. Fathers were expected to maintain contact with their children following parental separation and mothers expressed strong views if fathers were 'absent'. Twenty-five of the 43 lone mothers interviewed reported contact between fathers and children. In three of the families, children lived with their fathers at weekends.

For many mothers, sustaining children's relationships with others involved negotiating the risk others could present to children. This was especially prominent where mothers considered the neighbourhoods in which they lived to be risky for children or that ongoing paternal or family contact could be harmful to children. For example, Charlotte feared the potentially negative influence upon her daughter of some local children:

> You have to set your rules. ... If you aren't there to say don't do that or I want you in by a certain time then she will go astray. We have this little gang that hangs about outside, down the street. It is like basically not getting involved in the wrong crowd. (Charlotte, 42, three children)

Child development responsibilities

Providing stimulating interaction, setting behavioural standards and encouraging development were also critical concerns for many of the mothers. There were several examples in the research where encouraging children's development was clearly presented as an important aspect of being a good (lone) mother, especially in the context of social expectations that children's development could suffer due to parental separation, conflict or lone motherhood. For example, many of the mothers gave accounts similar to Hazel's, of supporting their children's education:

> I can't let things happen from day to day. I have made a conscious commitment to be a success. Everything that happens I have got to work it out. I have to wash their uniform each day ready for the next day. If they are ill at the weekend I wrap them up, give them paracetamol and just look after them really well. I don't like them missing off school, I don't want them to get that habit. (Hazel, 36, four children)

However, child development processes were also constructed as biologically driven or children themselves as being more self-directive. Here, maternal responsibilities are informed by everyday theories of child development, and notions of children's rights and capabilities. Some of the mothers were concerned about how far they should or could direct their children's development; and how best to support their child's development. For example, Alex and Sue debated the advantages and disadvantages for their children (and themselves) of after-school leisure and educational activities:

> I tried taking them to swimming lessons and drama classes. We did it, and it was hard financially. But we found it too stressful. We were going from school to the swimming pool, not getting back till late. They were getting tired. It was so stressful. I don't do it now, I think they need that time, to get the time, before bed, just to do their own thing. (Alex, 34, two children)

> I know friends who are always visiting each other, always taking their children to activities and clubs. The school runs some and [my daughter] wants to do them. But then she is tired and miserable. I try to keep things nice and relaxed. Just a ten minute walk or sitting and talking in the evenings. (Sue, 37, three children)

Some of the mothers, possessed of a stronger sense of maternal authority, challenged some of New Labour's policy messages about parental involvement in child development. Justine, a working class mother, 'tried not to worry too much' about her mothering and wanted to help her children to be independent in their school work:

> I try not to worry too much about if I am doing the right thing. Am I bringing up my children right? Do they have enough clothes? Do they eat well? Are they eating a balanced diet? Not important, not really! Just as long as a child eats three meals a day, the occasional snack. My children can eat healthy but still be miserable! ... If they need help they know where I am. … But I prefer if they don't overburden me with their problems. (Justine, 27, three children)

Melissa, an Afro-Caribbean mother, felt strongly about her own right to discipline her daughter in ways she deemed appropriate:

> People are always telling you what you should do with your kids. I listen to all of what's around and I make up my own mind about it. And I will occasionally smack. I will use everything possible, my eyes, my voice. I am telling you don't do that. ... Round here the parents are more afraid of the children than the children are of the parents and that is no good, they are wild. They look to you for guidance. (Melissa, 28, one child)

Others were concerned about 'excessive child dependency' on mothers, particularly in the context of being the only resident parent. Heather explained this in the following way:

> One of the worst things is that I am too close to him. I sometimes feel that that I am too involved. I am too wrapped up in him. I am very worried about him and what he is going to be like, and that might be detrimental to him. (Heather, 28, one child)

These accounts of mothering demonstrate high levels of concern for responsible parenting and children's welfare but individual differences in how children's needs and maternal responsibilities are perceived and practised. Mothers positioned themselves as central to their children's everyday welfare, especially in the context of being the sole resident parent. Maternal presence was stressed within the accounts of children's needs for care, maternal attachment, guidance and protection from risk. Responsibilities were also furnished by a sense of authority and informed by reflection upon the needs of their children growing up in a particular personal and social context. Maternal practices risk being judged as inappropriate because they deviate from an increasingly prescriptive policy environment which fails to recognise these complexities to contemporary parenting and mothering.

Situated interpretations of responsibilities: Economic self-sufficiency and paid work

While many of the mothers did aspire to achieve economic self-sufficiency and take up or sustain paid work, others were concerned about the effects of labour market participation on their children. Much depended on the conditions and hours of paid work, the mother's conception of her children's needs and their sense of maternal (and paternal) responsibilities for meeting those needs.

For those in paid work, employment was indeed a means of income generation, social inclusion, realising personal aspirations and providing a role model for their children. Lauren, for example, identified the importance of paid work for her in the following ways:

> I am better off working. It gives you the incentive to get up and go. It makes you feel like a human being again. Being unemployed … life is hell! The boredom and depression. When you are working or studying life is totally different and people treat you differently. They don't talk down to you. When you are working you feel like you are doing something, being useful, you are starting to afford to buy a few more extras. (Lauren, 35, five children)

There was evidence though that while many mothers perceived such benefits to arise from paid work, they also felt that their engagement with paid work could be detrimental to their children's welfare. This could be expressed in a number of ways. For example, Mandy valued the benefits of paid work for herself whilst being ambivalent about whether her working hours were in her children's interests. Mandy described how becoming a single mother as a teenager had disrupted her education and led to conflict with her parents. Mandy further detailed the difficulties she had faced in raising her daughter, living in poverty and being vulnerable to homelessness which culminated in her daughter being placed on the social services 'at risk' register. Training and employment as a care support worker had, for Mandy, been a 'life turnaround'. She was now 'even aspiring to buying her own house' and had 'a good life' – a success story in terms of the empowering implications of participation in the labour market. However, her long part-time working hours meant she regularly had to work evenings and some weekends. This caused internal conflict and anxiety as Mandy attempted to balance her aspirations to raise her family income, her enjoyment of her employment and her daughters' needs for maternal attention, time together and guidance:

> I have got this big guilt thing about not bringing them up very well and not being there for my younger one. I found out about an incident at school three weeks after it happened. It is like "Where is Mum? Oh she is at work!" I feel like I have failed two children. (Mandy, 35, two children)

Charlotte and Sarah gave up paid work due to conflict between their paid work aspirations and children's welfare. Charlotte had sought to increase her family income by taking on a retail job in the run up to Christmas, a decision she then regretted given the negative impact it had on her family life:

> I found when I was working more I would get home at seven. Then I had the housework. I was finding it fairly stressful. Taking it out on the children! I couldn't have kept it up. I wanted to because then we could have had a holiday but I was getting tired and it was best not to work and be happy at home than to work and be giving everybody a hard time! (Charlotte, 42, three children)

Sarah, who had postgraduate qualifications and described her previous income as 'high', also expressed commitment to employment for personal and family reasons. However, she left her advertising design job because of the risks to her own, and her daughter's, well-being:

> I worked full-time for two years, which was really stressful. It was a really good time in my life too. It was the only time since becoming a single parent that I was supporting myself. Your self-esteem goes way up there! I wasn't on benefits, I was paying everything myself, I was meeting people, I was being creative, I was enjoying what I was doing. But I had major deadlines. It got to the point where I felt so torn. I was just really knackered. ... I am now clear that I can only work between 9.30 and 3, and otherwise my relationship with my daughter would suffer. (Sarah, 32, one child)

Even parents with high educational qualifications can experience intense family/work conflicts. There was also evidence that children themselves aired concerns about their mothers' working hours. The quote from Mandy above demonstrates this as does the account provided by Janet, who recounted her own aspirations to increase the family income and buy her son desirable consumable items; but also her son's complaints about her absence from the home.

Mothers within the study differed in their aspirations for economic self-sufficiency. Some reflected assumptions of maternal dependence on a male breadwinner or shared parental responsibilities for providing for children. Fourteen of the mothers received regular maintenance from their children's fathers and fathers in general were heavily criticised for not providing child maintenance. There was also evidence of maternal assumptions of economic dependence on men or the state, although this was expressed in relation to facilitating mothers' caring role rather than as a means of escaping personal responsibilities for paid work or income maintenance. For example, Kim described herself as an 'independent' lone mother: she felt that she cared adequately for her children, she supported her own mother, she undertook 'men's' jobs in the house and managed her family finances without accruing debt or arrears. However, the largest part of Kim's income came from Income Support. Welfare receipt in this case was not perceived as 'economic dependency'; rather, it was seen as the provision of a low income for her as a full-time caring mother.

Maternal responsibilities, capabilities, resources and opportunities

Maternal accounts of responsibilities for their children were fused with narratives about parenting capacities and constraints affecting their ability to fulfil their responsibilities. New Labour policy discourses specifically identify parenting knowledge, childcare services, employability and income as common support needs. However the lone mothers involved in this study provided accounts both of enhanced parenting capacity on becoming a lone mother (due to increases in income security, reductions in family conflict or closer maternal/child relations) or they referred to additional constraints less recognised in policy discourses such as inappropriate government expectations, the demands of child-rearing, a lack of support, financial insecurity (whether they were in or out of paid work), work/family conflict, labour market disadvantage and negative social attitudes (for example, towards lone mothers and employed mothers). Accounts of increased parenting capacity as a lone mother highlight how lone mothers can experience this family formation as a positive experience for themselves and their children (Duncan and Edwards 1999). The discussion below, however, focuses on identifying the internal and external resources and constraints furnishing maternal responsibility (Duncan and Edwards 1999; Himmelweit and Sigala 2004). 'Inner' resources such as caring skills, attentiveness to others, practical life skills or self-confidence furnish maternal agency as well as external financial, practical and emotional support; opportunities and services; and adequate time or material resources (Himmelweit and Sigala 2004).

Parenting and internal constraints

Lewis and Guillari (2005) argue that parenting capabilities need to be understood as reflecting cultural and social influences as well as the realisation of human potential. The mothers involved in this study indicated that parenting knowledge and skills were important but were also mediated by the status conferred upon mothers in caring for children and cultural ambiguities as to what constitutes good mothering. The empirical data suggested that confidence in one's mothering informs agency; and that a perceived lack of expertise could lead to uncertainty in child-rearing decisions. This would suggest a role for sharing parenting experiences and gaining advice but this advice would need to be sensitive to maternal concerns for reducing family conflict, sustaining nurturing relationships and being flexible to children's particular needs. The issue of discipline, for example, seemed to involve much uncertainty and concern:

> Bedtime is becoming a real nightmare. It always has been. She is always pushing me to stay awake and I end up shouting. But then again, I am not very good with the boundaries thing. I tend to be quite easy going and then react! (Sarah, 28, one child)

Perceptions of capability could also be deeply connected to gendered self-identity. Kim and Janet portrayed deep-seated attitudes towards difficulties, as women, 'disciplining' their older sons – viewing their sons' fathers as having a critical role here. Mandy referred to being too much of a 'me person' to provide her children with enough maternal attention. Maternal emotional and physical well-being was also portrayed as connected to capacities for being attentive to children's needs. The quotes above from Lauren, Sarah and Charlotte all refer to their limited capacity to provide care for their children when tired, ill or stressed.

Parenting and external constraints

Turning to 'external' resources and opportunities, many of the mothers referred to financial, temporal, practical and cultural constraints, and insufficient informal and formal support. A major theme was the demanding nature of undertaking training and/or paid work as a lone mother even if paid work motivation and rewards were high. Only two of the employed lone mothers perceived a secure employment future or little conflict between their employment and family roles. Lauren described practical and temporal constraints in dealing with the demands of the transition from welfare benefits to paid work:

> When starting work, you need to sort everything out, all the paperwork. There is not enough time. You are trying to work and take care of the children as well. It is finding the time to do it all! (Lauren, 35, five children)

Problems of sustaining employment went beyond those of childcare or employability constraints. Melissa recounted how internal and external constraints led her to reassess her aspirations for economic self-sufficiency and a new career:

> I try to fit in my studying while Lucy is at school. But you need the shopping in and before you know it it's one o'clock. Then at three o 'clock you have to go. When Lucy says "Mum come and do this, come to the park", I might say "No, I need to do some work". And the tears come and I can't handle it! I say, "Oh lets go to the park!!" And I just forget about the work and concentrate on her. At the end of the day I am pleased that we have lived that day to the fullest and she is happy but I am too exhausted to study ... I think I made a mistake trying to do it all on my own. So I have taken six months off my course. (Melissa, 28, one child)

Whether in paid work or receiving out of work welfare benefits, many of the mothers struggled to provide financially for their families. Moving from welfare into paid work did not necessarily improve a mother's income; four of the mothers had experienced a loss of income on taking up paid work due to errors, delays and problems in receiving their first wage. All returned to welfare benefits a short while later, accruing debt in the meantime.

Beyond meeting children's basic needs, there could be problems financing educational and leisure opportunities. Lucinda expressed difficulties financing opportunities for fun 'time together' and enjoyable holiday activities, a common problem among parents with low incomes:

> I think probably the thing we go without the most is just doing stuff and enjoying going places. I have this image of all these middle class women jumping in the car and taking their kids to places. We never go to them. It's like the summer holidays, what can you do? There is only so much you can do. (Lucinda, 27, one child)

Five of the mothers were members of a local lone parent group, which they valued as a source of cheap and enjoyable social activity for themselves and their children.

An additional concern was cultural perceptions of good or inadequate mothers. For example, Heather, who described herself as having a middle class 'normal', 'happy' and 'comfortable' upbringing, felt she had 'failed' her son by separating from his father and becoming a lone mother. For Heather, moving back in with her parents and not being economically self-sufficient was a source of personal and social failure which she felt unable to talk about with many of her friends or with her parents. Rasheene, an Asian lone mother of Pakistani ethnic origin, felt she had been 'rejected' by her family due to the social stigma of divorce and marital abuse. Negative attitudes were also described in relation to being both welfare reliant and working mothers. Beverley explained how she had confronted her daughter's school teachers' views about her full-time hours as a working mother, while Janet and Lauren (above) expressed concerns about being 'looked down on' when reliant on welfare support:

> At school some teachers make comments. The Head Teacher has said, "Oh Lisa you are the first person I see in the morning and the last person I see at the end of the day". Last year my daughter really wasn't getting on with her teacher. The teacher said my daughter was too tired from her long day at school and she finds it hard being away from me. But she has never been used to me picking her up from school at three and yet she has been really happy at school! (Beverley, 33, two children).

Contrasting Discourses of Responsibility

Both policy and lay perspectives construct parents as having responsibilities as well as rights in relation to children and child-rearing. New Labour has emphasised income maintenance, paid work and child-rearing responsibilities with policies also acknowledging the need for enhanced childcare, employment and professional support. Mothers, however, can have differing views on these priorities; and their accounts reflect cultural ambiguities about the appropriate relationship between paid work and mothering, and parental involvement and child development. Mothers' accounts also demonstrate a concern with meeting the particular needs of their children which can change over time. Some of the mothers aired concern over social expectations of good mothering and referred to the risks and constraints they faced in attempting to meet these expectations. While some of these constraints are recognised in policy discourses, difficulties in balancing paid work with lone motherhood, cultural ambiguities about children's needs, dealing with negative social attitudes towards working or lone mothers, and in-work poverty were less recognised.

Other studies, based on a more purposeful sample of lone mothers, have also sought to explain differences between policy and grounded notions of maternal responsibility. Duncan and Edwards (1999) argued that mothers act according to 'gendered moral rationalities' that can differ according to social class, ethnic background and social networks. They suggested that in relation to paid work there are mothers who believe good mothering involves the stay at home ideal (especially white working mothers), mothers who primarily identify themselves as paid workers and mothers who view maternal paid work as in children's interests (particularly Afro-Caribbean mothers) (Duncan and Edwards 1999). Other studies have sought to establish the social origins of these maternal identities (for example, Graham and McDermott 2005; Lister 2004; Reynolds 2002; Skeggs 1997).

The comparison of policy and maternal accounts of responsibility presented in this chapter also resonates with feminist ethic of care and citizenship theory debates. In ethic of care debates, the active, attentive and reflective process of needs interpretation that many of the mothers detailed above constitutes an essential aspect of a caring orientation. For Williams (2004), there is a fundamental tension between New Labour's welfare to work, educational and parenting reforms in that the quality of parenting has become a focal concern and yet formal labour market participation rather than care work defines active citizenship. Kittay (2001) has further argued that Third Way conceptions of citizen responsibility mobilise a gender bias in two ways. First, citizens are modelled on a 'male norm' as autonomous agents devoid of care needs or responsibilities (Kittay 2001, 530). Secondly, it is economic and social order responsibilities that are the focus of responsibility debates rather than care giving and receiving activities: activities women disproportionately engage in and identify with, and activities which contribute towards social reproduction (Kittay 2001, 526). For these policy analysts, governments have a duty of care to carers which, in turn, needs to be balanced against the work ethic and involves supporting and rewarding caring as active citizenship. According to Kittay 'single parent poverty could be remedied by adequate support for dependency [care] work' (Kittay 2001, 538).

A further aspect of the analysis of policy and maternal perspectives relates to the issue of the politics of family policy making under New Labour. Policy makers are in the position of having to respond to social problems. They are engaged in setting normative social standards for behaviour and welfare, establishing the nature and level of collective state action and publicly justifying policy decisions. Hence, the balance between personal and state responsibilities for welfare becomes critical, with policy proposals often and necessarily examined on a cost–benefit analysis. In contrast, the mothers in this study detailed their personal experiences of mothering and personal beliefs on family responsibilities against the backdrop of social policies. Their concerns related to their perceptions of their own and their children's interests and needs (as well as wider social interests). Their accounts brought sharply into focus their own justifications for their actions and the implications of policy initiatives at the level of personal experience. In this chapter, though, I have argued that many of the mothers did not view some of New Labour's policy objectives as in their own or their children's interests, raising social justice concerns. Social justice concerns are raised if responsibility is conferred without a balanced consideration of issues of structural influence or respect for cultural diversity (Matravers 2007; Williams 2004). Others have argued that these conflicts of interest are underpinned by debates about the role of social policy in relation to the family. As family policy, which has arguably long been a vehicle for sustaining the social order, has become critical to realising economic and law and order policy objectives (Lister 2006), counter-narratives have stressed the need for human welfare priorities. Consideration needs to be given to neglected issues such as the relationship between adult welfare and child welfare; responsibility and capability; and care and economic productivity.

In conclusion, New Labour family orientated reforms have gone far in extending public support for childcare, in-work support, education and parenting training. There has also been an emphasis on explicitly defining parental responsibilities and regulating parenting. However, policy perspectives can be at odds with mothers' conceptions of their responsibilities, neglect the significance of responsiveness to children's changing and varied needs, downplay the increasing demands being placed on parents (which are arguably keenly felt by lone mothers and fathers) and ignore the multiple influences on children's outcomes. This in turn raises critical questions about whose interests are served by New Labour's family orientated policies and the politics of responsibility discourses within social policy.

References

Bennett, F. (2006), 'Paying for Children: Current Issues and Implications of Policy Debates' in Lewis, J. (ed.), *Children, Changing Families and Welfare States* (Cheltenham: Edward Elgar).

Blair, T. (1998), *The Third Way: A New Politics for the New Century*, Fabian Pamphlet 588 (London: Fabian Society).

Blair, T. (2006), *Speech on Social Exclusion*, accessed 2 January 2007 at www.epolitix.com/EN/News/200609/83f43492-4145-4f17-a2a0-90ea840bf108.htm.

Bochel, H. and Defty, A. (2007), *Welfare Policy under New Labour: Views from inside Westminster* (Bristol: Policy Press).

Cameron, D. (2007), 'Why Fathers Must Not Avoid Their Responsibilities', *The Telegraph*, 22 February 2007.

Churchill, H. (2007), 'New Labour versus Lone Mothers' Discourses of Parental Responsibility and Children's Needs', *Critical Policy Analysis* 1:2, 149-162.

Department for Education and Skills (2003), *Every Child Matters*, Cm 5860 (London: TSO).

Department for Education and Skills (2004), *Ten Year Childcare Strategy* (London: TSO).

Department of Health (2006), *Our Health, our Care, our Say: Making it Happen* (London: TSO).

Department of Social Security (1998), *New Ambitions for our Country; A New Contract for Welfare* (London: TSO).

Department of Work and Pensions (2006), *A New Deal for Welfare: Empowering People to Work*, Cm 6730 (London: TSO).

Duncan, S. and Edwards, R. (1999), *Lone Mothers, Paid Work and Gendered Rationalities* (London: Macmillan).

Evans, M., Harkness, S. and Arigoni Ortez, R. (2004), *Lone Parents Cycling Between Work and Benefits*, DWP217 (London: TSO).

Freud, D. (2007), *Reducing Dependency, Increasing Opportunity* (Leeds: TSO/Corporate Document Services).

Graham, H. and McDermott, E. (2005), 'Qualitative Research and the Evidence Base of Policy: Insights from Studies of Teenage Mothers in the UK', *Journal of Social Policy* 35:1, 21-37.

Henricson, C. and Bainham, A. (2005), *The Child and Family Policy Divide* (York: Joseph Rowntree Foundation).

Hills, J. and Stewart, K. (eds) (2005), *A More Equal Society? New Labour, Poverty, Inequality and Exclusion* (Bristol: Policy Press).

Himmelweit, S. and Sigala, M. (2004), 'Choice and the Relationship Between Identities and Behaviour for Mothers with Pre-school Children: Some Implications for Policy from a UK Study', *Journal of Social Policy* 33:3, 455-78.
Home Office (2003), *Respect and Responsibility – Taking a Stand Against Anti-Social Behaviour* (London: TSO).
Home Office (2006), *Respect Action Plan* (London: Respect Taskforce).
Kittay, E.F. (2001), 'A Feminist Public Ethic of Care Meets the New Communitarian Family Policy', *Ethics* 111, 523-47.
Lewis, J. (ed.) (2006), *Children, Changing Families and Welfare States* (Cheltenham: Edward Elgar).
Lewis, J. and Giullari, S. (2005), 'The Adult Worker Family Model, Gender Equality and Care: The Search for New Policy Principles and the Possibilities and Problems of a Capability Approach', *Economy and Society* 34:1, 74-104.
Lister, R. (2006), 'An Agenda for Children: Investing in the Future or Promoting Well-being in the Present?' in Lewis, J. (ed.), *Children, Changing Families and Welfare States* (Cheltenham: Edward Elgar).
Matravers, M. (2007), *Responsibility and Justice* (Cambridge: Polity Press).
Office of National Statistics (ONS) (2006), *Social Trends 37* (London: ONS).
Office of National Statistics (ONS) (2008), *Labour Force Survey*, available at www.statistics.gov.uk, accessed 17 April 2008.
Reynolds, T. (2002), 'Re-analysing the Black family' in Carling, A., Duncan, S. and Edwards, R. (eds), *Analysing Families: Morality and Rationality in Policy and Practice* (London: Routledge).
Ritchie, H., Casebourne, J. and Rick, J. (2005), *Understanding Worklessness, People and Communities: A Literature Review*, RR255 (London: HMSO).
Skeggs, B. (1997), *Formations of Class and Gender: Becoming Respectable* (London: Sage).
Social Exclusion Unit (2006), *Reaching Out: An Action Plan on Social Exclusion* (London: SEU/ Cabinet Office).
Williams, F. (1999), 'A New Paradigm for Welfare Research' in Williams, F., Popay, J. and Oakley, A. (eds), *Welfare Research: A Critical Review* (London: University College London Press).
Williams, F. (2004), *Rethinking Families* (London: Gulbenkian Foundation).

Chapter 5

State Responsibility and the Abuse of Vulnerable Older People: Is there a Case for a Public Law to Protect Vulnerable Older People from Abuse?

John Williams

Introduction

The end of the 20th century saw an increasing awareness of the abuse, in a variety of different settings, of people at risk. The Field-Fisher Report into the death of Maria Colwell highlighted the inadequacies of the existing law protecting children from abuse within their home environment (Field-Fisher 1974, 120). This was the first of a series of reports identifying weaknesses in child protection law and procedures. More recently, Lord Laming's report into the death of Victoria Climbié concluded that

> Not one of the agencies empowered by Parliament to protect children in positions similar to Victoria's – funded from the public purse – emerge from this Inquiry with much credit. (Laming 2003, para 1.18)

Law, policy and procedures were in place, but human and institutional failings contributed to her death. In the late 1960s Erin Pizzey challenged the perception that domestic violence did not happen, or that if it did happen it was a 'working class' phenomenon justified by some as being the exercise of a male prerogative.[1] When Pizzey opened her refuge in Chiswick, it confirmed that domestic violence was extensive and not confined to one social class. Pizzey could be summing up the attitude towards elder abuse when she wrote,

> It would probably take a Charles Dickens to do full justice to the labyrinth of indifference, red tape, callousness, and simple incompetence that exists between people in need and so many of the agencies that are meant to help them. (Pizzey 1974, 91)

She refers to 'hands being compassionately washed in all directions'. The refuge attracted people from all parts of the country, classes and roots (Pizzey 1974, 23). Increased awareness of domestic violence has led to practical, procedural and legal

1 For an interesting discussion on this point see Doggett 1992, 1-10.

reforms (Part IV, Family Law Act 1996). It would be complacent and misleading to suggest that these reforms have ended domestic violence; clearly they have not! However, they have increased public awareness, required agencies such as the police and housing authorities to respond, and provided civil law remedies for the victims of violence. In addition, domestic violence is now more likely to be regarded as a crime rather than as a purely 'social', 'domestic' or 'welfare' matter (Cretney and Davis 1996).

Elder abuse is finally following suit. It has left the denial stage and has entered the 'something must be done' stage. However, there remains a governmental reluctance (in Wales and England) to address it anything other than in a minimalist way. It is disturbing that given the experience of domestic violence and child abuse, we continue to debate whether there is a need for legislation to protect older people at risk. The private law remedies under the Family Law Act 1996 may be available to some victims of elder abuse. But not everyone is covered. Social exclusion, poverty, and lack of support and advocacy services often prevent vulnerable older people from availing themselves of private law remedies. This chapter considers whether there is a need for a public law designed to protect vulnerable older people (and adults at risk in general) from abuse. If so, how should the responsibility of the state towards older members of society be balanced against the state responsibility to ensure respect for their private and family life? How intrusive should such a law be?

Unlike the law of children, the legal responsibility of the state towards older people is found in a labyrinth of statutes that are complex, lacking in consistency and thoroughly confusing. It is ironic that we still rely on the National Assistance Act 1948 (albeit in amended form) as the key piece of the legislative framework for 21st century community care. Contrary to common belief, the National Health Service and Community Care Act 1990 did not provide a codified law on community care services; in many respects it added to the complexity. In seeking to describe the responsibility of the state towards older people in general, and vulnerable older people in particular, the best that can be said is that it is welfarist in its approach and focused on the provision of welfare-based services. For example, section 47 National Health Service and Community Care Act 1990 provides a right to be assessed if a person may be in need of community care services; once assessed the person may be entitled to the provision of services depending upon eligibility criteria (Department of Health 2003). The 'right' to be assessed is one of the few rights that exist in this area of law; the provision of services is rarely an absolute right and eligibility criteria are often dependent upon availability of resources.[2] However, in some instances the law imposes a responsibility on the state additional to welfare provision. This tends to be targeted on specific groups and not of general application. For example, section 135 of the Mental Health Act 1983 enables an approved social worker to make an application to a magistrate for a warrant authorising the police to enter private premises to search for and remove to a place of safety an adult believed to be suffering from a mental disorder. The rarely used section 47 of the National

2 See Lord Clyde in *R v Gloucestershire CC ex parte Mahfood* [1997] 2 WLR 459 at 474 and Lord Woolf MR in *R v Sefton MBC ex parte Help the Aged* (1997), 1 CCLR 57 at 671; see also Department of Health 2003, para. 52.

Assistance Act 1948 enables a local authority to apply to the magistrates for an order removing a person from their home on the grounds of 'grave chronic disease or, being aged, infirm or physically incapacitated, is living in insanitary conditions'.

Despite these and other provisions under, for example, the Care Standards Act 2000, the basic responsibility of the state, and in particular local authorities, is the provision of welfare support rather than protection from abuse. This restricted form of state responsibility is directly challenged by the Human Rights Act 1998 (HRA 1998). Section 6 HRA 1998 states that it is 'unlawful for a public authority to act in a way which is incompatible with a Convention right'. As will be discussed below, the Article 3 rights not to be subjected to inhuman or degrading treatment impose a positive obligation on the state to protect vulnerable older people from abuse. The provision of welfare support alone is inadequate. This chapter will consider whether the state is adequately meeting its responsibilities under the European Convention on Human Rights (ECHR) towards vulnerable older people at risk of, or experiencing, abuse.

Protection versus Autonomy

Any public law protection for older people at risk of abuse would be controversial and fraught with difficulty. While such a law might well meet the responsibility of the state under Article 3 of the ECHR to protect people from inhuman and degrading treatment in public it might undermine the right under Article 8 to respect for a family and private life. And it might, in effect, undermine the individual autonomy of older people. We must ask how far the state can go in its interference with an individual's right to autonomy and self-determination. Is it possible to incorporate adequate safeguards into any developed public law that would ensure an appropriate balance between the two rights? The following case studies identify some of the dilemmas that arise in trying to formulate a protection of adults at risk law.

1. Sioned is 85 years old. She is physically very frail and is reliant on her son and daughter-in-law for mobility, personal hygiene, nutrition and for getting into and out of bed. Mentally she is very alert and completes *The Times* crossword every day. Tom, her social worker, and Megan, her doctor, are very concerned about bruising on Sioned's body; the bruising is consistent with regular and severe beatings. Both professionals have serious concerns about Sioned's personal safety. When questioned, Sioned tells Tom and Megan to 'mind their own business'.
2. Steffan is 60 years old and suffers from severe bouts of depression; he lives at home with his younger brother Dafydd, although he is relatively independent and has a part time job at the local hospital. Steffan enjoys living with Dafydd – it gives him some security and he fears (rightly or wrongly) that if this arrangement broke down, he would have to live in some form of sheltered accommodation. Steffan is aware that Dafydd steals between £10 and £20 a week from his wallet. This leaves Steffan short of money, although he thinks that this is a 'price worth paying' for Dafydd's company.

3. Beth and Siôn have been married for 50 years. It has been a stormy relationship, but things are better now. On occasions, Beth will slap Siôn; these are rare occurrences, but they do produce bruising. For most of the time the relationship works better than it has ever done. This is important for Siôn.

Each of these scenarios identifies a tension between the protection older people might need and their autonomy. They invite a response from professionals about what would be a proportionate form of intervention; this is the contentious issue.

What is Elder Abuse?

Within the United Kingdom, there is relatively little research into elder abuse; this is in contrast to the United States of America, where there is a significant body of research, including studies into the legal response to abuse. One consequence of the paucity of United Kingdom research is that there is no settled definition of the term 'elder abuse'. An agreed definition would enhance the quality and quantity of research undertaken into the issue.[3] It is also a prerequisite to any form of statutory or guidance-based intervention procedures. In formulating a definition, it is necessary to identify its key components. A research seminar, hosted by the Department of Health,[4] and consisting of an interdisciplinary group of participants, identified the following key components of any definition:

- An understanding of the scale and variance of vulnerability, including the impact of perceived as well as actual vulnerability;
- Abuse and its different components e.g. financial, sexual, physical, psychological, social, neglect;
- Abuse in its different settings e.g. home, institution, sheltered housing, day care;
- Abuse in terms of the different responses required e.g. research, direct services, information provision, and advocacy;
- The role of different types of carers, the interaction between them and those in receipt of such caring, and the dynamics of caring that might contribute to or exacerbate abuse;
- Whether or not an element of trust is required between the abuser and the abused (in relation to the definition of abuse) (Action on Elder Abuse 2002).

In broad terms, these components require the definition to identify the class of people to whom it applies and the form of the abuse. Linked to that second aspect are issues such as the setting, the relevance of a relationship of trust and the nature of the abuse (physical, financial, sexual, etc). An abuse of trust is a key component of any definition. Action on Elder Abuse define elder abuse as:

3 For an interesting overview of the various definitions, see Glendenning 1997, 13-41.

4 Held on 20 January 2002.

> A single or repeated act or lack of appropriate action occurring within any relationship where there is an expectation of trust which causes harm or distress to an older person. (Action on Elder Abuse 1995)

This usually involves a family member, a carer or a professional care worker.

The definition of 'elder' for the purposes of elder abuse is also important. It would serve as the threshold for intervention – which may range from a watching brief to some form of criminal investigation and possible prosecution. There is much discussion and disagreement on the definition of 'old age'. In itself, being 'old' does not mean that a person should be treated differently from anyone else. The key element at issue is not really age at all, but the degree of vulnerability. Age may increase the likelihood of vulnerability, but not inevitably. Vulnerability arises in consequence of disability (physical or mental), lack of capacity, frailty, or through heavy dependency on an abuser. Thus, the definition has to address vulnerable older people rather than just older people.

In assessing vulnerability, the autonomy of the individual and his or her right to a private life under Article 8 is relevant. The proportionality of the state's response to elder abuse must be informed by the need to balance the duty to protect the person against their right to determine how they would wish to live. In scenario (2) above, for example (where a few pounds was stolen by the brother), the older person may appropriately concede that the loss does not matter: the continuation of the relationship with the brother is of more value than the money stolen. In addition, the individual may be concerned that, unless the statutory agencies can match the level of practical support that the carer provides, intervention would be detrimental. Whereas the carer's 'abuse' might be 'wrong' and ideally should be 'dealt with', it is difficult to deny the competent and independent older person the right to prevent intervention; their decision to live their life in this way is worthy of respect even if it may cause anxiety for professionals. The position may be different if the older person was also vulnerable as a result, for example, of a severe physical disability (see scenario (1) above, for example, in which the older person is confined to a wheelchair). In such cases, vulnerability and the need for protection may outweigh the right to respect for a private life.

The Department of Health and the Welsh Assembly have also addressed the problem of defining vulnerability. Their guidance on developing and implementing multi-agency vulnerable adult abuse protection procedures, *No Secrets* (Department of Health and Home Office 2000) and *In Safe Hands* (National Assembly for Wales 2000) follows the wording proposed in the Lord Chancellor's consultation paper, *Who Decides* (Lord Chancellor's Department 1997, para 8.7). A vulnerable adult is a person,

> who is or may be in need of community care services by reason of mental or other disability, age or illness; and who is or may be unable to take care of him or herself or unable to protect him or herself against significant harm or exploitation. (paras. 2.13 and 7.3 respectively)

The reference to 'community care services' in this definition incorporates section 46(3) of the National Health Service and Community Care Act 1990, which defines them as services which a local authority may provide, or arrange to be provided, under Part III of the National Assistance Act 1948, section 45 of the National Health Service and Public Health Act 1968, section 21 of and Schedule 8 to the National Health Act 1977, and section 117 of the Mental Health Act 1983.

The advantage of this definition is that it links adults at risk and protection procedures to a client group identifiable for the purposes of eligibility for community care services. However, whether a person is or may be in need of community care services under the 1990 Act is not directly relevant to whether they are vulnerable for the purposes of adult protection procedures. An older person may be vulnerable, but not in need of community care services. A physically and mentally fit older person coerced into parting with money by an abusing relative will be in need of protection rather than community care services. Indeed, they may be ineligible for community care services under the 1990 Act. Similarly, some forms of psychological abuse may be driven by the strength of the abuser's personality rather than the need of the abused person for community care services. The link with eligibility for community care services illustrates a welfarist approach to abuse.

It is interesting to note the language used when discussing such behaviour towards older people. We talk about elder abuse. This is not the language another adult would use to the police to describe an attack – even by a non-stranger. Criminal or quasi-criminal language – 'assault', 'attack' and 'grievous bodily harm' – is most likely to be used. This choice of language reflects, or may cause, a decriminalisation or a 'welfarisation' of such behaviour. The abuse of older people is perceived of solely as a welfare problem that requires a welfare-based response.

The second part of the *No Secrets* and *In Safe Hands* definition deals with an essential component of vulnerability, namely the inability to protect against 'significant harm or exploitation'. This may arise because of the physical or mental frailty of the individual; it may also arise because of financial dependency, care dependency or the dominant personality of the abuser.

The Scottish Law Commission in its report, *Vulnerable Adults*, also discussed the definition of 'vulnerable'. The Commission recommended that,

> A vulnerable adult should be defined for the purposes of this report as an adult who is unable to safeguard his or her personal welfare, property or financial affairs, and is:
> (a) in need of care and attention arising out of age or infirmity or
> (b) suffering from illness or mental disorder; or
> (c) substantially handicapped by any disability. (1997, para 2.17)

The Commission felt that short-term protective measures should be linked to longer-term responsibilities possessed by local authorities. Section 94(2) of the Social Work (Scotland) Act 1968 provided a useful basis for the 'person in need' concept used in paragraph (a) of the recommendation.[5] The justification for this approach is revealing

---

5 Section 94(2) of the 1968 Act at the date of the report stated that 'persons in need' means persons who, '(a) are in need of care and attention arising out of infirmity, youth or age; or (b) suffer from illness or mental disorder or are substantially handicapped by any deformity or disability; or … (d) being persons prescribed by the Secretary of State who have asked

and based on the need to limit the extent of local authority responsibility in this area. In rejecting a dictionary-based definition of 'vulnerable', the Commission stated,

> A much narrower definition of vulnerable was said to be needed, many respondents commenting that at some point in their lives almost everyone was vulnerable in the sense we used in our discussion paper. We appreciate the force of this criticism. A wide definition would place too great a strain on local authority resources and would make it impossible for the local authority to confine its attentions to those genuinely in need of them. (Scottish Law Commission 1997, para. 2.13)

The first sentence makes a reasonable point; vulnerability is something that we all experience, very often only as a transient status because of illness or an accident. To propose that statutory or guidance-based procedures should be available to everybody is unrealistic. In the discussion paper preceding the report the Commission proposed a dictionary definition:

> "vulnerable" should refer to people who were "capable of being wounded, liable to injury, or hurt to feelings: open to successful attack: capable of being persuaded or tempted …" (para. 2.9)

At this stage, the Commission was not convinced that it was desirable to enumerate the possible causes of vulnerability. After considering the responses to the consultation exercise, the Commission concluded that there was a need to restrict the definition, partly, as noted above, in recognition of the resource implications.

In many respects the way forward may lie somewhere in between the discussion paper's tentative suggestion and that of the final report. It is necessary for the term to be context sensitive otherwise local authorities would spend much of their time investigating cases that could be dealt with in other ways. However, for that context to be defined according to welfare-based statutes, the concept of 'person in need' is unduly restrictive and reinforces the welfare response to abuse. It is, surely, sufficient that vulnerability is a consequence of age or disability rather than that the person happens to fall within a definition designed for other purposes.

The Adult Support and Protection (Scotland) Act 2007 introduces a self-contained definition of 'adults at risk'. It severs the link between vulnerability and welfare-based legislation:

> (1) "Adults at risk" are adults who—
> (a) are unable to safeguard their own well-being, property, rights or other interests,
> (b) are at risk of harm, and
> (c) because they are affected by disability, mental disorder, illness or physical or mental infirmity, are more vulnerable to being harmed than adults who are not so affected.
> (2) An adult is at risk of harm for the purposes of subsection (1) if—
> (a) another person's conduct is causing (or is likely to cause) the adult to be harmed, or
> (b) the adult is engaging (or is likely to engage) in conduct which causes (or is likely to cause) self-harm.

---

for assistance, are, in the opinion of a local authority, persons to whom the authority may appropriately make available the services and facilities provided by them under this Act.'

Two points should be noted. First, there is no specific reference to age. Second, it includes self-harm, which presumably may involve professionals making judgements about the way people choose to live their lives. To what extent do we allow people to adopt a style of life that may put them at risk of harm?

The Prevalence of Elder Abuse

There have been many attempts to estimate the prevalence of elder abuse. The House of Commons Health Committee stated that the only estimate then available was that half a million older people at any one time were experiencing abuse (House of Commons Health Committee 2003, para. 31). At a more specific level, Mr Denzil Lush, Master of the Court of Protection, in his evidence to the Joint Committee on the Draft Mental Incapacity Bill put forward his 'hunch' or 'instinctive assessment' that financial abuse occurs in about 10 to 15 per cent of cases involving enduring powers of attorney. Of this, 2 or 3 per cent was probably criminal in nature; the remainder was 'unethical' (Joint Committee on the Draft Mental Incapacity Act 2002a). This is rather ironic given that enduring powers are intended as a form of protection from abuse.

A major United Kingdom study of the abuse and neglect of older people was undertaken by King's College, London, and the National Centre for Social Research (Mowlam et al. 2007). It does not include stranger crime nor does it include abuse in institutional settings. The findings reveal that there are approximately 342,400 people aged 66 years and over who are subject to some form of mistreatment. This figure only covers people living in private homes (including sheltered housing) and involves incidents involving neighbours and acquaintances. This means that approximately 4 per cent of that age group experience abuse. Neglect is the main form of abuse, reported by 1.1 per cent of the age cohort. This is followed by financial abuse (0.7 per cent), psychological abuse (0.4 per cent), physical abuse (0.4 per cent), and sexual abuse (0.2 per cent). Fifty-one per cent of the perpetrators were spouses or partners; 49 per cent were other family members. Care workers represented 13 per cent and 5 per cent were close friends. Respondents were able to mention more than one person in their responses.

The impact of abuse on older people was significant. The report concluded,

> The impacts included a raft of psychological impacts including emotional distress, loss of self-confidence and self-esteem, depression, thoughts of suicide and/or self harm and, in extreme cases, long-term abuse could result in uncharacteristic and unplanned physical retaliation. Some respondents became socially isolated; others experienced a loss of independence. Also evident were negative impacts on physical health, financial loss, and a change to family relationships.
>
> Respondents would typically experience a combination of different types of impacts, such as emotional distress, social isolation and a loss of self-confidence. Impacts described by respondents were often multiple in nature and those such as emotional distress, social isolation, depression and loss of self-esteem and self-confidence were typically experienced across a wide range of different cases. (2007, 44)

Government Guidance

No Secrets and *In Safe Hands* aim to provide a 'framework for action within which all responsible agencies work together to ensure a coherent policy for the protection of vulnerable adults at risk of abuse and a consistent and effective response to any circumstances giving ground for concern or formal complaints or expressions of anxiety' (2000, para. 1.1). The HRA 1998 places a responsibility upon governments to consider how best to respond to growing concerns about elder abuse. Article 3 of the ECHR imposes a positive duty on states to protect against inhuman or degrading treatment. *X v Netherlands*[6] and *A v UK*[7] reinforce the fact that this duty applies regardless of the locus of the abuse and of the identity of the perpetrator; they also emphasise that the duty under the Article is all the more compelling in respect of vulnerable people. At the same time, the state has a duty under Article 8 to protect the right to a private life, especially decision-making autonomy. If the state wishes to interfere with that right, then it must ensure that such interference is ECHR compliant. Prior to *No Secrets* and *In Safe Hands*, there was little by way of formal guidance to ensure that authorities had appropriate regard to the need to balance these two competing sets of rights. Many local authorities had introduced adults at risk protection procedures, although their effectiveness was questionable as they lacked the backing of central government guidance. *No Secrets* and *In Safe Hands* adopt the same interdisciplinary approach as the child protection equivalent, *Working Together* (Department for Education and Skills 2006). It sets out the roles and responsibilities of different agencies, outlines the manner in which joint agency working can be achieved, sets out processes that should be followed when abuse is suspected, and emphasises the importance of training and development. However, one crucial difference between the two documents is that whereas *Working Together* exists within a clear and cohesive statutory framework, *No Secrets* and *In Safe Hands* operate within a legal vacuum. In child protection cases the Children Act 1989 provides legal authority for intervention in the form of care orders (s. 31), child assessment orders (s. 43), emergency protection orders (s. 44), and a general police power to remove children at risk from dangerous situations (s. 46). Of particular importance is the existence of a statutory duty on local authorities to investigate cases of suspected child abuse (s. 47). This is supported by powers to assist in the discovery of children who may be in need of emergency protection (s. 48). It is unacceptable indiscriminately to incorporate principles of child protection law into any vulnerable adult protection law. Nevertheless, the ability to reinforce the principles in *Working Together* by reference to the statutory code enhances the effectiveness of the interdisciplinary approach.

This statutory basis is lacking in cases of the abuse of those who are older and at risk. The National Health Service and Community Care Act 1990 does not permit compulsory intervention in the lives of abused adults; it simply provides for the assessment and possible provision of services for those deemed to be in need. Whereas the child protection worker will have recourse to the Children Act

---

6 (1985), 8 EHRR 235.

7 (1998), 5 BHRC 137.

1989 if action is required and the family or carers are being obstructive, the adult services worker must rely on professional skills; these may be inadequate to protect the abused person.

No Secrets and *In Safe Hands* were issued under section 7 of the Local Government Social Services Act 1970:

> Local authorities shall, in the exercise of their social services functions, including the exercise of any discretion conferred by any relevant enactment, act under the general guidance of the Secretary of State.

The need to adhere to guidance has been emphasised in a number of recent cases. In *Re C (Adoption: Religious Observance)*,[8] for example, Wilson J said 'although only guidance, it is issued under section 7 of the Local Authority Social Services Act 1970, with the result that agencies are required to act under it' (at para. 35). However, the ability of local authorities to adhere to the guidance is compromised by a lack of adequate funding. In its evidence to the Joint Committee on the Draft Mental Incapacity Bill, the Association of Directors of Social Services said,

> It must be emphasised that Local Authorities have not been resourced for the additional responsibilities given to them under the "No Secrets" guidance, and are not in a position to undertake additional responsibilities effectively without further resources. (Joint Committee on the Draft Mental Incapacity Bill 2002b)

The lack of a statutory duty to investigate cases of suspected abuse alongside a lack of resources makes it difficult for local authorities to meet their wider responsibilities.

No Secrets and *In Safe Hands* emphasise the need to report cases of suspected vulnerable adult abuse. As abuse almost inevitably involves the commission of a criminal offence, it emphasises the importance of reporting concerns to the police. *No Secrets* states,

> early referral or consultation with the police will enable them to establish whether a criminal act has been committed and this will give them the opportunity of determining if, and at what stage, they need to become involved. (para. 6.8)[9]

The necessity to report is not confined to serious criminal offences, but to any form of abuse. Minor offences such as petty theft fall within the paragraph. In part, this enables an accurate profile to be constructed; unless such incidents are logged, it is difficult to identify whether a particular incident was an isolated incident, or part of a pattern of abuse. Involving the police does not necessarily mean that a full criminal investigation is commenced. A proportionate response is necessary that has regard to the autonomy of the individual as well as their right not to be subjected to inhuman or degrading treatment.

---

8 [2002] 1 FLR 1119.

9 See, too, National Assembly for Wales 2000, para. 8.6.

Is there a Case for New Legislation?

In its report, *Mental Incapacity*, the Law Commission made a number of recommendations for the reform of the public law protecting vulnerable people at risk (Law Commission 1995). It pointed out the inadequacies of existing law, namely its ineffectiveness and insensitivity to people's civil rights. The recommendations included placing social services departments under a duty to investigate the circumstances where they have reason to believe that a vulnerable person is suffering or likely to suffer significant harm or serious exploitation (paras. 9.15-16). Where their efforts were being frustrated, the authority should have power to enter premises and interview the person concerned (para. 9.19); apply to the court for an entry warrant (paras 9.21-23), an 'assessment order' (paras 9.24-26), or a 'temporary protection order' (paras 9.28-34).

To take account of self-determination, the Commission recommended that where the person objects, the powers should not be exercised, unless that person is unable to make a decision because of 'mental disability.' Finally, it recommended that magistrates' courts should have power to grant warrants or make orders for the protection of adults at risk.

The government responded to these proposals with a consultation paper, *Who Decides?* (Lord Chancellor's Department 1997). It challenged the need for public law measures. The Lord Chancellor, in a statement to the House of Lords said,

> The Government believes that, although there may be merit in some of the Law Commission's recommendations concerning these new provisions, there may not be a pressing need for reform in the light of powers which already exist in this area.[10]

In *Who Decides?* the government was not specific as to what the 'powers that already exist' are. It said that 'a number of initiatives have been undertaken to address the particular problem of elder abuse, and these cannot yet be fully evaluated' (Lord Chancellor's Department 1997, para. 8.6). *Who Decides?* did not refer to the public law proposal.

In questioning the need for further reform the government upheld the 'right of individuals to live in isolation', better known as autonomy (Lord Chancellor's Department 1997, para. 8.6). Medical law reinforces autonomy. In *Re T (Adult: Refusal of Treatment)*,[11] which involved the refusal of a blood transfusion, Lord Donaldson MR said that a person with legal capacity has the right to consent to, or refuse medical treatment 'notwithstanding that the reasons for making the choice are rational, irrational, unknown or even non-existent' (at 653). The judiciary's commitment to this principle is illustrated by its recognition that a woman has a right to refuse a caesarean operation,[12] and a patient advised that the amputation of his leg was essential to save his life, has the right to refuse the treatment.[13] This emphasis

10 Hansard, HL, vol. 584, col. 157 (10 December 1997).

11 [1992] 4 All ER 649.

12 See *St George's Healthcare NHS Trust v S (No 2)* [1998] 3 WLR 936.

13 *Re C (Refusal of medical treatment)* [1994] 1 All ER 819.

on autonomy is recognised in the Mental Capacity Act 2005. Section 1(4) of that Act preserves the right to make an 'unwise decision'.

The incorporation of the ECHR into our domestic law by the HRA 1998 imposes a duty on the courts and 'public authorities' to guarantee enjoyment of Convention rights. Under Article 8(1) private life includes (but is not confined to) the notion of the 'inner circle'.[14] This inner circle embraces the right of people to enjoy their private life without interference from the state – a right to 'live in isolation'.

The other argument against new legislation is that existing law and procedures are adequate. However, current law does not provide a unified and coherent response to elder abuse; it fails to address the need for clearly defined powers in extreme cases. Whereas *No Secrets* and *In Safe Hands* have ensured the introduction of protection policies and procedures across England and Wales, they exist within a legal vacuum. They are a useful start and contain a framework for a better interdisciplinary approach to vulnerable adult abuse, but they do not provide adequate protection in extreme cases.

Perhaps the most compelling argument in favour of new legislation is that vulnerable adult abuse is still with us. However, it is important not to overstate the impact that law can have. Child abuse is still with us, yet we have had child protection legislation for over one hundred years. Laws do not solve social problems like these, but they may contribute to a much broader, interdisciplinary approach to the prevention of abuse. *Re F*[15] highlights the shortcomings of existing law. An 18-year-old woman, T, with a mental age of between five and eight years lacked legal capacity. The local authority accommodated her, with the consent of her parents, just before her 17th birthday. But her parents later withdrew their consent. Butler-Sloss P in the Court of Appeal described T's family background as follows:

> The case for the local authority disclosed a picture of chronic neglect, a lack of minimum standards of hygiene and cleanliness in the home, a serious lack of adequate parenting and worrying exposure to those engaged in sexual exploitation and possible sexual abuse of one or more of the children including T. The eight children were said to be suffering significant harm and at risk of so doing, based upon these numerous allegations. (at 1742)

The consultant paediatrician examined T and found that she had suffered penetrative sexual abuse. As T was 18 years old, the child protection legislation and wardship jurisdiction were no longer available to her. T's mother sought T's return to the family home. If she returned home or had regular contact with her parent there were serious grounds for concern about her safety. The Court considered the possibilities. It rejected guardianship under the Mental Health Act 1983 but noted that guardianship under the Mental Health Act 1959 'might well have been sufficient to meet the needs of T as set out by the local authority' (at 1743). Under the 1959 Act a guardian could restrict 'to such extent as he thinks necessary the making of visits to the patient and may prohibit visits by any person who the guardian has reason to believe may have an adverse affect on the patient' (r. 6(2) of the Mental Health (Hospital and

14 *Niemietz v Germany* (1993), 16 EHRR 97.

15 *Re F (Adult Patient)* [2000] 3 WLR 1740.

Guardianship) Regulations 1960). However, the 1983 Act changed this: it reduced the 'powers' of the guardian to a point where, even if available, they would have little impact in this case. The other factor preventing use of guardianship under the 1983 Act was that in an earlier hearing[16] the court decided that T's wish to go home was not 'seriously irresponsible conduct' within s. 1(2) Mental Health Act 1983.

The Court was in a dilemma; it was unable to use the child protection legislation, wardship or the Mental Health Act 1983. Would it have to stand by and see T returned to an abusive and unsafe home environment? What other options were open to the local authority, which was anxious to protect T? The Court noted the lack of a statutory jurisdiction. Butler-Sloss P said,

> A local authority was a creature of statute and there was no statutory justification for the control sought by the local authority to restrict where T should live or who should contact her. Although the local authority had duties under the philosophy of "care in the community", the care was voluntary and not directive. (at 1747)

The Court was compelled to use the doctrine of 'necessity'. Sedley LJ stated the problem faced by the Court in the following terms:

> T is so unable to judge what is in her own best interests that no humane society could leave her adrift and at risk simply because she has reached the age of 18. (at 1756)

He concluded that, following *Re F (Sterilization: Mental Patient)*,[17] the common law of necessity would in appropriate cases permit otherwise tortious interferences with the personal integrity of the mentally incapacitated. The court granted a declaration in favour of the local authority that T should remain in their care with limited family contact. In reaching this conclusion it referred to the proposals by the Law Commission. However, until legislation was in place, the courts were compelled fill the gaps in the law.

Butler-Sloss P pointed out the limitations of the case-by-case approach.

> The assumption of jurisdiction by the High Court on a case by case basis does not, however, detract from the obvious need expressed by the Law Commission and by the Government for a well-structured and clearly defined framework of protection of vulnerable, mentally incapacitated adults, particularly since the whole essence of declarations under the inherent jurisdiction is to meet a recognised individual problem and not to provide general guidance for mentally incapacitated adults. Until Parliament puts in place that defined framework, the High Court will still be required to help out where there is no other practicable alternative. (at 1752)

The Court did not feel that the principle of necessity would provide the breadth of protection necessary. Sedley LJ said,

> If returning to her mother is in truth a source of danger to her, I agree that ... the court may, by declaring what is in T's best interests, sanction not only the provision of local

---

16 *Re F (Mental Health Act: Guardianship)* [2000] 1 FLR 192.

17 [1989] 2 FLR 376.

> authority accommodation (which in any case needs no special permission) but the use of such moral or physical restriction as may be needed to keep T there and out of harm's way. (at 1756)

This illustrates the weakness of the local authority's legal position, namely the problem of enforcing the declaration of the court. As Sedley LJ makes clear, the local authority has power to provide accommodation under the Community Care Act 1990 and National Assistance Act 1948. How could it ensure that this protective regime endures? The best he can suggest is that the authority resorts to 'moral or physical restriction'. Such restrictions are vague and of dubious legality especially since the advent of the HRA 1998. What happens if the parent of T ignores the moral or physical pressures? What statutory fallback is there, given that local authorities must have a legal (and invariably a statutory) basis for their actions? Historically the courts have been reluctant to undertake an ongoing responsibility for supervising orders that they make. Although it is impossible to disagree with the outcome of the case, the legal difficulties that it highlights re-emphasise the need for legislation. However useful necessity and best interests may be in a medico-legal context, they do not translate easily into the *Re F* circumstances, without straining the sinews that bind law and good practice to breaking point.

Another very important factor is the impact of the Human Rights Act 1998. The ECHR supports the status quo by emphasising the importance of autonomy. However, it also provides the basis for a much more compelling argument in favour of new law; indeed, it can be argued that the current lacuna in our law on vulnerable adult protection violates the ECHR.

The Impact of the HRA 1998

A number of ECHR rights are relevant in addressing the need for comprehensive legislation. They may be summarised as follows.

Inhuman and degrading treatment

Article 3 ECHR states that: 'No one shall be subjected to torture or to inhuman or degrading treatment or punishment.'

There has been a great deal of debate within the European Court about the meaning of 'inhuman or degrading treatment', and it is clear that a level of severity must be present. However, inhuman treatment that causes intense physical and mental suffering and degrading treatment that arouses in the victim a feeling of fear, anguish and inferiority capable of humiliating and debasing the victim and possibly breaking their physical or moral resistance, falls within Article 3.[18] One important factor in determining such treatment is the vulnerability of the victim. In *Ribitsch v Austria*,[19] the European Court emphasised that the vulnerability of the victim – in this case a person detained by the Vienna police – was a relevant factor in

18 See *Ireland v United Kingdom* (1978), 2 EHRR 25.

19 (1995), 21 EHRR 573.

deciding whether Article 3 ECHR was violated. Similarly, in *X v Netherlands*[20] the European Commission found that the sexual abuse in a privately run nursing home, of a 16-year-old woman with learning difficulty, caused mental suffering leading to psychiatric disturbance, and fell within Article 3.

This approach reinforces the argument for legal powers in relation to direct abuse by the state or somebody who falls within the definition of 'public authority' under s. 6(3) of the Human Rights Act 1998. The Court in *A v United Kingdom*[21] discussed this point. The case involved the chastisement with a garden cane of a nine-year-old child by his stepfather. The court acquitted the stepfather of assault occasioning actual bodily harm, relying on the defence of 'reasonable chastisement'. The child took the case to the European Court arguing that there was a breach of Articles 3 and 8 of the ECHR. The Court held unanimously that there had been a breach of Article 3. The United Kingdom argued that, unlike corporal punishment in schools, the state was not directly responsible under the ECHR for its use in the home. The Court rejected this argument. It said,

> The Court considers that the obligation ... under Article 1 ... to secure to everyone within their jurisdiction the rights and freedoms defined in the Convention, taken together with Article 3, requires States to take measures designed to ensure that individuals within their jurisdiction are not subjected to torture or inhuman or degrading treatment or punishment, including such ill-treatment administered by private individuals. Children and other vulnerable individuals, in particular, are entitled to State protection, in the form of effective deterrence, against such serious breaches of personal integrity. (para. 22)

Thus, the state has a positive obligation not only to avoid directly violating this right, but also to ensure that its laws are sufficiently robust to ensure that vulnerable people have adequate protection against such treatment in whatever setting. It is unlikely that in the context of vulnerable adult abuse, the United Kingdom could successfully argue that it fulfils this duty.

Respect for private and family life, home and correspondence

Article 8(1) ECHR states, 'Everyone has the right to respect for his private and family life, his home and his correspondence.'

A crucial part of our private life is the right to self-determination. The government's assertion of the right to 'live in isolation' and to be free of interference by the state was one of the arguments against a new public law on vulnerable adult abuse. As noted above, in medical law the right to self-determination receives the utmost respect from the courts, as does the Mental Capacity Act 2005. It would be undesirable, and in violation of the ECHR, if new law introduced compulsory intervention in the lives of older people, on the basis of their age and our desire to 'do what is best for all of them'. A balance between autonomy and protection is required; in many respects, identifying the point of intervention is the challenge for any new legislation. For people who lack capacity, the decision on intervention is easier. As they cannot decide for themselves,

20 (1985), 8 EHRR 235.
21 (1998), 5 BHRC 137.

it would be wrong to ignore their plight. Whether the 'best interest' criterion is an adequate basis for intervention is debatable, but the need for intervention is clear. The Mental Capacity Act 2005 now provides a statutory basis for decision making for people who lack capacity. More difficulty arises when the person has capacity, but is vulnerable and at an unacceptable risk, for example the person described in scenario (1) above (mentally alert, but physically dependent person).

Under the ECHR, the right to private life is not absolute. Article 8(2) ECHR narrowly defines the circumstances in which Article 8(1) may be restricted by the state.[22] The law must define the boundaries of the restriction to prevent arbitrary interference in private life. Unless intervention is authorised by the law, it cannot fall within Article 8(2). The law must ensure that the restrictions are reasonably precise and foreseeable. The European Court in *Halford v United Kingdom*[23] said it was entitled to look at the quality of the law forming the basis of the interference with Convention rights. It said,

> In terms of the quality of the law, the Commission notes that the law must be compatible with the rule of law in providing a measure of protection against arbitrary interference by public authorities and, in this context, it must be accessible to the person concerned who must moreover be able to foresee the consequences of the law for him. (at para. 61)

In addition, there must be adequate safeguards against the arbitrary use of any powers under an adults-at-risk public law. The European Court of Human Rights in *HL v United Kingdom*[24] considered whether the House of Lords in *R v Bournewood Community and Mental Health NHS Trust, ex parte L (Secretary of State for Health and others intervening)*[25] were right to say that detention of an incapacitated patient was justified by the doctrine of necessity. The European Court concluded that 'this absence of procedural safeguards fails to protect against arbitrary deprivations of liberty on grounds of *necessity* and, consequently, to comply with the essential purpose of Art 5(1) of the Convention' (at para. 124).

Article 8(2) determines that any restrictions on Article 8(1) may be legitimate if based on, inter alia, public safety, protection of health or morals, the prevention of disorder or crime, or the protection of the rights of others. No other reason than those found in Article 8(2) can justify a violation of Article 8(1). Seeking to justify intervention because it is 'necessary' or 'in the best interests of the client' will not be sufficient.

Finally, the restriction must be necessary in a democratic society: the Court in *Sunday Times v United Kingdom*[26] stated,

> It is not sufficient that the interference belongs to that class of the exceptions listed [in 8(2)] which has been invoked … the Court has to be satisfied that the interference was necessary having regard to the facts and circumstances prevailing in the specific case before it. (at para. 65)

22 See *Sunday Times v United Kingdom* (1979), 2 EHRR 245.
23 (1997), 24 EHRR 523.
24 [2004], 40 EHRR 761.
25 [1998], 3 All ER 289.
26 (1979), 2 EHRR 245.

Thus, intervention must depend upon the circumstances of each case and not result from the application of a general policy or overarching principles. For example, a law based entirely on the fact that an individual has obtained a certain age would be disproportionate and unnecessary to achieve the objective of the law.[27] A balance is necessary between the state's responsibility to prevent abuse and the protection of the individual's human rights.[28] Sweeping and disproportionate policies are unacceptable.[29]

The three scenarios outlined above involve adults at risk refusing to 'consent' to intervention. Putting aside, for the moment, the possibility of duress, the question arises whether there ought to be any limits on an individual's autonomy in these circumstances. The case of *Laskey v United Kingdom*[30] involved a group of sado-masochists who had been successfully prosecuted under the Offences Against the Persons Act 1861. In their application to the European Court of Human Rights they emphasised that all those involved were willing and consenting. The United Kingdom argued that the state was entitled to punish violence irrespective of the consent of the victim. It likened some of the acts to torture and maintained that no state could be obliged to tolerate such behaviour simply because it took place in a consensual context; the state is entitled to prohibit acts because of their potential danger. The European Court found that the restrictions imposed on these activities were not a violation of Article 8 ECHR because they were necessary in a democratic society for the protection of health (under Article 8(2)). *Laskey* demonstrates that the responsibility of the state to protect the health of its citizens can override or restrict the autonomous interests of freely consenting adults. How much stronger, therefore, is the case for imposing such restrictions, through state intervention, on involuntary and vulnerable victims.

Guaranteeing the rights in the Convention

Article 1 of the ECHR requires the signatories to 'secure to everyone within their jurisdiction the rights and freedoms defined in article 1 of this Convention'. The European Court said in *Osman v UK*,[31] a case on the Article 2 right to protection of life, that it was sufficient,

> for an applicant to show that the authorities did not do all that could reasonably be expected of them to avoid a real and immediate risk to life of which they ought to have knowledge. (para. 116)

This is consistent with the positive obligation referred to earlier in *A v United Kingdom.*[32]

---

27 *Handyside v United Kingdom (Application 5493/72)* (1976) 1 EHRR 737.

28 *Soering v UK* (1989) 11 EHRR 439.

29 *Open Door Counselling and Dublin Well Woman v Ireland (Applications 14234/88, 14235/88)* (1992), 15 EHRR 244.

30 (1995) (Application 21627/93) (18 January 1995, unreported).

31 (1998), 5 BHRC 293.

32 (1998), 5 BHRC 137.

Freedom from discrimination

Article 14 prohibits discrimination in the enjoyment of ECHR rights on the grounds of 'sex, race, colour, language, religion, political or other opinion, national or social origin, association with a national minority, property, birth or other status'. The words 'other status' are capable of wide interpretation and include age and disability. This supports the view that the state has a responsibility for ensuring that vulnerable older people are adequately protected, in appropriate circumstances, from abuse.

Conclusion

The debate on a new public law designed to protect vulnerable older people is complex. At the one extreme, we could simply adapt current child protection legislation so that it includes vulnerable adults. Despite the problems identified by Lord Laming and others in the working of child protection legislation, the Children Act 1989 as amended is a tried and tested piece of legislation and provides a sound legal framework for public intervention. Brogden and Nijhar comment on this approach as follows:

> A central tenet has been that children and elder persons are similarly vulnerable. The abuse paradigm that dominated research into elderly victimisation made key mistakes in drawing on this child abuse research. The latter led elder victimisation into a welfare trap. False parallels kept elder victimisation outside criminological concerns. (Brogden and Nijhar 2000, 18)

Tempting though it may be, there are dangers in drawing analogies between children and vulnerable adults at risk of abuse. Children (putting aside the *Gillick* principle)[33] do not enjoy the same degree of autonomy as adults. Paternalism is a concept that we normally apply to children. Arguably, the Law Commission based its proposals too firmly on child protection principles.

At the other extreme is the view that we do not need a new public law because the existing legal protection is adequate. There is an array of laws that can be used to protect vulnerable older people. These include the criminal law; there are offences that would cover financial, physical, sexual and psychological abuse. Section 44 Mental Capacity Act 2005 introduces the offence of ill-treating or wilfully neglecting a person who lacks capacity or whom the perpetrator reasonably believes to lack capacity; a similar provision is found in section 127 Mental Health Act 1983 in relation to patients under that Act. However, limited use is made of the criminal law – as noted above, the 'welfarist' approach risks screening out the possibility of criminal prosecutions in all but a few cases. Brogden and Nijhar argue that the label 'abused' implies incapacity to determine one's own fate. The term 'pathologises victims by denying them competence. It renders them – in their own interest – outside of normal criminal law protections.' (2000, 14). Even with the special

33 *Gillick v West Norfolk and Wisbech AHA* [1986] AC 112.

measures available under the Youth Justice and Criminal Evidence Act 1998, the state's welfarist approach to the abuse of older people has to be overcome.[34]

In addition to the criminal law, public law measures exist that might be helpful in addressing acts of abuse or preventing their occurrence.

The Care Standards Act 2000, the Mental Health Act 1983 and the National Assistance Act 1948 make require or permit the intervention by public bodies in cases of abuse. However, they fall short of a coherent and widely applicable public law.

Between these two extremes, there is an approach that allows a sensitive response to be made to individual cases of abuse. The proposition is that it is possible to devise a public law permitting (indeed requiring) intervention by local authorities in cases of suspected abuse. Such a law would need to address the balance, discussed above, between the state's responsibility to protect (in particular from inhuman or degrading treatment) and the state's responsibility to respect and promote autonomy and independence. Such a public law can play its part in addressing abuse, but it is only one part of a more complex solution involving changing attitudes amongst young and old, abusers and abused, and society in general. In very broad terms, law may perform an educative role and help change attitudes. Nevertheless, public law has a role to play. Commenting on the American experience of elder abuse, Weed argues,

> Until we can find a solution to the problem at its roots, and thus eliminate the problem, it is necessary to prevent as much of the suffering as possible. By providing an efficient and immediate method for intervention in life-threatening situations, with little sacrifice of autonomy, [the statute] takes a large step in the right direction. (1997, 903)

Public law should allow timely intervention by social workers, or others, before the point of unacceptable risk. The current guidance, *In Safe Hands* and *No Secrets*, is not enough. It is soft-law, without the backing of legislation.

What powers of intervention should be included in a new public law? The proposals in *Mental Incapacity* were noted above. The American model of mandatory reporting should be considered (Gardner Cravedi and Halamandaris 1981; Santo 2000; Silva 1992; Velick 1995). A duty to investigate along with powers of entry would allay some of the concerns of professionals. There must be procedural safeguards to ensure that intervention is lawful and compatible with the state's responsibilities under the ECHR; for example, it must meet the stringent conditions laid down in Article 8(2) of the ECHR. Such safeguards should include clearly defined criteria for intervention; restricting emergency intervention to a limited period; ensuring that a court or tribunal considers the appropriateness and legality of the intervention; and providing the subject of the intervention with an opportunity to be heard.

Who would a new public law be designed to protect? The California definition of 'endangered person' provides a possible working definition:

---

34 This Act introduces special measures that may be taken to assist defined categories of vulnerable adults in criminal proceedings (for example, giving evidence by live link, video-recorded evidence in chief, and the services of a support person).

> a dependent or elder adult who is at immediate risk of serious injury or death, due to suspected abuse or neglect and who demonstrates the inability to take action to protect himself or herself from the consequences of remaining in that situation or condition.[35]

How relevant is the consent or refusal of the alleged victim? Should autonomy prevail or should the state's responsibility to protect from harm override the consent of the individual? Consent is relevant, and in many situations will be the determining factor. Respect for autonomy will normally be decisive. However, an adult protection law must include the power to intervene even where the victim refuses help. In some cases the duty to respect private life should give way to the duty to protect life and limb. In making this judgement, issues such as level of risk, degree of vulnerability, and the very important doctrine of undue influence, are relevant. The doctrine is familiar to, but little used by, social welfare lawyers in Wales and England. It featured in *Re T (Adult: Refusal of Treatment)*[36] where Lord Donaldson MR had to consider the effect of outside influences (the patient's mother) on the free will of the patient. He said the question to ask is 'is it such that he can no longer think for himself?' (at 662).

Drafting such legislation will be very difficult. However, the Scottish legislation illustrates that it is possible to address the delicate balance between respect for autonomy and fulfilment of the responsibility to protect without relying on child protection principles. Similarly, the experience of America is that constitutional safeguards against the misuse of power by the state can be reconciled with protection laws.

There is a growing awareness of elder abuse. Help the Aged and Action on Elder Abuse jointly launched a campaign in 2006 to raise awareness of elder abuse. A new public law would be timely and would provide some protection for a particularly vulnerable section of society. It would also send out a message that elder abuse is something that the state takes seriously and that there can no longer be a blanket prohibition against state intervention based on an overstated case for autonomy.

References

Action on Elder Abuse (1995), 'What is Elder Abuse?', available at http://www.elderabuse.org.uk/What%20is%20abuse/what_is_abuse%20define.htm, accessed 10 December 2007.

Action on Elder Abuse (2002), 'Research into Elder Abuse', available at http://www.elderabuse.org.uk/Media%20and%20Resources/useful%20downloads/AEA/AEA%20research%20paper.doc, Research seminar held 2 January 2002, accessed 10 December 2007.

Brogden, M. and Nijhar, P. (2000), *Crime, Abuse and the Elderly* (Cullompton: Willan).

Cretney, A. and Davis, G. (1996), 'Prosecuting "Domestic" Assault', *Criminal Law Review* 162.

35 Article 2, CA Wel & Inst § 15700.

36 [1992] 4 All ER 649.

Department for Education and Skills (2006), *Working Together to Safeguard Children: A Guide to Inter-agency Working to Safeguard and Promote the Welfare of Children* (London: TSO).

Department of Health (2003), 'Fair Access to Care Services – Guidance on Eligibility Criteria for Adult Social Care', available at http://www.dh.gov.uk/en/Publicationsandstatistics/Publications/PublicationsPolicyAndGuidance/DH_4009653, accessed 4 January 2008.

Department of Health and Home Office (2000), *No Secrets: Guidance on Developing and Implementing Multi-agency Policies and Procedures to Protect Vulnerable Adults from Abuse* (London: Department of Health).

Doggett, M. (1992), *Marriage, Wife Beating and the Law: Victorian England* (London: Weidenfield and Nicholson).

Field-Fisher, T.G. (1974), *Report of the Committee of Inquiry into the Care and Supervision Provided in Relation to Maria Colwell* (London: Department of Health and Social Security).

Gardner Cravedi, K. and Halamandaris, V. (1981), *Elder Abuse: An Examination of a Hidden Problem* (Comm. Print 1981), 97th Cong., 1st Session.

Glendenning, F. (1997), 'What is Elder Abuse and Neglect?' in Decalmer, P. and Glendenning, F. (eds), *The Mistreatment of Elderly People* (London: Sage).

House of Commons Health Committee (2003), *Elder Abuse* (HC 111-1).

Joint Committee on the Draft Mental Incapacity Act (2002a), *Draft Mental Incapacity Bill, Vol 2 Oral and Written Evidence* (House of Lords – House of Commons Joint Committee) Session 2002-03, HL Paper 189-II HC 1083-II, Ev 188 Q 505.

Joint Committee on the Draft Mental Incapacity Bill (2002b), *Supplementary Memorandum from the Association of Directors of Social Services* (House of Lords – House of Commons Joint Committee), Session 2002-03, HL Paper 189-II HC 1083-II Ev 182, 24.

Laming, Lord (2003), *The Victoria Climbié Inquiry* (London, Home Office).

Law Commission (1995), *Report on Mental Incapacity* (Law Commission Report No. 231) (London: HMSO).

Lord Chancellor's Department (1997), *Mental incapacity – Who decides?: Making Decisions on Behalf of Mentally Incapacitated Adults* (London: HMSO).

Mowlam, A., Tennant, R., Dixon, J. and McCreadie, C. (2007), *UK Study of Abuse and Neglect of Older People: Qualitative Findings* (London: Department of Health and Comic Relief), available at http://www.comicrelief.com/docs/elder-abuse/ComicRelief-ElderAbuse-Summary.pdf, accessed 10 December 2007.

National Assembly for Wales (2000), *In Safe Hands*, Guidance issued under s. 7 of Local Authority Social Services Act 1970.

Pizzey, E. (1974), *Scream Quietly or the Neighbours Will Hear* (Harmondsworth: Penguin).

Santo, N. (2000), 'Breaking the Silence: Strategies for Combating Elder Abuse in California', *McGeorge Law Review* 31, 802.

Scottish Law Commission (1991), *Mentally Disordered and Vulnerable Adults: Public Authority Powers* (Discussion Paper No. 96) (Edinburgh: The Stationery Office).

Scottish Law Commission (1997), *Vulnerable Adults* (Report No. 158) (Edinburgh: The Stationery Office).
Silva, T. (1992), 'Reporting Elder Abuse: Should it be Mandatory or Voluntary', *Health Span* 9:4, 13.
Velick, M.D. (1995), 'Mandatory Reporting Statutes: A Necessary yet Underutilized Response to Elder Abuse', *Elder Law Journal* 3, 165.
Weed, M.C. (1997), 'Law Enforcement Intervention on Behalf of Endangered Adults', *Pacific Law Journal* 28, 903.

PART 2
Constructions of Children's Responsibilities

Chapter 6

Responsible Children and Children's Responsibilities? Sibling Caretaking and Babysitting by School-age Children

Virginia Morrow[1]

Introduction

Dominant ideas about children in English society tend to construct childhood as a period of dependency, signifying children's lack of 'responsibility' (Morrow 1996; Such and Walker 2005). News media imagery depicts children and young people in stereotypical ways, as 'out-of-control' and 'irresponsible' (Holland 1992), and these images are often reinforced by ideas embedded within social policies, particularly in relation to juvenile crime, with children and young people seen as 'problems to be solved' (James in this book; Keating in this book). Children are rarely credited with the positive capacity to take on responsibilities for others. This chapter discusses children's responsibilities, from a sociological perspective. It describes an aspect of children's activities outside school, as carers for younger siblings, and babysitting in their neighbourhoods, drawing on social historical material, and data from three empirical research projects with school children in England conducted during the 1990s (Morrow 1992; 1994; 1998; 2001), as well as recent research about children's work (for example, Howieson et al. 2006) and children's understandings of responsibility (Such and Walker 2005). It discusses the extent to which childhood is constructed as a period of dependency, signifying children's 'lack' of responsibility while, at the same time, there is evidence that children undertake care-related tasks that involve elements of trust and responsibility – in this case, being entrusted with the responsibility of caring for younger children. This chapter suggests that dominant understandings of children and childhood render children's responsibilities and work contributions invisible, and prevent us from detecting what may be reciprocal relations between family members and other people in the community. It argues that there are inherent contradictions in the ways in which older children are regarded in relation to the responsibilities bestowed upon them by adults, and concludes that a more consistent consideration of ideas of responsibility and trust in relation to children's roles could usefully be embarked upon.

1 Thanks to Priscilla Alderson, Margrét Einarsdóttir and Berry Mayall for very helpful suggestions on a previous draft of this chapter.

Background

A structural understanding of childhood highlights the ways in which children have been gradually removed from paid work, childhood has become increasingly institutionalised and extended, and the emphasis on education and protracted learning (scholarisation) tends to site children as learners and dependents. These are powerful forces shaping adults' ideas about normative childhood and children's roles (Mayall 2002). Yet secondary school children are expected to 'take responsibility' for their (own) school work (Mayall 2000) and children are allowed by law to have a part-time job from the age of 13, although the hours and forms of work they may undertake are restricted by a confusing array of local byelaws and national regulations. Generally, though, children are almost invariably perceived as the recipients of adult work and care rather than as workers or care-givers in their own right, an exception being child carers who look after ill or disabled parents and siblings (see Becker et al. 1998). However, even here there has been an emphasis on seeing child carers as 'children-in-need' or 'victims', rather than acknowledging and respecting their contributions as intrinsically useful (see Olsen 2000; Warren 2007). The tendency for children to be understood as demanding burdens appears to be increasing rather than diminishing (with increased dependency at the early stages of the life course and delayed transition to adulthood), and there is an implicit assumption that children do not, and should not, care for other people.

However, research over the past two decades has demonstrated that large numbers of secondary school children undertake various forms of work, broadly defined. As Hobbs and McKechnie (1997) note in their summary of UK research on children's paid employment, the findings are fairly consistent:

> There are approximately 3.5 million children aged 11-15 in Britain, and between 1-1.7 million are working at any particular time. If we look at how many will have worked by the time they reach the school leaving age, then the figure rises to 2.2-2.6 million. (1997, 92)

Thus they conclude 'it is the norm for children to mix employment will full-time education' (1997, 92). However, these figures only relate to children's participation in paid work outside the home, but children also undertake work (paid or unpaid) inside their homes (Morrow 1996). Less well-researched are aspects of children's marginal economic activities, such as babysitting, and children's domestic labour within their own families (Morrow 1996). At any rate, the extent of children's work contributions shows that children have the capacity to take on a range of responsibilities.

This chpater draws on data generated in three qualitative sociological research projects conducted with school children during the 1990s in England that explored firstly, children's involvement in work, broadly defined (Morrow 1992; 1994; 1996); secondly, children's understanding of the concept of family (Morrow 1998), and thirdly, children's social capital (social networks and experiences of their environments) (Morrow 2001). These were not directly intended to be studies about 'responsibility' *per se*, but the data produced raise interesting questions about children's competencies and responsibilities that this chapter discusses. All three studies were based upon the theoretical frameworks developed within the 'new' sociology of childhood, which move beyond psychologically based models, that construct childhood as a period of socialisation and development, towards attempting to understand children as active social agents who shape, and are shaped by, the structures and processes around them, at least at the micro-level, and whose relationships are worthy of study in their own right (Mayall 2002; Prout and James 1990; 1997). In all three studies, data were generated by children in response to open questions, and the emphasis in each project was to explore aspects of children's everyday lives from their points of view, mostly in the form of written descriptions of what they do outside school and who is important to them, but also in group discussions and using other participatory (visual) methods.

Child Caretaking as a Form of Children's Domestic Work

Evidence from social historians, oral history and childhood autobiographies shows that in the past children were an important source of domestic labour, particularly looking after younger brothers and sisters, and this persisted during the first half of the 20th century (Wade in this book). Anna Davin, in her classic social history of childhood in London during the period 1870-1914, describes the double standard that existed as girls but not boys were kept at home to help. This was perceived as an acceptable reason for girls' absences from school. She cites the 1902 Committee on Children's Employment, which found that:

> Girls' usual task to get younger children dressed and fed and take toddlers to infant school or crèche affected afternoon as well as morning punctuality [at school] ... Workers at the Stepney crèche in 1895 noticed a child who every morning brought "an infant she was hardly able to carry", and then went back to Whitechapel (perhaps a mile) for another child, old enough to walk much of the way, but whom she carried a good deal so as to get to school herself. ... The unpredictable last-minute demands of child care and domestic crisis contributed to making girls late more frequently than boys, as well as to keeping them away more often. (Davin 1996, 105; see also Parr 1980 and Roberts 1975, 15)

Until 1944, children were allowed to leave school a year early on the condition that they were entering 'beneficial' employment. During the 1930s, 'helping mother at home' appears to have been understood loosely as 'employment' in the heated debates about the nature of 'beneficial' employment for school leavers (Morrow 1992). The 1936 Education Act, raising the school leaving age to 15, had a clause specifically allowing children to leave school a year early 'for the purpose of enabling the child to give assistance in the home' if the local education authority was satisfied that 'exceptional hardship would otherwise be caused' (Education Act 1936; although this Act was repealed in 1939 at the outbreak of the Second World War).

There are very few studies of children's activities outside school in the post-war period, although Pearl Jephcott's (1942) study of young working women provides illustrations of how girls had helped their mothers at home: for example, one of her respondents recalled that

> When I was about eight I started to mind Iris, and I looked after her for about three months ... then I minded Stanley. His father was a bricklayer and his mother was a dressmaker. ... This went on till I was twelve. ... I've never been paid for minding them. (Jephcott 1942, 70)

Children's care of younger siblings is occasionally mentioned in research on childcare in general. Jackson and Jackson, in their study of childminding, found that

> in poorer districts there is a great deal of minding being carried out by older children, though this shows up in none of the official statements. Sometimes it is done by teenage children who should still be at school, but whose schools are neither anxious to have them back nor active in pursuing them. Sometimes it is a result of the shift system, and we have come across children – often very young – who are essentially childminded from 4pm till midnight – but at this point the acceptable borderline between childminding and "babysitting" … is very shadowy. (Jackson and Jackson 1979, 167)

Petrie and Logan (1986), in an early study of children's out-of-school care carried out with 379 children in London in 1982, found that during the summer holidays in particular 'it was not unusual for children … to be left at home to take care of themselves … for many of these children another, older, child (that is up to the age of 13) was at home, but not necessarily to take care of the younger one'. They also found that 'children from different social backgrounds were equally likely to look after themselves' (Petrie and Logan 1986, 11).

Assuming responsibility for other (younger) children is rarely mentioned in the sociological literature about children's everyday lives, and a cursory reading would lead one to suppose that children's involvement in domestic labour has declined as their school work has increased (Qvortrup 1987). Feminist studies of domestic labour during the 1980s and 1990s tended not to explore the extent to which children may act as sources of assistance in their homes (but see Solberg 1990), except minimally in studies of (girls') socialisation, where such tasks are understood as a rehearsal for domestic roles in later life and not as intrinsically useful (see, for example, Bates 1993; Mayall 2002; McRobbie 1978; Oakley 1974). Social anthropology is richer in highlighting children's domestic labour contributions in differing cultural contexts, where studies of children's work activities have found large amounts of sibling caretaking by older children (see, for example, Nieuwenhuys 1994; Poluha 2004; Punch 2001; Weisner and Gallimore 1977).

Evidence for Children's Childcare Activities

There had been a lack of research in the UK into children's work in general and their domestic contributions in particular. The study of children's economic roles (henceforth referred to as *Children's Work*) was an attempt to fill this gap. It was based mainly upon a collection of written accounts of everyday life outside school, collected from 730 secondary school children (11-16 year olds) in schools in Birmingham and West Cambridgeshire (Morrow 1992; other data were gathered through interviews with children, teachers, an employer of children, and observations). Essays were coded and analysed quantitatively. Thirty-one percent of the boys (n = 106) and 53 per cent of the girls (n = 153) mentioned some form of domestic labour. Their precise contributions in terms of time input cannot be 'measured' and it is important to remember that these were children's accounts, not their parents'. Cases were summarised and data broken down into themes that were explored in depth. Children mentioned a range of chores which were categorised under the following themes: general domestic chores, such as washing up, ironing, tidying, dusting, hoovering; care of or babysitting siblings; care of or helping other relatives such as grandparents, or babysitting younger cousins; shopping for the household; and outdoor tasks such as gardening, lawn-mowing, or washing the car. The 1996-97 study *Understanding Families* involved 183 children aged between 8-14 in Cambridgeshire, and explored children's understandings of the concept of 'family'. A sub-sample of the younger children were Muslim children whose families originated from the Azad Kashmir/Mirpur region of Pakistan. One of the qualitative methods used was written descriptions of 'who is important to me and why?' (Morrow 1998; 1999). The third study I draw upon here, *Children and Social Capital*, was carried out with 101 children aged 12-15, exploring different components of the concept of 'social capital' (Morrow 2001) and was again based on children's accounts of out-of-school activities, and descriptions of who is important to them (amongst other methods).

In the next two sections, the findings from these studies are discussed with respect first to sibling caretaking and then the related phenomenon of babysitting (childcare outside the family).

Sibling Caretaking

There were several examples in the various studies of children describing how they looked after their younger brothers and sisters. In the *Children's Work* study, children mentioned that they looked after younger siblings while parents were working. For example, a 12-year-old boy wrote:

> During the holidays I look after my little brother on Mondays, Tuesdays and Wednesdays from 9 till 3.30 as my mum goes out to work. I get paid £10 for doing this.

Other children collected their younger siblings from school whilst their parents were at work. For example, a 13-year-old girl described how 'After school I pick my sister up from nan's and take her home with me (she is 11) … at 6 my mum comes home.' Children whose parents worked shifts helped by looking after siblings at other times of the day, for example, a 15-year-old boy wrote:

> Other nights I go to the coffee bar at school with my mates, and at 8.30 I have to go home to look after my sisters that are 2 years and 7 years old. I have to do this because my dad goes to work at 8.45 and my mum gets home at 9.10, I then go back out until 10.00. Although when I am skating just down the road my brother looks after my sisters, my brother is 13 years old.

A 12-year-old girl described how she looked after her baby sister 'when my mum sleeps in the day because she works at night'. Other children described babysitting and helping in general with younger brothers and sisters:

> I babysit for my parents whenever they go out (two sisters). I cook dinner, tidy up the house. Get my two sisters to bed, then relax. (13-year-old girl)

> My typical day starts at 7-7.30 … I go downstairs, make my breakfast and sometimes my mum's and [get my] brother's rusks. I then bring my baby brother downstairs. On Saturdays I … have David (my brother) so my mum can get ready. I then change his nappy and get him half dressed then mum takes over and finishes him off. (12-year-old girl)

One 14-year-old girl described the amount of childcare she undertook for relatives:

> I get a video either Friday or Saturday evenings … because my mum and dad sometimes goes out for a drink so I get lumbered looking after my sister, and I find it a bit boring sometimes. … Mostly some Fridays my auntie comes round my house and picks me up from after school because I go round hers for the whole weekend to look after my baby cousin who is only two months old. The reason for this is because when I leave school and can't get a job straightaway, I can look after my cousin in the daytimes while my auntie goes to work. (14-year-old girl)

Some girls understood their contribution to childcare and other tasks in the context of their family's health problems:

> I help my mum with the cooking and changing my baby brother and giving him baths … she and my dad has very bad arthritis. (13-year-old girl)

And another example:

> Every Saturday I go shopping for my mum and I take my little brother with me so mum can spend some time alone because my brother is hyperactive. (13-year-old girl)

Small numbers of children in both the *Understanding Families* study, and the study of *Children and Social Capital* (where work roles were not the explicit focus) mentioned looking after younger siblings, cousins, nieces and nephews, and generally helping parents with childcare, in their descriptions of who is important to them and activities outside school. Children explained how they looked after younger relatives; for example, one girl wrote: 'I help look after my nephew when they come over, because they live in [nearby village], and ... they usually come over on a Sunday and stay all day, and my mum and dad just talk to my brother [sic], they just like talk, so I take my nephew (age 1) out, and we just go over to the Rec.'

Children's responsibilities for looking after and playing with siblings were particularly marked among the children of Pakistani origin in the *Understanding Families* study, for example: 'My baby sister is important to me because she is smaller than me and I got every right to look after her', as was receiving help from siblings – 'My big sister is important to me because she helps me to do the housework and takes me to the library'. Reciprocal relationships between family members may reflect the central importance of family obligations and interdependence emphasised by Islamic principles contained in the Qur'an (Ahmad 1996; Dosanjh and Ghuman 1996; Morrow 1998). Traditional notions of interdependence and the importance of the family unit may take priority over individualism, although there is a danger of stereotyping here, and 'there is diversity of experiences and expectations within the Asian communities, as well as similarities between the Asian and other communities' (Ahmad 1996, 71-2). The overall aim of the research was to explore children's conceptualisations of 'family', and about half of the older children (12-14 year olds) used notions of mutual support and reciprocity in their definitions, regardless of ethnic background, for example: 'families are for caring for each other'; 'sharing'; and 'looking after each other' (for similar findings, see also Brannen et al. 2000; Hadfield et al. 2006; McIntosh and Punch, forthcoming).

There were also examples in the *Children and Social Capital* study of children caring for younger siblings and relatives. Bob, aged 14, wrote: 'I look after my baby brother (age 3) on Wednesday, Friday and Sunday nights.' Brenda, also 14, described how 'my dad left when I was 2. … Outside of school I normally do anything that doesn't involve doing my bedroom. I help my mum do the washing up and drying up and also sometimes hoovering that's if I feel like it. I sometimes walk down the shops for my mum to get some milk, so I then come home and play with my little 3 year old sister. She gets bored … so I play bricks and skittles with her. ... Sometimes she pulls your hair out till you're bald, and other times she is a little sweetheart' (see Morrow 2001 for full report).

Other recent studies of school children's work activities have found similar patterns of sibling caretaking in other parts of the UK, suggesting that this is a common practice. Often, however, caring for younger brothers and sisters is either overlooked, or perceived negatively. For example, Hodgson and Spours (2000) in a study of part-time work among 14-19 year olds, suggest that children from 'one-parent families' have 'difficult domestic contexts' that

> appeared to produce a more introverted outlook with much of the student's time being spent at home, caring for brothers or sisters or watching television or videos. These students had relatively low social horizons, lacked confidence and did not appear to be as socially active as their peers. (2000, 14)

In contrast, Cockburn, in a study carried out in the mid-1990s that included 216 secondary school children in Manchester, found that 54 per cent of children with younger siblings had looked after them at regular intervals, measured as at least once a week for more than an hour (Cockburn 2001). He notes:

> Looking after children and collecting younger siblings may seem a trivial point. However, the ability of some young people to do this is crucial for the family economy. Young people's work here, although generally unrecognised as work and considered superficial, often makes the difference between parents being able to undertake paid employment or not. (Cockburn 2001, 18)

Towards Interdependence

Some children, especially but not exclusively girls, appear to make an important contribution to the running of households by taking care of their younger siblings and in some cases it is possible to suggest that, from children's points of view, their parents rely on them for help. In some cases family members may be interdependent. However, the fact that childhood is constructed as a period of dependency prevents us from 'knowing' about those cases of children undertaking domestic work because such work, particularly caring, is socially defined as an adult role and is a marker of adult status. Birth order, age, family composition, parental employment patterns, parents' health status, ethnic background and religious beliefs are all likely to interact with gender to influence whether or not children contribute to childcare within their families. There appears to be a continuum, from children who make no contribution whatsoever to the domestic economy, to children whose contribution is crucial to the functioning to the household, with many children making contributions that fall somewhere in between the two extremes.

The construction of children as 'dependents' requiring socialisation (which continues to dominate social policy concerns) has arguably precluded acknowledgement of the extent to which children have responsibilities in their everyday lives, in the here and now. This dependency-assumption results in children being seen as mere consumers (of goods and services) rather than as possible contributors. Both sociology and developmental psychology could move forward, away from dualistic conceptualisations of childhood dependence as the opposite of adult independence, towards a model that sees family members as interdependent at different stages of the life course (Jones 1992; Morrow 1996; see also Solberg (1990) on Norwegian children's housework and self-care). This links to broader issues raised about babysitting/childcare by older children outside their families, discussed in the next section.

Babysitting and Childcare for Non-family

Babysitting was the most common form of income-generating activity undertaken by children (76 children, that is 12 per cent of the sample of 730, Morrow 1992). It is a highly gendered activity: 65 girls, compared with 11 boys, mentioned babysitting for other families than their own, and it was mostly undertaken by 14-15 year olds. Several girls described their babysitting duties in terms of how much they enjoyed working with children, or how 'good' they were with young children. One 15-year-old girl wrote:

> Most of my nights from eight till twelve I babysit for different families. I have six babysitting jobs, I enjoy doing this as I love to be with them. The youngest is 6 weeks which I've looked after since it was born, and the oldest is 12. So I get quite a lot of money but I don't do it because of that. I get on well with the children and I can communicate with them. There are 15 children in all I look after.

One 15-year-old girl in the sample use the term 'childminding' in describing her work: 'After school everyday I go to work, I am a childminder and I do 1 and a half hours. I get paid on a Thursday, I get £10 a week.' Another 15-year-old girl described long hours of work and childcare:

> On Saturdays I work on [a] market stall selling fruit and vegetables. I work from 8.30 am to around 5.30 pm and have a half hour lunch break. Saturday nights I quite often babysit from about 8pm to late. In the summer holidays I babysit for two boys aged 8 and 12. I do this from 8.30 am until around 6.30 pm. I have to make them lunch and sometimes tea and take them out to places such as the cinema, bowling etc.

Perhaps reflecting the assumption that babysitting is a typical form of work for girls, two 15-year-old girls in the *Children's Work* study wrote about how they had tried babysitting and didn't like it. One described how 'I don't do babysitting as I tried it once and the baby girl wouldn't stop crying. I don't know many people with young children that need babysitting.' The few boys who described babysitting explained that they babysat for purely instrumental reasons. A 12-year-old boy who, like many children in the study had several ways of earning money, wrote 'I go babysitting for my mum's boss every Saturday night and I usually get in between £10-15.' A 15-year-old boy wrote 'Whenever I am short of money, I ask my mum and dad if they know anyone who wants me to babysit for them. This is a nice easy way of getting money in your pocket'; another 15-year-old boy wrote 'On the weekend I go babysitting on Friday night and Saturday day', and a 14-year-old boy: 'My free time is a variety of work and play. I have three main jobs. I babysit four children. I babysit for two families. I earn up to £10 a week depending on how many hours I babysit.' It is likely that fewer boys babysit than girls for a number of reasons, including constructions of femininity and an idea that babysitting is not 'boys' work', reflecting childcare patterns in society in general.

Recent research suggests that babysitting outside the family remains an important form of work for school children, particularly for girls. In a national survey of Scottish secondary school children of approximately 18,500 13-16 year olds, conducted between 2003 and 2006, babysitting was a source of employment for 11 per cent of girls and 4 per cent of boys. Children identified the following attributes of babysitting as a form of work: it involved cooperation with, and supervision of, others as well as the potential for decision-making and developing skills and abilities, though babysitting was also the job that was least likely to have involved any training (Howieson et al. 2006; see also Penrose Brown and Blandford 2002). Babysitting is generally not analysed or discussed in any depth, and some studies of child employment deliberately exclude it as a form of work (MacLennan et al. 1985; Pond and Searle 1991) yet it is clearly a commonly accepted practice in English society.

It comes to public attention when older children are 'abandoned' to look after younger children in 'Home Alone' cases, reported with 'shock horror' headlines in the popular press. Usually such cases involve a mother going on holiday and leaving her young children in the care of a teenager. The mother is prosecuted on her return. A recent example is as follows:

> **Turkish holiday mother faces jail for leaving children**
> Christopher Williamson, prosecuting, said she placed her children in the care of an unrelated teenager, whose name and age cannot be published by order of the court. Rogerson arranged for the girl and the children to stay in a friend's flat, telling the teenager to say the children were staying with their maternal grandmother if their father asked. She gave the babysitter her bank card with permission to withdraw £180 a week for the children. Rogerson was arrested on her return … on June 28. By then her children had been taken into care and found to be unharmed before being placed with Rogerson's mother. Chris Bunting, defending, said: "I think it is important to make clear that it is not

> a case of abandonment of children. There is no evidence that the defendant's actions, directly or indirectly, have caused any harm to the children". (Stokes, 10 August 2005 *The Daily Telegraph*)

The babysitter in this case presumably acted competently in caring for the children. From the perspective of the sociology of childhood, it is notable that the degree of competence shown by under-age babysitters in such cases is rarely commented upon.

Meaning and Implications of Childcare

Babysitting, whether within or outside the family, is an unregulated form of work and it falls outside child employment legislation (legislation which is confusing and poorly enforced). Children who are employed in jobs such as newspaper delivery are required to have a work permit from their Local Education Authority. Babysitting, on the other hand, is informal and cash-in-hand. If a child is left with another child then, in the eyes of the law, it is the parents of the child being minded who are responsible (under the Children and Young Persons Act 1933). However, there is an implicit acceptance that babysitting by children does takes place, and various organisations publish guidance and advice for parents and babysitters. It is up to parents to judge whether the older child has the maturity to look after the younger child (see, for example, Children's Legal Centre 2006). The recommended age varies – the Royal Society for the Prevention of Accidents guidelines (RoSPA 2004) suggests a minimum age of 16, while the British Red Cross runs babysitting courses for children over the age of 14. The Injury Minimization Programme for Schools (IMPS), developed in Oxford by a group of health care professionals, has run since 1994 and works with Year 6 (10-11 year old) children to teach them about risks, possible outcomes, and how to deal with emergencies such as what to do if a toddler is choking. An evaluation of the project found that IMPS children demonstrated significantly greater knowledge (than a control sample) in three respects: calling 999, first aid for burns, and for choking (Frederick et al. (2000). Indeed, according to a recent newspaper report (*The Guardian* 1 May 2006) 'This year ... An 11-year-old IMPS graduate dislodged a bar of soap from his two-year-old brother's throat' (it is not clear whether the 11-year-old was looking after his younger brother).

Responsibility for Others: A Relationship Based upon Trust

What does babysitting – whether these are younger brothers and sisters or non-family children – involve? It is a form of caretaking, often of quite small babies and young children, and as such involves a good deal of responsibility. One could argue that older children who babysit are symbolically and socially (but not legally) taking over the role of parent for a period of time. The RoSPA Guidelines are explicit: 'Being a babysitter means that you have someone else's life in your hand and that in itself is a tremendous responsibility. Having to look after one or more children can be tiring, frustrating and sometimes difficult to cope with – even for experienced adults' (RoSPA 2004, 1).

It is possible that responsibility is not a relevant concept for the children concerned but, rather, a preoccupation that adults have about children. In the course of my research on children's work, it was adults who used the term 'responsibility' rather than children themselves – the one exception being a 16-year-old girl, who wrote:

> Saturday evenings usually once a month I babysit for a regular couple. I take on the *responsibility* of looking after a four-year-old girl and an 8 month old baby. I enjoy this and take care to make sure they are happy … [emphasis added]

An employer of children (in newspaper delivery) talked when interviewed about children being made aware of 'their responsibilities' to customers and to their employer. Two head teachers interviewed commented on the responsibilities that many of their pupils had in taking younger siblings to school. One head teacher saw this negatively, because it interfered with attendance and punctuality requirements; the other saw it is as a positive responsibility and said that such responsibilities were included in children's 'Records of Achievement'.

On the other hand, more recently, Such and Walker (2005), in a small-scale study with 19 predominantly middle-class children aged nine and ten in a primary school in the East Midlands, explicitly explored children's responsibilities in their families. Children were asked open-ended questions about their 'experience of helping out at home, the division of household tasks, and who looked after whom and in what way' (2005, 47). They found that children did use the language of responsibility, and that

> the nature of responsibility in the home meant doing things to help maintain the practical working of the household … The assumption of responsibility among children challenges the notion that childhood is a time that is "free" from responsibility. (48)

Within sociology, the concept of responsibility rarely seems to be deconstructed; rather a common-sense view of it is adopted. It is a nebulous concept, which is all the more surprising given the huge amount of recent rhetoric about it in various political and legal contexts. Dictionary definitions of 'being responsible' suggest that it involves being competent, accountable, answerable, capable, dependent, reliable, trustworthy and so on. These are not qualities that are usually associated with older children or teenagers because childhood is defined and constructed, at least in the industrialised West, as a period of incompetence, of freedom from the responsibilities of adulthood (James in this book; Wade in this book). On the other hand, one could also argue that the lack of responsibility attributed to children is regarded as particularly dangerous and threatening to the adult social order. Children themselves recognise and understand this (Mayall 2002, 47): 'unlike parents, children were free from major responsibilities … Indeed, children had a right to "free time", partly as a component of this absence of responsibility.'

Sociological analyses of work have explored job content and skill in discussions of responsibility, for example, Burchell et al. (1994) suggest that accepting responsibility 'for property, output, standards and people' is one of the many attributes required of job holders:

> Many jobs carry a wide range of responsibilities which are not only, or even mainly, dependent on skill however defined ... There can be no doubt that the burden of responsibility has an important bearing on the value of a job, a fact which is fully recognised in job evaluation. (Burchell et al. 1994, 165)

In the examples mentioned above, children are temporarily responsible for younger children, but this does not seem to be recognised or valued (see Such and Walker 2005 and also Thomson and Holland, who suggests that families are 'a haven *of* obligation, not a haven *from* obligation', 2002, 109). Taking on responsibility might be positive for many children, but children may face a dilemma, because they have to demonstrate maturity and responsibility if they are to exit the stigmatised space of childhood and (especially) 'adolescence', yet because they are characterised as irresponsible they are given few opportunities to demonstrate the maturity required (Hudson 1984, 36). Supposedly 'incompetent' children are given responsibilities, but these children are more or less hidden from view, and occupy an ambiguous and unacknowledged place between adulthood and childhood. Ironically, children are asked to list their work experiences and responsibilities on their records of achievement when they leave secondary school, but this recognition does not translate into a general societal recognition of the value of these responsibilities. Even the language used to describe this work activity is in itself indicative of how it is perceived: 'babysitting' sounds passive, as if the baby sleeps all the time, and the 'sitter' simply sits. Like nearly all forms of childcare, it is somewhat devalued and hidden as a form of work.

Notions of responsibility are bound up with concepts of trust, and the relationship between parent and child-caretaker is a prime example of a relationship based on trust because it necessarily involves a degree of risk. The concept of trust has been the subject of an increasing amount of interrogation within the fields of social theory (see, for example, Gambetta 1988; Giddens 1990; Khodyakov 2007; Luhmann 1982; Misztal 1996) and feminist political philosophy (Baier 1990), but, it has to be said, not with respect to children's roles. Annette Baier suggests that trust is 'letting other persons ... take care of something the truster cares about, where such "caring for" involves some exercise of discretionary powers' (1990, 288). Both Luhmann and Baier use babysitting as an example of a relationship involving trust. As Alderson notes, in her study of parents' consent to surgery for their children, and writing about the trust that parents place in doctors: 'trust is very complicated, elusive, sometimes hard to establish and sustain, and subject to many influences' (Alderson 1990, 161). She suggests that 'Trust involves putting a precious possession into someone else's power, and so risking harm, loss, or betrayal. Two things of greatest value to parents are their child's welfare and their self-identity as their child's primary care-takers' (1990, 179). Babysitting or childminding involves parents placing immense trust in the caretaker. Khodyakov in a recent analysis of the concept of trust within sociology (but writing in an entirely different context, that of Soviet transition societies) notes that social scientists have 'come to realise the centrality of trust in social organisation' (2007, 115). He also points out that

> a close analysis of the ways in which the term "trust" is used ... reveals a disagreement among scholars about the definition, characteristics, and even the nature of trust. The

multiplicity of meanings of trust creates a measure of conceptual confusion, because confidence, reliability, faith, and trust are often used as synonyms. (2007, 116)

He proposes that trust should be understood as a process, not as a variable (as it has tended to be used in social capital theorising, Putnam (2000) and derivatives), and proposes the following definition of trust:

> Trust is a process of constant imaginative anticipation of reality of the reliability of the other part's actions based on (1) the reputation of the party and the actor, (2) the evaluation of current circumstances of action, (3) assumptions about the partner's actions, and (4) the belief in the honesty and morality of the other side. (Khodyakov 2007, 126)

He points out that reliability is based on previous experience and reputation. This, it could be argued, relates to babysitting by children. The examples quoted above demonstrate clearly that children utilise their parents' or neighbourhood social networks to acquire babysitting jobs, and presumably parents trust their own children to care for younger siblings. However, Khodyakov also suggests that interpersonal trust depends on social interactions that tend to be reciprocal and symmetrical in nature – on the other hand, this doesn't work so well for my example, because children who babysit are not generally in symmetrical relationships with the adults who they babysit for. As Alderson argues, trust can be understood as an emotional journey from doubt, or fear, to confidence, along a range of moral emotions. Trust tends to be poorly analysed because it has been regarded as a reasoned, measured calculation, whereas it is largely a moral emotion, or feeling (Alderson 1990).

There is a wealth of research that reveals that older children are acutely aware of how adults around them tend to regard them with mistrust, especially in public places (see, for example, Matthews and Limb 2000; Morrow 2000). Yet the same young people seem to be 'trusted' in various private situations, when they are involved in undertaking responsible tasks within households and their communities. However, the social construction of childhood dependency, based as it is on ideas about children as developing, immature, irresponsible burdens on their families, masks the extent to which children are capable, competent, have agency and responsibilities in their own lives. This inconsistency in the ways in which children are viewed as competent in some instances, but not in others, has been noted in an entirely different context. Koren et al., in a paper published in the *Journal of Medical Ethics*, contrast generally accepted guidance for ethics in medical research in Canada, with 'what the same children are allowed and expected to do as babysitters' (1993, 142). They point out that

> The act of babysitting is a powerful example of a responsibility given to minors by parents and teachers, where the inherent risk associated with the job seems to be accepted by society. Not only does babysitting require children to take immense responsibility and exhibit maturity, there are now official courses given to 10-12 year old children, usually in their schools. (Koren et al. 1993, 142)

To bring this up to date, in Canada, the age of 12 has become the rule of thumb as the youngest age that a child can babysit: it is the legal age that a child can be left alone overnight (Canadian Parents 2004). As noted above, the British Red Cross and RoSPA have guidelines, but the recommended age varies.

Koren et al. analyse the content of US and Canadian babysitting courses in some detail, and highlight the inconsistency in the way societies understand children's maturity and competence:

> The babysitter, presumably between the ages of 10 and 15, is quite explicitly expected to function in a way usually expected of mature individuals, i.e. to be capable of dealing not only with regular activities requiring discretion and responsibility (such as feeding or bathing a baby) but also with acute emergencies, potentially bearing severe and even life-threatening implications. … The assumptions underlying the babysitting course are strikingly incongruent with the widely accepted notions concerning children's vulnerability, which are taken for granted in other domains of life. (1993, 146)

They also point out that:

> Unlike the child participating in medical research, the babysitter is often left on her/his own without proper explanation and/or information. In the research situation, the participating child may decline and withdraw from participation at any given moment, irrespective of the research procedure. (1993, 147)

In contrast, they point out, babysitters cannot withdraw from their situation. Of course, they also note that the difference between these two examples relates to the probability and magnitude of possible harm. A further fundamental difference lies in the economic aspects of these two examples, in that babysitters are paid for their activities, children who are subjects of medical research cannot be. They also point out that a common-sense argument that 'children do babysit, so it is sensible to instruct them how to do it right' doesn't work either, because society does not accept children's behaviours (such as smoking or taking drugs) just because they are being practised (1993, 147). And it is even more illogical that, at the same time, *Gillick*-competent children can consent to medical treatment (Alderson 1993). Research often overlaps with treatment, complicating an apparent dichotomy of *either* treatment, *or* research.

At any rate, examples of children caring for other younger children suggest that we should attempt to move away from generalised/social policy views of children as 'burdens': who, as social actors, do little more than consume goods and services. While children are dependent on their families, they also contribute to varying degrees within households. So, rather than seeing dependence and independence as polar opposites, we could use ideas about responsibilities within families to develop a more nuanced approach to the study of the interdependencies of family members (in the case of sibling care-taking) by paying attention to reciprocal relationships, exploring the meaning and nature of trust in how these relationships are practised in everyday life. The construction of childhood dependency, which leads to a normative view of children as irresponsible and non-productive, and which is likely to become particularly irksome for children and young people as they approach adulthood, prevents us from detecting what may well be, at the very least, reciprocal relations between family members, highlighted in the examples of children looking after younger siblings. It is too simplistic to see dependence and independence as binary opposites, because the relationship is more complex. Adults are frequently interdependent, but the high value placed on individualism and independence in adulthood in Western societies often masks this interdependence (see further, Oliver 1989 on disability). However, reconceptualising child/adult relations as interdependent is a complex and daunting task, because recent English social policies relating to children appear to be solidly based on the idea that children are developing, future 'becomings' (Qvortrup 1987), simultaneously in need of increasing amounts of 'education' and greater surveillance and control (Fawcett et al. 2004; James and James 2004; James in this book).

Conclusions

This chapter has described an under-researched phenomenon, children's responsibilities as child carers. It has shown that there is evidence that in the past, in English society, children (especially girls) undertook a good deal of childcare, minding their younger brothers and sisters. Children still babysit, or work as informal childminders, and it seems plausible to suggest that this is a static, widespread, and (possibly) cross-class phenomenon. Any form of work inevitably involves elements of trust and responsibility, and given that 65 per cent of children in the United Kingdom have some experience of work while at school, we need to recognise children as active contributors. Babysitting and childminding epitomise a relationship based on trust – they are 'responsible' jobs. The chapter suggests that we need to re-evaluate the concept of responsibility in relation to the roles and activities that children undertake in relation to childcare, whether within or outside their families. Often such work is conceptualised as problematic because it is perceived as conflicting with the overriding aim of 'being a child', in other words 'to become' educated, and the pressure on children to achieve is currently very great.

However, this will involve asking some difficult questions about adult power, children's agency, and relationships between generations. Societal denial of children's agency in a positive sense in turn fails to acknowledge interconnections between family members, generations and others in their communities (see Morrow 1999). Social policy rhetoric emphasises responsibility in relation to good citizenship, but misses the point that many children already actively contribute in various ways – babysitting being a specific example. Neo-liberalising tendencies to withdraw the welfare state intentionally overemphasise the importance of parents in children's lives, with enormous emphasis being placed on parents to socialise their children 'responsibly'. This is in contrast to a weaker shift towards recognising children as people with rights in line with the UN Convention on the Rights of the Child (1989, ratified by UK government in 1991). This links to ideas about rights and responsibilities in relation to children in English social policy. As Such and Walker note, policy 'is not clear as to what extent children and young people can be responsible for themselves and others' (2005, 40; James in this book). The more that parents' responsibilities are emphasised, and the more the importance of parents in children's lives is reified, then the more the contributions that children already make may be rendered invisible or slip from view. Newman suggests that 'children's instrumental worth may be due for a serious re-examination, as may the assumed superiority of cultures that render children economic dependants rather than prepare them for citizenship through participation in valued social roles' (2000, 335). We could also usefully recognise that this is a peculiarly Western construction and understanding of childhood. There is evidence of a great deal of sibling caretaking and childcare work undertaken by children in developing countries (see, for example, Miller 2005; Punch 2001). This alerts us to the socially constructed nature of childhood in respect of children's activities – in sub-Saharan African countries, children's responsibilities are acknowledged in legal instruments, such as the African Charter on the Rights and Welfare of the Child (OUA/African Union 1990). Article 31, entitled responsibilities of the child, stipulates that 'Every child shall have responsibilities towards his [sic] family and society, the State and other legally recognised communities and the international community. The child, subject to his age and ability … shall have the duty [amongst others] to work for the cohesion of the family, to respect his parents, superiors and elders at all times and to assist them in case of need'. Perhaps the time has come for the UK to recognise and value children's responsibilities more systematically than it has done in the past.

References

African Charter on the Rights and Welfare of the Child (1990), available at www.africa-union.org, accessed 14 May 2007.

Ahmad, W. (1996), 'Family Obligations and Social Change Among Asian Communities' in Ahmad, W. and Atkin, K. (eds) *'Race' and Community Care* (Buckingham: Open University Press).

Alderson, P. (1990), *Choosing for Children. Parents' Consent to Surgery* (Oxford: Oxford University Press).

Alderson, P. (1993), *Children's Consent to Surgery* (Buckingham: Open University Press).

Baier, A. (1990), 'Trust and Anti-trust' in Sunstein, C.R. (ed.), *Feminism and Political Theory* (Chicago: University of Chicago Press).

Bates, I. (1993), 'A Job Which is "Right for Me"? Social Class, Gender and Individualisation' in Bates, I. and Riseborough, G. (eds), *Youth and Inequality* (Milton Keynes: Open University Press).

Becker, S., Aldridge, J. and Dearden, C. (1998), *Young Carers and their Families* (Oxford: Blackwell Science).

Brannen, J., Heptinstall, E. and Bhopal, K. (2000), *Connecting Children: Care and Family Life in Late Childhood* (London: Routledge/Falmer).

British Red Cross (2005), *A Guide to Babysitting*, available at www.redcross.org.uk, accessed 8 May 2006.

Burchell, B.J., Elliott, B.J., Rubery, J. and Wilkinson, F. (1994), 'Management and Employee Perceptions of Skill' in Penn, R., Rose, M. and Rubery, J. (eds), *Skill and Occupational Change* (Oxford: Oxford University Press).

Canadian Parents (2004), *Babysitter's Guide*, available at www.canadianparents.ca, accessed 1 May 2007.

Children's Legal Centre (2006), *Home Alone*, available at www.childrenslegalcentre.com, accessed 14 May 2007.

Cockburn, T. (2001), 'Youth Employment Transitions and Citizenship: A Reflection on a Local Study of Young People's Transitions to Employment in the North of England', *Young* 9:4, 2-29.

Davin, A. (1996), *Growing Up Poor. Home, School and Street in London 1870-1914* (London: Rivers Oram).

Dosanjh, J. and Ghuman, P. (1996), *Child-rearing in Ethnic Minorities* (Clevedon: Multilingual Matters).

Fawcett, B., Featherstone, B. and Goddard, J. (2004), *Contemporary Child Care Policy and Practice* (London: Palgrave).

Frederick, K., Bixby, E., Orzel, M.-N., Stewart Brown, S. and Willett, K. (2000), 'An Evaluation of the Effectiveness of the Injury Minimization Programme for Schools (IMPS)', *Injury Prevention* 6, 92-95.

Gambetta, D. (ed.) (1988), *Trust. Making and Breaking Cooperative Relations* (Oxford: Blackwell).

Giddens, A. (1990), *The Consequences of Modernity* (Cambridge: Polity).

Hadfield, L., Lucey, H., Mauthner, M. and Edwards R. (2006), *Sibling Identity and Relationships: Sisters and Brothers* (London: Routledge).

Hobbs, S. and McKechnie, J. (1997), *Child Employment in Britain: A Social and Psychological Analysis* (Edinburgh: Stationery Office).

Hodgson, A. and Spours, K. (2000), *Earning and Learning. A Local Study of Part-time Work among 14-19 Year Olds* (London: University of London).

Holland, J., Thomson, R., Henderson, S., McGrellis, S. and Sharpe, S. (2000), 'Catching On, Wising Up and Learning from Your Mistakes: Young People's Accounts of Moral Development', *International Journal of Children's Rights* 8, 271-94.

Holland, P. (1992), *What is a Child? Popular Images of Childhood* (London: Virago).

Howieson, C., McKechnie, J. and Semple, S. (2006), *The Nature and Implications of the Part-time Employment of Secondary School Pupils* (Edinburgh: Scottish Executive), available at www.scotland.gov.uk, accessed 15 May 2007.

Hudson, B. (1984), 'Femininity and Adolescence' in McRobbie, A. and Nava, M. (eds), *Gender and Generation* (Basingstoke: Macmillan).

Jackson, B. and Jackson, S. (1979), *Childminder. A Study in Action Research* (London: RKP).

James, A. and James, A. (2004), *Reconstructing Childhood: Theory, Policy and Social Practice* (London: Palgrave Macmillan).

Jephcott, A.P. (1942), *Girls Growing Up* (London: Faber and Faber).

Jones, G (1992), 'Short-term Reciprocity in Parent-Child Economic Exchanges' in Marsh, C. and Arber, S. (eds), *Families and Households: Division and Change* (Basingstoke: Macmillan).

Khodyakov, D. (2007), 'Trust as a Process: A Three-dimensional Approach', *Sociology* 41:1, 115-32.

Koren, G., Birenbaum Carmeli, D., Carmeli, Y. and Haslam, R. (1993), 'Maturity of Children to Consent to Medical Research: The Babysitter Test', *Journal of Medical Ethics* 19, 142-7.

Luhmann, N. (1982), *Trust and Power* (Chichester: Wiley).

Luhmann, N. (2000), 'Familiarity, Confidence, Trust: Problems and Alternatives' in Gambetta, D. (ed.), *Trust: Making and Breaking Cooperative Relations*, Electronic edition, Department of Sociology, University of Oxford, Ch. 6, 94-107, available at www.sociology.ox.as.uk/papers/luhmann94-107.pdf, accessed 1 May 2006.

MacLennan, E., Fitz, J. and Sullivan, J. (1985), *Working Children* (London: Low Pay Unit).

Matthews, H. and Limb, M. (2000), 'Exploring the "Fourth Environment", Young People's Use of Place and Views on Their Environment', *Children 5-16 Research Briefing No. 9.*

Mayall, B. (2000), 'The Sociology of Childhood in Relation to Children's Rights', *International Journal of Children's Rights* 8, 243-59.

Mayall, B. (2002), *Towards a Sociology for Childhood. Thinking from Children's Lives* (Buckingham: Open University Press).

McIntosh, I. and Punch, S. (forthcoming), '"Barter", "Deals", "Bribes" and "Threats": Exploring Sibling Interactions', *Childhood* (forthcoming).

McRobbie, A. (1978), 'Working Class Girls and the Culture of Femininity' in Women's Study Group, *Women Take Issue* (London: Hutchinson).

Miller, P. (2005), 'Useful and Priceless Children in Contemporary Welfare States', *Social Politics* 12:1, 3-41.

Misztal, B. (1996), *Trust in Modern Societies* (Cambridge: Policy Press).

Morrow, V. (1992), *A Sociological Study of the Economic Roles of Children, with Particular Reference to Birmingham and Cambridgeshire*, PhD Thesis (Cambridge: Faculty of Social and Political Sciences, University of Cambridge).

Morrow, V. (1994), 'Responsible Children? Aspects of Children's Work and Employment Outside School in Contemporary UK' in B. Mayall (ed.), *Children's Childhoods. Observed and Experienced* (London: Falmer Press).

Morrow, V. (1996), 'Rethinking Childhood Dependency: Children's Contributions to the Domestic Economy', *The Sociological Review* 44:1, 58-76.

Morrow, V. (1998), *Understanding Families: Children's Perspectives* (York: Joseph Rowntree Foundation/YPS).

Morrow, V. (1999), '"We are People Too": Children's Perspectives on Rights and Decision-making in England', *International Journal of Children's Rights* 7, 149-70.

Morrow, V. (2000), '"Dirty Looks" and "Trampy Places" in Young People's Accounts of Community and Neighbourhood: Implications for Health Inequalities', *Critical Public Health* 10:2, 141-52.

Morrow, V. (2001), *Networks and Neighbourhoods: Children's and Young People's Perspectives* (London: HEA).

Newman, T. (2000), 'Workers and Helpers: Perspectives on Children's Labour 1899-1999', *British Journal of Social Work* 30, 332-8.

Nieuwenhuys, O. (1994), *Children's Lifeworlds, Labour, Gender and Welfare in the Developing World* (London: Routledge).

Oakley, A. (1974), *The Sociology of Housework* (London: Martin Robertson).

Oliver, M. (1989), 'Disability and Dependency: A Creation of Industrial Societies?' in Barton, L. (ed.), *Disability and Dependency* (London: Falmer).

Olsen, R. (2000), 'Families Under the Microscope: Parallels Between the Young Carers Debate of the 1990s and the Transformation of Childhood in the Late Nineteenth Century', *Children and Society* 14, 384-394.

Parr, J. (1980), *Labouring Children. British Immigrant Apprentices to Canada, 1869-1924* (London: Croom Helm).

Penrose Brown, J. and Blandford, S. (2002), 'Children's Experience of Work. An Examination of the Range of Children's Experience of Work', *Support for Learning* 17:4, 193-200.

Petrie, P. and Logan, P. (1986), *After School and in the Holidays. The Responsibility for Looking after School Children* (London: TCRU, Institute of Education, University of London).

Poluha, E. (2004), *The Power of Continuity. Ethiopia through the Eyes of its Children* (Uppsala, Sweden: Noriska Afrikaninstitutet).

Pond, C. and Searle, A. (1991), *The Hidden Army. Children at Work in the 1990s* (London: Low Pay Unit/Birmingham City Education Dept).

Prout, A. and James, A. (1990), 'A New Paradigm for the Sociology of Childhood', in James, A. and Prout, A. (eds), *Constructing and Reconstructing Childhood* (London: Falmer Press).

Punch, S. (2001), 'Household Division of Labour: Generation, Gender, Age, Birth Order and Sibling Composition' in *Work, Employment and Society* 15:4, 308-823.

Putnam, R.D. (2000), *Bowling Alone. The Collapse and Revival of American Community* (New York: Simon & Schuster).

Qvortrup, J. (1987), 'Introduction', Special Issue 'The Sociology of Childhood', *International Journal of Sociology* 17, 3.

Roberts, E. (1975), 'Learning and Living – Socialisation Outside School', *Oral History* 3:2, 14-28.

RoSPA (2004), *Promoting Safety with Young People. Babysitting Guidance. When Children Look after Children*, available at www.rospa.com/safetyeducation/advice/babaysitting.htm, accessed 16 September 2005.

Solberg, A. (1990), 'Negotiating Childhood: Changing Constructions of Age for Norwegian Children' in James, A. and Prout, A. (eds), *Constructing and Reconstructing Childhood* (London: Falmer Press).

Stokes, P. (2005), 'Turkish Holiday Mother Faces Jail for Leaving Children', *Daily Telegraph*, 10 August 2005.

Such, E. and Walker, R. (2005), 'Young Citizens or Policy Objects? Children in the "Rights and Responsibilities" Debate', *Journal of Social Policy* 34:1, 39-57.

Thomson, R. and Holland, J. (2002), 'Young People, Social Change and the Negotiation of Moral Authority', *Children & Society* 16, 1-13.

Warren, J. (2007), 'Young Carers: Conventional or Exaggerated Levels of Involvement in Domestic and Caring Tasks?' *Children and Society* 21, 136-46.

Weisner, T. and Gallimore, R. (1977), 'My Brother's Keeper: Child and Sibling Caretaking', *Current Anthropology* 18:2, 169-89.

Chapter 7

Being Responsible, Becoming Responsible and Having Responsibility Thrust upon Them: Constructing the 'Responsibility' of Children and Parents

Heather Keating[1]

Introduction

Within families, parents and children are in a continual process of negotiating responsibilities in the sense that the freedoms children enjoy and the boundaries that constrain them are dynamic. Indeed, a fundamental feature of parenting is reflecting on and responding to the capacity of children to be 'responsible' for their behaviour. Judging when a child is mature enough to take certain decisions and be answerable for the consequences can be problematic for both parents and children, not least because this process takes place against a backdrop of different (or changing) constructions of childhood (and, increasingly, of parenthood) and a deep-rooted ambivalence in society towards children. Further, while much of the child/parent relationship does and should operate within a 'privileged sphere', 'free from institutional constraint and censure' (Eekelaar 2006, 82), it is very clear that the sphere of privilege is increasingly (if somewhat inconsistently[2]) breached by state intervention. Thus, families are, at the same time, 'a private institution but … also provide the building blocks for safe and sustainable communities' (Gilles 2005, 75).

Given these tensions, it is not surprising that the law has also struggled to determine the point at which children should be responsible for their decisions and behaviour. One dimension of this is the extent to which parents bear responsibility instead of or as well as their children. This chapter will consider recent shifts in criminal law and policy to explore what is meant when children (and their parents) are held responsible for harmful behaviour.

Youth crime has been a major focus of political thinking and policy for at least the last 20 years. In recent years the theme of responsibility has loomed very large in political and governmental discourse. Most recently another, closely related, theme

---

1 This chapter develops the arguments initially advanced in Keating 2007.

2 I have argued elsewhere that the failure of the government to take a lead against the physical punishment of children is an important illustration of where the state has wrongly stepped back from intervention (Keating 2006).

has emerged: the 'Respect Agenda' of New Labour (particularly in its third term) (Home Office 2003; 2006). If this means anything, it seems to rest upon a belief in individual responsibility for criminal and anti-social behaviour within a framework of obligation to the community. In an attempt to address the 'me first' culture (Gilles 2005, 74) children must be made to accept responsibility for the harm they have caused. The parents of anti-social or offending children are also held to account. This has been described as the strategy of 'responsibilisation' (Garland 2001; Rose 2000).

The concept of responsibility is, thus, of great significance. Although it is true that 'responsibility' is used in many senses it has had a particular meaning within discussions of the age of criminal responsibility. My fear is that this meaning is being abandoned or sidelined in recent governmental responses to children's unacceptable behaviour. Most of this chapter will focus upon this transformation. It starts, however, with a brief discussion of its latest manifestation: the concept of respect.

Respect

In *Family Law and Personal Life* Eekelaar reflects on the role of certain values in personal relations, and alongside those one might have expected to find – friendship, truth and responsibility – is respect, identified as 'a pivotal value' (Eekelaar 2006, 77). Eekelaar believes that the concept of respect is worth exploring – both in the context of family relations and in terms of broader social interactions – and should not be summarily written off as simply the latest political slogan. Many years ago, prior to its current invocation, Darwell distinguished between appraisal respect and recognition respect (Darwell 1977) and although these are not watertight categories they are of use in trying to identify the essence of respect. This rests upon the recognition and acknowledgment of the integral worth of another person (or even thing) and not upon an appraisal of whether a person has, for example, done anything that marks them out as deserving of special respect. So at this level it is possible to support Eekelaar when he espouses the value of respect and, further, to echo his statement at the end of the chapter:

> Respect for a child demands more than the kind of respect one has for one's pet hamster. It is more than merely providing the child with a happy childhood. It involves recognising the gradual emergence of the child as an individual with interests and aspirations which are their own. (Eekelaar 2006, 102)

However, this does not lead Eekelaar to critique the government's Respect Agenda; instead, it is suggested that 'the policy goal is to try to instil in the members of the community a perception of the value of the community and people living in it'(2006, 81). While the communitarian ethos (Etzioni 1994; Macmurray 1995) behind the Respect Agenda is clear to see, this interpretation ignores the more disquieting aspects of communitarianism. A number of commentators have persuasively argued that the top-down form of 'control through community' (rather than genuine community control) that has been adopted in 'Third Way' politics has a rather fortress-like identity that could lead to 'an obsession with community defence' (Pavlich 2001,

57, 66). The danger is that exclusion is exacerbated and not reduced. Certainly the indications from much of the language employed by the government (and looking behind the occasional reference to words such as 'nurturing'[3]) are that this is the law and order lobby or a zero tolerance campaign by another name. It seems to have little to do with respecting children and much more to do with seeing them as a threat.

Constructing Childhood in Criminal Law

Behind much of the current debate about the behaviour of children is the issue of how we construct the notions of a 'child' and 'childhood' (and, as will be explored subsequently, that of parenthood).

It is commonly accepted that childhood is a construct that has changed over time rather than a natural state. It is clear that there are different constructions of childhood in different non-legal disciplines, and it is not surprising that there are also different constructions of childhood operating in different legal contexts. Although such differences are not, *per se*, unjustifiable it has been argued elsewhere that the stark differences that currently exist between the constructions of childhood operating in family law and criminal law have not, in fact, been justified (Keating 2007). In focusing upon the criminal law in this chapter we should not lose sight of the fact that a very different construct, based upon the child as 'vulnerable' and 'becoming' operates in family law. Underpinning recent developments in criminal law, on the other hand, is a construction of the 'unruly' child: one who is untrained, in need of control and, most recently, in whom respect for the social order must be instilled. As Fionda has commented, this is the image of childhood that the media employ when demonising child criminals – and is one that is extremely useful to politicians (Fionda 2001, 14).

> Young people who commit offences must face up to the consequences of their actions for themselves and for others and must take responsibility for their actions ... No young person should be allowed to feel that he or she can offend with impunity ... Punishment is important as a means of expressing society's condemnation of unlawful behaviour and as a deterrent. (Home Office 1997, 1-2)

But while, as will be seen, England and Wales have set the age of criminal responsibility at a low age, for hundreds of years the protective and developmental presumption of *doli incapax* existed alongside to protect younger children from the consequences of their actions.

---

3 'The respect drive is a cross-Government strategy to tackle bad behaviour and nurture good ... It's about nurturing and, where needed, enforcing a modern culture of respect. ... The police, local authorities and other agencies will be encouraged to use the full range of tools and powers to deal with anti-social behaviour.' (www.respect.gov.uk/article.aspx?id=9054) It is noteworthy that it is good behaviour and respect that are being nurtured here rather than children.

Constructing the Parent in Criminal Law

The concepts of parenthood and parenting can rarely have been under as much scrutiny as is currently the case in relation to both civil and criminal law. Historically, and still predominantly, parenting is understood by reference to rights, duties and responsibilities in relation to the relevant child. Most people would accept that parents owe a moral duty to care for their children (Eekelaar 1991) – but how this has translated into law has changed over time. Parenting in law has been transformed from an exercise of (paternal) authority[4] where intervention in family life was permitted only to protect children from harm into something much more imprecise. The key legal concept at civil law has become that of 'parental responsibility' by virtue of the Children Act 1989. The attempt this phrase makes to move from the language of parental rights to responsibilities has been much discussed (see, for example, Edwards and Halpern 1992; Eekelaar 1991) but other, less obvious yet highly significant, shifts have also occurred. While the Children Act 1989 did indeed have non-intervention in family life as one of its traditionally liberal guiding principles, there are now expectations about the way parenting is conducted that increases state intervention when parenting 'fails' (Bridgeman 2007; Gilles 2005; Reece 2006). This is most notable when children behave in an anti-social or criminal way: for such problem families the 'privileged sphere' is dramatically curtailed. In government discourse parenting is an important job: parents are expected to 'teach values, provide stability, offer the support that children need, and protect them physically and emotionally' (Home Office 2003, 3) and they 'should be the first defence against anti-social behaviour' (Labour Party 1997). But this is not only with a view to maximising the welfare of the individual child. One pivotal result of the communitarian policy developments is that parents are not only responsible for their children – they are responsible *to* the community for them as well and are expected to instil in children a respect for the community. Much of the language employed here is that of 'helping parents to recognise and meet [their] … responsibilities' (Home Office 1997, 3) and of 'supporting' parents to do a difficult job by the provision of information, advice and services. The reality of targeted support may well be experienced differently.

The Age of Criminal Responsibility: *Doli Capax*

As Lord Steyn recently commented 'ignoring the special position of children in the criminal justice system is not acceptable in a modern civil society'.[5] The criminal law thus sets an age below which children are exempt from criminal liability, employing an arbitrary and fixed cut-off point. At common law the age of criminal responsibility was seven. This was raised to eight in 1933 and to ten in 1963.[6] Section 4 of the

---

4 As exemplified by the decision in *Re Agar Ellis* (1883), 24 Ch.D. 317.

5 *R v G and Another* [2004] 1 AC 1034, para. 53.

6 The Children and Young Persons Act 1933, s. 50 as amended by the Children and Young Persons Act 1963, s. 16.

Children and Young Persons Act 1969 would have raised the age to 14 but this was never implemented.[7]

Below the age of criminal responsibility the child is irrebuttably regarded as *doli incapax*. A notable trend of late has been for governments to introduce controlling measures for children under the age of ten. Measures such as child safety orders (which can be imposed, for example, where a child under the age of ten has acted in an anti-social manner) under the Crime and Disorder Act 1998 have been condemned for blurring the boundaries of the criminal justice system (Monaghan et al. 2003). The government justifies them on the basis that 'Children under 10 need help to change their bad behaviour just as much as older children' (Home Office 1997, para. 99). In this context the concept of the age of criminal responsibility has been rendered meaningless.

Above the age of ten children are legally liable for their actions. It is true that the criminal law and criminal justice system do make certain allowances for youthful immaturity in some contexts, most notably in relation to mode of trial and sentencing but also in relation to, for example, the application of the partial defence of provocation to murder. In this latter instance, the reason for a young person's not being expected to have the same standard of self-control as an adult was explained very simply by Lord Diplock: 'to require old heads on young shoulders is inconsistent with the law's compassion to human infirmity'.[8] Gardner and Macklem have further considered the basis for the concession to youth in the context of provocation. They assert that,

> Arguably there is a role of being a teenager, in which being more temperamental is a good or fitting thing to be. Arguably that is how a teenager should be: impulsive, passionate, heedless. At the very least to be so seems morally acceptable in a teenager to the extent that it would not be in an adult. (Gardner and Macklem 2001, 826)

If the criminal law does, to some degree, accept that a 'proper, self-respecting teenager' *ought* to have a lower level of self-control than an adult, then what *ought* to be asked of a 'proper, self-respecting' child of ten or so in terms of control, awareness and understanding? The difficulty in answering this question is that the issue is not only one of determining the point at which, in developmental terms, individual children can be said to be responsible for their actions. As will be seen, other considerations such as the purpose of imposing liability, policy and politics have become deeply significant.

The presumption that a child between the ages of 10 and 14 was rebuttably presumed to be *doli incapax* was abolished after an unsuccessful attempt by the Divisional Court in *C v DPP*[9] to hold that the presumption no longer existed in English law. The House of Lords rejected this view, holding that any reform would have to come from Parliament.[10] The government, after only a cursory examination of the issues, included a provision abolishing the presumption in the Crime and

7 The provision was repealed by the Criminal Justice Act 1991, s. 72.

8 *DPP v Camplin* [1978] AC 705 at 717.

9 [1994] 3 WLR 888.

10 [1996] 1 AC 1.

Disorder Act 1998. However, section 34 is not without interpretative difficulties. Walker argued that all this section did was to abolish the presumption: thus, it would still be open to a child to plead that he or she was, in fact, *doli incapax* (Walker 1999). The courts ignored this persuasive argument until very recently. However, in *DPP v P* Lord Justice Smith stated that Walker might well be right and that if the mischief the reform sought to remedy was having to rebut the presumption in every case, it should still 'remain available in "genuine" cases'.[11] Although Lord Justice Smith acknowledges that her 'tentative' statements are *obiter*, it is a step in the right direction that the issue has been now been highlighted as requiring authoritative determination.

It is accepted that the test used to rebut the presumption of *doli incapax*, of knowing the difference between right and wrong, was flawed (see Keating 2007, 193). But it was, nevertheless, a crude developmental test: responsibility was judged not in years but on the basis of the understanding and judgement of the individual child. In this sense, therefore, there was a similarity between the presumption and the test of competence established in child law in *Gillick v West Norfolk and Wisbech Area Health Authority and Another*[12] (see Keating 2007, 193). Both could be seen to reflect, albeit imperfectly, our understanding of child development:

> Researchers broadly agree that there are fundamental differences between childhood thought, preoccupied as it is with practical issues to do with the here and now, and adolescent thinking which is much more sophisticated. This material suggests that the intellectual competence of young children aged up to about 11 to 12 is far less sophisticated than that of adolescents between the ages of 12 to 18. [Further, research] shows that the typical adolescent of 12 or 13 years of age cannot appreciate that there may be more than one solution to a problem or that individual acts or political solutions are not necessarily absolutely right or wrong. (Fortin 2003, 72-73)

Moreover, as late as 1990 the government accepted the importance of the presumption in protecting immature children from the consequences of their actions:

> The criminal law is based on the principle that people *understand* the difference between right and wrong. Very young children cannot easily tell this difference and the law takes account of this ... between the ages of 10 and 13 a child may only be convicted of a criminal offence if the prosecution can show that he knew what he did was seriously wrong. The government does not intend to change these arrangements *which make proper allowance for the fact that children's understanding, knowledge and ability to reason are still developing.* (Home Office 1990, para. 8.4) (author's emphasis)

This thinking was abandoned within the decade. The presumption was condemned as reflecting 'an outworn mode of thought'; as 'steeped in absurdity' and 'capable of operating capriciously' (Law Commission 1985, paras. 11.21-11.23). It was

11 [2007] 4 All ER 628, paras. 40, 43.

12 [1986] AC 118. It is worth noting also that 14 is the age at which child witnesses may give sworn evidence in criminal trials as long as they have 'a sufficient appreciation of the solemnity of the occasion and the particular responsibility to tell the truth which is involved in taking an oath': Youth Justice and Criminal Evidence Act 1999, s. 55(2).

argued that the presumption was 'contrary to common sense' (Home Office 1997, para. 4.14); that children grow up more quickly now (but see Keating 2007, 195); that with universal education children between 10 and 13 are 'plainly capable of differentiating between right and wrong' (Labour Party 1997) and the rationale for change was explained thus:

> A new balance has to be struck between the sometimes conflicting interests of welfare and punishment. First and foremost youth crime represents acts against other members of the community. Young offenders need to be held to account for their actions. The younger an offender the less developed their sense of responsibility. Nevertheless, a young person caught committing a crime must be challenged and a sanction must be applied to develop their sense of right and wrong and of the consequences which follow from offending. (Home Office 1998, 11)

Not only was the link between child law and criminal law severed but also criminal liability and punishment, it seems, could be imposed to *instil* responsibility rather than reflect it.

Criminal Responsibility and Parents

One interpretation of the landmark decision of *Gillick* was that parental responsibility diminishes (or even terminates) as the child gains maturity to make his or her own decisions. In relation to government policy on children's offending behaviour some acceptance of this view can be identified: 'As they develop, children must bear an increasing responsibility for their actions, just as the responsibility of parents gradually declines' (Home Office 1997, para. 4.1). However, the passage concludes that the responsibility of parents does not disappear altogether as the child approaches adulthood. Insofar as parents' responsibility is concerned this sounds remarkably similar to the subsequent interpretation of *Gillick* by the Court of Appeal in cases such as *Re R*[13] and *Re W*.[14] In the criminal law it provided the impetus for a series of controversial reforms such as binding over, parenting orders and parenting contracts which have increasingly held parents accountable for their children's anti-social or criminal behaviour – with measures dealing with parents of children under and over ten years old (Powers of the Criminal Courts Act 2000, s. 150; Crime and Disorder Act 1998, ss. 8-10; Anti-Social Behaviour Act 2003; see Hollingsworth 2007, 192-4). A parenting order may be imposed, for example, where a child has behaved anti-socially and the making of the order is desirable to prevent anti-social behaviour, the latter defined as behaviour which causes or is likely to cause harassment, alarm or distress (Anti-Social Behaviour Act 2003, ss. 26(3), 29(1)). Sutherland has observed that 'what amounts to "causing distress" is both breathtakingly broad and dazzlingly vague' (Sutherland 2005, 470).

These measures have had the effect of making *both* parent and child responsible for the child's actions and although it can be seen as part of a much larger government

13 *Re R (A Minor) (Wardship: Consent to Treatment)* [1992] Fam 11.

14 *Re W (A Minor) (Medical Treatment: Court's Jurisdiction)* [1993] Fam 64.

strategy of instilling respect or 'responsibilisation' (Garland 2001; Rose 2000), the illogicality of holding both to account has been highlighted by a number of commentators (Commission on Families and the Well-being of Children 2005, 33; James in this book; Koffman 2008). While it is true that government policy is riddled with inconsistency (or sleight of hand) especially in relation to the attribution of responsibility to children, the issue of dual responsibility needs to be unravelled further. This will be attempted after the next section.

Before leaving this issue, however, it is worth noting that it has been suggested that the initiatives have been welcomed by parents, citing, for example, a 60 per cent voluntary attendance rate at parenting classes (Arthur 2004, 319). However, others have pointed out that it is difficult to assess whether attendance is truly voluntary or is the alternative to the imposition of a parenting order (Sutherland 2005, 477) and Gilles has commented,

> Parents refusing all the government's offers to join the mainstream moral community are viewed as endangering their children's moral development, thereby threatening the well-being of the community as a whole. While hard line intervention … is pursued to protect society, the language of support and inclusion enables coercion to sound positively compassionate … The promise to "work with" and "support" wayward parents places a benevolent spin on what amounts to an authoritarian attempt to enforce conformity. (Gilles 2005, 84)[15]

Exactly the same spin is adopted in relation to the anti-social behaviour of children (and underpins the nurturing façade of the Respect Agenda). Moreover, the 'pathologising and deeply offensive notion that the parents of children in trouble wilfully refuse to accept their responsibilities' (Goldson 1999, 13) and that parents are always to blame for their children's anti-social behaviour needs challenging (Penal Affairs Consortium 1995). The parents may have been doing their utmost to deal with a child's behaviour. Further, research reveals that a significant proportion of the parents of children falling within the youth justice system have health or other social problems (Koffman 2006, 610). Thrusting responsibility upon parents in what may be very difficult family or personal circumstances, is, at the least, unlikely to produce the effect the government is seeking. Moreover, although there is evidence that truly voluntary programmes can have a positive effect on parenting, 'it is surely questionable that using compulsion and the threat of fines and imprisonment will change the behaviour of parents and their children' (Arthur 2004, 319). Sutherland suggests that there has been no 'ringing endorsement of mandatory parenting programmes' from studies, dismissing the initiatives as 'a desperate, political attempt to deal with juvenile offending through blaming parents' (Sutherland 2005, 467, 478; also Commission on Families and the Well-being of Children 2005, 31). Finally, although the government directs its policies towards 'parents', their impact is differentially experienced. It is most frequently mothers who are held responsible (Gilles 2005; Koffman 2006).

---

15 Koffman's research reveals that a negative or hostile attitude by parents to offers of support was an important factor in decisions to impose ASBOs etc. upon children (Koffman 2006, 610).

Being and Becoming Responsible

In what sense (or senses) is responsibility being used in the youth justice system today? To discuss this three strands will be unravelled: the core meaning of responsibility in criminal law (being responsible), the development of responsibility (becoming responsible) and the relationship between responsibility and punishment.

The core of criminal responsibility (being responsible)

It is argued here that the central and enduring foundation of the criminal law has been that it is addressed to responsible subjects. The judgement that the actor is responsible has to be made first – indeed that is *why* you are punishing them. It is permissible to blame them *because* we have made the judgement that they are a responsible actor (rather than, for example, someone found to be legally insane). The liberal concept of moral responsibility underpinning the criminal law is both complex and contested. In essence we could explain it in terms of

> the notion of rational agency … what we condemn the agent for is a failure to recognise, to accept or to be adequately motivated by, reasons for action … which *were within his grasp*. (Duff and von Hirsch 1977, 109-10) (author's emphasis)

An alternative way of expressing this is found in the work of John Gardner. He draws upon the notion of 'consequential' responsibility (where some or all of the moral or legal consequences of a wrong or mistake are the actor's to bear) (Gardner 2003)[16] and distinguishes this from what he calls 'basic' responsibility. The essence of responsibility is exactly what is suggested by the word: an ability to respond (Gardner 2003,161; see also Bridgeman and Keating in this book). He goes on to state:

> The distinctively human form of reason is one which grasps the meaning of things as well as their instrumentality, and hence depends on the ability to conceptualise and interpret that is part of being a human communicator … [Basic responsibility] depends not only on our ability to *have* a certain kind of explanation for what we do or think or feel, but also our ability to *offer* that explanation. (Gardner 2003, 163, 171)

Very young children are, thus, by these accounts of responsibility exempt from criminal liability and punishment (Hart 1967, 361) because we do not believe that reasons (or explanations) for action were within their grasp and, further, they lack the ability to communicate any explanation. It is this account of responsibility that is accepted in this chapter: competency or capacity is – or should be – central. There are times in governmental and political discourse when the liberal view of what responsibility entails appears to be accepted:

> An excuse culture has developed within the youth justice system. … We must stop making excuses for youth crime. Children above the age of criminal responsibility are generally mature enough to be accountable for their actions and the law should recognise this. (Home Office 1997, 1-2)

16 Drawing on the work of Dworkin (2000), at 287.

Of course, as Hart (1967, 361) makes clear, the *mechanism* by which very young children are exempt from criminal liability and punishment is of a categorical nature: age. The actual competency of individual children is, in this sense, irrelevant (Hollingsworth 2007, 195).[17] This is undeniably and, it is argued here, regrettably true with the abolition of the protective and individualised presumption of *doli incapax*.[18]

Developing responsibility (becoming responsible)

It was noted earlier that the government at times justifies the early imposition of criminal liability on the basis that it will help children to *become* responsible citizens. As such, the raft of measures against anti-social or offending children can be seen, not so much as part of the liberal tradition of responsibility, but as part of the communitarian endeavour to instil values and foster a sense of respect. While one can, at the very least, question the inconsistency of the government's usage of the concept of responsibility, the shift has caused several commentators to reflect upon the merits of using the criminal law to develop responsibility in children. Perhaps, it could be argued, this is what respecting children entails. Drawing upon the work of Cane and Honoré (Cane 2002; Honoré 1999), Hollingsworth acknowledges that 'one may disagree with the age set [but] … the conferral of criminal responsibility on children can be symbolically important' (Hollingsworth 2007, 196) because not to do so strikes at the identity of the actor. Hollingsworth argues that holding children legally liable serves the ontological function of responsibility, that is, it allocates 'ownership' of the conduct. This 'contributes to the formation and maintenance of our identities as individuals, and to our sense of being able to influence the course of events, and it is this which Honoré says we should be reluctant to deny to any group of people, even those lacking competency' (Hollingsworth 2007, 196). Hollingsworth continues:

> The point being made is simply this. It is justifiable on a conceptual level to distinguish between a child being *presumed* responsible in order to cross the threshold into the criminal law, thus fulfilling the ontological function of responsibility and giving effect to the child's autonomy, and then to take account of *actual* capacity once within the system. (Hollingsworth 2007, 197)

According to Hollingsworth, the reality of a child's vulnerability can be accommodated within the justice system by virtue of the explanatory and evaluative functions of responsibility identified by Cane: 'the skills a child needs to explain his behaviour may well be developed and improved with increased experience and exposure to those mechanisms such as a trial or a youth offender panel' (Hollingsworth 2007, 196). Although Hollingsworth does state that none of this implies that the age of

17 Note that Hart goes on to describe the possession of normal capacities as one of the most prominent criteria of the primary sense of responsibility: liability-responsibility (Hart 1967, 363).

18 Unless found (as, indeed, an adult might be) unfit to plead: see *SC v United Kingdom* [2004] 40 EHRR 10.

responsibility should be set at ten, anyone who remembers the travesty of the trial of Venables and Thompson for the murder of Jamie Bulger would find it hard to accept the developmental qualities of trial in the Crown Court (and this is true even after the concessions made subsequently). Even insofar as youth offender panels are concerned, new research reveals that very young children are often at a complete loss to understand the process that they are supposedly participating in (Newbury 2008).

However, Hollingsworth is not alone in arguing that conferral of responsibility at a young age can be seen to enhance a child's autonomy. Vaughan has argued that at least some elements of the Crime and Disorder Act 1998 represent a shift to regarding the child as an 'active citizen'.

> The Act ... might represent a real shift in the way youth are regulated and governed. There may be a move away from a paternalistic model of regulation that stresses the essential passivity of youth towards the cultivation of a more active subjectivity within young people who will be required to take more responsibility for their lives. (Vaughan 2000, 348)

However, as Diduck comments and Vaughan acknowledges (Vaughan 2000, 359), although 'there are images of autonomous and responsible children from which the law can and does draw to invest children with the capacity for social and legal agency ... Law's autonomous child exists but only on the law's terms ... It tells young offenders and their parents that children are legally responsible ... But does so in ... a punitive, moralising way that also incorporates ideas of parental or family failure' (Diduck 2004, 94).

Others are even more fundamentally sceptical. Fortin regards as 'astonishing' the government's claim that the change will 'contribute to the *right* of children appearing [in court] ... to develop responsibly for themselves' (Fortin 2003, 555). She cites Bandalli's view that this is 'profoundly disingenuous and distorted' (Bandalli 2000, 89). For some it demonstrates how easy it is for rights talk to be subverted. Not least among the difficulties encountered in the arena of juvenile justice is the rhetoric of government. The view taken in this chapter is that while respect for the community is undoubtedly important, and the government is entitled to promote respect, it is an abuse of the criminal law to use it to try to develop responsibility in children who lack capacity.

Responsibility and punishment

Many of the government initiatives in recent years can be seen less as a direct challenge to the concept of moral responsibility than as a sidelining of it. Rather than debating whether children aged ten or over do or do not have the capacity to understand the wrongfulness of their actions (what Fionda calls the legal view), the minimum age of criminal responsibility can be seen to reflect a capacity to accept punishment for their actions (the policy view) (Fionda 2001, 17). As part of her robust critique of New Labour's reforms Fionda argues:

> This view can be most clearly be seen in the European and other jurisdictions where the minimum age of criminal responsibility is much higher than that operating in England and Wales. Are we to believe, as proponents of the legal view would have it, that children under 18 in Belgium or under 16 in Spain, are incapable of understanding that their actions are seriously wrong? The only sensible way of understanding these higher minimum ages is in relation to the policy view that has been taken in such jurisdictions that it is wrong as a matter of policy, to subject young people to the rigours of the criminal justice process. (Fionda 2001, 18)

Further, it has been observed that:

> In many countries the "age of criminal responsibility" is used to signify the age at which a person becomes liable to the "ordinary" or "full" penalties of the law. In this sense, the age of criminal responsibility in England is difficult to state: it is certainly much higher than eight [as it was at the time]. (Home Office 1960, 30)

Policy undoubtedly plays an increasingly dominant role in the youth justice system, whether in determining the age of responsibility or the point at which children are no longer treated as special cases in relation to the penalties that may be imposed by the courts. But policy has to be shaped by something. It may be shaped in part by political considerations but somewhere along the line the question '*why* is it wrong to subject children to the criminal law?' has to be answered. If one accepts that moral responsibility is what links justice to punishment and that underpinning the criminal law is the notion of retributive punishment then not only is it inappropriate to make children criminally liable for their actions, it is also inappropriate to punish them. As Hart argues, 'a system or practice which did not regard the possession of... [capacity] as a necessary condition of liability and so treated blame as appropriate even in the case of those who lacked [it], would not, as morality is at present understood, be a morality' (Hart 1967, 362). The presumption of *doli incapax* that used to operate for children aged 10-14 provided, as Lord Lowry commented, a 'benevolent safeguard': protecting children from brutal punishments in cases where moral responsibility was absent.[19] Of course, children are no longer brutally punished by hanging, flogging, etc. But it is not true that they are no longer punished at all by the criminal law. This issue is vitally important – those who have argued for the abolition of the presumption have based their case, in part, upon the claim that children are no longer punished. Glanville Williams, writing in 1954 (but quoted at length in *C v DPP*) said:

> At the present day the "knowledge of wrong" test stands in the way not of punishment, but of educational treatment. It saves the child not from prison ... but from the probation officer, the foster-parent, or the approved school. (Williams 1954, 495)

In exploring these claims of welfare and treatment it is important to acknowledge that in the 1950s the welfare star was still moving up into its ascendancy of 1969. The construction of childhood as unruly or evil was in the process of being supplanted by a construction that was much more like that in family law: a welfarist view that saw crime as a symptom of underlying problems in the child's life. However, that

---

19 *C v DPP* [1996] 1 AC 1, para. 33.

star is certainly not shining as brightly as it once did. In 1993, at the time of the killing of Jamie Bulger, John Major infamously said: 'We should condemn a little more and understand a little less.' The system is not as child-centred as it was but is an eclectic mixture of measures with different objectives. Some parts of the youth justice system do attempt constructive work with children and their parents. The referral system established by the Crime and Disorder Act 1998 may, for example, trigger the provision of desperately needed assistance – and there is some truth in the notion that the youth court, in particular, 'mops up' society's problem children.[20] But punishment is clearly still a major and developing feature of the youth justice system. To find Glanville Williams, therefore, being extensively cited in *C v DPP* when the surrounding circumstances have changed so fundamentally adds to the doubts which exist as to the reasoning behind abolition. The view taken here is that trying to separate the capacity to understand one's wrongdoing (in a broad sense) from the capacity to accept punishment is misconceived. In order to maintain the link between justice and punishment the two forms of capacity should be seen as inextricably linked.

In summary, the claims made by those advocating responsibility at the age of ten is: children are responsible at this age and, if they are not we can make them responsible and in any event, we are not really punishing them as if they were adults. All of these have been disputed. One should also bear in mind that even where supposedly supportive measures are taken they will have been preceded by an arrest which will have triggered a forced collection of a DNA sample, and an entry on the police database that may be there for the rest of the child's life, and that subsequently the child may be unable to claim to be of good character. Moreover, the increasing use of controlling civil measures such as anti-social behaviour orders (ASBOs) introduced by section 1 of the Crime and Disorder Act 1998[21] as well as those discussed above, against children under ten who have not committed any offence, is a further indication of a deeply worrying emerging trend. All of this could be said to represent a fundamental danger to the traditional boundaries of criminal law.

Dual Criminal Responsibility

It was noted earlier that increasingly parents are held responsible as well as their children for anti-social or offending behaviour. At one level this is entirely illogical. If the child is a responsible, autonomous actor who, say, understands the difference between right and wrong, how can the parent be held to blame as well? If one were to

20 At the time Glanville Williams was writing the criminal court could choose between civil and criminal measures in the same proceedings. But care options were removed from the criminal courts by the Children Act 1989 s. 90, repealing the Children and Young Persons Act 1969, s. 7(7). Care orders in criminal proceedings were replaced by supervision orders with a residence requirement: Children and Young Persons Act 1969, s. 12AA. s. 90 also abolished the power of the court to make a care order under the Children and Young Persons Act 1969, s. 1(2) where 'the offence condition' had been satisfied.

21 An amendment to the Bill which would have raised the threshold age from 10 to 13 was resisted by the government.

confine oneself, therefore, to the liberal tradition of moral responsibility underpinning the criminal law, imposing criminal liability upon parents would be difficult to justify. But we have seen how deeply contested this version of responsibility is in both academic and policy discourse. Hollingsworth has argued that children should be responsible to fulfil the ontological function of responsibility, enabling them to own their actions, quite separate from the issue of moral responsibility. Parents who are held to account for their children's actions are not fulfilling the ontological function but the explanatory and evaluative functions of responsibility. It is not, therefore, necessarily illogical to hold both parents and children responsible at the conceptual level.

> This type of legal liability is underpinned by a desire to hold parents responsible in one of two other senses. First, the parent is being held responsible for indirectly *causing* their child's offending behaviour, but this is in a general sense … Second, the parent is being held responsible for fulfilling – or not – the role as parent. (Hollingsworth 2007, 199)

So parents are responsible in the historic sense (for having created the circumstances which allowed the child to offend) and in the prospective sense – the sense that Cane, for example, is more interested in (for ensuring that the child does not reoffend) (Cane 2002, 34). But as we have seen, the notion that parents have always, however indirectly, caused their child's behaviour is problematic in practice. Further, the idea that parents, who may have very chaotic lives themselves, can effectively police their child's future actions may be unrealistic.

In summary, differing concepts of responsibility can be and have been invoked to justify holding parents and children responsible; children may be seen as being or becoming responsible (or both); parents certainly have responsibility thrust upon them. Add the supposedly communitarian (but actually strongly authoritarian) policies driving government here and it is little wonder that initiatives are not only inconsistent but a misuse of the criminal law in order to restore some supposed golden age of respect.

Restoring Children's Responsibility

It is clear that pre-1998 the presumption of *doli incapax* was not fundamentally different from the test of competence in *Gillick*. While the former has been swept away, the latter is still extremely influential (see, as a recent example, *R (on the application of Axon) v Secretary of State for Health*[22]). The argument that there is no place today for the presumption should be strongly rejected. Just as the *Gillick* competence test can be seen as protecting children from bearing the brunt of decisions they are too immature to make, so the presumption of *doli incapax* protected children from the consequences of immature actions (Douglas 1998, 269). One simple solution would be to raise the age of criminal responsibility to, for example, 12, 13 or 14 (Allen 2006; Royal College of Psychiatrists 2006). This would answer criticisms by the UN Committee on the Rights of the Child, which

22 [2006] QB 539.

condemned abolition of the presumption and has repeatedly urged the UK to raise the age of criminal responsibility (Committee on the Rights of the Child 2002, para. 58).[23] However, such changes would not sit well with the developmental approach.

A second possibility is the creation of a *Gillick*-type test that would reflect an understanding of children's development as a gradual process. This is not to advocate a revival of the old 'did he or she know it was wrong?' test: as was pointed out almost 50 years ago a capacity to do this does not necessarily equate with responsibility on a par with that of an adult (Home Office 1960, para. 81). But the criminal law should continue to be underpinned by a theory of moral responsibility. This should not be taken as arguing that the criminal law is just about punishing criminals in a retributive sense. Rehabilitation, reparation and restorative justice all have a role to play. Further, it is acknowledged that the criminal justice system is also rightly concerned with protecting the public. But we should not pretend, where very young children are concerned, that it is legitimate to use the criminal law to secure these ends.

Conclusion

This chapter opened by acknowledging the existence of a privileged sphere of family life in which parents undertake the task of caring for and developing an autonomous, independent child. This privileged sphere is retracting especially in relation to the offending or anti-social behaviour of children with the result that increasingly both children and parents are held responsible in an attempt to improve social order and create respectful citizens. Insofar as very young children are concerned, in 2004, 900 children aged 10-11 were found guilty of offences (Home Office 2005, 62). In the same year 100 10-17 year olds were tried in the Crown Court with very little concession made for their youth. The use of measures such as ASBOs continues to increase, as does the number of parenting orders etc. being imposed (Koffman 2008).

In focusing upon the issue of the age of criminal responsibility, this chapter has tried to explore changing constructions of parenting and childhood and the senses in which those much used concepts 'responsibility' and (to a lesser degree) 'respect' are being used. Parents are now expected to be 'good' parents. The vast majority of parents clearly do their utmost to care for their children and prepare them for adulthood. Where parents experience difficulties in fulfilling this role it may well be that the provision of support on a voluntary basis would be welcomed and valuable. But the child is not 'a child of the state'. Despite apparent acknowledgement of this, the government's supposedly communitarian policies run the risk of transforming family life. Moreover, compulsory measures to enforce a certain mode of parenting are unlikely to succeed.

---

23 It would also meet the concerns of the Joint Committee on Human Rights, Tenth Report of Session 2002-2003, HL117/HC 81, paras. 35-38; Joint Committee on Human Rights, Eighteenth Report of Session 2002-2003, HL 187/HC1279, paras. 13-14. One could, indeed, go much further and link the age of criminal responsibility with the age of majority and the right to vote.

In relation to children it has not been argued that the different tests of competency in child law and criminal law are *per se* unjustifiable: 'the search for a single test of competency is a search for a Holy Grail' (Roth et al. 1977, 283). But there should be sound reasons for the differences that exist. Not only have these not been developed in relation to youth crime but also we seem, by all the measures adopted, to be moving closer to the demonisation or destruction of childhood itself and to using the criminal law as the weapon of first rather than last choice. To see this done in the name of regarding children as responsible or as part of a development of a culture of respect is deeply frustrating. It has been commented that:

> No civilised society regards children as accountable for their actions to the same extent as adults. The wisdom of protecting young children against the full rigour of the criminal law is beyond argument. The difficulty lies in determining when and where that protection should be removed. (Howard 1982, 343)

While the current answer seems to be 'forever younger', commentators must continue to press for a debate about the age of criminal responsibility and youth justice more generally that goes beyond the politics of respect or the latest manifestation of 'no more excuses'. Fionda is right to argue that what is needed is a radical change in our perception of young people's behaviour and for responses that are not shaped by the ambivalent choice of devil or angel (Fionda 2005, 259). We should not lose sight of the protection afforded by the *Gillick* test of competence and, formerly, the presumption of *doli incapax*. At the very least, whether they are flawed or not in theory and in practice, they play an important role: they signal that children in a transitional stage of their lives are special cases.

Lady Butler-Sloss has argued that:

> Children in trouble, particularly persistent offenders, are children in need of help. It is important that we take a holistic approach to the family and the welfare of children, and look at ways in which we can reduce the present rigidity between the criminal justice and child welfare systems. (Butler-Sloss 2004, 7)[24]

There is much that one would endorse in this statement but caution is also needed. The current danger is that punishment is sometimes imposed in the name of help or treatment or support. One would not wish to exacerbate this trend. This is, thus, not a call for a return to the welfare orientated policies of the 1960s that disempower children and their parents. But the point is that the criminal law and the youth justice system are ill-equipped to respond to the anti-social behaviour of young children. That some parts of the system are trying to deal constructively with the problems that young children present with – 'mopping up' society's disadvantaged – is not a good enough justification for holding young children responsible and transforming the criminal law in the process.

As has been shown elsewhere in this volume (Morrow in this book) children are certainly capable of acting responsibly and the developmental discourse has the potential to infantilise children and needlessly extend their period of dependency

24 At the launch of the Charities' Youth Justice Coalition Report (Monaghan et al. 2003).

(James in this book). Further, as Article 40.1 of the Convention on the Rights of the Child stipulates, states should treat children in a manner that reinforces the child's respect for the human rights and fundamental freedoms of others. However, Article 40.1 also requires states to treat children in a manner consistent with the promotion of their sense of dignity and worth, taking age into account. It is argued here that securing the balance between respect for the community and respect for a child means that they should be recognised as a responsible subject at a point at which this is truly meaningful.

References

Allen, R. (2006), *From Punishment to Problem-solving: A New Approach to Children in Trouble* (London: Centre for Crime and Justice Studies).

Arthur, R. (2004), 'Young Offenders: Children in Need of Protection', *Law and Policy* 26, 309.

Bandalli, S. (2000), 'Children, Responsibility and the New Youth Justice' in Goldson, B. (ed.), *The New Youth Justice* (Lyme Regis: Russell House).

Bridgeman, J. (2007), 'Accountability, Support or Relationship? Conceptions of Parental Responsibility', *Northern Ireland Legal Quarterly* 58, 307.

Butler-Sloss, Dame (2004), *Family Law* 34, 7.

Cane, P. (2002), *Responsibility in Law and Morality* (Oxford: Hart Publishing).

Commission on Families and the Well-being of Children (2005), *Families and the State: Two-way Support and Responsibilities* (Bristol: Policy Press).

Committee on the Rights of the Child (2002), *Concluding Observations of the Committee on the Rights of the Child: United Kingdom and Northern Ireland* (31st session) (Geneva: United Nations).

Darwell, S. (1977), 'Two Kinds of Respect', *Ethics* 88, 36.

Diduck, A. (2004), *Law's Families* (Cambridge: Cambridge University Press).

Douglas, G. (1998), 'The Child's Right to Make Mistakes: Criminal Responsibility and the Immature Minor' in Douglas, G. and Sebba, L. (eds), *Children's Rights and Traditional Values* (Aldershot: Ashgate).

Duff, A. and von Hirsch, A. (1997), 'Responsibility, Retribution and the "Voluntary": a Response to Williams', *Cambridge Law Journal* 56, 103.

Dworkin, R. (2000), *Sovereign Virtue: The Theory and Practice of Equality* (Cambridge MA: Harvard University Press).

Edwards, S. and Halpern, A. (1992), 'Parental Responsibility: An Instrument of Social Policy', *Family Law* 22, 113.

Eekelaar, J. (1986), 'The Eclipse of Parental Rights', *Law Quarterly Review* 102, 4.

Eekelaar, J. (1991), 'Are Parents Morally Obliged to Care for their Children?', *Oxford Journal of Legal Studies* 11, 340.

Eekelaar, J. (1991), 'Parental Responsibility: State of Nature or Nature of the State', *Journal of Social Welfare and Family Law* 13, 37.

Eekelaar, J. (2006), *Family Law and Personal Life* (Oxford: Oxford University Press).

Etzioni, A. (1994), *The Spirit of Community* (New York: Crown).
Fionda, J. (2001), *Legal Concepts of Childhood* (Oxford: Hart).
Fionda, J. (2005), *Devils and Angels: Youth Policy and Crime* (Oxford: Hart).
Fortin, J. (2003), *Children's Rights and the Developing Law* (London: Butterworths).
Freeman, M. (1997), 'The James Bulger Tragedy: Childish Innocence and the Construction of Guilt' in Freeman, M., *The Moral Status of Children* (The Hague: Martinus Nijhoff).
Freeman, M. (2005), 'Rethinking Gillick', *International Journal of Children's Rights* 13, 201.
Gardner, J. (2003), 'The Mark of Responsibility', *Oxford Journal of Legal Studies* 23, 157.
Gardner, J. and Macklem, T. (2001), 'Provocation and Pluralism', *Modern Law Review* 64, 815.
Garland, D. (2001), *The Culture of Control: Crime and Social Order in Contemporary Society* (Oxford: Oxford University Press).
Gilles, V. (2005), 'Meeting Parents' Needs? Discourses of "Support" and "Inclusion" in Family Policy', *Critical Social Policy* 25, 70.
Goldson, B. (1999), 'Youth (In)justice: Contemporary Developments in Policy and Practice' in Goldson, B. (ed.), *Youth Justice: Contemporary Policy and Practice* (Aldershot: Ashgate).
Hart, H.L.A. (1967), 'Varieties of Responsibility', *Law Quarterly Review* 83, 362.
Hart, H.L.A. (1968), *Punishment and Responsibility* (Oxford: Oxford University Press).
Hollingsworth, K. (2007), 'Responsibility and Rights: Children and their Parents in the Youth Justice System', *International Journal of Law, Policy and the Family* 21, 190.
Home Office (1960), *Report of the Committee on Children and Young Persons* (Ingleby Report), Cmnd 1191 (London: HMSO).
Home Office (1990), *Crime, Justice and Protecting the Public* (London: HMSO).
Home Office (1997), *No More Excuses: A New Approach to Tackling Youth Crime in England and Wales* Cm 3809 (London: TSO).
Home Office (1998), *The Crime and Disorder Bill: Youth Justice, Criminal Procedures and Sentencing* (Home Office Research Paper 98/43), available at www. parliament.uk/commons/lib/research/rp98/rp98-043.pdf.
Home Office (2003), *Respect and Responsibility – Taking a Stand against Anti-social Behaviour*, Cm 5778 (London: TSO).
Home Office (2005), *Criminal Statistics 2004, England and Wales* (London: TSO).
Home Office (2006), *Respect Action Plan* (London: TSO).
Honoré, T. (1999), *Responsibility and Fault* (Oxford: Hart).
Howard, C. (1982), *Criminal Law* (Melbourne: Law Book Co.).
Keating, H. (2006), 'Protecting or Punishing Children: Physical Punishment, Human Rights and English Law Reform', *Legal Studies* 26, 394.
Keating, H. (2007), 'The "Responsibility" of Children in the Criminal Law', *Child and Family Law Quarterly* 19, 183.
Koffman, L. (2006), 'The Use of Anti-Social Behaviour Orders: an Empirical Study of a New Deal for Communities Area', *Criminal Law Review* 593.

Koffman, L. (2008), 'Holding Parents to Account: Tough on Children, Tough on the Causes of Children?', *Journal of Law and Society* 35, 113.

Labour Party Shadow Consultation Paper (1997), *Tackling Youth Crime, Reforming Youth Justice* (London: Labour Party).

Law Commission (1985), *Codification of the Criminal Law* (Law Com 143) (London: HMSO).

Macmurray, J. (1995), *The Form of the Personal* (London: Faber).

Monaghan, G., Hibbert, P. and Moore, S. (2003), *Children in Trouble: Time for Change* (Charities' Youth Justice Coalition) (Ilford: Barnardo's).

Newbury, A. (2008), 'Youth Crime – Whose Responsibility?', *Journal of Law and Society* 35, 131.

Pavlich, G. (2001), 'The Force of Community' in Braithwaite, J. and Strang, H. (eds), *Restorative Justice and Civil Society* (Cambridge: Cambridge University Press).

Penal Affairs Consortium (1995), *Parental Responsibility, Youth Crime and the Criminal Law* (London: Penal Affairs Consortium).

Reece, H. (2006), 'From Parental Responsibility to Parenting Responsibly' in Freeman, M. (ed.), *Law and Sociology: Current Legal Issues Vol. 8* (Oxford: Oxford University Press).

Rose, N. (2000), 'Community, Citizenship and the Third Way', *American Behavioral Scientist* 43:9, 139.

Roth, L., Meisel, A. and Lidz, C. (1997), 'Tests of Competency to Consent to Treatment', *American Journal of Psychiatry* 134, 279.

Royal College of Psychiatrists (2006), *Child Defendants* (Occasional Paper 56) (London: Royal College of Psychiatrists).

Smith, J.C. (1996), 'Commentary to *W (A Minor) v DPP*', *Criminal Law Review* 320.

Sutherland, E. (2005), 'Offending and Offensive Young People: Why Mandatory Parenting Education is Not the Answer' in Bainham, A. (ed.), *The International Survey of Family Law* (Bristol: Family Law).

Vaughan, B. (2000), 'The Government of Youth: Disorder *and* Dependence?', *Social and Legal Studies* 9, 347.

Walker, N. (1999), 'The End of an Old Song', *New Law Journal* 64.

Williams, G. (1954), 'The Criminal Responsibility of Children', *Criminal Law Review* 493.

Chapter 8

Responsibility, Children and Childhood

Adrian James

The issue of responsibility has become progressively prominent over the last decade as the government has increasingly placed the relationship between rights, responsibility and citizenship at the heart of a new social contract between citizens and the state. This has raised some difficult problems in relation to children, however, since the concepts of childhood and responsibility do not, for many, sit easily together, partly because of the behaviour of some children themselves – because of their agency and their choice of actions – but also because many adults, focusing on children's biological immaturity, find it difficult (or prefer not) to see children as being able to exercise responsibility (Morrow in this book).

This has resulted in an array of social policies, across a wide spectrum of public services, which reflects the ambivalence of adults towards children: an ambivalence that rests on the knowledge that adults, whether within the confines of the family or in the community more generally, will almost always have the final say, whatever rights or responsibilities children may or may not have. As children's rights discourse has progressively permeated public policy, however, this social reality has produced and increasingly highlighted a number of ambiguities, which this chapter will explore in the context of some of the key sites in which such tensions are played out, including crime, the family and education.

Understanding Children and Childhood

Much of the tension between children's rights discourse and the social practices of the adult world is attributable to the way in which the large majority of adults have grown up and have absorbed their understandings of children and childhood. Central to this process is the pervasive influence of the developmental paradigm, which delineates and describes the process of children's psychological maturation. This is firmly rooted in the work of Piaget (1950) who described both children's cognitive and moral development as a series of discrete stages, each defined in terms of a specific cognitive structure. Initially egocentric, according to Piaget children only gradually achieve powers of reasoning that comply with expectations for rational adult thinking.

In essence, his theory implied that for all children, everywhere, there is staged progression to adulthood, central to which is children's inherent lack of skills and their subsequent acquisition of these through clearly defined stages, linked to clearly specified ages. Thus in Piaget's schema, age and competence become thoroughly intertwined – the developing child is determined by its developing body and thus childhood is the epitome of lack of competence, whilst adulthood is the model of competence. This necessarily defines children as being 'en route', as becoming rather than as being.

Recent developments in the multi-disciplinary study of childhood (see, for example, James et al. 1998) have increasingly challenged this orthodoxy, however. Drawing upon other cultural and historical contexts, attention has been drawn to empirical evidence that challenges the rigidities of the developmental perspective highlighting, for example, children at work – often essential in many parts of world – who are clearly able to think logically and act competently and responsibly, or children filling other very adult roles – as child soldiers, as caretakers of other children, or even as carers for ill or disabled parents or older relatives.

While in broad terms, children's capacities clearly do evolve with age, in practice the actual ages at which a child acquires competencies will vary according, on the one hand, to their life experiences and social and cultural environment and, on the other, the nature of the competencies and the situations in which they are required to be exercised. The model of staged progression offered by the developmental paradigm, however, produces images of a 'standard' child, with the consequence that children come to be defined as either stupid or gifted, normal or abnormal depending upon the extent to which they exceed or fail to meet the 'normal standards' of developmental progression.

Piaget's work has been increasingly criticised over the last 25 years. In particular, for example, Gilligan has argued that the stages do not fit female development because Piaget (and others of the same school of thought, such as Kohlberg) derived their stage norms from studying *only* boys and men. She therefore argues that the ideas are of limited application and that the cognitive developmental model embodies a far-reaching devaluation of women. More recently, Mayall has argued that because of the profound influence of developmental psychology, adults in the UK have been *taught* to find the idea of recognising the child as a moral agent difficult, even 'a contradiction in terms' (2002, 87). Thus, in the context of child/adult relations, children's moral agency is neither recognised nor respected, in spite of the fact that 'in their daily interactions and relationships with other children and with adults, children confront [and deal with] issues of justice, equal distribution and sharing' (Mayall 2000, 88).

As Woodhead (1999) has argued, therefore, the developmental paradigm emphasises children's relative incompetence, immaturity and dependency in ways that implicitly diminish their status. As a consequence, it also structures adult thinking and perceptions in such a way that it becomes difficult to recognise in children behaviour and evidence to the contrary because adults have been taught to underestimate their abilities. Thus, as Lansdown argues:

> It is increasingly clear, from an overview of recent research of children's own perspectives and experiences, that adults consistently underestimate children's capacities … [and] children are denied opportunities for participation in decision making and the exercise

> of responsibility in many areas of their lives, because of extended social and economic dependency and *an enhanced perception of the need for protection.* (Lansdown 2005, 30-1, emphasis added)

As Smart et al. also point out:

> One of the reasons that we find it hard in Western cultures to appreciate children as moral actors is because they are seen as so dependent upon their parents ... [this] leaves unsaid the extent to which adults are also dependent on others, including children, for emotional and material support. (Smart et al. 2001, 97)

In the UK, therefore, understandings and perceptions of children and childhood are rooted in a developmental paradigm that produces a view of children that is heavily normative: we have absorbed, from numerous sources and images, an understanding of children as not competent, as dependent, as becoming rather than being, an understanding that is based upon a particular view of what is 'normal' in terms of child development. This has enormous implications for children, however, for as Greene has argued, 'Normalization constrains all children since it determines people's expectations of them *and their own expectations of themselves*' (Greene 1999, 257, emphasis added).

The significance of this last point should not be lost: it clearly implies that by regarding children as not being capable of exercising responsibility, or of being inherently irresponsible as a consequence of their developmental immaturity, adults help to shape children's expectations of themselves and thus their behaviour. We must therefore be mindful of the ways in which

> children themselves respond to the power, authority and value systems through which their position, as children, is being shaped within and through these social structures and societal practices and thus how "childhood" is also, in this sense, being constructed by children too. (James and James 2004, 118)

When translated into areas such as education, another area where Piaget's work has been particularly influential, one of the consequences of the normative power of the developmental model is that children and young people risk being labelled as either lagging behind or precocious when they fail to meet, or exceed, expected levels of achievement. Importantly, such perspectives are not restricted to child psychologists or educationalists, who have been exposed to them as part of their professional training; they trickle down to parents in the form of common sense or received wisdom, which is reinforced by their contacts with teachers, doctors and other professionals, in whose training they are firmly and deeply rooted.

Children and Rights

The influence of such developmental perspectives is also evident in legal discourses exploring children's rights. Thus, for example, O'Neill has argued that 'There are good reasons to think that paternalism may be much of what is ethically required in dealing with children, even if it is inadequate in dealings with mature and maturing minors' (1992, 40). Likewise Eekelaar; although clear in his view that children must be understood and treated as individuals and observing that 'General theories of what comprises children's best interests will not in themselves suffice as grounds for decision-making' (Eekelaar 1992, 229), also reflects the pervasive influence of the developmental model in stressing, as he does, the importance of children's rights in terms of the adult people they will become.

Freeman, however, arguing the need for a continuing search for the moral foundation of children's rights, points us towards the crucial importance of both equality and autonomy in any theory of rights, contending that 'To respect a child's autonomy is to treat that child as a person and as a rights holder' (Freeman 1992, 65). In so doing, he implicitly identifies one of the primary obstacles standing in the way of developments that might enable children to be seen as responsible bearers of rights: that is, the deep-seated influence of the developmental perspective that not only informs the views of so many adults but also underpins the myriad ways in which adult/child relations are structured, both in the family and in society more generally, which serve to construct children as unequal to and dependent upon adults.

Such debates help us to understand why the emergence of a children's rights discourse over the last two decades following the government's ratification of the UNCRC, to which increasing emphasis is apparently being given in various areas of public policy, is particularly problematic. It is because so much uncertainty remains about the foundations, content and nature of the rights of children, an uncertainty that is underpinned by, and is also an expression of, adult ambivalence about children's capacity to accept and manage responsibility. In other words, adult uncertainty and ambivalence about children's capacity to be morally and practically competent. In such a context, tensions inevitably arise if children begin to be constructed as bearers of rights, not least because of the need to establish the relationship between children's rights and those of adults in general, and parents in particular.

This tension is lessened if children's rights are constructed primarily in terms of protection or access to certain resources. However, rights to participation, which have been the focus of the most heated debate, are far more problematic since greater participation by children means a reduction in the power and influence of adults. It is clear from recent research, for example, that although

> Children concede authority to their parents in most instances, and rarely question their parents' protective, nurturing orientation towards them … trust in their parents is not an uncritical and unreasoned one however, and relies on parents being able to demonstrate their competence to make "good decisions". (Butler et al. 2005, 74)

It is arguable therefore that an increase in the influence of a children's rights perspective on the dynamics of family life could lead to increasingly critical appraisals of parents' competence by children.

Children's participation can also be taken as a proxy for, or be presented as, a symbolic representation of attempts to enhance their citizenship status, to which subject I will return later. But participation does not equal citizenship: this, I suggest, is rooted in the social, political and therefore *legal* identity that is only conferred upon adults as bearers of rights. Only the *citizen* can, as an autonomous legal entity, seek to assert these rights *on their own behalf*. The legal identity of children, however, means that in most respects, they are dependent upon the state or upon individual adults to assert, or to seek to secure or enforce their rights, whether they relate to welfare, protection, provision or participation. Therefore, fundamental to children's social and political position is their economic (and perceived developmental/emotional) dependence upon adult carers. As Cockburn has argued, 'Children today, despite a vociferous "children's rights" movement, still live in almost unprecedented dependence upon adults' (1998, 114).

This high level of dependence is also framed by a reluctance on the part of the state and public agencies to intervene in the private world of the family: it is in the family that children are located, and it is as members of the family that they are primarily understood; it is the family that provides the social and categorical umbrella under which, for so many purposes, children are subsumed; and it is the family that is their proper and rightful place, unless their adult carers are failing in their responsibility to do sufficient to ensure that their needs, which they have the *right* to be met, are indeed being met.

Underpinning this particular phenomenon is the belief, which finds expression in various ways, that since children are developmentally 'incomplete', they belong in the family and therefore they 'belong' to their parents, who are thus responsible for ensuring their needs are met and their rights enforced: dependence is thus equated with belonging. Viewed in this way, the relationship between children and responsibility becomes even more problematic since children cannot be constructed as being responsible (let alone as responsible as adults) and therefore as being entitled to the rights and responsibilities of citizenship, so long as they belong to and with the adults who are responsible for them.

Thus the prevailing political context, central to which is the notion of 'no rights without responsibilities' (Giddens 1998), is having to address two very different and conflicting perspectives – on the one hand, children as bearers of rights and on the other, children as incapable of carrying responsibility. The implications of this important ambiguity will first be considered through an examination of children's responsibility in the contrasting contexts of criminal and family law.

Children in Law

James and James have argued that law plays a central role in the social construction of childhood and that:

> the concept of "childhood" – however and wherever it finds local expression – can be theorised in terms of the cumulative history of social practices and policies about children, expressed as Law, which have arisen in response to the activities of children in their ongoing engagement with the adult world and adults' views about those activities. (2004, 50-1)

They therefore identify law as the key mechanism through which social structures (including the social space of childhood) and social practices (including the day-to-day interactions between adults and children that constitute the lived experience of childhood) are linked. This understanding is central to the concerns of this chapter since law not only incorporates the principles on which social structures are founded, it also 'provides the means through which relationships between the State and citizens are ordered and conducted' (James and James 2004, 51), which in this context includes the issues of rights and responsibilities.

It might therefore be argued that the way in which adults and children negotiate their relationships – including the social practices that underpin family life – informs the conceptualisation of responsibility, not only in the family but also in the community, and should therefore contribute to the legal understanding of responsibility. Viewed from this perspective, the absence of substantive children's rights in the context of family life – i.e. rights that they can seek to enforce on their own behalf – is entirely consistent with their absence of rights more generally.

We should also consider, however, the possibility that in practice, this process might also work the other way around. The way in which children's responsibilities are legally constructed is an expression of social policy, and the social practices that underpin and inform policy-making, and are thus a reflection of the prevailing cultural politics of childhood (see James and James 2004) in the UK. From this perspective, the reluctance on the part of the government seriously to embrace and implement the rights of children under the UNCRC is clearly reflected in the polices and laws it promulgates, and thus it is no surprise to find an absence of rights for children in the context of family life.

The construction of the criminal law relating to children is particularly instructive (Keating in this book). Youth crime became an increasingly prominent political issue in the wake of the killing of Jamie Bulger (James and Jenks 1996). Apart from the human tragedy reflected by this event, it rapidly became symbolic of much larger issues, coming to represent not only the betrayal of adult ideals about childhood but the loss of 'innocence', which adults associate with children, and the 'evil' of Jamie Bulger's young killers. In addition, however, it also came to symbolise the consequences of parental neglect – the harmful influence of 'video nasties' (why did their parents let them watch them?) and fears about the persistent young offenders (why didn't their parents control them?) – and provided public confirmation of the long-standing links made by criminologists between family background (and parenting) and juvenile crime (Gelsthorpe 1999).

The clearest reaction to the political concerns raised by these events was in the provisions of the Crime and Disorder Act 1998, in which a clear link was established between youth crime, education, and parenting and in which a clear determination to address offending behaviour, even by young children, was made evident. Thus, in spite of a recommendation by the UN Committee on the Rights of the Child (which monitors signatories' progress on implementing the provisions of the Convention) that 'serious consideration' should be given to raising the age of criminal responsibility throughout the UK (DOH 1999, Appendix A, para. 36), the Crime and Disorder Act 1998 went in the opposite direction. Perversely, it ended the limited protection that the long-established presumption of *doli incapax* gave to children between the ages of 10 and 14, which required the prosecution to prove that a child being prosecuted for an alleged offence knew what they were doing was wrong. Effectively, this reduced the age of criminal responsibility to the age of ten.

In addition, as the Home Office guidance on the Act made clear, 'tackling youth crime is likely to require action to deal with some of the underlying causes of youth offending, such as truancy and school exclusions' (Home Office 1998, para. 2.13). Thus, the provisions of the Crime and Disorder Act 1998 – for example, the anti-social behaviour order (s. 1), parenting programmes made available through parenting orders (s. 8), or voluntary attendance on such programmes as part of a less formal mechanism used by Youth Offending Teams for dealing with offending behaviour – provide clear evidence of an extension of explicit control over children, a process continued by subsequent criminal justice policies and legislation.

Importantly, however, such measures also represented the beginnings of a determined drive to reassert the importance of parental responsibility for and authority over children and to seek to enforce this. They embodied a view of young people as a threat that must be controlled, by targeting them with a range of interventions, in a range of sites, in order to 'encourage' them to accept their responsibilities to the community but without any commensurate acknowledgement of their rights (Scraton 1997). They also signified the development of a similar approach to parenting, underpinned by the desire to make parents take responsibility for their children's anti-social and offending behaviour (James and James 2001), clearly illustrating what Muncie has described as the 'major preoccupation with the family and anti-social behaviour [that] has dominated Labour's legislative initiatives' (Muncie 2004, 138).

Such developments are also partly a reflection of what Garland (2001) has referred to as a 'responsibilisation strategy', a process

> in which state agencies activate action by non-state organizations and actors. The intended result is an enhanced network of more or less directed, more or less informal crime control, complementing and extending the formal controls of the criminal justice state … state agencies now adopt a strategic relation to other forces of social control … to persuade them to act appropriately. (Garland 2001, 124-25)

In this process of 'responsibilisation', the community has become 'the all-purpose solution to every criminal justice problem' (Garland 2001, 123), a process that is firmly rooted in the communitarian underpinnings of Labour policies (Bridgeman in this book; Keating in this book). As has been pointed out elsewhere (James and James 2001), however, in his exposition of communitarian ideology, Etzioni notes that 'there is a fundamental contradiction between the society's needs for order and the individual's quests for autonomy' (1996, 3), a contradiction which can place obstacles in the path of realising a communitarian agenda.

In the particular case of children, this difficulty is compounded since communities also have a clear responsibility to provide socialising structures that will foster children's autonomy, as they move towards adulthood, as well as their responsibility and ability to conform. Part of the 'problem' of children is precisely that they are still in the process of acquiring values, norms, meanings and identities. By virtue of their youth, they do not yet have a history that is fully shared with the community: they therefore cannot be assumed to accept the values of the community, even whilst being encouraged to do so; and they must therefore also be helped, with increasing age, to explore and develop their own values and beliefs. Thus children not only have to be controlled, they have to be encouraged to explore their agency, their difference, and their individuality, but within the broader, common societal framework (James 1993).

These developments have, in turn, led to what Muncie has termed a process of 'family responsibilisation', to be realised through 'a series of programmes which seek either to remove young people from the street or to provide them and their parents with coercive "retraining"' (2004, 139). Throughout these, as Goldson (1999) observes, 'lies the objective of compelling parents to take "proper" care and control of their children, whilst by the age of 10 children will be held fully responsible themselves' (cited in Muncie 2004, 139). This illustrates a further ambiguity, however: by making parents and families responsible for the offending behaviour of their children – for example, through giving courts the power to bind parents over (Criminal Justice Act 1991) or to make them subject to Parenting Orders (Crime and Disorder Act 1998 – hereafter, CDA) – the implication is that, in spite of lowering the age of criminal responsibility to ten, children are in fact not really responsible, or rather perhaps that they are irresponsible in relation to such issues.

Such developments have also led to a renewed interest in restorative justice as part of the response to the offending of young people, an interest reflected in the provisions of the CDA 1998 and the Youth Justice and Criminal Evidence Act 1999, both of which introduced elements of restorative justice into the systems for dealing with youth offending (Gelsthorpe and Morris 2002). Thus, for example, youth offender panels, introduced by the 1999 Act to deal with first time young offenders subject to referral orders and empowered to order reparation, curfews or school attendance, include not only professional and community members, but the child and their parent or guardian. Similarly, family group conferences, involving meetings between the young offender, their family and the victim, have been adopted in some areas as a way of encouraging young offenders (and, by implication, their families) to take responsibility for their offending.

The government's commitment to this approach was confirmed by the Home Office in its departmental response to the Green Paper, *Every Child Matters* (Treasury 2003 – hereafter referred to as ECM), in which it stated its intention to introduce measures aimed at:

> more actively engaging fathers, making sure both parents generally come to court and ensuring courts consider a Parenting Order where they fail to attend and provide parenting programmes for young offenders who are parents. And within their current target of ensuring that restorative processes are used in 80 per cent of youth justice disposals by the end of 2004, the Youth Justice Board would also encourage appropriate use of family group conferencing. (Home Office 2003, para. 9)

Such approaches have been criticised by some for further eroding the rights of young offenders (see, for example, Fortin 2003). Whatever merits they might have in terms of youth justice, however, they also serve to relocate the young person firmly within the framework of the family. Not only does this make the family responsible for the offending of young people, it also establishes it firmly as part of Garland's enhanced network of informal crime control measures, as part of the responsibilisation of both the community and the family.

Early intervention through schemes such as *Sure Start* also implicitly addressed such concerns. Through its focus on improving the social responsibility of children in later life and reducing their social exclusion by providing support to parents in families with multiple disadvantages, early intervention is justified in ECM on grounds of prevention for those children and families 'at risk'. Such intervention has also been given to children as a 'right', subsequently justified in ECM by the notion of safeguarding their future development; responding to the UN Committee on the Rights of the Child in 1999, the government claimed that 'early intervention is an "entitlement" and that such pre-emptive policies contribute to "the *right* of children to develop responsibility for themselves" (UK Government, 1999 [*Convention on the Rights of the Child: Second Report to the UN Committee on the Rights of the Child by the United Kingdom*, London: HMSO]: para. 10.30.2, italics added)' (cited in Muncie 2004, 141). This linguistic sleight of hand, which some might regard as little more than sophistry, adopts the language of rights, ignoring that fact that this right is imposed on families and children who are targeted for such interventions in order to ensure that they do develop such responsibility.

Such linguistic and conceptual contortions are also evident in the field of family law, as illustrated by the judgment of Dame Elizabeth Butler-Sloss P in *Re W* (*Re W (Contact: Joining Child as Party)* [2001] EWCA Civ 1830). In this case a father had appealed against an order, made by a district judge, that there should be no contact between him and his son. This order had been made on the basis of the son's view and an independent social worker's report, following a deterioration in the arrangements for the son to have staying contact with his father. Allowing the father's appeal, the President argued that 'the child had a right to a relationship with his father, *even if he did not want it*, and his welfare demanded that efforts be expended to make contact possible' (Bridge, C. 'Contact' (Case Report) [2003] Fam Law 225, emphasis added).

This uniquely judicial construction of the concept of the child's right, which does not embrace the right of the child *not* to have contact with his father, demonstrates not only the readiness of courts to deny children's ability to behave and decide responsibly and to set aside their wishes and feelings, it also demonstrates the power of the language of welfare and how it can be used to deny children's agency. Family law is therefore also worthy of closer consideration in the context of this discussion, since issues of rights and responsibilities are also central to its construction of parents and children as social and legal actors. In addition, the process of family responsibilisation is also evident in the field of family law and, as Day Sclater argued in the context of her research on divorce, 'the governance of the family through the family may now have achieved unprecedented heights' (cited in Reece 2003, 196-7).

Of particular interest in terms of these arguments is the recent emphasis on increasing the use of mediation as a means of resolving disputes between parents over children when marriages and other parenting partnerships break down. *Every Day Matters* (CAFCASS 2005) is the CAFCASS response to ECM. It stresses early intervention and maximising the use of dispute resolution/mediation in private law cases; in this context it also makes clear that CAFCASS expects parents 'to resolve their dispute about the care of their child or children through a shared parenting approach and will facilitate this' (2005, para. 21). Such a policy illustrates Day Sclater's contention that increased emphasis is being placed on the self-governance of families.

Every Day Matters also provides a clear example of the extension of informal and passive control mechanisms for the regulation of children, since it emphasises the responsibility of adults for resolving such disputes and deciding about the future arrangements for children. Thus, para. 21 argues that 'The opportunities for casework under Section 7 of the Children Act 1989 should be maximised, with a move to a much more limited use of reports', while para. 34.1 *et seq.* also identifies reports as an area of practice that represents an inefficient use of professional time (CAFCASS 2005). However, nowhere in this section of *Every Day Matters* is there any consideration of the role of the welfare report in identifying and conveying a child's wishes and feelings to the court.

This shift of emphasis to dispute resolution is presented as being desirable in terms of achieving a better use of resources. One consequence of such a shift, however, is that the process of making decisions about children's futures in such cases will become even more firmly embedded in the adult-dominated process of negotiation and bargaining with and between parents that constitutes dispute resolution. This shift of emphasis means that, in spite of children's rights under the UNCRC to participate in such decisions, the large majority of children will find themselves even less directly involved in the process. As King (1987) has suggested, contested family proceedings are often less about child welfare and children's perspectives and more about

> the symbolic representation of parenthood, past, present and future. In other words, parents are arguing about, and judges and magistrates are determining, not the interests of the child, but rather the image that parents will take away from the proceedings about themselves and their relationship with their children. (1987, 6)

Thus, as James and James (1999) have argued, adults involved in such family proceedings (including Family Court Advisors) continue to work within the framework of a set of perspectives on childhood that, in effect, may still limit severely the extent to which children's voices can, in fact, be heard (see also, for example, Buchanan et al. 2001; O'Quigley 2000; Sawyer 1999; Smart et al. 2001).

The conclusion must then be that, in the context of family law, the changes that appear to have occurred, in relation to children's right to participate in decisions that affect their future, are more rhetorical than real. The adult world in general, and the courts in particular, have been slow to respond to what would be, in effect, a major shift of emphasis in the relationship between adults and children. This is partly because, as Sawyer has argued, 'In the family law paradigm, the idea of the child is dependent on the family; the child rarely has a positive separate legal identity' (2006, 1).

In contrast to mediation and as noted above, the preparation of a welfare report, whatever the limitations of these (see, for example, James et al. 2004; Sawyer 1999) does at least provide an opportunity, given the right approach to practice, for children's views to be ascertained and put directly to the court. There is no doubt that the financial constraints under which CAFCASS has to work are very real but in spite of the language in (and thinking behind) *Every Day Matters*, and the stress it places on the importance of children's participation and the child's right to be heard, the loss of this opportunity for children's participation is not acknowledged.

This points, once again, to the ambiguity surrounding adult, and particularly professional, attitudes towards children when it comes to the question of their right to participate in decisions affecting their future. This ambiguity and ambivalence was made clear by recent research into how welfare professionals in family law proceedings construct their understandings of childhood (James et al. 2004). In response to the specific question, 'What is the best thing about being a child?', it was clear that the Family Court Advisors interviewed saw this, in essence, as 'freedom from responsibility'. This was defined in a variety of different ways: no decisions to make; security, trust, being loved and cared for; being carefree, being able to play, spontaneity and innocence; and exploration and development. Implicit in these somewhat idyllic images of childhood was the notion of not knowing about or having to care about the realities of adult life.

In response to the question, 'What is the worst thing about being a child?', however, respondents did not identify the opposite of this: 'not being able to take responsibility'. Instead, they talked of 'the experience of powerlessness', in other words, the experience of not being *given* responsibility. This, too, was defined in various ways: lack of control; lack of information; not being listened to; dependence/loss of family; vulnerability. This lack of an exact opposite is of particular interest, however, since to have identified 'not being given responsibility' as the worst thing about childhood would have resulted in significant cognitive dissonance for practitioners, given the limited involvement given to children in family proceedings. Indeed, James et al. (2004) argued that such responses reflected the fact that children *cannot* be allowed to experience and exercise power/responsibility in such circumstances since for welfare professionals, the protection of children from the pressures of taking responsibility for determining what are regarded as adult issues is an important element of their practice.

This is reflected in the recent consultation paper (DCA 2006) on the separate representation of children in private law proceedings, a measure that would, if enthusiastically implemented, have gone some way to offset the growing and almost complete exclusion of children from divorce proceedings compared with public law proceedings. This proposes that party status, which would allow the direct involvement of the child who would then be able to instruct their own solicitor, 'is given to children only when there is a legal need to do so, for example where the child has evidence or a legal submission to make that cannot be given by another party' (2006, para. 23). This recommendation is made on the basis that 'party status and separate representation is not in the best interests of the child in all section 8 cases and can cause undue stress to the child' (2006, para. 21).

Such perspectives also, however, reflect another facet of adult beliefs about children more generally, which is evident in relation to health policies and practices and particularly so in relation to sexual health and education – that to give children responsibility (by allowing them to be informed, to participate in, and to decide or at least to influence decisions) involves their loss of innocence. Thus it might be argued that, apart from children's behaviour in public spaces, freedom from responsibility and innocence provide, in many respects, a *leitmotif* for childhood, at least in terms of adults' idealised images of children and childhood.

The courts have to some extent clarified this in the context of considering the balance between the rights of parents and those of children in *Gillick v Wisbech and West Norfolk Area Health Authority* [1986] AC 112, a judgment the principles of which were recently reaffirmed in *R (Axon) v Secretary of State for Health* [2006] EWHC 37 (Admin). The fact that the *Axon* case came to court, however, is worth noting, since it was a challenge to the guidance given by the Department of Health (2004) on the confidentiality to be afforded by medical practitioners to young people seeking advice on contraception and related issues. Its particular significance lies in the fact that it was a challenge made in spite of the decision in *Gillick*. As such, it clearly reflects the continuing unease of many parents about potentially being excluded from discussion of such matters by their children and the medical profession. Indeed, as Fortin argues:

> Overall, perhaps what is most interesting about the Axon case is that 6 years after the implementation of the Human Rights Act 1998, Sue Axon and her legal advisers thought that she had a good chance of succeeding in her application. This surely indicates their continuing reluctance to engage with the notion that children have rights under the European Convention which may actually override those of their parents. (Fortin 2006, 759)

This ambivalence about giving children responsibility also needs to be considered in the light of the shift apparently represented by the Children Act 1989, not only towards greater participation by children but also away from parental rights and towards parental responsibility (Bridgeman in this book). As Bainham (1999) argues, in this context parental responsibility is defined as a technical legal concept that includes the rights, duties, powers, responsibility and authority in relation to a child and their property: thus parental responsibility and rights are the same thing (Sawyer 2006). In this way, in spite of the apparently significant change of emphasis, in practice the Act perpetuates the importance of parental rights whilst telling us nothing about children's rights, or their responsibilities. Thus, not only the language but the concept of the rights of parents over their children continues to underpin conflict in divorce, even though as a result of the Act, such conflicts are now constructed and conducted in terms of the language of the child's best interests (James 2003).

It is also worth noting in passing that the responsibilisation of the family has now been extended to family law so that in cases of conflict over children, under the powers contained in s. 1 of the Children and Adoption Act 2006, the family law equivalent of the parenting order in criminal proceedings can be imposed in order to make parents behave responsibly. Even the title of the consultation document that preceded the Act (DCA 2005) is informative, juxtaposing, as it does, parents' responsibilities and children's needs.

The failure of the Children Act 1989 to effect a fundamental shift in the relationships between adults and children in the context of family law, and to lead to a meaningful increase in children's participation has been commented on by several observers (James et al. 2004; O'Quigley 2000; Roche 2002; Sawyer 1999), and as Roche has observed,

> Some of the disappointing jurisprudential and policy developments since the Children Act 1989 came into force testify to the fragility of the children's rights project. They serve to underscore the idea that it is a cultural project which necessarily straddles the public and the private sphere and requires adults to rethink their attitudes towards children and childhood. (Roche 2002, 74)

Even the landmark judgment in *Gillick* (*Gillick v Wisbech and West Norfolk Area Health Authority* [1986] AC 112), referred to above, has proved to have less of a lasting impact than had been expected, leading Freeman to argue after only ten years that:

> there are clear signs of a judicial resilement from *Gillick*, the Children Act (and I would add the Convention, if it were the case that the judiciary had ever got to grips with it). The most notorious instances are the cases overruling a child's refusal to consent to [medical] treatment. (Freeman 1998-99, 57)

Although the recent judgment in *Axon* has clearly served to reinforce that in *Gillick*, as Hall has argued,

> No matter how strongly the Children Act's promotion of parental "responsibilities" over "rights" is emphasised, proprietorial attitudes to parenthood persist. Conflicting social norms prevent parents from controlling their children's lives, while at the same time (for example the government's "Respect Agenda") requiring them to take responsibility for their children's moral education and to be accountable for their children's actions and decisions. (Hall 2006, 319)

Indeed, as Masson has pointedly observed, it can even be argued that those changes that have taken place can be seen as simply reactive and instrumental – that is, they are based not on a belief that children *should* be involved with the courts or that the legal process *should* change in order to accommodate children but simply 'on a need to comply with international standards' (2003, 80).

The way in which children are constructed and treated in law therefore highlights the ambivalent attitudes of the state and of adults towards children. The criminal law regards them as being responsible for their actions and, when they behave irresponsibly, seeks to return control of them to their parents, while family law regards them as being not capable of (or needing protection from) taking responsibility. By situating the child firmly in the institution of the family, both perspectives have the effect not only of masking or denying children's agency, their capacity for autonomous decision making, and their rights, but also of making parenting and the family synonymous (see also Qvortrup 1996). As James argues, this culturally-defined concept of 'parenting', made visible in social policy and family law,

> is essentially adult-centric and welfarist – that is, it is broadly conceived as something that is done to children, a view which takes little, if any, account of children's own

> subjectivity; and that from within this model of "parenting", children are regarded as being fundamentally vulnerable, dependent and in need of protection. (1999, 182)

and, if we add criminal law, in need of control. Therefore both perspectives fail to acknowledge the potential of children to behave responsibly and to accept responsibility for their decisions, albeit that the concerns of the criminal law are to control children and of family law to protect them.

As James argues, within such an adult-centric and welfarist model 'children can only be envisaged as passive recipients of "outcomes" of the process of parenting' (1999, 183), an envisioning that is clearly evident in the five outcomes for children articulated by the government in ECM. It is only where 'parenting' is under threat or subject to scrutiny by agencies external to the family, either through the divorce of parents or the offending of children, that the child's perspective or potential to act responsibly comes into consideration. In such situations the prevailing response, which is clearly evident in social policies and practices, is to reaffirm the centrality of 'parenting' by denying that the child can act responsibly: in the case of criminal law, this is achieved by declaring them to be culpable, their behaviour to be anti-social and therefore, by definition irresponsible and in need of parental control; and in the case of family law, by declaring them either to be in need of protection from the responsibility of making decisions, or to be incapable of making responsible decisions by reason of their immaturity. Thus, in the context of family proceedings (Family Proceedings Rules, S.I 1991, No. 1247 (L.20), Rule 9.1), the definition of a child as 'a person under disability' is telling: as Sawyer comments, 'their fundamental disability elides easily into abdication of their recognition as members of the polity' (2006, 13).

Children in Education

Such responsibilisation of parents and the increased embedding of children within the family, in a way that seeks to ignore their perspectives and subdue their agency, is also evident in relation to other areas, such as education. As part of a process of 'tightening the net' of social control, by increasing the monitoring and regulation of children's lives and the consequent reduction in the opportunities children and young people have to be relatively free from adult control (Valentine 1996), there has also been a narrowing of the gap between 'home' and 'school' as institutional sites of childhood. In this context too, as noted elsewhere (James and James 2001), political pronouncements have been made about the adequacy of some parents – criticism has been made of their failure to get their children out of bed in the morning, to ensure their children get to and stay at school, to ensure they do their homework, etc. As the Audit Commission argued, 'successful approaches to tackling truancy and disruptive behaviour often involve parents, who may condone absence from school' (1996, para. 34). Parent–school contracts, which emphasise parental responsibilities rather than children's rights, are part of a strategy for dealing with such issues whilst, simultaneously, the government has placed increasing pressure on parents to give children more help with their homework, further bridging the gap between home and school.

Such examples reflect what Wyness describes as the incorporation of parents into the 'broader project of educating children', by making them more responsible for what their children do (2000, 44). That children are seen as valuable human capital and as significant for the communitarian agenda is made explicit in the White Paper, *Excellence in Schools* (1997), which encourages 'parents and local communities [to be more] effectively involved in the education of children' (cited in Wyness 2000, 44). But in reasserting that parents and communities are responsible for children, the opportunities for children to act as autonomous social agents and to develop responsibility for themselves are correspondingly reduced.

Also central to Labour's commitment to develop a 'third way' in politics is the notion of citizenship and participation. Based on communitarian principles, this was heralded as bringing about a cultural and political revolution. It has become apparent, however, that in spite of children's participation rights under the UNCRC and the introduction of citizenship education in schools in 2002, embedded in the promised revolution lies the considerable risk that children's participation will actually be reduced through the reinforcement of ideologies of 'childhood' that emphasise children's marginality as citizens.

The expressed intention of citizenship education in English schools was to instruct children in the art of 'active citizenship' so that, literally and metaphorically, children will, as they grow up, come to know their place:

> Active Citizenship is based on the principle that young people learn to be effective citizens through meeting real needs in the school and wider community. Active learning in the community becomes part of the mainstream curriculum. Young people develop social responsibility and political literacy through becoming actively involved in the school and wider community. (Britton 2000, vii)

The citizenship curriculum was designed to cover, *inter alia*, 'the duties, responsibilities, rights and *development of pupils into citizens*' (DfEE 1998, 22, emphasis added). It is no small irony that this statement clearly identifies the place that children are expected to come to know: by confirming their non-citizenship and by highlighting the requirement that they *develop into* citizens, the government has made it clear that pupils are not viewed as citizens. Such policies reflect a particular representation of childhood, central to which is the belief that children lack responsibility. They also illustrate the role of 'policy as discourse' – i.e. the role of policy as a mechanism for agenda setting and for framing the context within which thinking about children and childhood takes place, and therefore in which the relationship between children and adults and citizenship is defined and understood. As Cockburn has argued, 'Children's exclusion from citizenship takes a variety of forms and can be clearly demonstrated by examining the ideological and normative representations of children' (1998, 105).

Thus it is simply not sufficient to *assert*, on moral or philosophical grounds, that children *are* citizens, or to believe that international agreements such as the UNCRC transform children into citizens by making them the bearers of rights, particularly if those rights cannot be exercised independently of adults. Such arguments must necessarily first influence the policy discourse before the relationship between adults and children, and their respective rights and responsibilities, can begin to be redefined.

Children as Citizens

In the light of this analysis, it is necessary to consider briefly the nature of the relationship between rights and citizenship and the proposition that, regardless of the rhetoric about children's rights, only the citizen can, as an autonomous legal entity, seek to assert their rights on their own behalf. The legal status and identity of children, as argued above, means that in most situations, they are entirely dependent upon the state or upon individual adults to assert, or to seek to secure or enforce their rights, whether these relate to welfare, protection, provision or participation. It follows therefore that children cannot be expected to be responsible, and therefore be entitled to the rights and responsibilities of citizenship, as long as adults are responsible for them.

To consider briefly the nature of citizenship a little more closely, Marshall's (1950) work is, for many, the starting point. He argued that citizenship comprises three elements – political, civil and social rights, each of which is embedded in different aspects of law. Each of these rights does, of course, imply the ability to participate – in voting or taking industrial action; in being able to speak freely or have recourse to the justice system; and in attending school or receiving the benefits or protection provided by the welfare system. Significantly, however, for Marshall citizenship was something that was conferred only on people with full membership of and participation in the community; for him, therefore, children were only citizens *in potentia*.

Although it might be argued therefore that children do have some aspects of citizenship conferred upon them, particularly with regard to their social citizenship and their rights to education or protection, it remains the case that such rights are mediated by and through adults. Indeed, they are not only mediated by adults, in practice they can only be exercised *by* adults *on behalf of* children. This raises an important question – what kind of rights are they that cannot be exercised independently by the individual holder of those rights, and what does this imply about the responsibility of the holder of those rights? So although having social citizenship rights may be a necessary part of citizenship, it is not sufficient to make the bearer of such rights into a full citizen, especially since rights such as the right to education are, as Qvortrup (2007 – forthcoming) has argued, not primarily a right to benefit an individual but a provision that is of benefit to society as a whole.

As Qvortrup has also pointed out, it might be argued that withholding full citizenship rights from children is defensible, particularly if one argues that:

> in a life long perspective there is … a certain justice in such a perspective, since [children] will sooner or later reach adulthood themselves and therefore, "if we treat the young one way and the old another, then over time, each person is treated both ways. The advantages (or disadvantages) of consistent differential treatment by age will equalize over time. (Daniels 1988, 88, cited in Qvortrup 2007 – forthcoming)

Whilst this argument may offer a seductive justification for denying children's citizenship, it must be pointed out that older people continue to be citizens, whatever their age, and unless they are declared to be legally (as opposed to socially) incompetent through failing mental health, they continue to be defined as both autonomous citizens and competent *legal* actors. As such, they are able to pursue their rights independent of others, since there are no legal impediments (except in very clearly defined circumstances) to prevent any adult citizen, no matter what their age, having recourse to law in order to seek to enforce their rights. For children, there are.

This raises some fundamental questions: are there any qualities of children and childhood that are, or should be, obstacles to children being full citizens, with all of the rights and responsibilities of citizens? If so, what are these? And are the notions of childhood and citizenship inherently incompatible, or is it simply that they are seen to be so by adults? As Hill and Tisdall (1997) have argued, a key issue in answering these questions is how childhood and citizenship are defined and this, as we know, is varyingly influenced by both the impact of the developmental paradigm and the specifics of different political and cultural settings.

As Hendrick reminds us, 'we should never forget the *political* nature of the social construction of childhood' (1997, 60, emphasis in original) and in this context, ECM provides an important insight into how childhood is currently being defined discursively through policy, since it embraces a broad swathe of children's policies and services and therefore offers a clear reflection of government thinking. Central to the context in which the policies embodied in ECM have been framed is the emergence of the 'social investment state' and its construction of children as citizen-workers of the future (Lister 2003) as opposed to children with rights in the present. By positioning them as being conditionally and generically 'in need', children require 'safeguarding' in the present against the 'risks' posed by potential long-term adverse outcomes. ECM therefore sets out to promote a raft of policies that are, in effect, creating a 'national childhood' (Hendrick 1997) that revolves around full participation in education in order to ensure future participation in the labour market, the community and the polity.

It represents the culmination of two decades of social policy that have evolved progressively to render children as the passive recipients of the educational process, rather than as active participants in it. Despite the government's liberal use of the rhetoric of children's rights and their apparent ideological commitment to children's participation, ECM reveals a rather different normative and ideological representation of children. Indeed, it is through the ever-closer regulation of children and childhood and their instruction in the context of citizenship education about how to be 'proper children', in institutions that they are under compulsion to attend, that a vision of a national childhood has been progressively constructed over the last 20 years. With a few exceptions, rather than creating meaningful opportunities for children to learn through 'doing' citizenship and 'being' citizens in the sense of acting as political entities – through, for example, the exercise of rights and participation in the running of schools – the emphasis on *teaching* them to be citizens has effectively denied them those very rights of participative citizenship.

Conclusion

Central to any discussion of the relationship between responsibility, law and the family in Britain at the beginning of the 21st century is the changing relationship between the state, the community and the individual, a relationship that reflects changing political philosophies that can be charted through the changes in social policy and its expression in law (Bridgeman in this book; Keating in this book). In this context, the communitarian ideology that underpins the thinking of 'New' Labour is of crucial importance since, 'In contrast with the Hobbesian version of the social contract that defined the relationship between the individual and the state, the Third Way defines the relationship between the individual and the community' (James and James 2001, 224).

The particular significance of this as it relates to the traditional view of children is that they are of only categorical significance to the state – i.e. they exist as a social category and as such, might be the target of various policies – since they are not members of the polity and are therefore seen and treated as non-citizens, without rights. At the level of the relationship between the individual and the community, however, children are much more visible as social actors and thus much more significant. As a consequence of the shift of focus effected by the Third Way, therefore, the relationship between children and the community has become much more visible, both conceptually and in reality – as Moore and Statham observe, 'most published evidence indicates that young people "hanging around" is actually one of the most significant problems to communities, as perceived by adults' (2006, 469). In the process, therefore, the relationship between generations has become more problematic.

The increasing focus on and responsibilisation of the community has also resulted in greater attention being given to the family and to parents, when their children are seen to be problematic to other adults in the community. This is inevitable since parents are seen to be responsible *for* their children and thus responsible *to* the community for their children's misbehaviour. There has thus also been an increasing responsibilisation of the family.

Much less is known about what happens in the context of the privatised world of the family when this is seen to be functioning properly and responsible parents are ensuring the responsible behaviour of their children. What this new perspective omits, however, is any account of or reference to the views and understandings of children and how they understand their rights and responsibilities. As outlined above, however, what research has clearly demonstrated is children's moral competence and their ability, if given the opportunity and therefore, arguably, if given the rights, to accept and behave with much higher levels of responsibility than their enforced dependence on adults currently allows.

Children's sense of moral agency and awareness is clearly evident from recent research with '"ordinary" children drawn from ordinary communities' (Butler et al. 2005). As the researchers argue, 'it is important to recognise the importance that children's claims to "fairness" have in the context of the limited forms of democracy practiced [sic] by families' (Butler et al. 2005, 75): because of their relative powerlessness in the absence of rights, 'fair process (if not a fair outcome) is important to children and should be understood as a legitimate moral claim on the actions of adults, especially where adults seek to engage children in formal participatory processes' (2005, 78).

This is a message that the adult world must take to heart, since much of what is currently happening to children in terms of the social policies and social practices that are being developed towards them seems likely to fail the test of fairness. If this is, indeed, the case, the lessons that children will draw about the nature of politics and adult power do not bode well for their developing perception and understanding of the relationship between the state and citizens, and politicians will continue to be puzzled by and worry about the declining levels of political participation by young people.

The mantra of 'no rights without responsibilities' has come to symbolise the approach of the government to the relationship between the individual, the state and the community. Whilst its meaning is fairly well understood in relation to adults, what, precisely, it means in relation to children and young people remains far from clear. Indeed, given the reality of the currently parlous state of children's rights in Britain, it is necessary to pose some pointed questions: to what extent can and should this apply to children as opposed to adults? What is the nature of the social contract between children, the state and the community? And what rights do responsible children have? Until we are much clearer about such issues and about the rights children have, it is difficult to be clear what responsibilities they should have and the extent to which these are commensurate with their rights.

References

Audit Commission (1996), *Misspent Youth: Young People and Crime: Summary* (Audit Commission: London).

Bainham, A. (1999), 'Parentage, Parenthood and Parental Responsibility: Subtle, Elusive Yet Important Distinctions' in Bainham, A., Day Sclater, S. and Richards M. (eds), *What is a Parent?* (Oxford: Hart).

Britton, F. (2000), *Active Citizenship: A Teaching Tool Kit* (London: Hodder and Staughton).

Buchanan, A., Hunt, J., Bretherton, H. and Bream, V. (2001), *Families in Conflict* (Bristol: Policy Press).

Butler, I., Robinson, M., and Scanlan, L. (2005), *Children and Decision Making* (London/York: NCB/JRF).

Children and Family Court Advisory and Support Service (2005), *Every Day Matters: New Directions for CAFCASS.* A Consultation paper on a new professional and organisational strategy (London: CAFCASS).

Cockburn, T. (1998), 'Children and Citizenship in Britain', *Childhood* 5:1, 99-117.

Department for Education and Employment (1997), *Excellence in Schools* (London: HMSO).

Department for Education and Employment (1998), *Education for Citizenship and the Teaching of Democracy in Schools* (London: TSO).

Department of Constitutional Affairs (2005), *Parental Separation: Children's Needs and Parent's Responsibilities, Next Steps* (London: TSO).
Department of Constitutional Affairs (2006), *Separate Representation of Children: Consultation to Inform the Content of New Court Rules* (London: DCA).
Department of Health (1999), *United Nations Convention on the Rights of the Child: Second Report to the UN Committee on the Rights of the Child by the United Kingdom, 1999* (London: TSO).
Department of Health (2004), *Best Practice Guidance for Doctors and other Health Professionals on the Provision of Advice and Treatment to Young People under 16 on Contraception, Sexual and Reproductive Health* (London: TSO).
Eekelaar, J. (1992), 'The Importance of Thinking that Children Have Rights' in Alston, P., Parker, S. and Seymour, J. (eds), *Children, Rights and the Law* (Oxford: Clarendon).
Etzioni, A. (1996), 'The Responsive Community: A Communitarian Perspective', *American Sociological Review* 61, 1-11.
Fortin, J. (2003), *Children's Rights and the Developing Law* (2nd edition) (London: LexisNexis UK).
Fortin, J. (2006), 'Children's Rights – Substance or Spin?', *Family Law* 36, 757–60.
Freeman, M. (1992), 'Taking Children's Rights More Seriously' in Alston, P., Parker, S. and Seymour, J. (eds), *Children, Rights and the Law* (Oxford: Clarendon).
Freeman, M. (1998-1999), 'The Right to be Heard', *Adoption and Fostering* 22:4, 50-9.
Garland, D. (2001), *The Culture of Control* (Oxford: Oxford University Press).
Gelsthorpe, L. (1999), 'Youth Crime and Parental Responsibility' in Bainham, A., Day Sclater, S. and Richards, M. (eds), *What is a Parent?* (Oxford: Hart).
Gelsthorpe, L. and Morris, A. (2002), 'Restorative Youth Justice: The Last Vestiges of Welfare?' in Muncie, J., Hughes, G. and McLaughlin, E. (eds), *Youth Justice: Critical Readings* (London: Open University/Sage).
Giddens, A. (1998), *The Third Way: The Renewal of Social Democracy* (Cambridge: Polity).
Gilligan, C. (1982), *In a Different Voice: Psychological Theory and Women's Development* (Cambridge, MA: Harvard University Press).
Greene, S. (1999), 'Old Themes, New Directions' in Woodhead, M., Faulkner, D. and Littleton, K. (eds), *Making Sense of Social Development* (London: Routledge).
Hall, A. (2006), 'Children's Rights, Parents' Wishes and the State: The Medical Treatment of Children', *Family Law* 36, 317-19.
Hendrick, H. (1997), 'Constructions and Reconstructions of British Childhood: An Interpretive Survey, 1800 to the Present' in James, A. and Prout, A. (eds), *Constructing and Reconstructing Childhood: Contemporary Issues in the Sociological Study of Childhood* (2nd edition) (London: Falmer).
Hill, M. and Tisdall, K. (1997), *Children and Society* (London: Longman).
Home Office (1998), *Guidance on Statutory Crime and Disorder Partnerships: Crime and Disorder Act 1998* (London: Home Office Communication Directorate).
Home Office (2003), *Youth Justice – The Next Steps* (London: Home Office).

James, A. (1993), *Childhood Identities* (Edinburgh: Edinburgh University Press).

James, A. (1999), 'Parents: A Children's Perspective' in Bainham, A., Day Sclater, S. and Richards, M. (eds), *What is a Parent?* (Oxford: Hart).

James, A. and James, A.L. (2004), *Constructing Childhood: Theory, Policy and Social Practice* (London: Palgrave Macmillan).

James, A. and Jenks, C. (1996), 'Public Perceptions of Childhood Criminality', *British Journal of Sociology* 47:2, 315-31.

James, A.L. (2003), 'Squaring the Circle – The Social, Legal and Welfare Organisation of Contact' in Bainham, A., Lindley, B., Richards, M. and Trinder, L. (eds), *Parent–Child Relationships and Contact* (Oxford: Hart Publishing).

James, A.L. and James, A. (1999), 'Pump Up the Volume: Listening to Children in Separation and Divorce', *Childhood* 6:2, 189-206.

James, A.L. and James, A. (2001), 'Tightening the Net: Children, Community and Control', *British Journal of Sociology* 52:2, 211-28.

James, A.L., James A. and McNamee, S. (2004), 'Turn Down the Volume? – Not Hearing Children in Family Proceedings', *Child and Family Law Quarterly* 16:2, 189-202.

James, A., Jenks, C. and Prout, A. (1998), *Theorising Childhood* (Cambridge: Polity Press).

King, M. (1987), 'Playing the Symbols – Custody and the Law Commission', *Family Law* 17, cited in G. Davis (1998), 'What Works in Family Court Welfare', *Probation Journal* 45:2, 87-91.

Lansdown, G. (2005), *The Evolving Capacities of the Child* (Florence: UNICEF Innocenti Research Centre/Save the Children).

Lister, R. (2003), 'Investing in the Citizen-workers of the Future: Transformations in Citizenship and the State under New Labour', *Social Policy and Administration* 37:5, 427-43.

Marshall, T.H. (1950), *Citizenship and Social Change* (London: Pluto).

Masson, J. (2003), 'Paternalism, Participation and Placation: Young People's Experiences of Representation in Child Protection Proceedings in England and Wales' in Dewar, J. and Parker, S. (eds), *Family Law* (Oxford: Hart).

Mayall, B. (2002), *Towards a Sociology for Childhood: Thinking from Children's Lives* (Buckingham: Open University Press).

Moore, S. and Statham, E. (2006), 'Can Intergenerational Practice Offer a Way of Limiting Anti-social Behaviour and Fear of Crime?', *The Howard Journal* 45:5, 468-84.

Muncie, J. (2004), 'Youth Justice: Responsibility and Rights' in Roche, J., Tucker, S., Thomson, R. and R. Flynn, R. (eds), *Youth in Society* (2nd edition) (London: Sage).

O'Quigley, A. (2000), *Listening to Children's Views: The Findings and Recommendations of Recent Research* (York: Joseph Rowntree Foundation).

O'Neill, O. (1992), 'Children's Rights and Children's Lives' in Alston, P., Parker, S. and Seymour, J. (eds), *Children, Rights and the Law* (Oxford, Clarendon).

Piaget, J. (1950), *The Psychology of Intelligence* (London: Routledge).

Qvortrup, J. (1996), 'Foreword' in Brannen, J. and O'Brien, M. (eds), *Children in Families* (London: Falmer).

Qvortrup, J. (2007 – forthcoming), 'Childhood in the Welfare State' in James, A. and James, A.L. (eds), *European Childhoods* (Basingstoke: Palgrave Macmillan).

Reece, H. (2003), *Divorcing Responsibly* (Oxford, Hart).

Roche, J. (2002), 'The Children Act 1989 and Children's Rights: A Critical Reassessment' in Franklin, B. (ed.), *The New Handbook of Children's Rights: Comparative Policy and Practice* (London: Routledge).

Sawyer, C. (1999), *Rules, Roles and Relationships: The Structure and Function of Child Representation and Welfare within Family Proceedings* (Oxford: Centre for Socio-Legal Studies).

Sawyer, C. (2006), 'The Child is not a Person: Family Law and Other Legal Cultures', *Journal of Social Welfare and Family Law* 28:1, 1-14.

Scraton, P. (ed.) (1997), *Childhood in 'Crisis'* (London: UCL Press).

Smart, C., Neale, B. and Wade, A. (2001), *The Changing Experience of Childhood* (Cambridge: Polity).

Treasury (2003), *Every Child Matters*, Cm 5860 (London: TSO).

Valentine, G. (1996), 'Children Should be Seen and Not Heard? The Role of Children in Public Space', *Urban Geography* 17:3, 205-20.

Woodhead, M. (1999), 'Learning Relationships with Children: Conceptual, Methodological and Ethical Issues', paper presented at the 'Sites of Learning' Conference, University of Hull, 14-16 September 1999.

Woodhead, M., Faulkner, D, and Littleton, K. (eds) (1999), *Making Sense of Social Development* (London: Routledge).

Wyness, M. (2000), *Contesting Childhood* (London: Falmer Press).

PART 3
Shifting Conceptions of Family Responsibilities

Chapter 9

Engaging Fathers? Responsibility, Law and the 'Problem of Fatherhood'

Richard Collier[1]

Introduction

> What has been missing from policy and reform discussions thus far is a debate about the nature of fatherhood and the transformation of the role of the father in response to changing expectations, norms and practices. How does the desire for gender neutrality and the ideal of egalitarianism play a role in the creation of a new set of norms for fatherhood? (Fineman 2004, 195)

There has occurred in recent years a growing debate about the 'future of fatherhood', an apparent heightening of social concern about the scope of fathers' responsibilities and rights.[2] Whether in relation to married or unmarried, cohabiting or separated, biological or 'social' fathers, law has an important role in these discussions, serving as a focal point for political frustrations, playing a central role in mediating disputes and operating as a symbolic 'authorised' discourse that provides an official, state-sanctioned account of what fathers' rights and responsibilities should be. For some, of course, what is at stake in these contestations is no less than the future of the 'family' itself (Blakenhorn 1995; David 1998; Duncan Smith 2007). Against this backdrop, a growing body of socio-legal scholarship, drawing on developments in both legal and social theory, has sought to explore diverse aspects of the way fathers have been understood, constructed and regulated within law (Collier and Sheldon 2008; Dowd 2000). Complementing a now well-established literature in the fields of sociology and social policy, history, psychology, gender and family studies (see, for example, Dienhart 1998; Doucet 2006; Lewis 2000; Lupton and Barclay 1997; Rosh White 1994), and dealing with diverse aspects of the role of fathers and the

---

1 I am grateful to Hart Publications for permission to reproduce material in this chapter drawing on R. Collier and S. Sheldon (2008), *Fragmenting Fatherhood: A Socio-Legal Study* (Oxford: Hart). I would like to acknowledge the support of the British Academy (BATOB0607/SG42903) and, in particular, thank Sally Sheldon, with whom the ideas discussed in this chapter have been developed.

2 Whilst the issue of how to promote ongoing, 'healthy' relationships between men and children is a subject with a long history, the question of what is happening *to* contemporary fatherhood has become a ubiquitous feature of a range of cultural artefacts. It is, I shall suggest in this chapter, central to conversations about the shifting parameters of the (heterosexual) family and the scope of parental responsibilities in law.

idea of fatherhood, this work explores the contours of the 'father-figure' (McKee and O'Brien 1982) as drawn in law and social policy. Reflecting the increased political and cultural prominence of fathers' rights groups and a 'fathers' rights movement' internationally (Collier 2005; Collier and Sheldon 2006; Smart 2004), the position of the separated father, in particular, has received critical attention (see further Wilson 2006).

The focus of this chapter concerns, in contrast, some recent developments relating to men's responsibilities as fathers in the context of subsisting marital relationships. I wish to consider how paternal responsibility has emerged as a distinctive *kind* of problem to be addressed by law in this specific context. Marriage has long played a central role in how law has sought to attach men to their children (Lind in this book). It remains a legal ideal lauded by politicians from across the political spectrum as the best possible framework in which to raise children. However, a complex amalgam of economic, cultural, technological and political change, as well as shifts in the nature of law's governance itself (Dewar 1998; van Krieken 2005; Reece 2003), have served to challenge the possibility of relying on marriage as a way of grounding legal fatherhood and the rights and responsibilities which have traditionally accompanied it. In what follows I will chart a significant shift in how law has approached the responsibilities of fathers within marriage.[3] This has involved, more specifically, a move away from the idea that a 'good father' need be only a remote disciplinarian and breadwinner towards an increased expectation that men will be 'engaged', 'hands-on' fathers, parents who will 'be there' for their children. There has occurred, more recently, a growing concern at a policy level to promote what has been termed 'father inclusive' practice in the delivery of services (Bartlett et al. 2007; Burgess and Bartlett 2004), a development that I suggest is further redrawing social and legal understandings of what it means to be a 'father' and what responsibilities and obligations should accrue to that status.

The structure of the argument is as follows. In section one I briefly trace the development of family law and policy from a position where men held exclusive rights over their children to one in which, by the mid-20th century, fathers had been reconstituted primarily as familial 'breadwinners'. During this period, as women displace men as legal guardians, the question of what being a responsible father entails is reframed primarily, although by no means entirely, by reference to the economic link between a man and his family. I proceed, in section two, to explore how a move from legal rights to responsibilities has taken a further turn in recent years. Encapsulated in the idea of the 'new fatherhood', contemporary fathers are now widely expected to have, and to desire, a closer, more emotionally involved and nurturing relationship with their children. This shift has been described as a move from 'cash to care' in how fatherhood is now positioned across a number of areas of law and policy (Hobson 2002). British fathers 'are now expected to be accessible and nurturing as well as economically supportive to their children. They are, it is

3 This does not mean, of course, that policy debates discussed in this chapter do not relate to other categories of fathers (for example, non-marital and separated dads). See further Collier and Sheldon 2008.

suggested, increasingly self-conscious about juggling conflicts between looking after children and having a job' (O'Brien 2004).

In section three I consider key assumptions underscoring these debates and the extent to which understandings of fathers' responsibilities have been marked by what is in fact both continuity and change. Dealing with different discourses around a distinctive 'problem of men' (Scourfield and Drakeford 2002) in debates around fatherhood has, I will suggest, become a key feature of contestations around parental responsibility and the changing nature of family life. Unpacking the conceptual basis of these shifts around fathers' responsibilities in law, however, reveals diverse, and frequently contradictory, beliefs about the gendered nature of divisions of labour, paid employment, sexualities, class and masculinities. Recent developments raise questions not just about the 'gap' between *cultures* of change in fatherhood and understandings of fatherhood as a social *practice*, but also about the issue of what can, and cannot, be expected from law reform in seeking to change parenting practices.

(Re)Constructing Fatherhood: From Rights to Responsibility

At common law, married fathers were invested with sole rights of custody and control over their legitimate children.[4] By the early 19th century inroads had been made into this model of paternal rights and a move away from the 'empire of the father' had begun (Diduck and Kaganas 2006, 305; Maidment 1984). The law at this time was not so much concerned with the care of children, still less with what the practical role of fathers might be in practice. Rather, fathers' rights were seen as symbolic, the embodiment of patriarchal authority, a man's control within, and over, his family interlinked to the maintenance of social order and the orderly transmission of property. Whilst equitable doctrines developed by the Court of Chancery subsequently sought to lessen the harshness of the common law rules, divorce remained severely restricted and permeated by sexual double standards. This understanding of fathers' responsibilities reflected the dominant attitudes of the period towards family, parenting, gender and class (Holcombe 1983).

During the latter part of the 19th century and first half of the 20th, significant reforms were introduced which enabled mothers to seek custody and access to their children, albeit in prescribed circumstances.[5] The Guardianship of Infants Act (1925), in particular, provided that the court, in deciding questions relating to the custody or upbringing of a child, should henceforth have regard to the welfare of the child as the 'first and paramount consideration' (Cretney 1996; Eekelaar 2006, 140-4). This 'paramountcy principle' continues to inform child law to the present

4 Writing in the eighteenth century, Blackstone had declared that it was only at the time when a child reaches the age of 21, that the 'empire of the father ... gives place to the empire of reason'. The mother, in contrast, 'is entitled to no power, but only to reverence and respect': Blackstone's *Commentaries on the Law of England*, 1765 Vol. 1: 453; *Re Agar Ellis* (1883), 24 Ch D 317, per Bowen LJ at 338.

5 For example, Custody of Infants Act 1839; Divorce and Matrimonial Causes Act 1857; Custody of Infants Act 1873; Guardianship of Infants Act 1886.

day, now enshrined in the 1989 Children Act[6] as amended and further elaborated as a result of the Human Rights Act 1998 (Choudhry and Fenwick 2005; Fenwick 2004). For the purposes of this chapter, and noting the indeterminate nature of the welfare principle itself (Reece 1996), it is necessary to look more closely at how, throughout this period of apparently egalitarian and progressive reform, ideas about fathers and fatherhood were reconstructed in some far-reaching ways.

Law, culture and fatherhood

In approaching fathers' responsibilities in law it is important to note the potential disjuncture between the ideas about parenting contained in law and the diverse material realities of fathering practice. It cannot be assumed, for example, that a model of paternal responsibility underscored by the 'separate spheres' ideology, as above, was ever diffused throughout the social order (Richards 1987, 27). However culturally resonant and embedded in law these ideals may have been in the late 19th century, they did not necessarily map to the social experience of all men and women. Class, geographical (for example, rural/urban), religious and ethnic differences have divested the legal authority of fathers in different ways and at different moments (Gillis 1996; Mangan and Walvin 1987; Tosh 1999). This does not mean that to talk of shifting representations of fathers' responsibilities within statute and case law has no value however. Legal changes tell us much about social attitudes to parenthood, childhood and child welfare, equality and power (see further Boyd 2004). Legal constructions of the rights, obligations and responsibilities of fathers must, however, be socially, economically and politically located within the context of broader and longer-term changes in family structures, adult/child relations, gender configurations and forms of governance (van Krieken 2001; 2005). The shifts that occurred around fatherhood are the product of a complex interweaving and inter-discursive nexus of law, medicine, psychology, religion and science, all of which (in different ways) are implicated in the production of normative beliefs about 'family life', children and childhood, health and illness, sexuality, social class, 'good' parenting and so forth.

Importantly, during the shift within the 20th century 'from rights to responsibilities' there emerges a new way of talking about (gendered) parenthood in which, while mothers are subject to levels of surveillance, scrutiny and regulation by laws in ways that fathers were not (Boyd 2003; Diduck 1998; Fineman and Karpin 1995; Silva 1996), ideas about the married 'family man' and the 'good' father are also transformed. It is to this reconstruction of paternal responsibility and reassessment of the responsibilities of fathers in the context of a model of the family as an egalitarian, complementary household unit that I now turn.

6 S. 1(1) of the Children Act 1989 provides that when a court determines any question with respect to a range of circumstances concerning children 'the child's welfare shall be the court's paramount consideration'.

Making the modern father: The 'family man' as breadwinner

By the mid-20th century the assumption that households would be organised on a sexual division of labour between (male) primary breadwinner and (female) childrearer was entrenched across a range of areas of law and policy. At the macro-level, beliefs about fathers as breadwinners were embedded in the model of the 'male wage' and the idea of 'providing for the family', binding men as financial providers to an economic system which structured household economies via the allocation to one family member (usually the man) the role of primary wage earner (Land 1980). Post-war debates about the level, structure and distribution of wages, taxes and welfare benefits reflected this idea that men and women had differential primary commitments towards their families. Sociological research, showing that fathering practices in the UK were themselves contingent on socio-economic background and region, further reflected the extent to which these divisions had become embedded in household economies and prevailing cultural norms (e.g. Young and Wilmott 1957; 1973). During the 1950s and 1960s, the assumption that a father's primary family responsibilities lay as breadwinner was reproduced extensively within the domains of leisure, advertising and the media (Segal 1990, 1). The texts of law (cases, statutes) of this period are, unsurprisingly, replete with assumptions about the 'natural' familial roles and responsibilities of men and women, whether it be in relation to child care, (pre-989) child custody (Boyd 2003; Smart and Sevenhuijsen 1989), ideas about domestic labour (Auchmuty 2007), paid employment or the respective positions of mothers and fathers within the workplace and the home (Atkins and Hoggett 1984; Smart 1984).

Understandings of fathers' familial responsibilities, as well as of normative paternal masculinities, are here mobilised primarily, if not exclusively, as an economic resource (Connell 1987, 106), a theme reflected perhaps most clearly in the legal history of the obligation to maintain (see further Finer and McGregor 1974; Wikeley 2006). Judges have subsequently sought to introduce notions of fairness into the legal recognition of domestic labour and child care as work of equal significance to paid employment, notably through the development of principles of equity (Diduck 2001; Eekelaar 2006, 144-5). However, fathers' primary commitments to work have been seen as largely, if not entirely, precluding extensive participation within child care and domestic labour (Collier 2001a; 2001b). It is to significant changes in relation to these ideas of the father as responsible 'family man' (Coltrane 1996) that I now turn.

Fragmenting the 'Family Man': Reshaping Paternal Responsibility

Fathers have been constituted as a desirable presence within families via reference to three key themes, each of which draws on distinctive ideas about men's responsibilities that are being challenged, undermined and fragmented in recent years (see further Collier and Sheldon 2008). These are, first, beliefs about fathers as heterosexual (the sexual father); second, about the father as family breadwinner (the worker father, as above); and, third, around the idea of the father as a rather 'distant' figure of authority and prerogative within the household (the father as patriarch). Each is subject to significant challenge as a result of political, social, economic and cultural shifts in the context, importantly, of legal frameworks marked by a commitment to formal equality and gender neutrality (Boyd 1989; 2003; Fineman 1991; 1995; 2000). At the same time a profound rethinking of the place of the father in child welfare and development, linked to a growing research base challenging 'deficit' perspectives on fathering (Hawkins and Dollahite 1997), informs the emergence of social care agendas that have, over the past decade especially, redrawn the parameters of fathers' responsibilities.

The heterosexual father

First, ideas about fathers' responsibilities in law are historically enmeshed with beliefs about the normative nature of heterosexuality (Carabine 1996; Collier 2000). Legal marriage, the mechanism by which law has historically sought to attach men to children, has been, and remains, an institution by statute open only to men and women (s. 11 Matrimonial Causes Act 1973). However, social, demographic, cultural and technological change has undermined the model of responsibility which, in the past, legally bound fathers to families in law. Marriage is no longer the sole vehicle used in family law to safeguard (legal) fatherhood, and a range of other legal concepts and techniques are now used to attach men to children. The recognition in law of civil partnerships (Mallender and Rayson 2006) and of the social parent within same-sex households,[7] meanwhile, alongside an expansion of the remit of paternal responsibility linked to growing numbers of non-marital births (Barlow et al. 2005, 1, 2) (what has been seen as a 'rolling out' of paternal responsibility),[8] further fragments hetero-normative understandings of family life and challenges the place of marriage as the primary determinant of paternal rights. These developments generate an increased emphasis within law on biological fatherhood and the biological and relational bonds between parent and child, rather than the traditional family based on marriage between a man and a woman.

The worker father

Second, as we saw above, fatherhood has historically been constructed in law via reference to sexual divisions and gendered assumptions, not least about paternal masculinity, that have underpinned the cultural legitimacy of men's disengagement from child care and domestic labour (Collier 1995, 213-4). This model of the father as breadwinner, however, is challenged by demographic and relational shifts

---

7 Pre-dating the 2004 Act note *Fitzpatrick v Sterling Housing Association* [2000] 1 FLR 21; *Ghaidan v Godin-Mendoza* (2004), 2 AC 557. Note *Wilkinson v Kitzinger* [2006] EWHC 2022 *Fam* 121.

8 The increased legal recognition of the relationships of unmarried cohabitants and related developments in case law, policy and legal practice (for example, in the field of adoption), has further diminished the former primacy of the marriage tie between husband and wife in determining legal paternity. See Collier and Sheldon 2008, Ch. 6.

around the contours of intimacy and 'personal life' (Giddens 1992; Jamieson 1998; Smart 2007). Shifting patterns of economic labour market participation on the part of women and men (Crompton 1999; EOC 2007), in particular, have driven the emergence of policy agendas seeking to 'bring fathers in the frame' (O'Brien 2004). A political concern to encourage and facilitate the employment of women, and tackle the social pressures resulting from their increased participation in the workforce, is seen as disturbing a model of fathers' responsibilities based on these kinds of assumptions about men's subjective and material disengagement from child care and domestic labour.

It is against this backdrop that men's commitment to paid employment and understandings of its consequences for families and individuals emerges as a key political and policy issue and, more specifically, as an obstacle to promoting both women's employment and functional, 'balanced' family life within the new globalised economy (as evident, notably, in the debate about 'work–life balance'). Accordingly, it is argued, what are required are legal reforms directed at providing a more 'modern' infrastructure of economic and social support that might, in turn, promote the caring commitments of *both* mothers and fathers within, and beyond, families (EOC 2003; Hatten et al. 2002; Warin et al. 1999). This has taken the form of a heightened policy debate about how law might promote the idea of the 'involved father' in family life, via policies aimed at 'engaging fathers' in ways which transcend the traditional economic nexus between men and families (see further below).

The father as (distant) patriarch

Third, and bound up with each of the above, a social shift has occurred in understandings of normative paternal masculinities, of what now constitutes a 'good father' and 'family man'. The interlinking in economic responsibility with ideas of male authority and prerogative has, in a sense, been the 'hidden history' of fatherhood in law. As Hearn observes, 'the social and historical meaning of fatherhood includes the treatment of children as possessions … even a man who is a "nice" father carries with him the possibility of becoming a "nasty" or violent one' (Hearn 1990, 76). Concerns about fatherhood, risk and violence remain central to policy debates across many areas of law, not least in the area of post-separation contact. The dualism between the 'good dad/bad dad' (Furstenberg 1988) continues, moreover, to be mediated by assumptions about class, race, ethnicity and sexuality, by ideas about 'safe' and 'dangerous' masculinities (Collier 2003). At the same time, however, not only are ideas of what constitutes socially 'acceptable' male behaviour subject to considerable change, research across disciplines is contributing to the increasingly held view at a political and policy level that fathers have a significant, positive contribution to make to families, one which transcends the traditional role of provider (Flouri 2005; Hawkins and Dollahite 1997; Lewis and Lamb 2004; Marsiglio 1995). Whether in relation to subsisting marital relationships or the effects of divorce on children, therefore, fathers are now widely seen to make a vital contribution to child development and to offer a positive economic, social and developmental resource for children.

This has a number of implications for the model of the father as (distant) patriarch. In terms of a child's psychological health, future socio-economic status, educational achievement and adolescent development, social policy is increasingly informed by the view that that the mere physical presence of fathers in the home is not enough. This is a key part of the shift from 'rights to responsibility' encapsulated in the concept of parental responsibility in the 1989 Children Act, as above.[9] In this regard it reflects what had already become, by the late 1980s, a broader political and policy acceptance of the view that fathers' relationships with their children should, wherever possible, be encouraged by law. However, I shall argue in the next section, these three developments around marriage, employment and child welfare are, taken together, now serving not just to reframe fathers' responsibilities in law. They are reconstituting fatherhood itself as a particular kind of social problem and object of intervention.

The 'New Father', 'New Family' and the Problem of Men

There is at present some agreement, cutting across political divides, that law has a significant role to play in the promotion of 'good', socially desirable fathering. It is via law reform, at least in part, that a new form of social responsibility and parenting practice on the part of men, one in keeping with the social changes discussed above, can be encouraged and facilitated. Two elements of this development are of particular significance for discussion of fathers' responsibilities. First, there has occurred a wide-ranging attempt, across diverse fields of law and policy, to refigure understandings of paternal responsibility. Second, this has involved a distinctive conceptualisation of a 'problem of fatherhood' that involves different ideas about how fathers can be seen, at a policy level, as a 'solution' to a range of social problems. I will address each of these points in turn.

Father-inclusive practice: promoting the 'good father'

Over the past decade in Britain there has occurred an explicit attempt to promote, via the use of law, a range of 'father-inclusive' practices across diverse areas of social policy and service delivery (Burgess and Bartlett 2004). In different ways, and in the last three years alone, measures such as the Childcare Act 2006,[10] the Equality Act

---

9 Section 2(1) of the Act provides that, in cases where a child's father and mother are married to each other at the time of birth, they shall each have parental responsibility for the child. 'Parental responsibility' encompasses 'all the rights, duties, powers, responsibilities and authority which by law a parent of a child has in relation to the child and his property', including 'the rights, powers and duties which a guardian of the child's estate … would have had in relation to the child and his property' (s. 3(1)).

10 By which local authorities in England and Wales must identify parents and prospective parents who are considered unlikely to use early childhood services (for example, fathers who are specifically mentioned) and facilitate access to those services (http://www.surestart.gov.uk/resources/general/childcareact).

2006[11] and documents such as *Every Parent Matters* (2007),[12] alongside a range of National Service Frameworks, guidance and other developments,[13] seek to increase expectations and change the practices of local authority and health care providers, as well as other organisations, around the need to include fathers, regardless of social background, in the delivery of services. 'Engaging fathers' has itself become a strategic requirement for all children's services in England and Wales and a range of initiatives now seek to develop and support work with fathers, in particular socially vulnerable fathers, as a key element of engaging with families within a diverse, multi-faith and multi-ethnic population.

These initiatives are informed not just by a rethinking of how fathers impact on children, as above, and of the role of fathers in child protection. Underscoring these developments are the values of social justice, emancipation, equality and social cohesion, integral elements of the economic and social policy agendas of the Labour government since 1997 (Annesley 2001; Featherstone and Trinder 2001; Giddens 1998). These values shape policy objectives which engage, quite explicitly, with the responsibilities of fathers; in relation, for example, to the promotion of equality between women and men; in attempts to facilitate 'work–life balance';[14] in concerns to protect the vulnerable; and, importantly, in the belief that parental responsibilities must be negotiated, joint and lifelong, that to *be* a responsible citizen, whether male or female, is to be economically productive (Plant 2003). Paternal responsibility more generally is a recurrent theme in policy debates around crime, social order and citizenship (Day Sclater and Piper 2000; Piper 2007), as well as 'family life', welfare benefits and social care.

In the case of the latter, whilst these initiatives around father-inclusive practice track to political and policy concerns that predate 1997, the 'ratcheting up' of social care agendas over the past decade (Lewis 2007) draws, quite explicitly, on the three

---

11 This places upon public bodies (including health, education and children's services) the requirement to publish an 'action plan' for promoting gender equality, to undertake a 'gender impact assessment' and to gather information and consult on how services impact on men and women.

12 *Every Parent Matters* (London: Department of Education and Skills, 2007). This explicitly states, for example, that fathers 'irrespective of the degree of involvement they have in the care of their children … should be offered routinely the support and opportunities they need to play their parental role effectively'. It is now required that information is gathered about fathers and that fathers, across all social groups, are routinely consulted with in planning services.

13 For example, the *Children's Centre Practice Guidance 2006* and *Planning and Performance Management Guidance 2006*, which place specific requirements on including fathers; and the *Teenage Parents Next Steps: Guidance for Local Authorities and Primary Care* (London: DH and DCFS, 2007), which prioritises the need to work with young fathers in the development of service provision around pregnancy and birth.

14 See Collier and Sheldon 2008, Ch. 4. In the first Queen's Speech since Gordon Brown became Prime Minister ('Flexible Working Hours for Millions', *The Times*, 7 November 2007), the government announced a proposed extension of the right to request flexible working for those with children up to age 17. The literature on the subject of work–life balance is, of course, vast.

themes outlined in the previous section: on changing ideas of child welfare and development, the shifting labour market participation of women and wider social changes around marriage and parenting (see *Building on Progress* 2007; Collier 1999; Kilkey 2006). There are, however, I shall suggest in the next section, some significant limits and inconsistencies to this approach that relate to questions of both change and continuity in how fatherhood has been conceptualised in law.

On the 'problem of fatherhood'

In the emergence of a distinctive policy agenda around 'engaging fathers' (Bartlett et al. 2007), the role played by men in families has, I have suggested above, been firmly written onto the policy agenda. If we look closer, however, an ambiguity and complexity informs how fatherhood is being pulled in different directions in these policy debates. In an insightful analysis of how the 'problem of men' has been articulated within New Labour's social policy, Scourfield and Drakeford (2002) suggest that there is a degree of 'policy optimism' about men inside the home and, in contrast, a marked pessimism about men outside it (with the reverse being true for women). In relation to the home and family, we have seen above, attempts are made to encourage and facilitate men as fathers. There is an assumption, reflected in numerous ministerial and policy statements, not only that men are changing but also that men want to change. This perspective highlights the institutional and organisational barriers to 'changing men', the obstacles to achieving 'active fathering'. It envisages a key role for both law and government in making men 'better' fathers. Thus, fathers have, for the first time, a right to take parental leave, to restrict their maximum working hours, to request flexible working and so forth.[15] Funding, meanwhile, is provided to develop father-inclusive and father-friendly initiatives at both national and local level and to source information provision and policy development around fathers.

Outside the home, however, the position of fathers appears very different. Far from optimism about changing men a rather different understanding of men and masculinity as social problems calls into question ideas about fathers' responsibilities and behaviour. The development of law and policy around youth crime and criminality (Piper 2007), anti-social behaviour and the educational underachievement of boys (Epstein et al. 1998), questions around men working with children, of men's health and illness (Featherstone et al. 2007; Robertson 2007), child support and paternal 'irresponsibility' (Williams 1998) entail the deployment of ideas about fathers' responsibilities and masculinities that contrast starkly with the figure of the caring 'new father'. If a deficit model of fathering is being rejected inside the home, that is, in these other contexts, across diverse media and within a range of academic and political discourses, fatherhood is being contested in some rather different ways.

In accounting for these differences two observations can be made. First, the ideal of the 'new fatherhood' is itself, as Smart and Neale suggest (1999), an undifferentiated social phenomenon made up of several distinct elements in how both men and 'what men do' ('what men are *really* like') are conceptualised. Thus, it is unsurprising there

15 Discussed in detail in Collier and Sheldon 2008, Ch. 4.

co-exists in law a range of conflicting ideas about fathers' responsibilities. What we can see here are ideas about fatherhood as both a source of masculine identity, of fathers as symbolic enforcer of familial power and social order; and about fathers as carriers of legal *rights*. Increasingly, as above, the assumption that fathers are equal sharers of responsibilities is now positioned as a progressive discourse at the centre of social care agendas.

Secondly, just like the 'new fatherhood', the 'problem of men' is not, Scourfield and Drakeford (2002) observe, a unitary discourse. It 'does not arise from a homogenous set of concerns, but comes from several different directions and focuses on a variety of behaviours' (2002, 621). A number of 'fundamentally different' approaches define this kind of identification of fathers as a social problem: ideas of men as *perpetrators* and men as *victims*. The former envisages men as 'a source of danger and disorder, an anti-social influence' (2002, 621). Aligned to themes within both feminist and masculinities scholarship, the focus becomes how men are empowered in society, how dominant discourses of masculinity, a 'gender order', serves to privilege men. The latter, in contrast, highlights the disadvantages that befall men, the costs, if not crisis, of contemporary masculinity (Clare 2000; Faludi 1999), the 'displacement' of men from the workplace and the family that has itself become a key theme of fathers' rights discourse (Collier and Sheldon 2006).

Each of these perspectives inform contemporary understandings of fathers' responsibilities in the legal arena and it is against this backdrop of change and continuity, conceptual ambiguity and political differences, that debates about law and fatherhood are now marked by a simultaneous cultural devaluing (Burgess 1997, 19-20) and yet also celebration of fathers. 'Father absence' and 'father distance' are presented as indicative of men's individual and collective avoidance of their responsibilities (e.g. Campbell 1993; McMahon 1999) and, alternatively, as the products of institutional barriers to men spending more time with children (e.g. Burgess and Ruxton 1996; Stanley 2005). Both views can be aligned with strands of feminism, one emphasising men's agency and choice, the latter a vision of men as constricted by gender roles and institutional arrangements. Time use surveys, meanwhile, point to marginal, rather than significant, change in fathering practices (Dermott 2005; Office for National Statistics 2002; Office for National Statistics 2003). In relation to debates about crime and social disorder, tackling fathers' responsibilities is a key element of policy development aimed at addressing issues of respect, social exclusion, community and cohesion (Day Sclater and Piper 2000). As a strand of feminist legal scholarship seeks to reclaim a place for autonomy in the family (Fineman 2004), the 'gendered authoritarianism' (Scourfield and Drakeford 2002, 630) underscoring such initiatives is seen as further reconstituting the family as a site for the reassessment of 'acceptable' and normative behaviour on the part of both parents.[16]

---

16 'Where New Labour is optimistic, it tends to produce policies that are encouraging and facilitative. This is true of those policies that are designed to assist men as fathers and women as public figures. Where New Labour is pessimistic, it can produce policies that are authoritarian', Scourfield and Drakeford 2002, 623.

Concluding Remarks

This chapter has presented a reading of fathers' responsibilities in one particular social and legal context. Focusing on the constitution of the father as 'family man' (Coltrane 1996) within the context of subsisting marital relationships, I have unpacked how a number of conflicting assumptions inform the production of the paternal subject within legal discourse. Law, we have seen, has embodied and reproduced a range of ideas about how fathers do and should work and care for young children. These ideas map, although not in any straightforward way, to dominant theories of child development and welfare, as well as to infrastructures of care within and beyond family and kinship networks. In tracing a shift from 'rights to responsibility' in law, broadly from the late 19th to the late 20th centuries, in more recent years a coming together of economic, cultural and political shifts has served to reframe the question of what constitutes a 'good father' and responsible 'family man' in law.

On one level this 'story' of fatherhood in law can be read as a transition from the model of the father as a distant authority figure and breadwinner to a paradigm in which fathers are now viewed as having a central role to fulfill in meeting the day to day needs of children (e.g. see Stanley 2005). Yet this narrative is, I have suggested, more complex. It is certainly tempting to see here a linear progression in which the position of men in families has been 'modernised' and subject to changes which occur in identifiable stages. Such a view would, however, be misleading. Writing in 1987, Richards suggested that, as our historical understanding of fatherhood increases, so does our ability to understand the present (Richards 1987, 33-4). The shifts in the responsibilities of fathers traced in this chapter are much more complex than the modernisation thesis would suggest. Social class, race, ethnicity and geographical location (for example, under-explored regional variations in meanings of fatherhood) are important factors influencing family structures and fathering practices within specific locales and communities (Sayer et al. 2004; note also Gillies 2006). At the same time, the experience of caring and the social responsibilities associated with fatherhood are mediated by individual biography and life history. The micro-political realities of fatherhood, that is, the 'everyday' experience of breadwinning, domesticity and child nurturing, all occur at the interface of structure and individual agency. Significantly, given the distinction identified in this chapter between fatherhood as practice and fatherhood as culture, between descriptions and legal prescriptions of father's behaviour, a focus on shifting representations of the responsibilities of fathers in legal discourse runs the risk of subordinating fatherhood practices and experiences which might appear 'off the radar' to such a reading. This may be true, for example, for experiences of what is seen as paternal responsibility on the part of many non-cohabiting and separated fathers, grandfathers, young fathers, disabled fathers, gay fathers and ethnic minority fathers (see, e.g., Weeks et al. 2001).

The shifts charted in this chapter reveal how hitherto hetero-normative ideas about parenting and families are being disturbed, challenged and fragmented. At the same time, however, I have noted the continued legacy and hold, not least in terms of under-explored collective cultural memory, of earlier ideas about fatherhood (Smart 2007). In recognising the co-existence of change and continuity fathers remain, in certain legal contexts, situated as guarantors of social and familial order, as subjects of a primary economic obligation and responsibility. The idea that a father's primary commitment and identification will and should be with paid employment rather than full-time child care, for example, remains powerful, the obligation on men to provide financially for their children emphasised notably in relation to the provisions of the Child Support Act 1991, as amended (Wikeley 2006). The experience of fatherhood more generally continues to involve, for most men, a temporal and spatial trade-off between the domains of work and family (Crompton and Lyonette 2007).

In these debates around fathers' responsibilities it is important to consider how 'parental choice' is understood. What has often been unclear in these discussions is how choice is itself constrained and bound up with distinctive 'gendered rationalities' (Barlow and Duncan 2000a; 2000b; Barlow et al. 2002; Carling et al. 2002; Duncan and Edwards 2002; Duncan et al. 2003) that must be socially, economically and culturally located in ways that frame how men's capabilities and agency are understood in the policy promotion of responsibility (Hobson et al. 2007; Lewis and Guillari 2005; Sen 2003). As Lewis (2007) asks, regarding the limits of legal intervention:

> Are men to be cajoled or coerced? Probably not, but if it is increasingly assumed that women and men will be more self-provisioning – for example, in respect of pensions – then the bottom line is that women and men must be in a position to make genuine choices to work and to care.

Notwithstanding the policy packages outlined in this chapter, what remains unclear is how it might be made possible for fathers to 'choose to care'. Heterosexual relationships and the roles of men and women as parents continue in many respects to be ideologically reproduced in such a way that dominant ideas of fatherhood associate fathers with a sense of physical detachment and emotional disengagement from domestic labour and the 'day to day' care of children. Research highlights significant obstacles towards greater participation on the part of those men who do wish to care for children. In relation to policies such as the introduction of Sure Start services and emergence of father support groups within the context of social and health care provision (Gillies 2005; Lloyd et al. 2003; Williams and Churchill 2003), for example, fathers' take-up of support continues to be limited (Daniel and Taylor 2001; Ghate et al. 2000). Many fathers do not see *themselves* as in need of support (Edwards and Gillies 2004). A growing literature tracks the possible reasons for the low participation rates of fathers in family support services and the practical barriers which can deter them from accessing such services.

The way in which fathering practice is often mediated through the agency of mothers further complicates this picture. However, as Jane Lewis has argued, it is ultimately far from clear just what the policy aim has been in these debates around fathers' responsibilities (Lewis 2007; note also Dey and Wasoff 2006). Is it to promote gender equality or to foster child welfare and development? Or is it to improve the 'quality of life' of individuals? Is it primarily economic, to get mothers 'into work', whether by degrees of force or the subsidising of childcare services? It may well, of course, be each and all of the above, but this does not mean that these policy aims are compatible. Writing a decade before the election of the New Labour government, Lewis and O'Brien noted how the heterogeneity of styles of fathering serves to invalidate the making of any general claims about 'the father' (1987, 6). In the same way, the idea of the 'new' 'caring' fatherhood may itself be misleading, obfuscating as much as it reveals about the complexities of men's parenting.

I have suggested in this chapter that a model of the male breadwinner and the structure of welfare provision on which it has been based is fracturing as a result of the increased fluidity in civil status, rising rates of 'family breakdown' and labour market change. Far from interpreting these changes in terms of a modernisation narrative, however, as a 'progressive' embrace of gender neutrality and formal equality, it is possible to see developments in this area as embedded within broader trends toward fiscal conservatism and economic retrenchment (Boyd 2004). Political concerns to promote a privatisation of economic responsibilities in families over the past 30 years inform debates around fathers' responsibilities to a considerable degree. They pervade, in a particularly clear way, the history of the much maligned Child Support Agency, which sought since the early 1990s to oblige fathers to provide financial support for their biological children.[17] Intriguingly, at the very moment social care agendas are expanded in ways that reshape ideas of paternal responsibility, other, more established, social policies around care have either stagnated or contracted (Lewis 2007). Employers in England and Wales are not at present obliged to provide day care facilities for their workers' children.[18] Economic imperatives and the 'bottom line' of Treasury concerns around public expenditure, meanwhile, all too clearly frame these debates about the responsibilities of parents. More generally, the perceived demands of globalisation and market competition structure the labour market and work patterns in the UK in ways that continue to be profoundly 'family-unfriendly' for all parents, mother and fathers.

Far from presenting a narrative of decline in the father as breadwinner discourse, therefore, it is preferable to see the heightening of neo-liberal economic and political agendas within Western states as having resulted in a reframing of the economic and cultural terrain in which these debates about individual 'choice' take place. The 'father as breadwinner' model, and the ideas around masculinities with which it has been associated, have not been supplanted in law. Rather, they exist alongside, and in tension with, the new ideology of the 'father as carer'. It is assumed that both men and women should be engaged in paid employment. Yet the conditions in which they do so are marked not only by 'gendered rationalities', as above, but also by increased insecurity, high levels of casualisation (Lewis 2002) and an entrenched polarisation within the workforce. In such a context, significantly, much child care and domestic labour now passes to third parties, whether statutory or market providers; or, increasingly, in certain parts of the country and amongst some privileged social groups, to migrant workers. Such a passing on of care and domestic labour does not mean that structures of power and inequality have faded way. Rather,

---

17 The CSA has now been replaced by the Child Maintenance and Enforcement Commission.

18 For a visioning of the scale of reform required to institute such changes, see Fineman 2004.

they are being displaced within an increasingly global and mobile economy in ways which cut across traditional gendered class and race divisions.

References

Annesley, C. (2001), 'New Labour and Welfare' in S. Ludlam and M.J. Smith (eds), *New Labour in Government* (London: Macmillan).

Atkins, S. and Hoggett, B. (1984), *Women and the Law* (Oxford: Blackwell).

Auchmuty, R. (2007), 'Unfair Shares for Women: The Rhetoric of Equality and the Reality of Inequality' in Bottomley, A. and Lim, H. (eds), *Feminist Perspectives on Land Law* (London: Routledge Cavendish).

Barlow, A. and Duncan, S. (2000a), 'New Labour's Communitarianism, Supporting Families and the "Rationality Mistake": Part I', *Journal of Social Welfare and Family Law* 22:2, 23.

Barlow, A. and Duncan, S. (2000b), 'New Labour's Communitarianism, Supporting Families and the "Rationality Mistake": Part II', *Journal of Social Welfare and Family Law* 22:2, 129.

Barlow, A., Duncan, S. and James, G. (2002), 'New Labour, the Rationality Mistake and Family Policy in Britain' in Carling, A., Duncan, S. and Edwards, R. (eds), *Analysing Families: Morality and Rationality in Policy and Practice* (London: Routledge).

Barlow, A., Duncan, S., James, G. and Park, A. (2005), *Cohabitation, Marriage and the Law: Social Change and Legal Reform in the 21st Century* (Oxford: Hart).

Bartlett, D., Burgess, A. and Jones, K. (2007), *A Toolkit for Developing Father-Inclusive Practice* (London: Fathers Direct).

Blakenhorn, D. (1995), *Fatherless America: Confronting Our Most Urgent Social Problem* (New York: Basic Books).

Boyd, S. (1989), 'From Gender Specificity to Gender Neutrality? Ideologies in Canadian Child Custody Law' in Brophy, J. and Smart, C. (eds), *Child Custody and the Politics of Gender* (London: Routledge).

Boyd, S. (2003), *Child Custody, Law and Women's Work* (Oxford: Oxford University Press).

Boyd, S. (2004), 'Legal Regulation of Families in Changing Societies' in Sarat, A. (ed.), *The Blackwell Companion to Law and Society* (London: Blackwell).

Building On Progress: Families, HM Government Policy Review (2007) (London: Prime Minister's Strategy Office).

Burgess, A. (1997), *Fatherhood Reclaimed: The Making of the Modern Father* (London: Vermillion).

Burgess, A. and Bartlett, D. (2004), *Working With Fathers* (London: Fathers Direct), available at www.fathersdirect.com.

Burgess, A. and Ruxton, S. (1996), *Men and their Children: Proposals for Public Policy* (London: Institute for Public Policy Research).

Campbell, B. (1993), *Goliath: Britain's Dangerous Places* (London: Methuen).

Carabine, J. (1996), 'Heterosexuality and Social Policy' in D. Richardson (ed.), *Theorising Heterosexuality: Telling It Straight* (Buckingham: Open University Press).

Carling, A., Duncan, S. and Edwards, R. (eds) (2002), *Analysing Families: Morality and Rationality in Policy and Practice* (London: Routledge).

Choudhry, S. and Fenwick, H. (2005), 'Taking the Rights of Parents and Children Seriously – Confronting the Welfare Principle under the Human Rights Act', *Oxford Journal of Legal Studies* 25, 453.

Clare, A. (2000), *On Men: Masculinity in Crisis* (London: Chatto and Windus).

Collier, R. (1995), *Masculinity, Law and the Family* (London: Routledge).

Collier, R. (1999), 'Feminising the Workplace? (Re)Constructing the "Good Parent" in Employment Law and Family Policy' in Morris, A. and O'Donnell, T. (eds), *Feminist Perspectives on Employment Law* (London: Cavendish).

Collier R. (2000), 'Straight Families, Queer Lives? Heterosexual(izing) Family Law' in Stychin, C and Herman, D. (eds), *Sexuality in the Legal Arena* (London: The Athlone Press).

Collier, R. (2001a), 'A Hard Time to be a Father?: Law, Policy and Family Practices', *Journal of Law and Society* 28:4, 520.

Collier, R. (2001b), 'In Search of the 'Good Father': Law, Family Practices and the Normative Reconstruction of Parenthood', *Studies in Law, Politics and Society* 22, 133.

Collier, R. (2003), 'Men, Masculinities and Crime' in C. Sumner (ed.), *The Blackwell International Companion to Criminology* (Oxford: Blackwell).

Collier, R. (2005), 'Fathers 4 Justice, Law and the New Politics of Fatherhood', *Child and Family Law Quarterly* 17, 511.

Collier, R. and Sheldon, S. (eds) (2006), *Fathers' Rights Activism and Legal Reform in Comparative Perspective* (Oxford: Hart).

Collier, R. and Sheldon, S. (2008), *Fragmenting Fatherhood: A Socio-Legal Study* (Oxford: Hart).

Coltrane, S. (1996), *Family Man: Fatherhood, Housework and Gender Equality* (Oxford: Oxford University Press).

Connell, R.W. (1987), *Gender and Power* (Cambridge: Polity Press).

Cretney, S. (1996), '"What Will Women Want Next?" The Struggle for Power within the Family 1925–1975', *Law Quarterly Review* 12, 110.

Crompton, R. (1999), *Restructuring Gender Relations and Employment: The Decline of the Male Breadwinner* (Oxford: Oxford University Press).

Crompton, R. and Lyonette, C. (2007), 'Gender, Attitudes to Work and Work Life Balance in Britain', GeNet Project 7: Class, Gender, Employment and Family, available at http://www.gnet.ac.uk/projects/project7.htm.

Daniel, B. and Taylor, J. (2001), *Engaging with Fathers: Practice Issues for Health and Social Care* (London: Jessica Kingsley Publishers).

David, M.E. (ed.) (1998), *The Fragmenting Family: Does It Matter?* (London: Institute for Economic Affairs Health and Welfare Unit).

Day Sclater, S. and Piper, C. (2000), 'Re-moralisng the Family? Family Policy, Family Law and Youth Justice', *Child and Family Law Quarterly* 12:2, 135.

Daycare Trust (2003), *Informal Childcare: Bridging the Childcare Gap for Families* (London: Daycare Trust/One Parent Families).

Dermott, E. (2005), 'Time and Labour: Fathers' Perceptions of Employment and Childcare' in Pettinger, L., Parry, J.,Taylor, R. and Glucksmann, M. (eds), *A New Sociology of Work?* (Oxford: Blackwell/The Sociological Review), 91.

Dewar, J. (1998), 'The Normal Chaos of Family Law', *Modern Law Review* 61, 467.

Dey, I. and Wasoff, F. (2006), 'Mixed Messages: Parental Responsibilities, Public Opinion and the Reforms of Family Law', *International Journal of Law, Policy and the Family* 20, 225.

Diduck, A. (1998), 'In Search of the Feminist Good Mother', *Social & Legal Studies* 7:1, 129.

Diduck, A. (2001), 'Fairness and Justice for All? The House of Lords in *White v White*', *Feminist Legal Studies* 9, 173.

Diduck, A. and Kaganas, F. (2006), *Family Law, Gender and the State: Text, Cases and Materials* (2nd edition) (Oxford: Hart).

Dienhart, A. (1998), *Reshaping Fatherhood: The Social Construction of Shared Parenting* (Thousand Oaks: Sage).

Doucet, A. (2006), *Do Men Mother? Fatherhood, Care and Domestic Responsibility* (Toronto: University of Toronto Press).

Dowd, N. (2000), *Redefining Fatherhood* (New York: New York University Press).

Duncan, S. and Edwards, R. (eds) (2002), *Analysing Families: Morality and Rationality in Policy and Practice* (London: Routledge).

Duncan, S., Edwards, R., Reynolds, T. and Alldred, P. (2003), 'Motherhood, Paid Work and Partnering: Values and Theories', *Work, Employment and Society* 17, 309.

Duncan Smith, I. (2007), 'Now They Want to Abolish Fatherhood', *The Mail on Sunday*, 18 November 2007, 29.

Edwards, R. and Gillies, V. (2004), 'Support in Parenting: Values and Consensus Concerning Who to Turn to', *Journal of Social Policy* 33:4, 623.

Eekelaar, J. (2006), *Family Law and Personal Life* (Oxford: Oxford University Press).

EOC (Equal Opportunities Commission) (2003), *Fathers: Balancing Work and Family* (Manchester: Equal Opportunities Commission).

EOC (Equal Opportunities Commission) (2007), Facts about Men and Women in Great Britain 2006 (Manchester: Equal Opportunities Commission).

Epstein, D., Elwood, J., Hey, V. and Maw, J. (eds) (1998), *Failing Boys? Issues in Gender and Achievement* (Buckingham: Open University Press).

Every Parent Matters (2007) (London: Department of Education and Skills).

Faludi, S. (1999), *Stiffed: The Betrayal of the Modern Man* (London: Chatto and Windus).

Featherstone, B. and Trinder, L (2001), 'New Labour, Families and Fathers', *Critical Social Policy* 21:4, 534.

Featherstone, B., Rivett, M. and Scourfield, J. (2007), *Working With Men in Health and Social Care* (London: Sage).

Fenwick, H. (2004), 'Clashing Rights, the Welfare of the Child and the Human Rights Act', *Modern Law Review* 67:6, 889.

Fineman, M. (1991), *The Illusion of Equality: The Rhetoric and Reality of Divorce Reform* (Chicago and London: University of Chicago Press).

Fineman, M. (1995), *The Neutered Mother, the Sexual Family, and Other Twentieth Century Tragedies* (New York: Routledge).
Fineman, M. (2000), 'Cracking the Foundational Myths: Independence, Autonomy, and Self Sufficiency', *Journal of Gender, Social Policy and Law* 13, 13.
Fineman, M. (2004), *The Autonomy Myth* (New York: Free Press).
Fineman, M and Karpin, I. (eds) (1995), *Mothers in Law: Feminist Theory and the Legal Regulation of Motherhood* (New York: Columbia University Press).
Finer, M. and McGregor, O.R. (1974), 'History of the Obligation to Maintain: Appendix 5' in M. Finer, *Report of the Committee on One Parent Families*, Cmnd 5629 (London: HMSO).
Flouri, E. (2005), *Fathering and Child Outcomes* (Chichester: John Wiley & Sons).
Furstenberg, F. (1988), 'Good Dads-Bad Dads: Two Faces of Fatherhood' in Cherlin, A.J. (ed.), *The Changing American Family and Public Policy* (Philadelphia: University of Pennsylvania).
Ghate, D., Shaw, C. and Hazel, N. (2000), *Fathers and Family Centres: Engaging Fathers in Preventative Services* (York: Joseph Rowntree Foundation).
Giddens, A. (1992), *The Transformation of Intimacy* (Cambridge: Polity).
Giddens, A. (1998), *The Third Way* (Cambridge: Polity).
Gillies, V. (2005), 'Meeting Parents Needs? Discourses of "Support" and "Inclusion" in Family Policy', *Critical Social Policy* 25:1, 70.
Gillies, V. (2006), *Marginalised Mothers: Exploring Working Class Experiences of Parenting* (London: Routledge).
Gillis, J.R. (1996), *A World of their own Making: Myth, Ritual and the Quest for Family Values* (Cambridge, MA: Harvard University Press).
Hatten, W., Vinter, L. and Williams, R. (2002), *Dads on Dads: Needs and Expectations at Work and Home* (Manchester: Equal Opportunities Commission).
Hawkins, A.J. and Dollahite, D.C. (1997), *Generative Fathering: Beyond Deficit Perspectives* (Thousand Oaks: Sage).
Hearn, J. (1990), *Child Abuse and Men's Violence*, in Violence Against Women Study Group (ed.), *Taking Child Abuse Seriously* (London: Unwin Hyman).
Hobson, B. (ed.) (2002), *Making Men into Fathers: Masculinities and the Social Politics of Fatherhood* (Cambridge: Cambridge University Press).
Hobson, B. with Duvander, A.Z. and Halldén, K. (2007), 'Men's Capabilities and Agency to Create a Work Family Balance: The Gap Between European Norms and Men's Practices', paper delivered to the Conference 'Fatherhood in Late Modernity: Cultural Images, Social Practices, Structural Frames', Centre for Interdisciplinary Research, Bielefeld University, Germany, April 2007 (copy of paper with author).
Holcombe, L. (1983), *Wives and Property: Reform of the Married Women's Property Acts* (Toronto: University of Toronto Press).
Jamieson, L. (1998), *Intimacy: Personal Relationships in Modern Society* (Cambridge: Polity Press).
Kilkey, M. (2006), 'New Labour and Reconciling Work and Family Life: Making it Fathers' Business?', *Social Policy and Society* 5, 167.
Krieken, R. van (2001), 'Legal Informalism, Power and Liberal Governance', *Social & Legal Studies* 10:1, 5-22.

Krieken, R. van (2005), 'The "Best Interests of the Child" and Parental Separation on the "Civilising of Parents"', *Modern Law Review* 68:1, 25.

Land, H. (1980), 'The Family Wage', *Feminist Review* 6, 55.

Lewis, C. (2000), *A Man's Place in the Home: Fathers and Families in the UK* (York: Joseph Rowntree).

Lewis, J. (2002), 'Individualisation, Assumptions about the Existence of an Adult Worker Model and the Shift towards Contractualism' in Carling, A., Duncan, S. and Edwards, R. (eds), *Analysing Families: Morality and Rationality in Policy and Practice* (London: Routledge).

Lewis, J. (2007), 'Balancing Work and Family: The Nature of the Policy Challenge and Gender Equality', GeNet Project 9: *Tackling Inequalities in Work and Care Policy Initiatives and Actors at the EU and UK Levels*, available at http://www.genet.ac.uk/projects/project9.htm at 2.

Lewis, J. and Guillari, S. (2005), 'The Adult Worker Model Family, Gender Equality and Care: The Search for New Policy Principles and the Possibilities and Problems of a Capabilities Approach', *Economy and Society* 34:1, 76.

Lewis, C. and Lamb, M.E. (2004), 'Fathers: The Research Perspectives' in *Supporting Fathers: Contributions from the International Fatherhood Summit 2003: Early Childhood Development, Practice and Reflections* (The Hague: Bernard van Leer Foundation).

Lewis, C. and O'Brien, M. (1987), *Reassessing Fatherhood: New Observations on Fathers and the Modern Family* (London: Sage).

Lloyd, N., O'Brien, M. and Lewis, C. (2003), *Fathers in Sure Start: The National Evaluation of Sure Start (NESS)* (London: Institute for the Study of Children, Families and Social Issues, Birkbeck, University of London).

Lupton, D. and Barclay, L. (1997), *Constructing Fatherhood: Discourses and Experiences* (London: Sage).

Maidment, S. (1984), *Child Custody and Divorce: The Law in Social Context* (London: Croom Helm).

Mallender, P. and Rayson, J. (2006), *The Civil Partnership Act 2004* (Cambridge: Cambridge University Press).

Mangan, J. and Walvin, J. (eds) (1987), *Manliness and Morality: Middle Class Masculinity in Britain and America 1800-1940* (Manchester: Manchester University Press).

Marsiglio, W. (1995), *Fatherhood: Contemporary Theory, Research and Social Policy* (New York: Sage).

McKee, L. and O'Brien, M. (eds) (1982), *The Father-Figure* (London: Tavistock).

McMahon, A. (1999), *Taking Care of Men: Sexual Politics in the Public Mind* (Cambridge: Cambridge University Press).

O'Brien, M. (2004), *Shared Caring: Bringing Fathers into the Frame* (Manchester: Equal Opportunities Commission, Winter 2004-2005).

Office for National Statistics (2002), *UK Time Use Survey*, 2000 dataset (2nd edition) (London: ONS).

Office for National Statistics (2003), *2001 Census Key Statistics for Local Authorities in England and Wales* (London: ONS).

Piper, C. (2007), 'Feminist Perspectives on Youth Justice' in Diduck, A. and O'Donovan, K. (eds), *Feminist Perspectives on Family Law* (London: Routledge Cavendish).
Plant, R. (2003), 'Citizenship and Social Security', *Fiscal Studies* 24:2, 153.
Reece, H. (1996), 'The Paramountcy Principle: Consensus or Construct?', *Current Legal Problems* 49, 267.
Reece, H. (2003), *Divorcing Responsibly* (Oxford: Hart Publications).
Richards, M. (1987), 'Fatherhood, Marriage and Sexuality: Some Speculations on the English Middle-Class Family' in Lewis, C. and O'Brien, M. (eds), *Reassessing Fatherhood: New Observations on Fathers and the Modern Family* (London: Sage).
Robertson, S. (2007), *Understanding Men's Health: Masculinities, Identity and Well-being* (Buckingham: Open University Press).
Rosh White, N. (1994), 'About Fathers: Masculinity and the Social Construction of Fatherhood', *Journal of Sociology* 30:2, 119.
Rotundo, E.A. (1987), 'Patriarchs and Participants: A Historical Perspective on Fatherhood' in Kaufman, M. (ed.), *Beyond Patriarchy: Essays by Men on Pleasure, Power and Change* (Toronto: Oxford University Press).
Sayer, L., Gauthier, A.H. and Furstenberg, F. (2004), 'Social Class Differences in Parental Time with Children: Cross-National Variations', *Journal of Marriage and the Family* 1152.
Scourfield, J. and Drakeford, M. (2002), 'New Labour and the 'Problem of Men', *Critical Social Policy* 22, 619.
Segal, L. (1990), *Slow Motion: Changing Masculinities, Changing Men* (London: Virago).
Sen, A. (2003), 'Capability and Well-being' in Nussbaum, M. and Sen, A. (eds), *The Quality of Life* (Oxford: Oxford University Press).
Silva, E. (ed.) (1996), *Good Enough Mothering? Feminist Perspectives on Lone Motherhood* (London: Routledge).
Smart, C. (1984), *The Ties That Bind: Law, Marriage and the Reproduction of Patriarchal Relations* (London: Routledge and Kegan Paul).
Smart, C. (2004), 'Equal shares – Rights for Fathers or Recognition for Children', *Critical Social Policy* 24, 484.
Smart, C. (2007), *Personal Life* (Cambridge: Polity).
Smart, C. and Neale, B. (1999), '"I Hadn't Really Thought About It": New Identities/New Fatherhoods' in Seymour, J. and Bagguley, P. (eds), *Relating Intimacies: Power and Resistance* (Basingstoke: Palgrave Macmillan).
Smart, C. and Sevenhuijsen, S. (eds) (1989), *Child Custody and the Politics of Gender* (London: Routledge).
Stanley, K. (2005), *Daddy Dearest? Active Fatherhood and Public Policy* (London: Institute for Public Policy Research).
Tosh, J. (1999), *A Man's Place: Masculinity and the Middle-Class Home in Victorian England* (New Haven and London: Yale University Press).
Warin, J., Solomon, Y., Lewis, C. and Langford, W. (1999), *Fathers, Work and Family Life* (London: Joseph Rowntree Foundation/Family Policy Studies Centre).
Weeks, J., Heaphy, B. and Donovan, C. (2001), *Same Sex Intimacies: Families of Choice and Other Life Experiments* (London: Routledge).

Wikeley, N. (2006), *Child Support: Law and Policy* (Oxford: Hart).

Williams, F. (1998), 'Troubled Masculinities in Social Policy Discourses: Fatherhood' in Popay, J., Hearn, J. and Edwards, J. (eds), *Men, Gender Divisions and Welfare* (London: Routledge).

Williams, F. and Churchill, H. (2003), *Empowering Parents in Sure Start Local Programmes*, Sure Start National Evaluation Report 018 (London: HMSO).

Wilson, G.B. (2006), 'The Non-Resident Parental Role for Separated Fathers: A Review', *International Journal of Law, Policy and the Family* 1.

Young, M. and Wilmott, P. (1957), *Family and Kinship in East London* (Harmondsworth: Pelican).

Young, M. and Wilmott, P. (1973), *The Symmetrical Family* (Harmondsworth: Penguin).

Chapter 10

Responsible Fathers: Paternity, the Blood Tie and Family Responsibility

Craig Lind[1]

Introduction

In this chapter I wish to explore the relationship between our understandings of paternity and the responsibility which fathers have for children. The chapter will focus on the way in which paternity has been constructed in the cases on the determination of paternity under the Human Fertilisation and Embryology Act 1990 (HFEA 1990). I wish to examine those constructions in the light of insights into the nature of paternity that emerge from other areas of family law. The chapter will examine in some detail the traditional (common law) ascription of paternity to a particular man. But it will also note legal and social developments in relation to adoption, fostering, step-parenting, same-sex parenting, single parenting and 'absent' parenting which will, I hope, cast some analytical light on the problems that are introduced by assisted reproduction and disputes about paternity in that context.

Before exploring these issues it is as well to note that I have chosen to use 'paternity' rather than 'fatherhood' for a simple reason. The distinction is, I believe, not unlike the one Andrew Bainham employs when he distinguishes between parentage and parenthood (Bainham 1999). 'Paternity', particularly in legal sources, seems to relate more closely to genetics[2] than does 'fatherhood'. 'Fatherhood' has more of the connotations of the social attributes of parenting than does 'paternity'.[3]

---

1 This chapter started as a lecture delivered at the Institute of Advanced Legal Studies, University of London on 23 June 2004. It was then developed for the Symposium on Family Responsibility held at the University of Sussex on 15 September 2005. I am grateful to participants at these two events and to numerous others for their contributions to the thinking that has materialised in this piece.

2 The Concise Oxford English Dictionary defines paternity as 'the state of being someone's father' (thus linking it to genetics). See Oxford Reference Online Premium at: http://www.oxfordreference.com/views/BOOK_SEARCH.html?book=t23&subject=s7, accessed on 29 January 2008.

3 'Father' in the Concise Oxford English Dictionary is defined both by reference to genetics ('a man in relation to his child or children') and in terms of social – familial – responsibility ('a man who provides care and protection'). See Oxford Reference Online Premium at: http://www.oxfordreference.com/views/BOOK_SEARCH.html?book=t23&subject=s7, accessed on 29 January 2008.

'Paternity' seems more overtly tied to the 'fact' of male parentage and 'fatherhood' to the social attributes of male parenting.

But while I wish to note the distinction I am reiterating here I wish also, throughout this chapter, to keep questioning it. If some changes that have occurred over the last few decades are noted, my reasons will become apparent: although parental status and parental responsibility were intricately linked until the mid-20th century, parental responsibility as a concept was 'invented' in the Children Act 1989 and a potential separation with parental status introduced. After the passage of that Act it became possible to be a parent – to have the status of parent – without having (exercisable) parental responsibility. More recently we have begun to cloud the distinction again by allocating 'parental responsibility' to factual fathers (under CA 1989, s. 4) where they are to have no power in relation to their children.[4] We also try to encourage fathers who have no parental responsibility to achieve it and to exercise it. We are, in short, trying to recreate the powerful tie between the fact of fatherhood and the responsibilities of fatherhood (Collier in this book; Sheldon 2005). The status father (as opposed to the functional father) is gaining a measure of responsibility. That (re)encroachment has made me wonder about the allocation of status to fathers, a concern which manifests itself most obviously in assisted reproduction cases.

Thus, although I use 'paternity' to imply a status relationship and 'fatherhood' to imply one which is functional (about responsibility), I am aware that that distinction has become unstable once more. My interest is, therefore, (in this chapter) in the connection between status and functional and in the way in which status has gathered importance in terms of paternal responsibility. We have begun to reassert the importance of status in the allocation of responsibility to adults. But where we have flexibility in the allocation of status we have not embraced it (Diduck 2007). We are not, as fully as we are able in law, allowing those whose ambitions are to care for children to be regarded fully as the adults responsible for their well-being.

My analysis will start with a quote from Thomas Hardy which encapsulates some of what I feel about this subject:

> The beggarly question of parentage—what is it, after all? What does it matter, when you come to think of it, whether a child is yours by blood or not? All the little ones of our time are collectively the children of us adults of the time, and entitled to our general care. That excessive regard of parents for their own children, and their dislike of other people's, is, like class-feeling, patriotism, save-your-own-soul-ism, and other virtues, a mean exclusiveness at bottom. (Hardy 1995, 253)

Paternity at Common Law

The social fact of paternity

I will start with an analysis of paternity in the common law. And I will spend more time here than, perhaps, seems justifiable. But I believe that the common law

4 See, for example, *Re S (Parental Responsibility)* [1995] 2 FLR 648 CA.

position has much to offer us which the era of rapid changes in family life may have obscured and complicated.

Paternity, we are given to believe, is a matter of fact, and a common sense matter of fact at that. We all – or most of us – know our fathers (if not in person, then certainly as a matter of identity).[5] He is the man we are told (usually since birth) is our father. If we were to discover that he was not 'really' our father (by, for example, genetic testing, or some other circumstantial evidence that proved the unlikelihood or impossibility of his procreative role in our birth we would (usually) be shocked at the revelation, but we would also recognise the mistake as real if the (genetic) evidence were convincing. In this society – in which significant numbers of children are raised by men who are not their 'real' fathers – we teach children to distinguish between their 'real' fathers and the people (commonly their step-fathers) who raise them in the responsible way we would like to expect of a father.

Paternity is, therefore, a notion so ordinary that we are all taken to understand it instantly. We take for granted the *fact* of paternity. That fact is based upon a blood relationship (or a genetic tie). Men are fathers if their genes were party to a particular procreation.

Common law paternity

The law, like the society it serves, also believes paternity to be a matter of fact. However, the law also accepts that, unlike maternity, the fact of paternity is not so easily proved.[6] While we can see motherhood established, there is no parallel, overt evidence of paternity being established. The evidence of the *factual* relationship between a child and a man is – traditionally – in the 'blood' but that blood relationship could, for most of our history, not be confirmed by evidence. Before medical science, and consequently the courts, acquired the ability to know definitively (by reference to reliable evidence) who the father of a child, in fact, was, evidence of paternity was always circumstantial. We sought out the circumstances of conception which would, as reliably as possible, suggest factual paternity. And the major circumstance to which the common law turned was marriage.[7]

To avoid problems of evidence in the determination of paternity the law, therefore, operated (for the longest time) a presumption of paternity. Until relatively recently that presumption seemed to meet the difficulties of evidence and managed

---

5 Estimates about the number of people who think they 'know' their fathers' identities but who are then mistaken range from 2 to 8 per cent. There are some quite high estimates (in the region of 21 per cent but these tend to apply to skewed populations of men – like prisoners – where other factors may explain the higher incidence of 'mistaken' identity) (see Sasse et al. 1994; Cerda-Flores et al. 1999 (I am grateful to Martin Johnson for these two references); and Anderson 2006). There is a website dedicated to the collection of information about misattributed paternity (from both academic and non-academic (newspaper) sources): see http://www.childsupportanalysis.co.uk/analysis_and_opinion/choices_and_behaviours/misattributed_paternity.html, last accessed on 24 January 2008.

6 Which is proved by parturition at common law: see *The Ampthill Peerage Case* [1977] AC 547.

7 *Ampthill Peerage* note 5 above.

to serve a society quite strictly governed by the social and legal importance of the marriage relationship in fostering child rearing. Where a child was born to a married woman her husband was deemed to be the father of that child.[8] Until the mid-20th century this presumption successfully settled paternity in most cases (whether or not it was, in fact, true). Other *social* pressures bolstered the results achieved by this presumption and made the presumption seem reliable (notably the pressure to marry before engaging in sexual activity). The legal presumption, then, taken with social pressure worked to identify a father and to link him to a responsible fathering role. He had exclusive parental authority of his child (in preference to the mother) (Cretney 2004, 566). Because marriage was almost indissoluble, he was also actively engaged in fostering the child's well-being on a day to day basis (although usually materially, rather than in term of providing actual care).

There were, of course, instances where married women gave birth to children who were not the children of their husbands. In some cases the secret would have lasted to the grave – so that none of those involved were ever affected. A man – not a father – was, in law, father and bore both social and legal responsibility for 'his' child. But occasionally the issue was open. Either an affair was declared and acknowledged or, in some cases, the parties were complicit in the 'deception' (as, for example, where infertile men arranged – with their wives' cooperation – to have children by 'borrowing' another man and his progenitive material). There is some authority for the proposition that the legal presumption of paternity was, in some jurisdictions and at some moments in history, irrebuttable (Boberg 1977, 324). But by the early part of the 20th century it had become a rebuttable presumption.[9] However, the seriousness of the issues that were raised where allegations of illegitimacy were made resulted in a demand that the evidence used to rebut the presumption of paternity be proved at the criminal standard – beyond a reasonable doubt (Lowe and Douglas 2007, 275).

That evidential burden gave way to the civil standard in 1969 (Family Law Reform Act 1969, s. 26). The authorities continued to demand especially weighty evidence, however. They reminded us that the ordinary civil standard takes account of the seriousness of the allegations made in assessing the amount of evidence that is required to shift the balance.[10] Of course, evidence of the fact of a genetic relationship between a man and a child became significantly more reliable in the latter part of the last century so that talk of the 'standard of proof' is now almost entirely academic.[11]

---

8 *Ampthill Peerage* note 5 above. This civil law presumption – with the latin tag, *Pater est quem nuptiae demonstrant* – seems to have been imported into England by the 12th century (Lowe and Douglas 2007, 321).

9 See *Serio v Serio* (1983), 4 FLR 756.

10 See *Serio v Serio* (1983), 4 FLR 756. For a version of this idea, extended into the difficult area of child sexual abuse see *Re H (Minors) (Sexual Abuse: Standard of Proof)* [1996] 1 FLR 80.

11 There will, of course, continue to be very occasional instances in which the presumption and circumstantial evidence will be determinative (where, for example, DNA material is not available from the alleged father because he has disappeared or has died in a way that has made obtaining his DNA impossible).

Of course, women who bore children when they were not married were also subject to these rules of evidence to establish paternity. No presumption assisted them, but proof on the same basis could be put to the courts – once again in an attempt to discover the truth of paternity.

In the era before dependable scientific evidence of paternity the marital presumption was, clearly, not always a reliable indicator of the fact of paternity.[12] Neither was the fact that circumstantial evidence of paternity was sought to establish paternity of children born to unmarried women (or even to married women whose husbands were able to disprove their paternity). The common law presumption must, sometimes at least, have yielded a father for a child who was not, in fact, the father. Where a married woman was, for example having a sexual relationship with someone else, while at the same time continuing in her sexual relationship with her husband, either man could have been the father of her child. But the husband would have been presumed in law to be the father. Evidence to dislodge that presumption would not have been forthcoming. A simple 'competition' for fatherhood would not have been enough to swing the balance against his paternity (especially where the standard of proof was more onerous than the simple civil standard). The husband would remain, in law, the father of the child in question. And, significantly, that would have imposed upon him the legal responsibilities of fatherhood (notably the support obligation).

Thus, although the premise of paternity was a factual blood relationship, the evidence of that relationship was, for a long time, unreliable. Given this unreliability it is probable that a significant number of children grew up thinking a man to be their father when, in 'fact' – the 'fact' admired so in law – he was not. That man was, however, raising the child.

Social Developments in the 20th Century

There were further social developments in the 20th century that began to reveal the need to resolve the problems associated with the legal determination of paternity. Perhaps the earliest change was the rising significance of social adoption at the beginning of the century (which eventually led to the legalisation of adoption in 1926).[13] It began to create inroads into the stable sense of significance that existed between paternity (status) and fatherhood (social function). Men (and women) who were not fathers (and mothers) of children were raising them and the law's response was to try to make them fathers (and mothers) so that their responsibilities were appropriately borne. Legal adoption introduced children into families which were not, in 'fact', theirs.

In the latter half of the century, however, change began to be swift. The sexual revolution of the 1960s embraced a much more open sexuality which saw an increasing toleration of sexual relations outside of marriage. As a result, pregnancy outside marriage attracted much less opprobrium; unmarried motherhood no longer

12 Cretney reflects that 'disputes about *paternity* were commonplace' in the early part of the 20th century (2004, 530).

13 Adoption Act 1926.

attracted the sense of shame and disgrace that it had once attracted. When, in the late 1960s, a relatively easy legal divorce was introduced[14] (reflecting a changing attitude towards the need for stoicism in relationships) a much more tolerant attitude towards divorced people and multiple sexual relationships began to emerge. The social stigma associated with relationship termination began to wane. Cohabitation rates increased, and births outside marriage began to rise (Haskey 2001). In addition to these demographic changes, the state also began to loom large as the protector of children treated badly by their parents (Cretney 2004, 586). It began to allocate the care of children to different adults who were better able to raise them, and who created new family forms. Foster parents gained some status both in law and in society.

In this new social context the common law presumption of paternity became much less reliable than it had once been in determining the 'real' father of a child. And where there was no presumption (because there was no marriage) or the presumption had been rebutted, finding a father for a child also became less reliable. It was more likely that alternative potential fathers might exist. It is no surprise, therefore, that medical science was forging ahead with techniques that would create a more certain genetic world. By the end of the 20th century it had become possible to link a child to a father using reliable scientific evidence (Johnson 1999).

By the end of the 20th century, then, family life had altered so dramatically, achieving such different ways of being a parent, that the law was compelled to adapt. Social fostering and adoption led to legally invested power for foster carers and a law on adoption. Step-parents, same-sex parents, and single parents were all, gradually, brought within the ambit of the legal regulation of the family (in particular through the flexibility introduced into child law in the Children Act 1989 (CA 1989, particularly in Part II of that Act). In each of these cases the parents of tradition – both social and legal tradition – had been displaced, at least to some extent, by substitute parents whose status in the lives of child unsettled the status of traditional 'real' parents. But these developments took place against the background of the growing reliability of evidence which could identify who those 'real' parents actually were.

The tension that began to emerge, therefore, was one between social and genetic (or biological) parents. This tension led to a debate in law about the relative significance of each in the lived lives of children. Trying to order the status of each in relation to the other (and in relation to children) became the problem law had to resolve, usually when disputes about the responsibilities of the various actors were brought before the courts. In whom did legal responsibility vest? Was it with genetic parents, or did these new social parents acquire some entitlement to exercise responsibility for children? And was that responsibility legally inscribed with power (particularly against the competing desires of 'real' or genetic parents)?

Aside from the (adapting) adoption legislation that was passed during the course of the century, the most important legal step in creating a regulatory framework for these non-genetic participants in child rearing was the enactment of the CA 1989. And perhaps its most important characteristic (in this respect) was the separation of 'parent' from 'parental responsibility' (CA 1989, ss. 2-4, 12 and 14C). While

14 Divorce Reform Act 1969.

the Act makes it relatively easy for parents to acquire parental responsibility (often automatically, or almost automatically (CA 1989, ss. 2 and 4)) it also makes it possible for people who were not parents to do so (in particular, step-parents: CA 1989, s. 4A, but also anyone else: CA 1989, ss. 8, 10 and 12). The law embraced social parenthood as something separate from genetic parentage. Under the CA 1989 it left the courts a considerable discretion to resolve the significance of each – and, in particular, the relative importance of each in relation to the other (CA 1989, s. 1).

While these legal developments impacted upon both women and men, it is clear that the impact was not entirely even. Same-sex parenting and step-parenting are the most obvious circumstances in which the unevenness of the application of the rules on genetic and social parenting has come to have significant gender differences. Same-sex parents raising children are more likely to be women than are men (Weeks et al. 2001, 159). Step-parents involved in the rearing of children are, on the other hand, more likely to be men (Clingempeel et al. 1984, 466; White and Gilbreth 2001, 155). The parent/child relationship is much more likely to be a (physically, if not emotionally) close one for step-fathers than it is for step-mothers. Conversely the genetic parental relationship is likely to be a much looser one between genetic fathers and their children than between genetic mothers and their children where the genetic parents have separated.

The Advent of Medically Assisted Conception

I have left out of account so far developments in medicine that have made it possible to seek assistance with procreation where 'natural' procreation has failed. Of course, some of this capacity is not entirely new. Surrogacy and sperm donation have always been possible. But the common law had, in the light of what might be described as traditions of surrogacy and sperm donation, never deviated from its fact-based assertions of parenthood. Mothers were the women who gave birth to children (and were genetically related to those children anyway). And fathers remained those who could be proved – by the evidence (however unreliable) – to have been the progenitors of children; the circumstantial evidence of a genetic link remained all important.

But medically assisted reproduction has introduced much greater complexity. Women can now carry children genetically unrelated to them, and men can donate sperm without knowing who is to procreate using it and without wishing to become parents as a consequence. Furthermore, gametes can be stored so that they can be used in procreation at some future time, in cycles of treatment that are more and more likely to be successful (as medical techniques are perfected, and because repetition increases the chances of success). These altered circumstances have introduced new problems into the determination of parentage. In particular they have raised the problem of parentage where those who set about procreating use genetic material not their own. Who, in these changed circumstances, should be the parents of children thus created? Are the parents the people whose genes were used in their procreation, or are they the people who wish to be the parents of the children born as a consequence of the medically assisted procreative project? Is it genetics or the prospect of bearing responsibility that matters most to the acquisition of parental status? Perhaps the most intractable problem concerns the circumstances in which the female gamete is implanted in a woman who is not its author. In those circumstances the 'blood tie' itself becomes confused.

Following the report of the Warnock Committee (Warnock 1984), the HFEA 1990 was passed to resolve these (and other) issues. For only the second time in a century[15] the statute resolved the issue by accepting that in some circumstances parentage should not be determined by a blood tie or a genetic link (HFEA 1990, ss. 27-30).

The Act resolved that maternity would continue to be dependent on giving birth (irrespective of the author of the genetic material that resulted in that birth) (HFEA 1990, s. 27). But paternity was less easily resolved. It was clear that the Act wished to end the parental relationship of gamete donors. This it does by formalising a form of donation that allows men to dissociate themselves from their prospective progeny. They will not be the fathers of children born as a result of the use of their gametes (HFEA 1990, s. 28(6)). Like the involvement of men in 'natural' procreation, their (relative) involvement in medically assisted reproduction is fairly limited. If the Act was to divert paternity from the genetic progenitor, therefore, it had to find some other anchor for the ascription of parental status. Like the common law it opted, in the first instance, for marriage (HFEA 1990, s. 28(2)). A social fact – marriage – was used to link a child to an adult through the relationship that that adult had with an undoubted parent (the mother). This was done, no doubt, because that adult was most likely to bear and exercise real social responsibility for the child. The father was not the genetic progenitor but the man who was set to participate in the rearing of the child. In this respect the Act is exactly like the common law. It lends its powerful allocation of status to a man who (whether or not he is 'really' the father) will perform as we expect fathers to perform. The only exception which arises under the Act in relation to husbands arises where they do not consent to their wives' assisted conception treatment. Again, in these circumstances, we might surmise that this is because they would not, in fact, be involved in the rearing of the resulting child and there is no reason in equity to expect them to take responsibility for them.[16]

If there were no husband, or the husband could not be the father because of his failure to consent to his wife's treatment, the Act goes on to find a father elsewhere. Again, the anchor sought is a social one. If a women becomes pregnant 'in the course of treatment services provided for her and a man together' the man in question will be her child's father (HFEA 1990, s. 28(3)). An assumption about the desire of the man to be a responsible father is made because of his involvement in a procreation project (see Probert 2004).[17] His apparent desire to be a father attracts legal respect

---

15 The first had occurred when adoption was introduced as a 'full legal transplant' of parentage in the Adoption Act 1926.

16 Although, see *Leeds Teaching Hospital NHS Trust v A* [2003] EWHC 259 (QB) (discussed below).

17 *Re B (Parentage)* 2 FLR 15.

in the law's ascription of paternity to him. The consequence, we hope, will be a man who accepts responsibility for participating in raising the resulting child.[18]

Although issues of both maternity and paternity were ethically difficult in the debates leading up to the legislation (Warnock 1984) it is the paternity provisions that have created the greatest problems. Given the social developments that were noted above this should come as no surprise. Men are (statistically) more likely to have parent/child relationships which are disrupted by shifting family patterns. Fathers – in the 'fact' based sense – are more likely to be the 'absent' parents of children than are mothers. And social fathers are more likely to be present in raising children not – in genetic terms – their own. This is further complicated by a developing idea – at both the personal and the state level – that absent (genetic) fathers should develop and maintain good active and emotional relationships with their children. This is what responsible (absent) parents would do (Reece 2006).[19]

Paternity in the Cases under the 1990 Act

It is, therefore, to the determination of paternity that I wish to return. I will start with a brief analysis of three important cases in England and Wales which have highlighted these issues. In relation to each I will say something about the result I would have preferred to have seen achieved in each case. My analysis will reveal the extent to which I take issue with Lady Justice Hale (as she then was) when she said (in another case):

> We can only guess at the feelings of someone who has suffered as Mrs U has suffered, but we can sympathise and even empathise with them. There is a natural human temptation to try to bend the law so as to give her what she wants and what she truly believes her husband would have wanted. But we have to resist it.[20]

My analysis will also reveal the extent to which I think that the judges in these cases could have rendered a decision different from the one delivered. To what extent were they powerless to follow their sympathetic instincts? I am interested in the extent to which they really are reliant on Parliament's desire to make changes to the paternity scheme in each case in order to alter its apparent prescriptions.[21] Finally, I will attempt to outline some of the concerns I have with the decisions and with the way

---

18 But see *Re R* [2003] EWCA Civ 182 (discussed below).

19 This is further evidenced in the trend in adoption law to allow for openness and in the statistics on contact with birth relatives after adoption (even if only in adulthood). It is also evidenced in the growing pressure to allow children to have access to identifying information in relation to donor genetic material: government announcement to change the rules on tracing.

20 *Centre for Reproductive Medicine v U* [2002] EWCA Civ 565, para. 29. Similar expressions of sympathy were expressed in *Evans v Amicus Healthcare Ltd* [2004] EWCA (Civ) 727, para. 69.

21 See Brownsword (2004): he expresses the view that in ethically contentious debates the best we can hope for is a process that fully and acceptably allows for full participation in reaching a decision that cannot bridge ethical divides (see also Reece (2003 and 2006)).

in which they are conceptualising paternity. These concerns will be raised in the light of the history of paternity and fatherhood which I have attempted to outline above. In the section which follows I will go on to deal with the way in which the proposed amendment to the statutory structure (in the Human Fertilisation and Embryology Bill 2008) is likely to reinforce the views that judges have taken in these cases and make it even more difficult to achieve the kind of paternity (with its relationship to responsibility) that I would like to see the law develop.

But first, the decisions themselves.

Re R (A Child)[22] *and Re D (A Child)*[23]

In this case a couple approached a clinic for infertility treatment because both had problems which undermined their ability to conceive without assistance. A long process ensued during which embryos were created (using donor sperm) and a treatment cycle was attempted. Conception failed at this first attempt. The couple separated, but the woman returned to the clinic to use the remaining embryos in a second cycle of treatment. At this stage she misled the clinic as to the status of her relationship with the man with whom she had begun to receive treatment services. This time the treatment was successful. A child was conceived. The man discovered the pregnancy and when the child was born sought parental responsibility and contact (under CA 1989, ss. 4 and 8).

In order to succeed in a claim for parental responsibility he had to be the father of the child. As he was not related by blood, he had to satisfy the court that he was the *man together with whom the mother had been provided with treatment services by the clinic* (HFEA 1990, s. 28(3)). In the Court of Appeal Lady Justice Hale, delivering the unanimous judgment of the court, held that, at the relevant time – the time of the second implantation – the treatment services could not have been provided for the woman and the man together because they were no longer a couple on a project to create a child whom they would both parent. The man did not, therefore, satisfy the statutory conditions and was not the father of the child. The court found that whether or not he was party to the treatment services was a simple question of fact, established by the evidence at the time of the second implantation. As he was not party to the relationship at that time the evidence indicated that treatment was not provided for both of the couple.

If one were to read the majority of the commentary on this case it is clear that Lady Justice Hale was right to make this determination. A couple not in a relationship could not, self-evidently, receive treatment services together (see Sheldon 2005). However, I have argued (at length) that the decision was not self-evident and that I would have preferred a different outcome (Lind 2003). My argument attempted to demonstrate how that outcome might have been achieved within the terms of the statute. Despite that argument, however, the courts continue to prefer an ordinary reading of the statute; the House of Lords upheld the Court of Appeal's decision (a similar attitude also was evident in the decisions in *Evans*[24]).

22 [2003] EWCA Civ 182.

23 [2005] UKHL 33.

24 *Evans v Amicus Healthcare Ltd* [2004] EWCA (Civ) 727 (discussed below).

The courts have not embraced the complexity and the sophistication of both the medical and the social events at issue.

Despite the interesting variety of ways in which the superior court decisions in this case can be read to recreate parenthood (Fovargue 2006; Sheldon 2005) I continue to wish for a different conceptualisation of paternity in cases like these. The decisions frame deviation from 'natural' (genetic) parenthood as something difficult to achieve. This is done despite the fact that the creation of non-genetic paternity was deliberately made possible by the statute; paternity could be legally reconstituted against the proscriptions of genetics. Because the language used to achieve that end was convoluted and unclear it seemed possible adopt a flexible understanding of the conditions for the recreation of paternity. The courts could have embraced the policy of the Act to alter paternity where a different strategy towards procreation was chosen than 'natural' conception. As I have said elsewhere (Lind 2003) the man in *Re R* was a much more active participant in the procreation of the child in that case than are many (if not most) men who are genetically (and in law) the fathers of their children. It is that active involvement in the process of procreation and the ambitions he has for responsible parenthood that should be honoured under the statutory scheme (Lind 2003).

Leeds Teaching Hospital NHS Trust v A[25]

Leeds is an even more desperate case. In this case a married couple approached a clinic for infertility treatment. This time the treatment sought involved using the sperm of the husband. The treatment appeared to be successful but when the children (twins) were born it was clear that the husband was not their father. The couple where white; their twins were mixed race children. An investigation revealed that the clinic had *mistakenly* used the sperm of another (the wrong) man in the treatment process (that man and his wife were also trying to have a child using the assistance of the clinic).

The question of paternity was, therefore, before the court. The mother's husband intended to raise the children as their father (and the genetic father had no intention of involving himself in their upbringing). But was the mother's husband their father in law? Section 28 of the HFEA 1990 was engaged because of the clinical intervention in conception. Had the husband's sperm been used, he would have been the father under the statute (which reiterated the common law presumption of paternity: HFEA 1990, s. 28(5)). But because his sperm had not been used the court had to consider whether or not paternity vested in him under section 28(2); was he a husband who had consented to his wife's treatment?

In this respect the court found that it was clear that the treatment for which the husband's consent had been obtained was materially different from the treatment that had been provided; he had consented to treatment using his sperm. The treatment his wife had been given used the sperm of another man. The court held, therefore, that he did not satisfy the conditions of the section and he was not the father of the child.

25 [2003] EWHC 259 (QB).

Once again this decision yields a result I think the law should have avoided. It is also one I am convinced could have been rejected; a different judge might have argued it to a different conclusion. The decision revels in the technicalities of the statute where those technicalities defy the empathy for the parties that the facts raise (the 'donor' is not a formal donor whose consent has been appropriately obtained to distance himself from paternity of the child (he is a man whose sperm is being held for use on his own wife), and the husband's consent is narrowly construed to be about treatment to his wife using his sperm, not simply treatment to achieve a pregnancy). The court also found the will of Parliament to be patently clear where, it is submitted, it could not possibly be that clear (especially given the strange circumstances of the case).[26]

In the circumstances the court found that the man who would be the active father of the child – who would perform as a responsible father, in practice – would have to adopt the children to establish his paternity. The man who had no interest in raising the children would be their father in law (and would, without adoption, be legally responsible for their support and well-being: see, for example, the Child Support Act 1991, s. 1(1)).

Like *Re R* this case harks back to a paternity of genetics and fails to embrace the attribution of paternity to a social relationship which the Act attempted to create. A court demonstrated (for the second time in a week)[27] that the Act's embrace of different criteria for paternity could only operate in the clearest, most technical circumstances.

Evans v Amicus Healthcare Ltd[28]

Evans is perhaps the most difficult of the cases that I wish to analyse here. In this case I have sympathy for the plight of the judges having to determine the issue, despite my great empathy for Ms Evans (Lind 2006).

Two women wished to use embryos which were created during the currency of their relationships with two men. But they wished to use those embryos when those relationships had ended and when the consent to the use of the male gametes had been withdrawn (under the terms of the statute). One of the women – Ms Evans – had, just after the harvesting of her eggs, undergone surgery for ovarian cancer and would never be able to have children genetically related to her again if she could not use those embryos.[29]

---

26 Having found that the husband was not the father because he had not given the particular consent required by s. 28(2) the court would not go on to find that he could be the father under s. 28(3) (as a man together with whom a woman had been provided with treatment services by a licensed clinic) despite the fact that the husband patently satisfied all these conditions (para. 32).

27 *Re R* was decided on 19 February 2003 (in the Court of Appeal) and *Leeds* was decided on 26 February 2003 (in the High Court).

28 *Evans v Amicus Healthcare Ltd, Hadley v Midland Fertility Services Ltd* [2003] EWHC 2161 (Fam), *Evans v Amicus Healthcare Ltd* [2004] EWCA (Civ) 727, and *Evans v United Kingdom* [2006] 1 FCR 585 (ECHR).

29 Although the *Evans* and *Hadley* decisions were made together, the circumstances of Ms Evans were much more difficult that those of Ms Hadley. It is, therefore, no surprise that

On a number of technical arguments the court was not prepared to interpret the Act so as to remove the power of the men to withdraw their consent to the use of their gametes in procreation. Nor was it prepared to use the Human Rights Act 1998 to declare this interpretation of the HFEA 1990 to be incompatible with the Convention rights which the 1998 Act had incorporated into English and Welsh law. Estoppel, the court found, was also of no use to the claimants in their attempts to use the embryos. It could not operate to prevent a man from withdrawing his consent to the use of his gametes in procreation where an Act of Parliament gave him that power.

The underlying problem in this case revolves around the extent to which a person can control her or his gametes so as to control her or his procreative potential. It is most acute when the gametes of two people are brought together in an embryo in respect of which each wishes to make a different decision. It is a problem that has been with us ever since the possibilities of medically assisted reproduction were first mooted.[30] And the solution is as intractable now as it has always been. The observation, for me, that is more relevant, however, as the outcome of these decisions is that they, too (like *Re R* and *Leeds*) enunciate a doctrine of parenthood that harks back to a preoccupation with genetics as the principle criterion of parental identity. People who will 'really' be parents (genetically) must be *absolutely* able to control the procreative uses to which their gametes are put. Despite the legal capacity to sever genes from parenthood under the Act, the court reiterate a view that genetics – rather than real (performed) parental responsibility – is what matters in the determination of paternity.

Analysing the Case Law

I wish to turn to some general comments on these cases and the way in which paternity, as an issue, is affected by them. In this part of the chapter I will be much more questioning and much less prescriptive than might seem to have been the case thus far.

Family responsibility and the control of procreative material

Despite the fact that the courts do not regard embryos as property, their analysis of the control which individuals are taken to exercise over their gametes does, particularly in *Evans*, approximate an unfettered property right (which includes the right to destroy). Because of the consent provisions of the HFEA 1990 the courts appear to accept that Parliament wished to see genetic material controlled by those who were its authors in the most profound way. There is no analysis of the extent to which ideas of (family) responsibility ought to be incorporated into any test of the way in which their decisions are made.

Ms Evans took her concerns all the way to the House of Lords and then to the European Court of Human Rights.

30 For decisions similar to this case see the US and Israeli cases referred to in the ECtHR decision in this case: *Evans v United Kingdom* [2006] 1 FCR 585 (ECHR).

What I find interesting about the pervasive sense of control, which emanates from the consent provisions of the legislation and the courts' interpretation of it, is the significance it attaches to genetic ties. Controlling my gametes becomes, it seems, central to my capacity to determine my most important relationships. Not only am I enabled to choose to use my gametes so as to create a life with which I will have no relationship and in relation to whom I will bear no responsibility at all (as a gamete donor), but that control is extended to the product of the use of my gametes – where another's gametes become involved – provided only that the gametes have yet to be implanted so as to achieve a greater potential for human life.

I have serious reservations about this supreme controlling capacity. People, and men in particular, do not always (or even often) behave responsibly with respect to the uses to which they put their gametes when they are not brought within the context of clinically assisted reproductive treatment. Pregnancies are often 'accidental'. And the responsibility consequences are often confused and complex.[31] In this context the HFEA 1990 and the courts appear to exaggerate the extent to which such pervasive control ought to be exercised over gametes in the case of clinical interventions. This assertion seems to me to become more powerful when we acknowledge the law's capacity (evidenced in the Act) to divorce genetic paternity from social fatherhood and the responsibility to which it gives rise.

If we add to this some simple observations about the nature of the significant relationships we have, we begin to see the danger of extending an exaggerated control over procreative potential. My most important relationships are not necessarily blood relationships – even those that appear to be blood relationships are made important socially and not by virtue of the 'blood tie'.[32] Step-fathers are often more important to their step-children than are their genetic fathers (White and Gilbreth 2001). What matters most to us are the relationships which serve to meet our (emotional and material) needs. What matters to children must be the relationships that result in adults exercising beneficial responsibility for them. This is not – especially in the context of assisted reproduction – dictated by genetic contributions. The shifting family patterns of the last half-century have demonstrated this. The law seemed to have followed suit until disputes under the 1990 Act began to be settled by the courts.

Identity

Of course, the position I take is undermined by another social development: the rise in importance of genetic identity. Since it has become possible to test the (scientific) truth of paternity there is a general eagerness for that truth to be known – or at least

31 Men who are 'accidental' fathers bear unavoidable financial responsibility for children (under the Child Support Act 1991 (as amended)) however thorough their precautions against conception. But they may not have any other responsibility for the child – and may not even have a relationship with them.

32 It is perhaps noteworthy that, in modern Western thought, perhaps the most important relationship in any life is not a blood relationship but a social one (the marriage/partner relationship).

to be available where it is sought to be known.[33] This tendency is developing apace in adoption (Adoption and Children Act 2002, s. 60), and is gathering momentum in the context of clinically assisted reproduction (HFEA 1990, s. 31). In this context, there is clearly a move to reassert control over the uses to which an individual's gametes might be put. Thus, if a child is to trace a genetic parent at some point later in life, the genetic parent is deemed to require a right to control the use to which their genes can be put. But I wonder if that right is necessary? Once again this query is raised in the context of the variety of circumstances in which an individual is a parent (genetically) but is limited in his capacity to exercise responsibility (or attempt to exert rights).[34] In those cases it is clear that a man may create an identifying relationship with a child (where they will know of each other's existence, and of their genetic tie to one another) but in which that tie will in no way undermine the responsibility which the caring parent has for the child. The parental functional relationship is entirely unaffected.

Diverging social trends in paternity/fatherhood recognition

The two concerns raised above also evidence a set of divergent trends: one is the trend towards the greater recognition (and consequent empowerment) of social fatherhood; the other is the trend towards the greater recognition, for the purposes of individual identity, of genetic ties. Giving social parents powerful attributes of parental responsibility must be affected (probably negatively), it is submitted, by a trend which sees a rising desire to trace genetic heritage. The problems of child rearing, must, in these circumstances, be exacerbated by the desire of children to discover their 'real' parents.

These divergent trends clearly create a problem for any regulatory regime which seeks to weaken the control that people have over their genetic material. And yet I would resist the tendency to think that because genetic identity complicates paternity, genetic control should be enhanced in people who have donated their gametes. I take the view that responsibility is what matters a great deal more. It has material and emotional consequences which are of much greater significance than the identity consequences of genetic association and identity.

Absent fathers

For several decades political attention has, periodically, focused on the 'problem' of 'absent fathers' (see, for example, Bennet 2007; Burgess 2004). The pressure to empower absent fathers is already evident in some court decisions.[35] Absent fathers

---

33 This is so even where material changes to the rearing of the child may take place which seem to be disadvantageous to the child: See *Re H & A (Paternity: Blood Tests)* [2002] 1 FLR 1145.

34 See *Re S (Parental Responsibility)* [1995] 2 FLR 648 CA where the court makes it clear that the acquisition of parental responsibility by an unmarried father will not enable him to intervene in the life of his child.

35 *A v A (Shared Residence)* [2004] EWHC 142 (Fam).

acquire parental responsibility relatively easily.[36] They are encouraged in almost every social realm to take a more active role in the lives of their children. And they remain liable for their support (Child Support Act 1991, s. 1(1)) and are subject to inheritance rights on death (Inheritance (Provision for Family and Dependants) Act 1975), ss. 1 and 2).

For people who, although raising children, have no paternal status in their lives it is much more difficult to cement those relationships in law. They usually require leave to apply for a residence order and have additional hurdles to overcome in order to do so (CA 1989, ss. 8 and 10). Even if they are able to create a relationship of responsibility under the 1989 Act, it is not a lifelong legal relationship (unlike the parental relationship) (CA 1989, s. 91). Their relationships with those children seem almost always to be much more tenuous.[37] In relation to step-parents the problems may have been eased by recent legislative amendments (CA 1989, s. 4A), but in the context of parenting by unmarried cohabitants the problems persists.

Where we refuse to recognise willing (responsible) fathers under the HFEA 1990 because they do not satisfy the technical requirements of the sections (interpreted narrowly) we undermine the capacity of those men to assert and develop a relationship with a child which, as I have argued elsewhere (Lind 2003), is much more a consequence of their efforts than are most children born as the result of 'natural' conception. Their responsibility has been demonstrated in their long involvement in and commitment to the procreative process and ought to be rewarded by a real recognition of their status as responsible parents (Probert 2004).

Genes and paternity

In the light of the quote from Thomas Hardy with which I opened this chapter I have another concern about the direction of developments in relation to assisted reproduction. I worry about the ease with which the courts and the statute itself are prepared to reiterate as unproblematic the primacy that people attach to having their own children. This is particularly the case in *Leeds* and *Evans*. In each of these cases the problems would have been reduced considerably had the parties (and the regulatory regime) not been pedantic on the issue of the very particular uses to which their gametes could be put. If we took a broader view of the idea of bearing and raising children not genetically our own (which the Act is designed to foster) the problems in these cases might have disappeared completely. If the law were better able to negotiate the link between the parental status and family responsibility that was being fostered by the HFEA 1990, better decisions would be made (see Freeman, in this volume). And that may require a clearer mapping of that relationship in future legislation.[38]

---

36 *Re H (Local Authority: Parental Rights)* [1991] 1 FLR 214.

37 See, for example, *Re DW* [1984] 14 *Fam L* 17 (where, because a child's father leaves his step-mother, with whom he has an exceptional relationship over eight years, the child is moved to his mother's custody). See too *Re G (Children)* [2006] UKHL 43 (where a lesbian 'step-mother's' relationship with a child is regarded as less significant than the relationship the child has with the genetic mother).

38 It is worth noting that the relationship between parental status and parental responsibility that was (partially) detached in the CA 1989 has, over time, become cloudier

Equality

My final concern is a limited, and technical one. The judgments in all of the cases discussed above considered questions of human rights compliance. In none of them was I convinced by the courts' considered decisions. In human rights discussions there is always scope for legitimate disagreement. But in relation to *Evans* one line of enquiry did strike me as so powerful as to demand proper consideration in the case (which it did not receive).

In *Evans* the court dismissed an assertion that the HFEA 1990 works in a discriminatory manner as between men and women by giving men an unfair veto on the use of embryos. The court held that each of the parties had an equal right to veto further use of the embryos. They were being treated equally. However, I wonder if this is true. The court outlined the way in which a man might be caught in the same bind that had trapped Ms Evans. If he had testicular cancer and had had sperm removed and used in the creation of embryos before the testes were destroyed he too would have lost the chance of genetic parentage if his partner changed her mind about the use of her gametes in procreation.

There is a superficial equality which seems very appealing. But if we consider the social and medical circumstances in which the notion of equal treatment is said to work we are compelled, it is submitted, to see the equal application of the rules very differently. The problem is elaborated in the judgment itself. Sperm freezing is not difficult, nor is it uncommon. Egg freezing, on the other hand, is both uncommon and much less easy to achieve successfully. That simple gender difference makes the decisions that a man and a women take when they have parallel illnesses that will destroy their genetic procreative capacity very different. If Mr Johnston was discovered to have testicular cancer but was able to harvest sperm before having his testes removed his sperm would simply have been stored. Ms Evans had to store embryos. She had to rely on a man's participation in order for her procreative potential to have been rescued. Men and women are not, then, in an equal position when offered assisted reproductive treatment. As I have argued elsewhere, the failure to treat them so as to take account of this significant difference does amount to discriminatory treatment which ought not to have been sanctioned by the court (Lind 2006).

Reform of the Statutory Regime

A long process has been underway to reform the HFEA 1990 (Department of Health 2006). There are a number of concerns about its effectiveness in some of the cases that have come before the courts and in some of the medical developments that have taken place. However, the reform that has been proposed – in the Human Fertilisation and Embryology Bill 2007 (currently[39] before Parliament) – is, it is submitted, a relatively conservative one. Although parental status is extended in

---

again (see Eekelaar 2001). It is perhaps time that the CA 1989, and the HFEA 1990 recaptured the relationship between these two concepts in clearer language.

39 In January 2008.

some progressive ways – for example, to same-sex couples (clauses 42, 43, and 54 of the Bill) – the reform proposed has set out to clarify the law so as to give effect more clearly to a legal position to which the courts in the cases discussed here have subscribed. Instead of opening up the scope of parental status – and the status of fathers in particular – to embrace those who would (and, it is submitted, should) bear responsibility for children, the reformed legislation tries to tighten control of the ascription of parental status. Clearer rules on the allocation of paternity are being formulated so that the cases discussed here do not arise again (see clauses 35-38), but not so that different (better) decisions could be reached. The reform seems to be backward looking; it resolves the problems of the past. But it does not attempt to come to terms with what the status of parents – and in particular, fathers – should be. Nor is there a principled view of the relationship between that status and the responsibility which fathers ought to have for their children. The distinction set out in the CA 1989 between parent (and father, in particular) and parental responsibility has not been clarified in this reform package. That is to be regretted.

Conclusion

The HFE Act 1990 was designed (in part, at least) to disrupt genetic paternity (and maternity) where there was clinical intervention. Deliberate non-genetic parents were to be given the same status as parents and, therefore, the same presumptive responsibilities of parents to raise children. For the first time in law, outside of adoption, a child would be the child of a person, or people with whom it shared no genetic link. Those people would actually raise it and would have presumptive responsibility for it. The only significance of the genetic 'parents' would be as a mark of identity which the child could later access. The Act was designed to acknowledge the importance – in terms of status and responsibility – of the people who were most responsible for its procreation (parents, in a truly social sense). In cases where a project to procreate involved outside clinical assistance the Act allowed for a breach of the parental relationship normally established by virtue of a genetic link between an adult and a child.

In this respect the Act might be said to hark back to the days of a fiction of paternity (the common law presumption of paternity). The social fact looms larger than the genetic one. Paternity determination defies a particular kind of evidence: in the case of the common law presumption, circumstantial evidence that casts doubt on paternity, but does not persuade us that the husband is not the father of a child; in the case of medically assisted conception, the genetic evidence that attempts to undermine the social evidence of the project to procreate.

In other words, a presumption arises out of social involvement in procreation rather than out of the genetic link. Husbands were fathers of children by presumption whether or not their genetic material had created the child because their involvement in the child's procreation was presumed to arise out of the marriage and to be performed in the family life that would ensue. They would conduct themselves both as responsible parents and as responsible spouses. Assisted reproduction seemed designed to follow that pattern; social involvement in the procreative project would be followed by social involvement in parenting. The law allowed responsibility to follow (an amended) status. We should be wary of interpreting or amending our law to reduce its capacity to foster this flexible association of a man with a child, an association which has sought out a new future for responsible parenting by harking back to the productive and responsibility inducing fictions of the past.

References

Anderson, K.G. (2006), 'How Well does Paternity Confidence Match Actual Paternity? Evidence from Worldwide Non-paternity Rates', *Current Anthropology* 47, 513-21.

Bainham, A. (1999), 'Parentage, Parenthood and Parental Responsibility: Subtle, Elusive Yet Important Distinctions' in Bainham, A., Day Sclater, S. and Richards, M. (eds), *What is a Parent?* (Oxford: Hart Publishing).

Bainham, A., Day Sclater, S. and Richards, M. (eds) (1999), *What is a Parent?* (Oxford: Hart Publishing).

Bennet, R. (2007), 'Absent Fathers Face Automatic Fines and Mandatory Fees', *The Times* (6 June), available at http://www.timesonline.co.uk/tol/news/politics/article1890476.ece, accessed on 25 January 2008.

Boberg, P.Q.R (1977), *The Law of Persons and the Family* (Cape Town: Juta).

Brownsword, R. (2004), 'Regulating Human Genetics: New Dilemmas for a New Millenium', *Medical Law Review* 12, 14.

Burgess, A. (2004), 'Absent Fathers Need Not Just be Seen as Walking Wallets', *The Guardian* (20 November), available at http://www.guardian.co.uk/comment/story/0,,1355535,00.html, accessed on 25 January 2008.

Cerda-Flores, R.M., Barton, S.A., Marty-Gonzalez, L.F., Rivas, F. and Chakraborty, R. (1999), 'Estimation of Non-paternity in the Mexican Population of Nuevo Leon: A Validation Study with Blood Group Markers', *American Journal of Physical Anthropology* 109, 281-93.

Clingempeel, W.G., Brand, E. and Ievoli, R. (1984), 'Stepparent-stepchild Relationships in Stepmother and Stepfather Families: A Multimethod Study', *Family Relations* 33, 465-73.

Cretney, S. (2004), *Family Law in the Twentieth Century: A History* (Oxford: Oxford University Press).

Department of Health (2006), *Review of the Human Fertilisation and Embryology Act: Proposals for Revised Legislation (including establishment of the Regulatory Authority for Tissue and Embryos)* (Cm 6989) (Norwich: HMSO).

Diduck, A. (2007), '"If Only We Can Find the Appropriate Terms to Use the Issue Will be Solved": Law, Identity and Parenthood', *Child and Family Law Quarterly* 19, 458.

Eekelaar, J. (2001), 'Rethinking Parental Responsibility', *Family Law* 31, 426.

Fovargue, S. (2006), '*Re R (IVF: Paternity of Child)*: Assisting Conception for the Single Infertile', *Child and Family Law Quarterly* 8, 423.

Hardy, T. (1995), *Jude the Obscure* (London: Wordsworth).
Haskey, J. (2001), 'Cohabitation in Great Britain: Past, Present and Future Trends – and Attitudes', *Population Trends* 103, 4.
Haskey, J. (2001), 'Demographic Aspects of Cohabitation in Great Britain', *International Journal of Law, Policy and the Family* 15, 51.
Johnson, M. (1999), 'A Biomedical Perspective on Parenthood' in Bainham, A., Day Sclater, S. and Richards, M. (eds), *What is a Parent?* (Oxford: Hart Publishing) 47.
Lind, C. (2003), '*Re R (Paternity of IVF Baby)* – Unmarried Paternity Under the Human Fertilisation and Embryology Act 1990', *Child and Family Law Quarterly* 15, 32.
Lind, C. (2006), '*Evans v United Kingdom* – Judgments of Solomon: Power, Gender and Procreation', *Child and Family Law Quarterly* 18, 576.
Lowe, N. and Douglas, G. (2007), *Family Law* (10th edition) (Oxford: Oxford University Press).
Probert, R. (2004), 'Families, Assisted Reproduction and the Law', *Child and Family Law Quarterly* 16, 273.
Reece, H. (2003), *Divorcing Responsibly* (Oxford: Hart Publishing).
Reece, H. (2006), 'From Parental Responsibility to Parenting Responsibly' in Freeman, M. (ed.), *Law and Sociology* (Oxford: Oxford University Press), 459.
Richards, M. (1999), 'A Biomedical Perspective on Parenthood' in Bainham, A., Day Sclater, S. and Richards, M. (eds), *What is a Parent?* (Oxford: Hart Publishing).
Sasse, G., Muller, H., Chakraborty, R. and Ott, J. (1994), 'Estimating the Frequency of Non-paternity in Switzerland', *Human Heredity* 44, 337-43.
Sheldon, S. (2005), 'Fragmenting Fatherhood: The Regulation of Reproductive Technologies', *Modern Law Review* 68, 523.
Warnock, M. (1984), *Report of the Committee of Enquiry into Human Fertilisation and Embryology* (The Warnock Committee) (London: HMSO).
Weeks, J., Heaphy, B. and Donovan, C. (2001), *Same Sex Intimacies: Families of Choice and Other Life Experiments* (London: Routledge).
White, L. and Gilbreth, J.G. (2001), 'When Children Have Two Fathers: Effects of Relationships with Stepfathers and Noncustodial Fathers on Adolescent Outcomes', *Journal of Marriage and the Family* 63, 155-67.

Chapter 11

Being Responsible: 'Good' Parents and Children's Autonomy

Amanda Wade[1]

> Amanda: When you look at your grandchildren's lives and think about your own, what do you see as the biggest changes?
>
> Madge: Well, they have more freedom haven't they? And they have far too much.
>
> Wilf: It's a different world.

Madge and Wilf are two people I interviewed as part of a three-generational study of parenting.[2] In characterising contemporary childhoods as being distinguished by the freedom children are now permitted, they were far from alone. Interviewees from across the sample depicted children today as being permitted a level of self-expression and of personal choice that differentiates them from other, earlier, generations. Some, like Madge and Wilf, inferred that this is to be regretted; that it is a process that has been allowed to go too far, leaving children without the clear guidelines and boundaries that they need. Others were more positive, viewing it as a welcome development; an indication that children are no longer seen as lacking competence due to their immaturity, but as persons in their own right whose views and feelings should be respected. Whatever the perspective, the term 'freedom' was used as shorthand covering a range of behaviours and beliefs, but notably to refer

1 My thanks to Inge Bates with whom an early version of this chapter was discussed. Also to Carol Smart and my former colleagues at the Centre for Research on Family Kinship and Childhood at the University of Leeds for their support when this research was undertaken.

2 ESRC R000239248. The study used parenting as a lens through which to examine changes in parenting practices; transformations in family relationships (including shifts in the way children are thought of and in the relations of care between parents and children); and the impact of social and life events on the construction of meaning. Qualitative biographical interviews were carried out with 80 people (21 men and 59 women), aged between 100 and 21 years, from 27 families. In most cases I interviewed at least one member of each of three generations (referred to for simplicity as the grandparent, parent, and grandchild generations) from each of these families, although in one case, I was able to interview across four generations of the same family. The term 'grandchild' is somewhat misleading in referring to members of the youngest cohort, as all interviewees in this category were over the age of 21and some were parents themselves. Members of the oldest generation were the first to be recruited into the study and, in order to capture a diverse range of family experience, were drawn from three localities with contrasting socio-economic characteristics.

to autonomy. And, like Wilf, older interviewees invariably associated it with other, wider, social changes that have led to the creation of a 'different world', so that their own childhoods seem to them to have been lived in another dimension as well as another time.

These viewpoints are, of course, not new. Whether in everyday conversations, media discussions, or academic debates, the transformations brought about in social relations over the past century by processes of individualisation are the subject of considerable analysis and controversy. In the literature, as far as family life is concerned and in particular in the relations between parents and children, there is broad agreement that there has been a discernible trend towards more democratised family arrangements (Beck 1997; Beck and Beck-Gernsheim 2002; Giddens 1999). The emergence of 'progressive' child rearing practices among sections of the UK middle and working classes during the early 20th century (when rising standards of living and the declining birth rate facilitated the expression of individual affection towards children), and the subsequent growth of awareness of children's emotional needs (especially in the aftermath of World War Two and the family separations that this had entailed), are widely portrayed as contributing to an erosion of the hierarchical and authoritarian relations that had previously pertained and, social historians suggest, represent a shift that has become ever more pronounced (Bertaux and Thompson 1993; Davidoff et al. 1999; Hendrick 1997; Roberts 1995). Contemporary families, it is suggested, are more participative and democratic (Brannen et al. 2004; Smart et al. 2001). Generational relationships, and especially the boundaries and power relations between parents and children, have been progressively restructured, and this is expressed, in particular, in practices around autonomy, control and participation (Tomanovic 2003). Within the home, evidence for children's participation in everyday family life is demonstrated in their involvement in decision-making (which school to attend; what leisure pursuits and activities to engage in); the exercise of personal choice (what to eat, what to wear); and their scope for expressing their feelings and opinions. Outside it, social policy and legislation increasingly recognise and promote the importance of listening to, and taking account of, children's views, opinions, and experiences (Fortin 1998; James and James 1999; Smart et al. 2005).[3]

This is not to suggest that this has been simple, one-directional process. The brief sketch that I have outlined above inevitably disguises a far more nuanced picture. Recent research indicates that how family democracy manifests itself can vary greatly and is by no means characteristic of all (Brannen 1996; Morrow 1999; Smart et al. 2001; Williams 2004). Parents vary both in the extent to which they regard their children as persons with views, feelings and desires of their own, and in their willingness to accommodate and compromise in the face of these considerations. The scope that children have for the expression of autonomy and personhood intersects with beliefs about the obligations and responsibilities that parents have

3 For example, s. 1(3) (a) of the Children Act 1989 placed a statutory duty on the courts to have regard to children's wishes in welfare cases, while s. 52(2) of the Criminal Justice Act 1991, abolished the competency test that had for so long placed barriers in the way of children giving evidence in criminal proceedings.

towards their children. As Austin says, we 'intuitively believe that parents have certain obligations and rights with respect to their children that others do not have' (2007, 4), these obligations including the provision of care and 'helping children become autonomous pursuers of a good life' (2007, 8). Given that autonomy implies self-sufficiency, the ability to provide for oneself and to act on one's choices, it is simply not possible to argue that it is something that children innately have. Rather, it is something that they acquire as their knowledge and understanding of the world, and capacity for self-direction, expand. And it is here that parents have a central role, the responsibility for raising their children necessarily involving the obligation to nurture and promote their potential, eventually, to live independently. Nevertheless, how this should be done is open to wide interpretation. So, while some see young children, in particular, as being in need of clear parental protection and guidance, and the process of becoming independent as a very gradual one, others emphasise children's capacity from an early age to make sense of the world, pointing to the exploratory behaviour of infants (see, Winnicott 1964),[4] and the persistence with which those as young as three or four years pursue answers to the questions that intrigue them (see Dunn 1996; Tizard and Hughes 1984).

In this chapter I explore some of the shifts that have occurred over three generations in attitudes and practices around the obligations and responsibilities of parents, and the autonomy to be accorded to children. In particular, I examine the suggestion that contemporary family practices accord children more scope for autonomy and self-determination than was the case in earlier generations. I should emphasise that in addressing this question I am not concerned with issues of measurement – it is doubtful whether autonomy is realistically quantifiable in this way – but in whether the locations of autonomy have shifted, thus giving rise to a (possibly misleading) impression of extensive social change.

In what follows I therefore explore the concepts of autonomy and responsibility through the lived experiences of the participants in my research study. Autonomy is considered as children's capacity for independence, whether in terms of action and activity; thought and expression; or the exercise of choice. So, I explore a number of dimensions of autonomy related to children's participation in everyday life, such as the possibilities for them to direct their own use of space and time; the extent to which they act independently in taking responsibility for themselves and others; and their options for expressing their opinions and for influencing decisions that affect them.

Sociologists, interested in children as competent social actors but acknowledging that children's worlds are largely determined by adults, often focus on the strategies that children adopt in order to attain a relative autonomy by subverting the limitations placed upon them by parental rules and guidelines (Punch 2001; Tomanovic 2003). It is likely that children will always have found ways around adult rules and prohibitions to a greater or lesser extent, depending on their circumstances, strength of character

---

4 Chapter 11, 'The Baby as a Person', demonstrates this clearly, while Chapter 19 contains a lovely account of a mother whose success in breastfeeding her infant rested on 'following him, letting him decide when to start and when to finish' (126).

and determination and, clearly, this is a rich area for investigation.[5] However, given that I am interested in shifting attitudes towards children, I concentrate on areas of autonomy that are socially sanctioned. So, rather than focusing on autonomy as expressed through resistance, I look instead at how children's autonomy intersects with ideas about responsible parenting. I use the term 'responsible' here in its everyday sense of moral accountability, and to denote parents' beliefs about the ways in which they 'should' raise their children, as expressed in and through their decisions about their children's upbringing. With this in mind, the chapter explores the dimensions of everyday life where children's autonomy is encouraged, promoted or expected by their parents. In presenting material from the data set to support my arguments, and to explore the traditional liberal/welfare assumption that opportunities for the expression of autonomy are progressive and increase with age, I give priority to experiences of autonomy in younger childhood and in relation to young people entering work.

Everyday lived experiences of childhood autonomy across a span of some 80 years are explored. The data are grouped into three broad sections corresponding to the 'grandparent', 'parent', and 'grandchild' categories of my research study. In the first section, I draw on data from interviews with the oldest participants, who reflect back on their childhoods and the manner in which they were raised. In the second section, these same interviewees speak about how they raised their own children, sometimes defining this in relation both to their depictions of the upbringing that they received and that they now see their grandchildren receiving. Additionally, I draw here on material from interviews with the second ('parent') generation of interviewees, who offer their own accounts of their childhoods. The third section, similarly, draws on the accounts both of the 'parent' cohort and of the 'grandchild' cohort.

I characterise the experience of childhood over the period of the study as moving through three broad phases. The first I term one in which children were expected to be responsible for themselves from an early age. Parental responsibility rested primarily in providing materially for the family, something that involved much time-consuming labour, leaving little opportunity for direct oversight of children. Thus children had to become self-reliant, and learn to subordinate their own wishes to the needs of the family as a whole. The second I define as a period of opportunity and social mobility, when parents saw themselves as responsible for helping their

---

5 At the time of writing, I am reading the autobiography of Alois Podhajsky. Born in 1898, the former director of the Spanish Riding School in Vienna recalls how his first riding lessons had to be 'stolen pleasures'. 'It had been my dearest wish as long as I could remember to have a horse of my own, a wish that was in one sense fulfilled about my third birthday when I was given a magnificent grey – unfortunately only a rocking horse. … Even though I enjoyed these early rides, my thoughts darted way beyond my trusty steed, building up a picture of a real horse, still the object of my dreams. I sometimes managed to persuade our servants to let me sit on one of my father's horses and make a round of the barracks square perched high on its back. … Later, I took clandestine riding lessons with some of the grooms who were fond of me. It was often terribly difficult to conceal the damage to my clothes and myself that resulted from these escapades, for my stern father would have none of his son's passion for riding, and my surreptitious excursions had to be kept from him.' *My Dancing White Horses*, 1964, 18-9.

children benefit from the life chances opening up. Equally, they felt responsible for their children's happiness and associated this with more companionable parent/child relations. The third phase I represent as one in which parental responsibility is expressed in equipping children to become competent in rational decision-making, and the strategic exercise of choice. Throughout, I attempt to tease out the interplay between autonomy and responsibility. Inevitably, the wide age-span of my interviewees means that they do not always fit neatly into age-banded cohorts, nor do their accounts map exactly onto the three categorisations, which inevitably are broad-brush-stroke. Nevertheless, I believe there is sufficient equivalence in participants' experiences across the three groupings to ensure that the generalisations that follow are meaningful.

The Responsible Child

As indicated above, I have characterised my oldest interviewees, most of whom were born during the 1920s and 1930s, as having had childhoods that ensured that they became responsible and self-reliant from an early age. Childcare manuals published around this time (see King 1937; Watson 1928) promoted behaviourist methods of raising children. They encouraged mothers to see themselves as professionals and, rather than behaving 'sentimentally' (that is, tenderly) towards their children, advocated a disciplined approach that centred on 'habit training'. The aim was to raise children who could quickly be relied upon to be well behaved, independent and self-reliant. None of my older participants referred to these authors, and it is unlikely that Truby King or Watson's work was read in their homes. Nonetheless, the ethos expressed in these manuals captures certain of the qualities of the older participants' childhood memories.

The members of the 'grandparent' generation who took part in the study were recruited from three Midlands/Northern localities with contrasting socio-economic characteristics: a deprived rural former mining village, a prosperous county town, and a large cosmopolitan city. Yet, despite the differences between the three locations, and differences in the social positions that the older participants had achieved during their lifetimes, their backgrounds were often remarkably similar. Except for three older women from professional or landed backgrounds, and five participants whose parents' occupations were classified as middle or lower-middle class, all had been raised in working class families, their fathers for the most part being either agricultural labourers or miners. They described childhoods in which their parents' primary concern, as parents, was to provide materially for their families. In many cases, the fathers worked long hours in their primary occupation and followed this with further work on an allotment where they grew the family's food. In some cases the family also kept chickens and in many, a pig was raised, slaughtered, and shared on a communal basis by groups of families. Mothers, like fathers, contributed to the economic support of the household. In addition to running a home, with all that this entailed (including making and mending clothes, and preserving the produce of gardens, hen coops and pig sties), many had paid part-time employment. Some worked as cleaners or shop workers; others were home workers, for example, collecting stockings from local factories, and stitching intricate silk patterns into the heels and seams.

The sheer physical labour and time that had to be devoted to supporting and running a working class household at this time required self-discipline and a contribution from everyone, including children. Some of my interviewees described warm relationships with their parents; families in which time had been made for cuddles and companionship, or in which some of the labour demanded by everyday life became the subject of family jokes, rituals and celebrations. One interviewee described, with affectionate amusement, a mother whose impatience with cooking meant that her cakes invariably had a burnt crust while remaining soggy and uncooked inside. Another recalled how the summer's crop of runner beans was always celebrated with a 'bean feast' in the garden to which her cousins were invited. But, in other households, the long hours of work demanded of parents meant that there was limited scope to give time, or become close, to their children and these parents were often viewed by their children as remote or authoritarian. Gwen, aged 72, remembered how, when she contracted an infectious illness that required isolation, she received no special attention:

> I was sent to stay with an aunt. Actually, my mother didn't have that sort of interest in me. Honestly, no. No. I mean, she would care for me. I remember the ... the doctor coming etc., etc. You know, there wouldn't be any neglect but there wouldn't be any pampering either. Well, in a way it wasn't possible, you know.

In these circumstances, it was vital that children should quickly become capable of looking after themselves both in the home and outside it; Lillian (aged 78), recalled how she would walk to Brownies by herself, even in the winter when it was dark, and described how her father had taught her to box so that she acquired the confidence to stand up for herself. If children were hurt or injured, they were not expected to show prolonged distress, but to control their feelings. This self-regulation extended to developing a willingness to subordinate their own wishes to those of their parents and the needs of other family members, and to contribute as necessary to the household. Their use of time was highly structured; there were household chores to be completed before and after school. Growing older meant that children acquired more responsibility within the family, rather than more scope for self-determination. Once of an age to take up paid employment, their choice of occupation was a matter for the family as much as for themselves. And, as long as they remained a member of their parents' household (which they tended to do until marriage), their wages were handed over to their mother, with a small amount of 'spending money' being returned for their own use.

Viewed from the present, such childhoods appear to offer little in the way of autonomy. Yet, in being independent and self-regulating, the children acquired a certain freedom and status. Parental rules and expectations were internalised from an early age; few participants remembered being taught what was expected of them; they simply 'knew'. All of this meant that they did not have to be subjected to close adult supervision. So, the manner in which children carried out their allocated tasks or responsibilities was largely a matter for themselves; moreover, where they went and how they occupied such free time as they had, was for them to determine as long as they returned home when expected, and did not become the subject of complaints from other people in the community. Furthermore, these children were regarded as contributors to, rather than dependents upon, the family. Their necessary contribution to the running of the home, or the family economy, meant not only that they acquired skills but that they were regarded as competent persons, and this not only by members of their families, but also by those outside it. An interesting factor arising from these interviews is the frequency with which participants speak of non-familial adults as childhood friends or companions; people who took an interest in them; treated them as equals; shared knowledge and activities with them, and passed on skills.

To illustrate some of these themes I will draw on an interview with Harry; a 75 year old, who was a member of a large extended family with a network of businesses that encompassed farming, a milk round, grocery shop, and undertaking. Harry described how:

> When, … I'd be about eleven or twelve-year old, I used to get up in the morning and I'd go down to that farm and … I'd put grain into these two horses to feed them, water them, harness them up, bring them out, put them in milk floats – we'd two milk floats … for me Uncle Arthur and them to go on the milk round. … And I'd take this money, always in bags, always silver, to the bottom of Boar Hill to Mrs. Brent's farm. And they used to put a fifteen gallon and a ten gallon on there, and … then I'd come back, go and get two buckets of coal for me Grandma, two buckets of coal for me Mother, go in Uncle Cyril's shop and make sure there was sticks to light a fire, and then I could probably have my breakfast and get ready to go to school.
>
> Amanda: Really? So, how long would you have spent working then, before you went to school? How many hours?
>
> Harry: Well, I should say, from four o'clock till probably half-past seven – three and a half hours most mornings. Yes. But it wasn't working … it was 'Go and help your Grandad', 'Go and help your Dad' … I took it as part of life, you know.
>
> Amanda: Yes? …You didn't think of it as working?
>
> Harry: No. It was just part of living. Aye. Part of living.

It is clear from this extract how tightly embedded Harry was in the network of relationships that made up the family economy, and it is telling that he does not see this activity as 'work' or a chore. Harry does not give the impression that he felt in any way exploited. He was expected to work hard but so was everyone else around him. In contributing to the family as he did, Harry's membership of the family unit was made explicit. Like his uncles, parents and grandparents, he had a part to play in the family's functioning.

What also became clear during the interview was that the range of business activities in which his family was involved invested Harry's life with considerable interest. There was always something to learn and contribute. And, he could organise some of his allocated tasks in such a way as to ensure himself time to combine these with the pursuit of interests of his own:

> But, same as I say, I enjoyed growing up. I mean, I used to unharness those two horses, rub them down, feed them, jump on Peg or Billy and down that hill … into the station yard, and lean over and open the gate and I'd say "Come on Peg" … and I'd ride the full length of the meadows, up over the hedge … with Billy running after us. … And off I'd go and that were it.

Autonomy, amongst this generation of children, can thus be found in the early competence and self-regulation that they acquired, and in their capacity for acting independently, taking responsibility for themselves and others, whether animals, or younger siblings. It is also evident in the opportunities that they created for finding pleasure in their activities and surroundings, despite the bounded contours of their lives. From the perspective of their parents, a 'good' parent is seen as needing to ensure that the children were equipped to become self-regulating and self-reliant in the desired manner, given that the demands of providing for and running a household allowed them little time to watch over the children. In this respect, the emphasis on hierarchical relations within the family, inculcation of a strong sense of duty, and exercise of firm discipline can be seen as constructive and a means of meeting their children's needs.

Opportunity's Child

In the main, this older generation of interviewees became parents themselves in the 1940s and early 1950s, in the aftermath of World War II. Liz Heron, herself a child of the time, has said that 'beyond 1945 and its immediate aftermath was the outline of a future permeated with hope' (1985, 156). This was a period when a new democratic emphasis guided much social thinking. After the dislocations of the war, the family became an objective into which many people channelled their desires for peace, intimacy and security. Children were central to this vision and, in a powerful reaction against authoritarianism of all kinds, there was a rejection of strict forms of discipline in favour of more liberal methods focusing on understanding and guiding the child (see Post 1947; Ribble 1943; Spock 1946; Winnicott 1957a and 1957b). Enjoyment and reciprocity were regarded as central features of the parent/child relationship: 'A child needs to feel he is an object of pleasure and pride to his mother; a mother needs to feel an expansion of her own personality in the personality of her child' wrote Bowlby (1953, 77).

Once again, many of these ideas emerge in the interviews I was given. Above all, what the interviews show is the importance placed by this generation of parents on their children's happiness. This is apparent in numerous ways but, conspicuously, emerges in the emphasis placed by interviewees on their children's development and well-being; their concern to nurture their children's interests and aptitudes; pursuit of more permissive and companionate forms of parenting; and willingness to put their own needs or wishes aside in order to promote their children's futures. Interviewees whose own relationships with their parents had been lacking in intimacy, or who had felt that their parents had had little time for them, were especially committed to this stance. Grace (aged 64), while somewhat younger than the majority in this cohort, expressed the essence of these ideas when she said:

> Our parents didn't seem to have time ... they didn't have time to do things like we do for ours. We found time. ... All I can say is [my childhood was] not a family life I'd like to go through again. Not like it is now. We tried to do as much as we could for our kids.

Clearly, in this she was successful for her daughter Nicci (aged 40) told me:

> I had a very happy childhood, a very cosseted childhood. ... I felt very loved, very much that ... I [was] the focus of my parents' life. That's the overwhelming feeling that they gave [my brother and me], and I wanted to please them. ... I always wanted to come home [from school] and tell them I'd done well, "The teacher said I'd done this good", and "look at my work" and "I can read this book".

In wanting to give their children opportunities that they, themselves, had not had some of my interviewees limited the size of their families. They did this in the belief that this would enable them to provide better, materially, for those children that they had, giving them better food, clothes and toys, and taking them on holidays. Fewer children in a family also meant that parents could more readily devote time to each child. Companionship became an important element of the relationship; a way in which intimacy and closeness could develop, not only fostering mutual enjoyment but also giving parents increased access to their children's internal worlds, and a means of monitoring their emotional well-being. This sensitisation to children's feelings was accompanied by a wish for their lives to be free of the demands and constraints that, as children, the parents had experienced. For Harry, as for many others I spoke to, this meant freeing their children from expectations that they should contribute to the running of the home and family. 'I gave them freedom', said Harry. 'As long as they were willing to do their schooling, they'd got their freedom.' This is reflected in the interviews given by the second generation of participants. Penny (47), for example, said:

> I don't recall being restricted in play. ... You could go out after your breakfast and mum never seemed to be worried where we were ... as long as we got back for lunch time and as long as we got back for tea time, it didn't really matter where we went. ... We were gone for hours on end, in the summer time anyway. During the winter there were fields with a slope and we'd go sledging if there was snow. ... I don't know, am I remembering it through rosy tinted glasses? ... I don't recall having many restrictions ... as long as you were in for your tea and in for your dinner and you had your breakfast, you had your food inside you (laughter) then we were quite happy.

As Penny admits, such a representation of childhood is frequently met with scepticism. Yet her account of temporal and spatial autonomy, of being free to use her time as she wished within the constraints of attending school and being at home for meal times, echoes those of the majority of interviewees in this cohort.

The data also indicate that ensuring a secure future for their children was a priority for many of the parents, with education being seen as central to achieving this:

> Jenny (aged 81): I wanted education for them. Because … the time was coming when education, you was going to need it if you wanted to get on in the world. And, they were never pushed. Never pushed, encouraged. You know, we'd buy educational – not toys – books … we'd watch what their schoolwork was like, but we never had any problems with them. ... I'm never saying they was top of the class for everything, they weren't. But they was always up at the top end, and happy … that was the main thing. We would never have pressurized them. … No, as long as they was happy. They did social things. Julie played the piano and Sally wanted horse-riding which they did. They were in Guides and Brownies, you know. They found their own measure. We didn't curb them an awful lot, just tried to guide them.

Jenny's memories capture much of the essence of the concept of 'good' parenting that emerges from these post-war accounts. Children were to be nurtured and encouraged; their happiness was a priority and harsh forms of discipline and training were to be abhorred. Jenny's comment that 'the time was coming' is indicative of how, as a responsible parent, she had to think not only of her children's present needs but also their future ones, requiring her to be responsive to changing social circumstances, and frame her parenting strategies accordingly. New opportunities were opening up, especially through education and, like many of her contemporaries, she wanted her children to be amongst those who benefited.

In addition to experiencing more scope than their parents for directing their use of space and time, this second generation of children exercised substantially more choice in terms of their future occupations. Whereas for their parents starting work had not meant independence, but new responsibilities associated with their enhanced means of contributing to the family economy, for many of these children a wealth of opportunities were available on the completion of their schooling. The expansion of further and higher education at this time put within the reach of lower-middle/working class young people a range of educational and career options, together with the life chances associated with them, that had been unavailable to their parents. A typical story is that of Penny, quoted above, who characterised herself as having been a shy child with low expectations. She described how, as a child, she had turned down a chance of music lessons at school not because she thought her parents would object but simply because, 'I was so sure that musical instruments cost too much and mum and dad would never have the money to buy me one'. Yet, as an adolescent she began to regret her erstwhile timidity, realising that:

> There were all these things that I wanted to do and I hadn't had the confidence. … I suddenly realised, you know, "This is silly, whatever I'm doing I'm stopping myself rather than somebody else saying no, … I'm putting up hurdles for myself". I really don't know if there was anything that first prompted that. It's just something I became aware of … I sort of thought "Right I'm going to have to do something or sit at home and do nothing forever", so I started to go on these holidays with [a friend] and we went pony trekking … and I went on the school trip up to Oban in Scotland to do sailing and canoeing and scuba diving. We did … all sorts of things.

Here, we have Penny representing her adolescent self as an autonomous person who made her own choices and decisions. There is no reference to discussion with her parents although (presumably) they paid for the holidays and school trips. Indeed, the lack of reference to money and implicit assumption of parental support is intriguing given her comments about her younger self, and is suggestive of the extent to which the shift in her expectations reflected cultural changes as much as a personal transformation. Whatever the explanation, Penny's account of her adolescent career choice is that of a self-directing agent:

> I thought, "Well … I don't want to be a teacher, I don't want to be a secretary and I don't want to work in a shop", which [was] … what they [school/careers adviser] seemed to be encouraging. … and, suddenly it was like a big flash, "I want to join the Navy, that's what I'm going to do, that's my whole purpose", and it was as sudden as that, that's what I'd been looking for. I wanted to do something different, not the run of the mill.

Having realised what she wanted to do, Penny set about achieving her ambition, finding out all the necessary information, and arranging and attending for an interview by herself. When I asked if this was something that her parents had encouraged, she responded:

> They said "Just find something you're happy with" but nothing specific, not "Well you seem to have a leaning towards this, why don't you think of that?" or "You don't appear to be very good at that so I should steer away from that". Nothing like that, but I can remember them always saying "Just find something you're happy with" so when I did say I wanted to join the WRENS, I don't know whether they could see the enthusiasm or whatever it was, then they said "Well go for it", they were really pleased that I had found something that I wanted to do.

This account epitomises the qualities of responsive, permissive parenting that many of my second-generation interviewees experienced. In electing to join the WRENS, Penny was stepping outside family tradition. Her father had been in a reserved occupation during the war, and no member of the family had been in the services. The careers open to women of her mother's generation, in the community in which Penny lived, were those that she described; teaching, and secretarial, factory or shop work. For her parents, Penny's decision to join the WRENS represented both something of which to be proud, but equally a loss, as it took Penny away from them both geographically and socially; the future trajectory of her life was very different to theirs. There was never a question, however, but that they would support her.

I use this example because, within the study, Penny's is not an unusual story. Harry, living in the same mining village, watched from the sidelines as his daughter passed her 'A' levels and gained a place at a university. He saw it as his role to foster, rather than guide, her ambitions and supported her financially and practically throughout her studies. Jenny, another village resident, similarly supported her children's aspirations although, in contrast to Harry, or to Penny's parents, she took a more active role in shaping their choices. Believing that she knew her children's characters and aptitudes, she did what she could to help them obtain the career openings she thought would suit them. Thus, knowing that her older daughter wanted to become a teacher, she contacted the Education Department and secured a post for her as a local teaching assistant before helping her through training college. Nevertheless, Jenny too felt that, in the end, it was her children who should decide what they would do. Having dissuaded her younger daughter from leaving school aged 15, she did not stand in her way when at 16, and having passed her 'O' levels, she decided that she did not want to go any further academically:

> She didn't want to stop on. … She left school and worked in a bank. No, she didn't want to go further on. We gave her the chance. We wanted them all to go further on but … I wouldn't put pressure on or anything.

From these accounts, it is clear that, certainly in terms of choosing their future careers, the decision was very much viewed as the young person's. Their parents had, themselves, exercised little choice in this area and, undoubtedly, this affected the views of many of them; several spoke in their interviews of their frustrated ambitions. At the same time, this was not simply a matter of wanting their children to have what they had not had themselves, but reflected a changing view of children. These parents regarded their children as having their own characters, aptitudes, and wishes. Promoting their development became central to parenting; as so many of the quotations I have selected show, what the parents strove for was their children's happiness, whether this were immediate, through opportunities for free play as youngsters; or longer-term, through self-fulfilment as adults. In this, the parents gave these second generation children considerable autonomy; having, as children, had scope to direct much of their own use of space and time, as adolescents and young people they had far more latitude when it came to deciding on their future direction and this at a time when more and more opportunities were opening up.

The Strategic Child

The 1970s, when many of the interviewees in the second cohort became parents, was a time when liberal and progressive movements of all kinds burgeoned, the children's rights movement (which advocated freeing children from institutional control, including that of the family) being no exception (see Berger 1972; Holt 1975). These authors anticipated contemporary sociological accounts of children as persons and advocated that children should be self-determining. Whilst such ideas were not yet part of mainstream thinking, there is nevertheless evidence that children were allowed to express themselves in a manner that would not have been permitted a generation earlier. Research by the Newsons (1968) showed that young children were permitted considerable freedom of speech within their families, while Benjamin Spock, in the 1968 revised edition of his classic work *Baby and Child Care*, commented:

> In America very few children are raised to believe that their principal destiny is to serve their family; their country or God. Generally we've given them the feeling that they are free to set their own aims and occupations in life according to their inclinations. (1968, 24)

Since the 1970s the association between seeing children as persons and encouraging them to express their views and feelings has become ever more central to constructions of childhood and representations of parental responsibility. Coveney, for example, recently argued that:

> [Children's] views have to be considered. These practices are, in fact, part of the role of today's "good" parent: the listener, the reflective adviser, the "sounding board" for children's thoughts, desires, and beliefs. ... teaching children autonomy and choice not only produces them as modern, moral subjects but also assists in the production of "good", that is, ethical, parents who can show the right concern for their children's views. (2000, 162)

Unsurprisingly, then, and having been allowed considerable latitude in shaping their own futures as adults, interviewees in the second cohort, when asked about their approach to parenting, frequently put emphasis on enabling children to become self-actualising. This perspective is even more pronounced in their children (cohort three), some of whom are also now parents, and is clearly apparent when comparing the way they speak of their children with that of the 'grandparent' generation. Jenny, discussed in the preceding section, believed that she was familiar with her children's characters and aptitudes. By contrast, younger interviewees, placing more emphasis on children as separate persons, represent them in a more fluid way, making fewer claims to 'know' them. This is apparent in one father's use of the metaphor of the 'stranger' for his daughter:

> Julian (37): I remember reading a book ... about your children being strangers ... you don't own them ... they are strangers given to you by God to care for and nurture ... And I've got that ... as a concept in my mind that [my daughter]'s not – I don't own her in any sense ... I think I've found that quite a helpful way to think about the way that my relationship with her will develop.

Similarly, it is evident in a mother's refusal to 'map out' her children's future:

> Vivianne (37): I see us all as people that are connected to each other. Whereas there are some families that are definitely "the whatever", the clans ... the clan thing means that they tend to map out their children's lives a bit more. They tend to believe what might happen in the future to them whereas we don't. I don't feel that, I feel that they have their own choices to make ... our children will have to decide for themselves what's important.

In representing their children as responsible for their own destinies, these parents' comments can be taken as inferring that autonomy is now firmly embedded in the creation of the self. However, other aspects of the data set point to a somewhat different interpretation. There is evidence that, despite their use of discourses of personhood, many of these parents (and especially those who are middle class) shape the way in which their children 'choose' to define their identities and futures. If 'choice' has become a defining characteristic of contemporary identity then, as 'responsible' parents, they want their children to become competent in its exercise. Coveney's reference to 'good' parents teaching their children autonomy is instructive here. The data support the view that children are encouraged to express their views and participate in family decisions but suggest that the emphasis placed by the parents on talk, communication and participation is, in fact, highly purposive. It can be seen as constituting a form of training; a means of ensuring that children will be equipped with skills they will need as they grow towards independence. In other words, parents encourage their children to think rationally and strategically, in the hope that when it comes to decisions that 'matter', they will make the 'right' choice. As the quotation from Lloyd (below) shows, this training begins early. He explains that by involving his seven-year-old son in decisions about misdemeanours, the boy will accept the penalties, but Lloyd can also be seen as training his son in making choices and decisions, and promoting his self-governance[6] by teaching him to 'willingly' moderate his wishes and impulses:

> Lloyd (45): I think that what started off the concept of right and wrong, is goodies and baddies … Superman does good things, good things are about saving and helping people, so that was already cast in stone before we started having conversations, and then it was about, "well, do you think this is a good thing, or do you think this is a bad thing?" … It was like, we were having the world cup in the garden with a few friends over, and just because Ben lost the ball he actually went and tripped somebody up, so I just pulled him to one side and … said "well, we're just playing in the garden but if this was a proper game, what would have happened?" "I would have got a red card", etc., etc., so it's kind of trying to reinforce the message by showing him examples of things he actually does, and then asking his opinion as to whether or not he feels it – because if he doesn't feel it's wrong then it doesn't really matter whether I tell him it's wrong, um, so – it's very much about asking him his opinion … it's about really involving him quite deeply in the whole decision … and by going through that route he now actually accepts the punishment because he's agreed to it, as it were.

The importance of teaching children to think strategically is especially apparent in the interview data on career choices. Such decisions matter considerably to parents, since future opportunities now depend far more on the early choices that young people make than they did 30 or more years ago (Wade 2004). Posy, a 21-year-old post-graduate student, sees herself as making her own decisions, but indicates (below), that her parents:

> always had an input into what I did. Outside of school I could really do what I wanted, they weren't really that strict, I mean within reason. … Academically, … it was quite difficult because I do like to do what I want to do and at GCSE and A level I had to take art as an extra subject because I really liked art and I was quite good at it. But they wanted, they preferred something more, academically things like English and history. Which I quite understand because it's a bit of a dossers' subject …

Posy described herself as 'arty' but recognised that her parents would have been far from happy had she focused on art, a subject they regarded as lacking sufficient academic status or rigour. So, for her 'A' levels and degree, she 'chose' to pursue a traditional academic course, the compromise being that having made the 'sensible'

6 The highly temporally structured childhoods many children now experience, having, as a result of the demands of their parents' jobs, to attend breakfast and after-school clubs or childminders, for example, can also be seen as promoting self-governance.

decision, she could do 'A' level art in her own time. In Posy's terms this meant 'I still did what I wanted anyway', but her statement 'I just had to create extra time for it' indicates the extent to which, in reality, she deferred to her parents' authority in this matter.

The risks associated by parents with children not thinking strategically about the future are shown in the case of Sally and her son Nick. Sally, like many of the members of my second cohort, has experienced considerable upward social mobility. Having come from a working class background, she and her husband are now firmly established members of the middle classes. Yet they are confronting the prospect of their son moving down the social ladder rather than up. Sally attributes her personal success to the educational opportunities available to her as a child, and the good use she made of them. Wanting to secure similar chances for Nick, she and her husband decided that he would be educated privately at a boarding school; something that they associated with privilege and hoped would increase his chances of going to college and entering a career 'with prospects'. However, Sally now sees this as increasingly unlikely as Nick has failed to complete two FE courses, and only ever worked in unskilled jobs:

> I think he now realises that he's 23 … he's wasted six years … and he'd desperately like to do something and knows that he doesn't want to be doing those sort of jobs – poorly paid jobs – forever. But you know, the older you get the harder it gets, doesn't it?

She now regrets having sent Nick away to school as she believes that this meant she was unable to influence him when it mattered, and contributed to his making what she sees as unrealistic choices about his future. When interviewed, Nick echoed his mother's remarks, saying that he had 'never got organised really' and commenting:

> I came to college up here but I didn't see that through … I had a good education and now I haven't got a really good job or anything, whereas my cousins have got really good jobs, earning lots of money. … I don't really have any big goals or anything like that … I'm quite apathetic really. … I wouldn't mind going back to college but … I'm too old now, like I've got to pay for it so I can't really afford to do it.

Nick is still relatively young and may yet achieve much. The point I want to make here is that while both he and Posy regard themselves as having 'chosen' the courses they applied for, the conditions under which their decisions were made differ in important ways. Arguably, Nick had the 'better' education but, living apart from his parents, he lacked their influence in shaping his thinking at a decisive moment and their close and sustained influence over his educational choices over the previous years. Their stories show how the apparently democratic, participative practices adopted by this particular cohort of parents can be seen as designed to 'fit' their children for the social necessities of the time, equipping them for a future when, as young adults, they will need to be skilled in the performance of choice.

Forms of Freedom: Generational Autonomy and Choice

In this chapter I have used biographical accounts of childhood and parenting to outline everyday understandings of parental responsibility and childhood autonomy over a span of some 80 years. A generational perspective dispels any easy assumptions that might be made about children today experiencing 'more' autonomy. It makes apparent that how autonomy is manifested varies greatly, depending on how childhood, and what is important for children, is understood. Whilst one generation may experience an absence of autonomy in one area, it nevertheless finds it in another. For example, the 'grandparent' cohort in my study had less freedom than their grandchildren to express their own views and opinions, but they were considerably more self-reliant from a younger age.

Interestingly, when comparing the three generations in this study, it is the middle, 'parent', generation who grew up in the 1950s and 1960s that appears to have enjoyed the widest range of freedoms. The experiences of the 'grandparent' and 'grandchild' cohorts may not map directly on to one another, and certainly there have been extensive changes in the concepts of childhood employed over the intervening years, but nevertheless certain parallels can be drawn between them. Both cohorts experienced considerable structuring of their use of time as children, and both had parents who took an active role in shaping their employment futures, in the one case parents expecting their children to contribute to the family economy at least until marriage,[7] and in the other, equipping their children to compete advantageously in an increasingly structured and competitive environment. By contrast, not only did the intervening generation enjoy significant temporal freedom, and freedom of expression, but they also had parents whose scope to influence their employment choices was circumscribed by the expansion of social and educational opportunities at the time. Rather than having a clear sense of what their children's futures would become, these parents often found themselves, in effect, watching from the wings as their children's lives evolved in ways very different to their own. Their ability to guide their children's choices from the basis of their own experience being diminished, their role in this instance became more one of encouragement and support.

The study demonstrates both the expansion and contraction of opportunities for social mobility over the course of the three generations and the implications of this for understandings of responsibility and autonomy. The majority of the first, 'grandparent', generation of participants in the sample were from working class backgrounds, but many of their children had a university education and moved with relative ease into the professions. By contrast, their grandchildren are experiencing a far more competitive social environment. The growth of the middle classes means that, as parents, the 'middle' generation has had to work that much harder to ensure

7 There is insufficient space to go into detail in the chapter on this subject, but there is considerable evidence in the data set of a young person's wage at this time being seen as a part of the family economy. Young people who wanted to step outside what were the traditional occupations in their family were often dissuaded or even barred from doing so. Women, but also some men, in the sample described how it was World War II that opened up employment opportunities for them.

that their children are able to hold onto what they themselves achieved. In the face of competition from ever increasing numbers of graduates there is a risk that children will slip back down the social ladder, hence 'holding on' itself constitutes an achievement.

The research points to the way in which the more 'democratic' family practices associated with contemporary families can be seen as a means by which parents are working to equip their children for the demands of a rapidly changing, but highly regulated, world. Equally, it demonstrates how they conceal subtle (and necessary) forms of adult supervision, and socialisation. It indicates that the recognition among sociologists of contemporary children's agency, and affirmation of their active participation in their own social worlds, has to be tempered by an understanding of the wider cultural and structural determinants that demarcate opportunities for self-determination, whether among adults or children. 'What to do? How to act? Who to be?' may, as Giddens has argued, be 'the focal questions for everyone living in circumstances of late modernity' (1991, 70). Nevertheless, the intuitive experience of social reality today is one of considerable regulation. Young people embarking on careers now face increasingly narrow entry regulations in the form of required qualifications (themselves highly regulated), and a future of performance management, through annual appraisals and routine audits. For their parents, responsibility thus takes the form of equipping children with the skills they will need to operate effectively in such an environment. The ability to communicate, analyse, construct an argument, be self-reflective, and effective in self-presentation can all be seen as skills that young people will require and which can be learnt within the crucible of a 'participative' family dialogue. Viewed in this way, contemporary opportunities for self-determination can be seen as constrained in complex ways. What is experienced or expressed as choosing may not necessarily be choosing but, rather, reflect a 'necessary' choice that is disguised through its expression in the language of self-actualisation.

If autonomy is understood as self-expression, and involvement in decisions that affect them, then the articulate contemporary child, used to expressing their views and having them listened to, might well be regarded as having more freedom than their grandparents. Yet, as Wilf said, they are living in 'a different world'. Social conditions are, as I have tried to show, a vital contributing factor to the ways in which children's autonomy is promoted. Equally, the study suggests that it is impossible to separate understandings of children's autonomy from those of parental responsibility. The responsibility that parents feel for their children may, to an extent, be self-imposed as well as culturally conditioned; a product of the commitment that grows through giving birth to and raising a child but it constitutes a powerful and life-long urge. It involves thinking not only about children's present needs but also anticipating those of their future and equipping them for this. The recognition of infants' early development of a sense of self and capacity to express this, or young children's considerable competence, challenges traditional views on the acquisition of autonomy as a linear development process. Nevertheless, while aspects of autonomy may be expressed at any age, there is a clear logic in the view that, in its strongest sense, autonomy involves experience of the world and that this is something that we all obtain over time. 'Good' parents will, then, tend to consider children's autonomy as a process, attempting to judge when to promote or even demand it and when to do so would be disadvantageous. Quite how they do so depends on the times.

References

Adams, P., Berg, L., Berger, N., Duane, M., Neill, A.S. and Ollendorff, R. (eds) (1972), *Children's Rights: Towards the Liberation of the Child* (London: Granada Publishing).

Austin, M.W. (2007), *Conceptions of Parenthood: Ethics and the Family* (Aldershot: Ashgate).

Beck, U. (1997), 'Democratization of the Family', *Childhood* 4:2, 151-68.

Beck, U. and Beck-Gernsheim, E. (2002), *Individualization* (London: Sage).

Berger, N. (1972), 'The Child, the Law, and the State' in Adams, P., Berg, L., Berger, N., Duane, M., Neill, A.S. and Ollendorff, R. (eds), *Children's Rights: Towards the Liberation of the Child* (London: Granada Publishing).

Bernstein, B. and Brannen, J. (eds) (1996), *Children, Research and Policy* (London: Taylor and Francis).

Bertaux, D. and Thompson, P. (eds) (1993), *Between Generations: Family Models, Myths and Memories* (Oxford: Oxford University Press).

Bowlby, J. (1953), *Child Care and the Growth of Love* (Harmondsworth: Pelican Books).

Brannen, J. (1996), 'Discourses of Adolescence: Young People's Independence and Autonomy within Families' in Brannen, J. and O'Brien, M. (eds), *Children in Families: Research and Policy* (London: Falmer Press).

Brannen, J. and O'Brien, M. (eds) (1996), *Children in Families: Research and Policy* (London: Falmer Press).

Brannen, J., Moss, P. and Mooney, A. (2004), *Working and Caring over the Twentieth Century* (Basingstoke: Palgrave Macmillan).

Coveney, J. (2000), *Food, Morals and Meaning* (London: Routledge).

Davidoff, L., Doolittle, M., Fink, J. and Holden, K. (1999), *The Family Story* (London: Longman).

Dunn, J. (1996), 'Family Conversations and the Development of Social Understanding' in Bernstein, B. and Brannen, J. (eds), *Children, Research and Policy* (London: Taylor and Francis).

Fortin, J. (1998), *Children's Rights and the Developing Law* (London: Butterworths).

Giddens, A. (1991), *Modernity and Self-Identity* (Cambridge: Polity Press).

Giddens, A. (1999), 'The 1999 Reith Lectures No. 4', *The Observer*, 2 May 1999, 16.

Hendrick, H. (1997), *Children, Childhood and English Society* (Cambridge: Cambridge University Press).

Heron, L. (ed.) (1985), *Truth, Dare or Promise: Girls Growing Up in the Fifties* (London, Virago Press).

Holt, J. (1975), *Escape from Childhood: The Needs and Rights of Children* (Harmondsworth: Penguin Books).

James, A. and James, A. (1999), 'Pump Up the Volume: Listening to Children in Separation and Divorce', *Childhood* 6:2, 189-206.

King, Sir F.T. (1937), *Feeding and Care of Baby* (Oxford: Oxford University Press).

Morrow, V. (1999), '"We Are People Too": Children's and Young People's Perspectives on Children's Rights and Decision-making in England', *International Journal of Children's Rights* 7, 149-170.

Newson, J. and Newson, E. (1968), *Four Years Old in an Urban Community* (London: Allen and Unwin).

Post, E. (1947), *Children are People and Ideal Parents are Comrades* (New York: Funk Wagnalls).

Punch, S. (2001), 'Negotiating Autonomy: Childhoods in Rural Bolivia' in Alanen, L. and Mayall B. (eds), *Conceptualizing Child–Adult Relations* (London: RoutledgeFalmer).

Ribble, M. (1943), *Rights of Infants* (Oxford: Oxford University Press).

Roberts, E. (1995), *Women and Families: An Oral History, 1940-1970* (Oxford: Blackwell).

Rubinstein, D. and Stoneman, C. (eds) (1970), *Education for Democracy* (Harmondsworth: Penguin Books).

Smart, C., Neale, B. and Wade, A. (2001), *The Changing Experience of Childhood* (Cambridge: Polity).

Smart, C., May, V., Wade, A. and Furniss, C., with Sharma, K. and Strelitz, J. (2005), *Residence and Contact Disputes in Court, Volume 2* (London: Department of Constitutional Affairs).

Spock, B. (1946), *Common Sense Book of Baby and Child Care* (New York: Duell Sloan).

Spock, B. (1968), *Baby and Child Care*, 179th printing April 1968; revised edition July 1968 (London: New English Library).

Tizard, B. and Hughes, M. (1984), *Young Children Learning: Talking and Thinking at Home and at School* (London: Fontana).

Tomanovic, S. (2003), 'Negotiating Children's Participation and Autonomy within Families', *International Journal of Children's Rights* 11, 51-71.

Wade, A. (2004), *Buffing the Pearl: Mothering, Work and Self-Actualisation* (Working Paper No. 35) (Leeds: Centre for Research on Family, Kinship and Childhood).

Watson, J.B. (1928), *Psychological Care of the Infant and Child* (London: Allen & Unwin).

Williams, F. (2004), *Rethinking Families* (London: Calouste Gulbenkian Foundation).

Winnicott, D.W. (1957a), *The Child and the Family* (London: Tavistock).

Winnicott, D.W. (1957b), *The Child and the Outside World* (London: Tavistock).

Winnicott, D.W. (1964), *The Child, the Family and the Outside World* (Harmondsworth: Penguin Books).

PART 4
Family, Responsibility and the Law

Chapter 12

Parental Responsibility, Responsible Parenting and Legal Regulation

Jo Bridgeman

Responsibility is a concept frequently evoked by parents to express their experience, and understanding, of their relationships with their children (Bridgeman 2005; Ribbens McCarthy et al. 2000). The legal basis of the relationship between parent and child is, as a consequence of the Children Act 1989, one of responsibility. In part, this reflects a change in the nature of the relationship from one in which parents enjoyed rights over their child; in part, it is an attempt to generate a shift from parental rights to responsibilities premised upon the view that to frame the parent/child relationship in terms of responsibilities would encourage parents to be more responsible (Eekelaar 1991, 49; Smith 1990). Secondly, in the terms of John Eekelaar's discerning analysis, the provisions of the Children Act 1989 place the responsibility for children with their parents rather than with the state,[1] with state intervention into the parent/child relationship only in those cases where it is necessary to protect a child from significant harm (Children Act 1989, section 31) or to provide services to support children in 'need' (Children Act 1989, sections 17-18). Shortly after coming to power in 1997, the Labour government issued a consultation paper, *Supporting Families*, which detailed its intention to support parents and, since then, has continued to express policy developments in family life and law in terms of supporting parents and supporting families (Home Office 1998).[2] Policy developments in family life which, when they relate to parenting, are either explicitly, or by implication, directed at 'support[ing] parents to *meet their responsibilities* in raising their children' (HM Treasury and DfES 2007, 1, emphasis added). The role of government is identified in *Building on Progress: Families* as one of supporting families to 'exercise their rights to manage their own affairs while living up to the responsibilities they have' and clarifying for parents their rights and responsibilities (Prime Minister's Strategy Unit 2007, 6-7). What are

1 Eekelaar, J. (1991), quoting the Secretary of State in the House of Commons Debates, vol. 151, col. 1107: 'The Bill's emphasis on the primary function of parenthood will, we hope, sharpen our perceptions and highlight the obligation on parents to care for their children and bring them up properly.'

2 Across a range of policy areas including: anti-social behaviour (Home Office 2003); post-separation contact (Department for Constitutional Affairs 2004) and joint registration of births (DWP 2007). A range of policy measures impacting upon the family are analysed by Churchill in this book.

the responsibilities of parents and how do they relate to the concept of 'parental responsibility', defined in section 3(1) of the Children Act 1989 as a bundle of 'rights, duties, powers, responsibilities and authority which by law a parent of a child has in relation to the child and his property'? This chapter examines the responsibilities of parents, support for responsible parenting and the concept of responsibility in order to explore the role of the law in regulating responsible parenting. In doing so, I seek to contribute to the development of a discourse of responsibility in the context of the parent/child relationship. Furthermore, I aim to explore the role that the state should adopt to support responsible parenting, including whether the law has a role to play in establishing the specific responsibilities of parents. In other words, I explore the responsibilities of parents and the parameters of the legal regulation of parental responsibility articulated by Baroness Hale in her speech in *Williamson*:

> Children have the right to be properly cared for and brought up so that they can fulfil their potential and play their part in society. Their parents have both the primary responsibility and the primary right to do this. The state steps in to regulate the exercise of that responsibility in the interests of children and society as a whole. But "the child is not the child of the state" and it is important in a free society that parents should be allowed a large measure of autonomy in the way in which they discharge their parental responsibilities.[3]

The Responsibilities of Parents

Anyone caring for a child, irrespective of whether they have parental responsibility, may do what is reasonable to safeguard or promote their welfare (Children Act 1989, section 3(5)). A child's carer has the powers they need to provide *care*, to make decisions affecting the immediate *well-being* of the child and *promote their best interests*. The Children Act 1989 continues to provide that *obligations* to children are not affected by whether a person has parental responsibility (Children Act 1989, section 3(4)). The specific obligations of those caring for a child, including their parents, are shaped by the general provisions of the criminal and civil law directed at the prevention and punishment of deliberate, reckless or carelessly caused harm, framed according to liberal understandings of responsibility which attribute moral responsibility for the chosen acts of the competent individual (Bridgeman 2007b; examined in the introduction to this book). Hence, parents or other carers who harmed a child will be prosecuted for offences contrary to the Offences against the Person Act 1861 or, if the child died, murder or manslaughter.

In addition, due to the dependency and vulnerability of children, specific legal *obligations* detailed in legislation impose *duties* upon those caring for a child to feed, clothe, house, obtain medical treatment for (Children and Young Persons Act 1933, section 1) and protect the child (Domestic Violence, Crime and Victims Act 2004, section 5); upon parents to ensure that the child is appropriately educated (Education Act 1996, sections 7, 8) and named (Births and Deaths Registration Act 1953); upon

3 *R (on the application of Williamson and others) v Secretary of State for Education and Employment and others* [2005] UKHL 15, para. 72.

absent parents to maintain (Child Support Act 1991, section 1); and justifies the use of physical punishment (Children Act 2004, section 58).[4] These are basic duties of care, financial provision and control (Freeman in this book). Generally, parents will go beyond these minimal legal *duties* but not because of any *legal* obligation. The extent to which parents are given the freedom to care for their children as they consider appropriate or there is intervention in the family to ensure that parents conform to norms of 'good' parenting is a matter for political determination (Bartlett 1988, 297). Do measures to support parents to meet their responsibilities change the nature of parental responsibilities or obligations?

As noted above, the Children Act 1989 does not give content to the concept of parental responsibility and, consequently, it has been left to the courts to define parental responsibility; to delineate what parental responsibility means for the adult possessed of it and for the child in relation to whom it is enjoyed. It is important to note the context in which judicial reflection upon the meaning and content of parental responsibility has occurred: most often in cases of fragmented families where fathers have applied to court for parental responsibility not conferred automatically or by agreement. From these cases three points emerge: a distinction between the allocation of parental responsibility as status and the exercise of parental responsibility (the allocation of parental responsibility in the context of assisted reproduction is examined by Craig Lind in this book); parental responsibility as distinct from primary, or day-to-day, care; and the importance of relationship (attachment, commitment and future intentions) to parental responsibility. These three aspects were noted by Sir Stephen Brown P as he sought to clarify the scope of the frequently misunderstood parental responsibility order:

> A parental responsibility order does not affect the day-to-day care of the children when they are in the care of the mother. That is the situation in this case. She has the primary responsibility for the children in her care. However, the parental responsibility order does in fact provide status for the father. In this case the father had, in the Justices' view, demonstrated his commitment to his children and the children had shown their attachment to him.[5]

First, parental responsibility has been described as 'conferring upon a committed father the status of parenthood for which nature has already ordained that he must bear responsibility'[6] and as an 'acknowledgement and declaration of … parental status'.[7] Parental responsibility thus amounts to legal recognition of an existing status as parent. But parental responsibility is more than merely status given that there is a close relationship between the conferral and the exercise of parental responsibility: one of the reasons a father who was in prison was denied parental responsibility was that his imprisonment limited his ability to exercise it.[8] Further, in the circumstances

---

4 Although not paid childminders, *Day Care and Child Minding (National Standards) (England) Regulations 2003* (SI 2003/1996), reg. 5.

5 *Re Smith (Minor)* [1995] 3 FCR 564.

6 *Re S (Parental Responsibility)* [1995] 2 FLR 648.

7 *Re H (A Child: Parental Responsibility)* [2002] EWCA Civ 542, para. 16.

8 *Re P (Parental Responsibility)* [1997] 2 FLR 722.

of a difficult relationship between the child's parents, the exercise of parental responsibility can be limited by specific issue orders (for example, that the mother of L was to have sole responsibility for medical decisions concerning a severely ill child) or constrained by prohibited steps orders.[9] In *Re H*, the order prevented the father from finding out, or attempting to find out, where his daughter lived, which inevitably placed severe constraints upon the exercise of parental responsibility simultaneously conferred upon him.

Secondly, what is involved in the exercise of parental responsibility is distinguished from the legal obligations imposed upon parents with respect to their children[10] – it is decision-making responsibility rather than primary, caring, responsibility.[11] In these cases, it has been emphasised that parental responsibility does not empower the holder to interfere with the day-to-day care of the child (although the primary carer of the child is also likely to enjoy parental responsibility).[12] It is a legal status which confers decision-making involvement upon an absent parent although, in many cases, the primary carer who enjoys parental responsibility will be able to make those decisions alone (Children Act 1989, section 2(7).[13] In the recent case of *Re D* in which a parental responsibility order was sought by the biological father of the daughter of a lesbian couple, Black J was of the opinion that the 'novel' family circumstances required a creative approach towards parental responsibility. Her ladyship accepted the offer of the father to agree to conditions upon the order to the effect that he would not 'intrude' in those areas where his involvement might present a problem.[14] Black J emphasised that parental responsibility was a status, which did not permit interference in the day-to-day care of the child, the exercise of which could, if necessary, be controlled by the use of section 8 orders. Conferring D's biological father with parental responsibility, the court constrained him from contacting D's school or those providing her with medical treatment without the permission of her mothers, whilst requiring that they keep him informed of D's progress and permit him to attend school events if D invited him. Black J noted that D's family was her mothers and sister with whom she lived, who took care of her and were her 'primary security'. Granting parental responsibility recognised Mr B as a 'different sort' of parent, one who should be informed of the major decisions regarding D made by her mothers.[15] Notably, and consistent with the Children Act 1989 which is structured around the relationship between parent and child irrespective of the state of the relationship between the parents (Smart 2003, 224), the decision whether to grant parental responsibility is dependent upon the quality of the parent/child relationship. Determination of the welfare principle, which as section 1 of the Children Act

9 *Re H (A Child: Parental Responsibility)* [2002] EWCA Civ 542, para. 16.

10 Ibid.

11 *Re G (Parental Responsibility: Education)* [1994] 2 FLR 964.

12 *Re P (A Minor) (Parental Responsibility Order)* [1994] 1 FLR 578.

13 Except where provided otherwise by statute or judicially created exceptions including decisions about sterilisation, change of surname and circumcision.

14 *Re D (Contact and Parental Responsibility: Lesbian Mothers and Known Father)* [2006] EWHC (Fam), para. 91.

15 Ibid. para. 93.

1989 applies, is the guiding principle,[16] is thus informed by demonstration of prior commitment, the presence of attachment[17] and future intentions. There is also judicial comment to the effect that conferring the status of parental responsibility may encourage responsible behaviour. The father in *Re P* had demonstrated his irresponsibility by committing offences for which, at the time of the hearing, he was serving a prison sentence. Ordinarily, and if he were not in prison, to have granted parental responsibility would 'no doubt encourage him to behave in a responsible way to those children'.[18] Granting parental responsibility might, on the other hand, be of benefit to the child. In *Re H*, contact occurred quarterly, indirectly, in the form of reports from the mother to the father, yet Thorpe LJ expressed the hope that to confer parental responsibility upon the father would 'take effect to the benefit of L in years to come so that she knows she has two parents, both of whom, in very differing ways, have a manifest responsibility for her continuing well-being'.[19]

The understanding of parental responsibility articulated by the judiciary in disputed cases is one of a legal status which entitles the holder to information, and involvement in major decisions, regarding the child. Parental responsibility may be conferred upon adults for the benefit of the child, to encourage responsible behaviour by parents or in recognition of prior commitment, a relationship of attachment and future intentions. Although, as Sally Sheldon has observed, 'whilst the intention behind the Children Act may have been one of encouraging greater parental *responsibility*, in practice the impact of the provision is largely to allocate parental *rights* (whether exercisable against the state or the other parent) to make certain decisions with regard to the upbringing of children' (Sheldon 2001, 95). Vaguely defined in the Children Act 1989 and given content in cases of disputes arising in fragmented families, the concept of parental responsibility has been developed into a confused, contradictory concept with little meaning in relation to the responsibility of caring for children. Section 3 of the Children Act 1989 is clearly something much more extensive as is the responsibility exercised and experienced by parents throughout their children's lives. As Peter Singer observed, in a case which was concerned with the powers of parents arising from their responsibilities, section 3 appears 'to be about as all-embracing a bundle of responsibilities as it is possible to contemplate'.[20] What is required is the development of a discourse of responsibilities towards children informed by the experiences and understanding of parents of their responsibilities to their children; parents' sense of responsibility, how they live, experience and aim to fulfil their responsibilities. That other conceptualisations of responsibility will be employed in the absence of a discourse of parental responsibility can be illustrated with reference to the portrayal of the responsibilities of parents in recent family policy.

---

16 Ibid.

17 Balcombe LJ considering the granting of a parental rights order under s. 4 of the Family Law Reform Act 1987, *In re H (Minors) (Local Authority: Parental Rights) (No. 3)* [1991] Fam 151.

18 *Re P (Parental Responsibility)* [1997] 2 FLR 722.

19 *Re H (A Child: Parental Responsibility)* [2002] EWCA Civ 542, para. 16.

20 *Re HG (Specific Issue Order: Sterilisation)* [1993] 1 FLR 587, which extended in that case to a responsibility to seek a decision of the court on the question of sterilisation of their child.

Supporting Parents to Meet their Responsibilities

The approach adopted in the consultation document, *Supporting Families*, in which it was stressed that the primary responsibility for the well-being of children rests with their parents, working with professionals in the health, education and social services and supported by advice, information and guidance, has continued across government policy and legislative reform in relation to children, parents and families (Churchill in this book; Home Office 1998). In *Supporting Families* the role of government was sketched out as that of supporting parents to support their children and together ensuring 'the best possible start in life' (Home Office 1998, 4). Areas for government action were identified as improving health, education and social services; providing advice, information and guidance; introducing fiscal measures supportive of families; legislating for family friendly working policies; strengthening marriage; and addressing serious family problems such as domestic violence and teenage pregnancy (Home Office 1998, 5). Practical support, however, was to be offered within the context of clarifying the rights and responsibilities of families and of the government.

The development of children's services placed on the agenda in *Supporting Families* became more urgent in the light of the findings of the Bristol Royal Infirmary Inquiry (Bristol Royal Infirmary Inquiry 2001) and of the Laming Inquiry into the death of Victoria Climbié (Lord Laming 2003). The Green Paper, *Every Child Matters*,[21] proposed a programme of change to ensure that all children have the opportunity, through promotion and preventative strategies, to fulfil their potential with specialist services for children in need and targeted services for vulnerable children (Chief Secretary to the Treasury 2003, 8). Child-centred, rather than parent- or family-centred, universal services will co-exist with targeted services and compulsory measures to ensure all children fulfil their potential and are protected from harm. The aim of *Every Child Matters* was to build upon changes already implemented to integrate services, improve the recruitment and training of the workforce in children's services, support parents and carers and protect children (Chief Secretary to the Treasury 2003, 7). To provide a focus upon enabling every child to realise their potential rather than, as in the past, identifying standards below which care must not fall, a 'shared set of goals' was identified for 'children, families, communities and public services': being healthy; staying safe; enjoying and achieving; making a positive contribution; and economic well-being (DFES 2004, 9).[22] The legislative framework for implementation of the *Every Child Matters* agenda was provided by the Children Act 2004.

Supporting Families proposed the introduction of another layer of support for parents beneath health, education and social services in the form of information and general advice about how to raise children (Home Office 1998, 6). *Supporting Families* identified the need for a cultural change: although advice and guidance on

---

21 In addition to the structure of public services for children, *Every Child Matters* covered a wide range of issues including poverty, truanting, sport in schools, bullying and child offending.

22 Developed into 25 outcomes set out in DfES 2004, 9.

how to raise their children should not be foisted upon parents, 'parenting support is relevant to all parents regardless of their circumstances. We want to change the culture so that seeking advice and help when it is needed is seen not as failure but the action of concerned and responsible parents' (Home Office 1998, 7-8).

> There's no doubt that children enrich our lives, but raising them is hard work. The hours are lousy, there's no annual leave, and crucially, you don't get training. While we all want to do our best and give our children a good start in life, it's often hard to know what we should be doing. ... The Government wants to help you to help your child. ... It's important that all parents know where to get information, and feel happy to use any support or advice they need. (DfES 2007, 1)

There is nothing novel about parents seeking advice – from family, friends, professionals or books – about problems with, or concerns about, children. What is distinctive is the message that the responsible parent will seek expert advice from official sources: government sponsored services directed at educating parents about their role in child development and learning whilst also providing advice to parents on specific problems. The proposals in *Supporting Families* which have since been implemented include a *National Family and Parenting Institute* (now the Family and Parenting Institute, http://www.familyandparenting.org/), a national parenting helpline to provide advice and direct parents to local sources of help and support (Parentline Plus, www.parentlineplus.org.uk) and the introduction of *Sure Start*. *Every Child Matters* developed these plans, proposing information meetings for parents at key points in their children's lives, support for fathers so that children develop positive relationships with both parents (through, for example, *Fathers Direct*, the national information centre on fatherhood, www.fathersdirect.com) and family learning programmes. Generally, parents should be educated, through childcare, early years education, social services and schools, to help their child's development, and assisted to support their child's learning. More recently, the 2007 policy review, *Aiming High for Children*, tied together the responsibilities of parents with outcomes for children, which were the focus of *Every Child Matters*. It spells out the responsibility of parents to work to improve outcomes for their children, supported by public services and government sponsored sources of guidance, information and advice. Support for parents will be enhanced by improved accessibility to information (a new service is to be developed using the model of Parentline Plus) and by clarifying information about entitlements to support (to be set out in a Parents' Charter) (HM Treasury and DfES 2007, paras. 4.9-4.10, 4.17).

As the focus has shifted to outcomes for children, so there has been a shift from government clarification of the rights and responsibilities of parents in a number of situations, for example, responsibilities within marriage, the financial responsibilities of non-resident parents, and the 'rights and responsibilities of parents, children and schools' (Home Office 1998, 32, 23, 40 respectively). More recently, the responsibilities of parents towards their children have been clearly expressed in communitarian terms of the interests of protecting society from failure of parents to meet their responsibilities: 'The Government has an important role to play in setting out the responsibilities that parents and carers have towards their children, in order that both children and the wider society are protected from the harm that would result from parental failure to live up to these responsibilities' (Prime Minister's Strategy Unit 2007, 24). Furthermore, the focus upon positive outcomes for children generating from *Every Child Matters* has now become firmly linked to responsibilities: 'Raising outcomes for children and young people relies on partnership between active, responsible parents and an empowered community, supported by enabling government' (HM Treasury and DfES 2007, para. 1.25).

To understand this approach to supporting parents to meet their responsibilities, we need to explore the communitarian conceptualisation of responsibility which, as Anne Barlow, Simon Duncan and Grace James have identified, has informed these developments:

> this policy emphasis can be seen as resulting from New Labour's prescriptive and moralistic version of communitarianism, one that emphasises individual responsibility at the expense of socio-economic reform, but also that this emphasis becomes naturalised where the sovereignty of individual preferences and behaviour is an axiom of the neo-classical version of social behaviour. This is, after all, the very foundation of rational economic man and, from this starting point, it does indeed make little sense to see the origins and causes of social problems as lying in wider social conditions. (Barlow et al. 2002, 116-117)

Concepts of Responsibility

Responsibility in communitarian thought

Although parental responsibility was recognised in law in 1989, the Labour government since 1997 has placed responsibility at the centre of its policies concerning individuals, parents, families and communities.[23] In this, communitarian thought has been influential. Although there are differences amongst its proponents, in general terms communitarians understand the family to be the primary location for moral education, supported by school, church and community; believe that individual rights need to be balanced with social responsibilities; and argue for regulation at as local a level as possible, with national government the last port of call except in empowering and supporting 'social subsystems' (Etzioni 1998, xxx). With respect to the family, Amitai Etzioni has argued, from a communitarian perspective, that two parents are preferable to one and in favour of marriage between men and women as equals both contributing to childcare and participating in paid employment. Rather than using the law to sustain marriage by making divorce more difficult, Etzioni has suggested that marriage should be strengthened through economic and practical measures and parenting supported by being ascribed greater value (Etzioni 1998, xiii). The model of the family assumed in *Supporting Families*, as Richard Collier has identified, 'marked by the qualities of emotional and sexual equality, mutual rights and responsibilities in relationships, a negotiated authority over children,

---

23 Frank Furedi has argued that there is now a gap between parental and state responsibility for children created by the absence of a concomitant community responsibility (Furedi 2001).

co-parenting and, a commitment on the part of both women *and* men to lifelong obligations to children', reflects this stance (Collier 2003, 246).

The responsibilities of parents are framed by the conceptualisation of responsibility more generally in communitarian thought. For example, Dallin Oaks' consideration of the relationship between rights and responsibilities in communitarian thought starts from the proposition that there has been too much importance attached to rights as a tool of social justice at the expense of consideration of responsibilities (Oaks 1998). Oaks suggests that there is a correlation to the extent that responsibilities may be imposed upon an individual as a consequence of another's rights. However, rights and responsibilities are not, in his view, coextensive; rather, some moral responsibilities are not legally enforceable but can, and should, be encouraged (Oaks 1998, 97-8). Oaks suggests that responsibilities can be encouraged through the 'power of example', by strengthening institutions in which moral development occurs such as the family, church, education and community and that the law can encourage responsibilities without enforcing them, for example, 'Making the existence of a right dependent on the prior fulfilment of a responsibility would surely contribute to restoring the status of responsibilities in our way of thinking' (Oaks 1998, 102-4).

In *The Parenting Deficit*, Amitai Etzioni offers a communitarian critique of the failure of parents to take responsibility for their children and the failure of community to support parents to meet their responsibilities (Etzioni 1993) central to which are concerns about social disintegration (Frazer and Lacey 1993, 130). His thesis is premised upon the view that parents have an obligation to the community to educate their children in moral values because the community suffers as a consequence of the anti-social behaviour of children, which results from poor parenting (Etzioni 1993, 54). The force of Etzioni's criticism is directed at parents whom he characterises as primarily preoccupied with their own career and the pursuit of material wealth at, he suggests, the expense of a commitment to care for their children (presumably understanding these as in opposition rather than, at least potentially, mutually beneficial). He suggests that parents need to reassess their priorities and be supported with flexible working, shared childcare, financial support and measures which discourage hasty marriages (which he believes are swiftly followed by divorce). Although Etzioni stresses that the community has a responsibility to support parents, the precise form which this might take is not clear from this pamphlet (Etzioni 1993, 6). Adopting this approach, a communitarian might endorse a policy permitting publication on the Child Support Agency's website of the names of non-resident parents who had been taken to court for non-payment along with details of the punishments meted out to them. The rationale given for this policy, which has since been abandoned, was that: 'We are making an example of non-resident parents who commit these offences to encourage others to give us the information we need straight away' (quote from CSA, reported by David Sapsted 2007). However, this approach is followed through into proposals for legislative change in the Child Maintenance and Other Payments Bill 2007. Whilst separated parents are to be encouraged to reach their own agreements about child payments or 'empowered to take responsibility', it is proposed that the Child Maintenance and Enforcement Commission will enforce these efforts through a variety of methods which include the imposition of curfews and confiscation of passports and driving licences from parents who fail to pay. Similarly, the Green Paper, *Joint Birth Registration*, proposes to make joint registration of birth a legally enforceable duty upon the child's mother and father. Supported by a publicity campaign and literature, the proposed legal duty is premised upon a view that it is the role of government to set out the rights and responsibilities of parents and ensure they know what they are: 'the Government identified joint registration of births as one area where it could do more to establish a clear sense of responsibility for unmarried fathers for the welfare of their children' (DWP 2007, paras. 22, 46). Registration of birth automatically confers parental responsibility upon unmarried fathers. For many unmarried fathers that status reflects a relationship of attachment, commitment and future intentions to secure the welfare of the child. The legal status, however, would be enjoyed even by those for whom a sense of responsibility has to be created and by those who take no responsibility for caring for the child.

As is apparent from this account of communitarian family responsibility there is, within communitarian approaches, a clear view of how the family should be structured, what daily family life should be like and what good parenting practice involves, grounded in traditional notions of the good life. As Val Gillies has argued, 'how' to parent is not considered to be a matter of individual choice; rather, there is a right way in which to parent (Gillies 2005). Individual liberty in parenting, so cherished within liberalism, is constrained by conformity with community norms. The responsibility of parents is to raise their children according to correct values, to guide and control them, to bring them up to be good citizens. As Gillies has commented, supporting parents thus involves supporting them to be good or responsible parents; to parent in accordance with given standards (Gillies 2005, 77). Within a communitarian approach, the responsibilities of parents for their children are not recognised in order to support intimate relationships but are imposed in order to ensure the 'proper' behaviour of parents and their children for the good of society or community. Stephen Driver and Luke Martell have observed that, translated into Labour policy, communitarianism is not a pluralistic communitarianism respectful of diversity: rather that, 'moral values [are] prescribed from above' and 'enacted from there'; moral values selected by politics and imposed by law (Driver and Martell 1997, 40).

Lacking a clear definition in the Children Act 1989, developed as a confused, contradictory yet essentially empty concept in family law jurisprudence, in recent family policy parental responsibility has been crafted in communitarian terms which stress the need for parents to be supported to behave as responsible parents countering the selfish pursuit of individual rights. The next section argues for an alternative understanding of parental responsibility informed by the feminist ethic of care as more appropriate for the intimate, personal, relationship between parent and child.

A feminist approach to parental responsibility

Having exposed the 'rationality' and 'morality' 'mistakes' in family policy, Barlow et al. suggest that the focus should be upon *relations* rather than upon form and upon the development of 'supportive and flexible legislative frameworks that do recognise the varying ways in which people take moral decisions' (Barlow et al. 2002, 122). They point to research in family sociology which suggests that moral decisions are negotiated and that in any situation the 'proper thing to do' depends on a variety of factors. This research reveals that 'people do not make rational cost–benefit responses to the law' (Barlow et al. 2002, 119); indeed, they often do not know the detail of the law. Furthermore, they suggest, this research demonstrates that social circumstances and family history have a greater influence upon individual decision-making than does the law (Churchill in this book). This conclusion first raises questions about the effectiveness of a communitarian approach to the responsibilities of parents adopted in the examples noted above (which will not be explored further in this chapter) and then raises the question of the implications of this conclusion for how we might understand parental responsibility.

Reflecting on this we should note two studies; one by Carol Smart and Bren Neale, *Family Fragments?*, and Mavis Maclean and John Eekelaar's study of *The Parental Obligation* (Smart and Neale 1999; Maclean and Eekelaar 1997). Both explore post-separation parenting and competing parental obligations to children and both reveal parents drawing alternatively upon concepts of justice and rights and upon care and responsibility. Importantly, the discourse of responsibility employed by the parents in these studies is very different from that of the communitarian approach based in assumptions of parental irresponsibility. The conceptualisation of responsibility within the family which the parents employed is that offered by the feminist ethic of care. It is this which I suggest should form the conceptual framework for our understanding of the responsibilities of parents to their children and consequently, the role of the law in regulating parental responsibility. I propose that we can understand, conceptualise and develop a discourse of responsibility in relationships and within family life through a conceptual framework of relational responsibilities, derived from the feminist ethic of care. The distinct contribution of the ethic of care is summarised in the following quotation from Selma Sevenhuijsen:

> the ethics of care involves different moral concepts: responsibility and relationships rather than rules and rights. Secondly, it is bound to concrete situations rather than being formal and abstract. And thirdly, the ethics of care can be described as a moral activity, the "activity of caring", rather than as a set of principles which can simply be followed. The central question in the ethics of care – how to deal with dependency and responsibility – differs radically from that of rights ethics: what are the highest normative principles and rights in situations of moral conflict? (Sevenhuijsen 1998, 107)

Selma Sevenhuijsen identifies responsibility and relationships as central moral concepts of the ethic of care. She notes the importance of the specific context and of care as an activity (which requires a caring disposition). The primary concern, as she explains, is not which right prevails in a particular conflict but how best to meet conflicting responsibilities arising from relationships.

Hilde Lindemann Nelson notes that parental duties have been understood as based in contract, utility and in deontological respect for others but, she argues, 'the connections among persons not only contribute to persons' sense of who they are, but are themselves the ground of many moral obligations' (Lindemann Nelson 1999,

120). It is the relationship with their children which makes an adult a parent and those relationships which establish the responsibilities of adults as parents.

In contrast to the way in which the self is understood in communitarian thought, from the perspective of the feminist ethic of care the individual is understood to be primarily connected to others and concerned to preserve their relationships with them. '[T]he ethic of care takes the idea of self in relationship as the point of entry for thinking about obligations and responsibility' so that, as Selma Sevenhuijsen observes, it is situated responsibility rather than duty which determines action (Sevenhuijsen 2002, 131). If responsibilities arise from relationships, the content of those responsibilities is, consistent with the feminist ethic of care, determined by the context of the relationship in which they arise. The relationship between parent and child is one in which the child is dependent, although the particular nature of the dependency changes over time (the needs of a six-month-old baby are very different from those of a 14-year-old child), and depends upon the circumstances (such as the particular abilities, or health, of the child). Furthermore, in any relationship, including that of parent and child, understandings of responsibilities are also shaped by social and cultural expectations:

> The experience and meaning of responsibility may be quite personal and individualized. Its meaning, however, is derived within a social context that defines ideal roles for persons engaged in particular relationships. Thus, while individuals to a certain extent choose the terms of their own relationships, the choices they make and the meaning given to those choices are strongly shaped by role expectations defined by the community. (Bartlett 1988, 299)

This conceptualisation of responsibility seems particularly suited to personal or intimate relationships such as between parent and child. Responsibilities are thus not conceived of as imposed by the state or arising due to another's possession of rights; rather, they arise from a concern to maintain the relationship with the other and a commitment to them (Bartlett 1988, 299). What people do, and what people feel they ought to do, is not confined to that which the other can demand of them. Consequently, the responsibilities of parents go beyond doing what they are obliged to do, in other words what they owe the child, to doing their best to meet the needs of the child and secure the best outcomes for the child. But what they are able to do, the extent to which they can fulfil their responsibilities, is affected by external factors which may be beyond their control.

Understanding responsibilities to arise out of relationships leads to an appreciation that whilst the primary relationship and primary responsibilities will be between parent and child, others also have relationships with, and hence responsibilities to, children. Other relatives, and other adults involved in the care and upbringing of children, for example, nursery staff, childminders, teachers, doctors, health visitors, will have responsibilities to children, the content of which depends upon their professional role and expertise as well as the particular needs of the child at the specific time.[24] Agents of the state such as doctors, social workers and the police

24 John Eekelaar suggests that communities also have responsibilities to children (Eekelaar 2006, 131).

have responsibilities to children although not, given the absence of a relationship, the state itself. Rather, children have rights against the state.

In this approach, responsibility does not mandate a particular action, it is not about telling parents what is the right thing to do, according to given norms of the community or those currently in vogue amongst experts. It offers a framework for deciding what to do in a given situation, informed by practices and understandings of responsibility. In *Parental Responsibility, Young Children and Healthcare Law*, I argue that, in the context of the responsibilities of parents for the healthcare of their children, a framework of relational responsibilities would consider the needs of the child as an individual, examine practices of caring responsibility (including different responsibilities arising from different relationships and roles) and explore the wider context in which those needs are met (Bridgeman 2007a). As I demonstrate, where children's healthcare is concerned, parents are generally seeking the best for their child but may have different opinions from the doctors caring for the child as to the best course of action arising from their different experience, expertise and relationship with the child. More generally, I suggest, we need to develop a discourse of responsibility informed by evidence of the sense of responsibility felt by parents and the extent to which parents experience and understand their relationship with their child in terms of responsibility. The next question which arises is what, if any, role does the law have in supporting parents to meet their parental responsibilities?

Legal Regulation of Parental Responsibilities?

Both the liberal and the communitarian approaches to responsibility understand responsibility as something which can be regulated by law although there are differences between advocates of communitarianism with regard to the extent to which the law should be used. Within this body of thought there is agreement that the law is the mechanism through which to respond to the most extreme violations of community values and, further, that the law has an important symbolic role in terms of identifying acceptable conduct (Etzioni 1998, 45). Whilst 'responsive communities define what is expected of people; they educate their members to accept these values; and they praise them when they do and frown upon them when they do not' (Etzioni 1998, xxxvi); there is less consensus as to whether the frowning community should use the law or non-legal and non-coercive measures to enforce community values. Ann Barlow, Simon Duncan and Grace James have identified the 'rationality mistake' in policy and law: 'If people do not act according to the model of rational economic man and the rational legal subject, then legislation based on such assumptions might well be ineffectual', quoting as an example the extent of failure to comply with the Child Support Act 1991 (Barlow et al. 2002, 111). Furthermore, they argue, legislation can compound the 'rationality mistake' with the 'morality mistake' where it is based upon false assumptions about people's behaviour and consequently seeks to make people behave in ways which they consider to be morally wrong.

Should the law be used to give effect to, and enforce, the responsibilities of parents and thus support responsible parenting? Clem Henricson has set out the case for a parenting code which would clarify the expectations of parents, could enhance the standing of adults as parents and affect attitudes to parenting. The parenting code Henricson envisages would delineate the rights of parents to support from the state and public services and clarify the obligations of parents: 'While the monitoring of child outcomes will always form the cornerstone of child protection policy, that policy would stand to gain from a preventative arm providing positively framed messages around expectations of parents' (Henricson 2003, 76). Whilst the current legal obligations imposed upon parents could be codified, can parental responsibilities?

John Eekelaar has suggested that responsibilities are very different from rights which are entitlements enjoyed by individuals, obligations (what, morally or legally, is owed to another), or duties. In his recent book, *Family Law and Personal Life*, John Eekelaar adopts John Gardner's concept of responsibility as 'the ability to give an account of oneself as a rational being' (Eekelaar 2006, 128, quoting Gardner 2003, 161). Consequently, John Eekelaar suggests that the distinction between rights and responsibility is that:

> when we think of responsibility in these circumstances, we signal an expectation that the agent should demonstrate an appreciation of the effects of their actions, or inactions, on other people by modifying their behaviour accordingly even if this means modifying claims to one's entitlements. It is a manifestation of recognition of "the other" and of acceptance of community. It is the counterpoise to the engine that drives the language of rights, which are the claims individuals make for recognition of the sectional interests of themselves and others similarly placed. (Eekelaar 2006, 128)

The distinction between obligations and responsibility is that whilst 'a responsible person follows their legal obligations, responsibility does not stop there' (Eekelaar 2006, 129). John Eekelaar concludes his analysis of responsibility with the view that by their nature responsibilities, in contrast with obligations, duties and rights, go beyond that which is expected and, as such, cannot be legislated for. From this perspective, the Children Act 1989 correctly identifies responsibility as something wider-reaching and more all-embracing than parental rights, duties, powers or authority. Adopting this approach, policies and laws can be used to encourage responsible behaviour but, as John Eekelaar argues, the very act of making it legally enforceable means that it can no longer be understood as responsible behaviour: it has been translated into a legal duty or obligation (Eekelaar 2006, 130-1). Parents have obligations to their children: the minimum they ought to do to provide for them financially, care for them and raise them. These can be legally enforced and should be in the interests of child protection and welfare. The practice of parenting is, as Katharine Bartlett has identified, a practice of 'judgment developed through experience and example' (Bartlett 1988, 302); parental responsibilities are contextual, particularistic and relational.

Conclusion

There is currently much talk about responsibilities, use of the concept in a range of policy areas and a renewed interest in theorising responsibility amongst academic lawyers. Current government policy is informed by communitarian approaches which assume that parents need to be made aware of their responsibilities, need to be made to take responsibility and need to be *supported* to *meet their responsibilities* in order to protect society from the damaging consequences of their failure to do so. In communitarian terms, responsibilities can be legally enforced and the law used to support parents to meet their responsibilities for their children. But parenting is a practice performed in the context of a relationship of attachment with a child, involving prior commitment and the intention to do the best for the child. Parents don't understand their responsibilities to their children in terms of obligations to community safety: rather, they are personal, contextual and needs-based. Andrew Bainham has pointed to the persuasive and constitutive aspects of law in addition to its punitive forms noting that in family law, which regulates intimate relationships, 'coercion seldom works' (Bainham, 1998). Rather, I argue, a discourse of parental responsibility needs to be developed which is informed by the understanding, and experiences, of parents who strive daily to fulfil their responsibilities to their children. I suggest that a starting point is offered by the feminist ethic of care in which the responsibilities of parents arise from their relationship with their child, respond to the child's particular needs as they seek to do their best for their child and which acknowledges the extent to which factors external to that relationship, including the law, have an impact upon the ability of parents to care. From this perspective the role of the law would be to support parents in the discharge of their responsibilities to their children and to foster the quality of the parent/child relationship, not to make parents meet their responsibilities.

References

Bainham, A. (1998), 'Changing Families and Changing Concepts – Reforming the Language of Family Law', *Child and Family Law Quarterly* 10, 1.

Barlow, A., Duncan, S. and James, G. (2002), 'New Labour, the Rationality Mistake and Family Policy in Britain' in Carling, A., Duncan, S. and Edwards, R. (eds), *Analysing Families: Morality and Rationality in Policy and Practice* (London: Routledge), 110-28.

Bartlett, K. (1988), 'Re-Expressing Parenthood', *Yale Law Journal* 98, 293.

Bridgeman, J. (2005), 'When Systems Fail: Parents, Children and the Quality of Healthcare' in Holder, J. and O'Cinneide, C. (eds), *Current Legal Problems, Volume 58* (Oxford: Oxford University Press), 183-213.

Bridgeman, J. (2007a), *Parental Responsibility, Young Children and Healthcare Law* (Cambridge: Cambridge University Press).

Bridgeman, J. (2007b), 'Accountability, Support or Relationship? Conceptions of Parental Responsibility', *Northern Ireland Legal Quarterly* 59, 307-24.

Bristol Royal Infirmary (2001), *The Report of the Public Inquiry into Children's Heart Surgery at the Bristol Royal Infirmary 1984-1995: Learning from Bristol*, Cm 5207(I) (HMSO: London).
Chief Secretary to the Treasury (2003), *Every Child Matters*, Cm 5860 (London: HMSO: London).
Collier, R. (2003), 'In Search of the "Good Father": Law, Family Practices and the Normative Reconstruction of Parenthood' in Dewar, J. and Parker, S. (eds), *Family Law: Processes, Practices and Pressures* (Oxford: Hart), 241-69.
Department for Constitutional Affairs, DfES and DTI (2004), *Parental Separation: Children's Needs and Parents' Responsibilities*, Cm 6273 (London: Department for Constitutional Affairs).
DfES (2004), *Every Child Matters: Change for Children* (London: DfES).
DfES (2007), *Every Parent Matters* (London: DfES).
Driver, S. and Martell, L. (1997), 'New Labour's Communitarianisms', *Critical Social Policy* 17, 27-46.
DWP (2007), *Joint Birth Registration: Promoting Parental Responsibility*, Cm 7160 (London: TSO).
Eekelaar, J. (1991), 'Parental Responsibility: State of Nature or Nature of the State?' *Journal of Social Welfare and Family Law* 37-50.
Eekelaar, J. (2006), *Family Law and Personal Life* (Oxford: Oxford University Press).
Etzioni, A. (1993), *The Parenting Deficit* (London: Demos).
Etzioni, A. (ed.) (1998), *The Essential Communitarian Reader* (Lanham: Rowman & Littlefield Publisher, Inc.).
Frazer, E. and Lacey, N. (1993), *The Politics of Community: A Feminist Critique of the Liberal-Communitarian Debate* (Hertfordshire: Harvester Wheatsheaf).
Furedi, F. (2001), *Paranoid Parenting: Abandon Your Anxieties and Be a Good Parent* (London: Allen Lane).
Gardner, J. (2003), 'The Mark of Responsibility', *Oxford Journal of Legal Studies* 23, 157.
Gillies, V. (2005), 'Meeting Parents' Needs? Discourses of "Support" and "Inclusion" in Family Policy', *Critical Social Policy* 25, 70-90.
Henricson, C. (2003), *Government and Parenting: Is there a Case for a Policy Review and a Parents' Code?* (York: Joseph Rowntree Foundation).
HM Treasury and Department for Education and Skills (2007), *Aiming High for Children: Supporting Families* (London: Crown Copyright).
Home Office (1998), *Supporting Families: A Consultation Document* (London: HMSO).
Home Office (2003), *Respect and Responsibility – Taking a Stand Against Anti-Social Behaviour*, Cm 5773 (London: TSO).
Laming, Lord (Chair) (2003), *The Victoria Climbié Inquiry* (London: TSO).
Lindemann Nelson, H. (1999), 'Always Connect: Towards a Parental Ethics of Divorce' in Ruddick, S. and Hanigsberg, J. (eds), *Mother Troubles: Rethinking Contemporary Maternal Dilemmas* (Boston: Beacon Press), 117-35.
Maclean, M. and Eekelaar, J. (1997), *The Parental Obligation: A Study of Parenthood Across Households* (Oxford: Hart).

Oaks, D. (1998), 'Rights and Responsibilities' in Etzioni, A. (ed.), *The Essential Communitarian Reader* (Lanham: Rowman & Littlefield Publisher, Inc.), 97-105.

Prime Minister's Strategy Unit (2007), *Building on Progress: Families* (London: Crown Copyright).

Ribbens McCarthy, J., Edwards, R. and Gillies, V. (2000), 'Moral Tales of the Child and the Adult: Narratives of Contemporary Family Lives under Changing Circumstances', *Sociology* 34, 785-803.

Sapsted, D. (2007), 'CSA Names and Shames 40 Absent Fathers on the Internet Website', *The Telegraph*, 27 June 2007.

Sevenhuijsen, S. (1998), *Citizenship and the Ethics of Care: Feminist Considerations on Justice, Morality and Politics* (London: Routledge).

Sevenhuijsen, S. (2002), 'A Third Way? Moralities, Ethics and Families: An Approach Through the Ethic of Care' in Carling, A., Duncan, S. and Edwards, R. (eds), *Analysing Families: Morality and Rationality in Policy and Practice* (London: Routledge), 129-44.

Sheldon, S. (2001), 'Unmarried Fathers and Parental Responsibility: A Case for Reform?', *Feminist Legal Studies* 2, 93-118.

Smart, C. (2003), 'Children and the Transformation of Family Law' in Dewar, J. and Parker, S. (eds), *Family Law: Processes, Practices and Pressures* (Oxford: Hart), 223-40.

Smart, C. and Neale, B. (1999), *Family Fragments*? (Cambridge: Polity Press).

Smith, R. (1990), 'Parental Responsibility – and an Irresponsible State?', *Childright* 71, 7-8.

Chapter 13

Family Law and Family Responsibility

Alison Diduck[1]

Changing Families; Changing Family Law?

Most people interested in family sociology and family law seem to agree that families are changing. Whether we look simply at the demographic data or at the more nuanced research that demonstrates changes in the nature, manifestations and experiences of personal commitment and responsibility (Diduck 2008), we all have to admit that something is happening. Some of us may be pleased by the changes and some of us disconcerted or even frightened by them, but research shows that 'family life' for many of us is lived outside the heteronuclear married norm and includes forms of group marriage, serial monogamy, unmarried different or same sex cohabitation, non co-resident intimate partnerships or living apart together, step-parenthood and/or lone parenthood (Carling 2002; Diduck 2005), not to mention other household communities (Budgeon and Roseneil 2004) including the non-conjugal homesharers with whom the Law Commission had so much trouble in 2002 (Law Commission 2002) and disregarded in 2006 (Law Commission 2006). Sociologists tell us that these relationships are important to people; they provide stability, intimacy, care, and companionship. They are central to people's core values. Family sociologists further tell us that friendship practices are changing so that there may be a blurring of lines between friends and family (Roseneil 2004). In all of these new family practices, connectedness operates in more various ways than simply through sexual intimacy or blood (Williams 2004).

What is law's relationship with these ambiguous or at least flexible family practices? What is family law to make of these other forms of 'connectedness', or, more to the point, of their personal and social consequences? One view is that family law has simply and appropriately responded to them. Whether we see these relationships as new or as only newly acknowledged, law has in the last decade extended its jurisdiction remarkably rapidly to encompass many of them simply by

1 I am indebted to Michael Freeman, Felicity Kaganas and David Seymour for taking time to read this chapter and offering their always insightful comments upon it. Thanks also for insights beyond the editorial from Craig Lind. I am also grateful to participants at the *Responsibility and the Family* Symposium for their views on the initial ideas for this chapter. Finally, ideas from this chapter were also presented at the *Changing Social Norms, Changing Family Law?* Seminar, part of the ESRC Seminar Series, hosted by the Nuffield Foundation in London and at the University of Edinburgh Faculty of Law and Lancaster University School of Law. I am grateful to participants in each of these sessions for their lively discussion and feedback.

acknowledging them as family connections. On this view, family law itself really hasn't changed; it has simply extended its remit to permit a wider range of people and relationships within it.

Another view, however, is that family law has not so much responded to social change as it has participated in it. Expanding family law may have helped to facilitate changing family practices and new 'personal familiarities' (Diduck 2005) and in this way has worked together with actual behaviour to legitimise the increasing diversity of ways in which we arrange our personal living. On this view, law is connected to the actions of people such that both constituencies are engaged in a continual process of 'meaning making'. Family law and family practices 'mutually shape each other as people challenge the partiality of legal conceptions through social action *and* challenge social patterns through legal discourse' (Minow 1985, 890, emphasis added). Meaning making does not begin from scratch, however; connection and mutuality 'invest legal forms with new meanings by reference in part to the meanings that are already established' (Minow 1985, 890). The *Fitzpatrick*[2] decision and those cases before it[3] which shifted the legal meaning of 'family' for the purposes of rent and housing legislation offer good examples of this process. In this series of cases, the legal definition of family was reshaped by the relationship practices first of heterosexual unmarried cohabitants and then same sex cohabitants. In both new 'shapes' though, the family roles adopted by the claimants owed a great deal to their married counterparts and their 'family' relationships were made with reference to the (legal) meaning already invested in the terms spouse and family (Diduck 2001).

In *Law's Families* (2003) I suggested that even through the diversity of their family practices people demonstrate a commitment to two ideal families: the romantic traditional family, with its preordained and presumed functions, duties and roles and the modernised, individualised democratic family with its negotiable and negotiated ones. I called this dichotomous ideal the family we live *by*. But I also suggested that in our everyday lives we negotiate these commitments in a variety of ways according to our personal and structural contexts from time to time and that these negotiations are more often than not messier than the simple alignment of the 'modern' with the 'traditional'. I went on to suggest that while the meanings of commitment and responsibility are made in these messy 'families we live *in*' they are also made within the normative framework of the dichotomous ideal – and legal – families we live by. While the inclusion of same sex families into law, for example, challenges one of the traditional bases of family – heteronormativity – it also instantiates a version of that ideal by absorbing the potentially far more disruptive gay or lesbian subject back into familiar roles and displacing his or her disruptive potential (Boyd 1999). Thus, the families created by *Fitzpatrick*, *Mendoza*[4] and the Civil Partnership Act and by

2 *Fitzpatrick v Sterling Housing Association* [2001] 1 AC 27.

3 *Gammans v Elkins* [1950] 2 KB 328 (married partners only) to *Dyson Holdings v Fox* [1976] QB 503 (long-term heterosexual cohabitants); *Harrogate BC v Simpson* [1986] 2 FLR 91 (same sex long-term cohabitants are not family) to Fitzpatrick (same sex long-term cohabitants are family).

4 *Ghaidan v Godin-Mendoza* [2004] UKHL 30.

Mr Fitzpatrick, Mr Mendoza and all those who have registered their partnerships, at the same time both restructure and reinforce that normative framework.

Perhaps the process is as much bound up with the power of language as it is with the power of certain legal forms. Both affect the conceptual and normative frameworks in which family living is understood. The terms we use for the familial roles we adopt bear both legal and social baggage. Research with lesbian parents, for example illustrates the difficulties many have in giving names to newly forged parental roles that sometimes resist and sometimes support their heterosexual and gendered foundations.[5] 'Mother' for many is associated with maternity so that the term 'co-mother' fails to describe accurately the parenting role and identity of her partner and new terms must be found to do so. In fact, 'mother', 'parent', 'father' and 'family' all may have diverse meanings in these families and disengaging those meanings from the familial norm is part of the work lesbian parent families do on a day to day basis. But their work is made more difficult by the lack of alternative language available for these relationships. Concepts and language are deep-rooted in the law so that family law 'in a sense, pre-empts ways of understanding new family structures.'[6]

And so, family practices exhibit both transgression and instantiation of norms. They and the law that regulates them are mutually reinforcing and transforming. And when the law changes, those reforms, whether judicial or legislative, are as likely to be pragmatic responses designed to promote equality or fairness for an individual or a particular class of people as they are to be part of any consistent principled or policy agenda. Equality was the government's stated interest in promoting the Civil Partnership Act, for example, while seeking fairness for dependent cohabitants was the declared motivation for the Law Commission's cohabitation project, and the redefinition of family in *Fitzpatrick* was necessary to prevent the claimant's eviction from his home of many years. Family law, like the common law generally, appears to 'stumbl[e] forward in the empirical fashion … blundering into wisdom' (Müller-Freienfels 2003, 40) with apparently little conceptual comprehensiveness and within an apparently shifting or uncertain normative framework.

John Dewar, writing in 1998 of similar phenomena, characterised them as evidence of law's normal but chaotic response to the chaos of changing family practices, including some form of individualisation of them, and indeed, my views about the ambiguity of these changes suggest something similar. Dewar said that family law exhibited normative incoherence (or contradiction, disorder, pluralism, even antinomy) or uncertainty and that this stemmed from uncertainty about its proper role or purpose. Is family law to enforce rights between family members, or to promote their welfare, for example, or is it to maximise utility and pursue an optimal outcome (1998, 490)? While family law's chaos or normative uncertainty ought to be taken seriously (1998, 469), Dewar also said that it need not be cause for concern. 'To the extent that family law deals in ideas of what families are, how their members should deal with each other, and what the role of law and the state

5 See discussion of recent research in Diduck (2007).

6 Dr Claire Sturge, para. 57 in *Re D (Contact and Parental Responsibility: Lesbian Mothers and Known Father)* [2006] EWHC 2 (Fam), [2006] FCR 556.

should be with regard to them, it is not coherent at all' (1998, 468). This was not a problem, however, at least partly because family 'engages with areas of social life and feeling – namely love, passion, intimacy, commitment and betrayal – that are themselves riven with contradiction or paradox' (1998, 468).

And then in 2000 Dewar wrote again about the 'discontents' or tensions in contemporary family law, once more uncovering what he saw to be a pervasive uncertainty about what family law is for, how it is to go about its tasks and how it should embody conventional notions of legality. He again saw this discontent positively, however, because the terms on which family life should be lived *are* uncertain and family life *is* more diverse than ever before. We ourselves, as families and family members, lack both consensus and clear object or focus (2000, 79). In this light, Dewar proposed that family law's discontents or chaos must be considered positively; they are what so far still offers an opportunity to conduct a continuing *conversation* about the terms on which family life should be lived and therefore contain the risk of 'family' being hijacked by ideological rhetoric. Law's discontent, therefore, provides a second form of politics of and for families. That I agree with this can be seen in both *Law's Families* and this chapter.

But Dewar then goes further and this is where he and I diverge. He says 'family law deals in the consequences of relationships and so far there is doubt about what those legal consequences should be' (1998, 481). He says that the doubt stems from a logically prior uncertainty – what meaning we should give to relations we have with others – specifically what marks off family relationships from other types of relation (ibid.) especially in light of growing dissociation of sex from marriage and procreation from intercourse and, I would add, of love/care/commitment from biological or conjugal connections. He says that law's pattern in making choices about relationship legitimacy is neither uniform nor consistent, but reflects wider uncertainties about what constitutes connection between individuals while also reflecting a logic of bolstering paternal authority drawing on whichever means are most conveniently at hand to link men to children (1998, 483).

In effect, Dewar and I see the same phenomena occurring in family law, but unlike him, I'm not convinced that they are necessarily evidence *only* of uncertainty or pluralism in legal norms, no matter how much of a positive spin we put on that uncertainty. To me, embedded within the pluralism and the tensions is the glimmer of a thread of normative consistency which may be only newly *expressed* in a plurality of ways, so as to appear to embrace diversity and plurality in family living.

My disagreement with Dewar may stem from our different emphases upon the role and place socially of family and family law. While he does not ignore family law's public role and the role that families themselves play in public life, Dewar seems to me to be concerned primarily with family law in its role as regulator of private relationships and with their consequences for the individuals concerned. His perspective emphasises the traditional view of family law as private law. My focus on the other hand, while not ignoring the individual private effects of family law, is more clearly upon the relationship between families and familiar roles and the state. It adopts the family law as public law perspective. So while Dewar rightly sees normative *uncertainty* beneath family law's search for determining the relationships deemed appropriately familial (should interfamilial obligation require a conjugal link? A genetic one? A social one? A contractual one?), I see beneath this search a degree of normative *certainty* or *consistency* about determining the public consequences of those relationships which are to be deemed appropriately familial. It is about the fundamental, primary role family is to play in society: care of dependants. For me, therefore, the legal regulation of private, *family* relations is also the regulation of these *social* and *political* relations. To be sure, family law is about promoting some idea of justice and welfare for, and perhaps even the rights of, individual members of the 'family' group, but it is also about the nature and public value of dependence and independence and about regulating the balance of political, social and economic power in society as much as in the family. On this view family law is about managing the personal and social consequences of interdependence, caring and intimacy, precisely because those roles have always been tied to the family (Law Commission of Canada 2002). Their effective management is therefore *dependent* in part on enduring yet malleable concepts of the family and family law and it is at this level that some normative consistency is evident.

Normative Coherence?

I wish to focus upon two of the public consequences of this thread of normative consistency in family law. Both relate to responsibility. The first is responsibility for caring and by implication for the more general costs of social reproduction. Family sociologist William Goode has suggested that 'no society can work very well that does not ensure a fair level of protection for its inept, and less able members of the family and society' (2003, 19). While the state has taken on more or less of this responsibility at various points in history in Britain, the family has traditionally been assumed to be the first and primary port of call, and we must not underestimate the importance of family law in ordering and re-ordering that balance of responsibility. As Brenda Cossman has said 'family law has always been about the public enforcement of private responsibilities of individual family members. But in an era of privatization, it has acquired a newfound importance' (2002, 69).

Martha Fineman observes that in the US also, caring remains the primary role for families. She goes on to say that while carers themselves are also dependent because they depend upon resources in order to undertake that care, it is always assumed that those resources are to be subsumed within the self-sufficient family (Fineman 2004) or are to be provided by private employers or often, charity.

> It is the family, not the state or the market, that assumes responsibility for both the inevitable dependent – the child or other biologically or developmentally dependent person – and the derivative dependent – the caretaker. The institution of the family operates structurally and ideologically to free markets from considering or accommodating dependency. The state is cast as a default institution, providing minimal, grudging and stigmatized assistance should families fail. (2004, 228)

The family is thus attributed with an autonomy or self-sufficiency that she calls mythical, but which is linked to its characterisation as a responsible family. The responsible family is the one that assumes the costs of care of its dependants, relieving the state from responsibility for sharing those costs.

In Canada, Fudge and Cossman say that there is a whole new set of assumptions about the role of government and the rights of citizens:

> In the new political and social order, governments are no longer responsible for the social welfare of their citizens but only for helping those citizens to help themselves. The social citizen is giving way to the market citizen who (quoting Brodie 1996) "recognizes the limits and liabilities of state provision and embraces her obligation to become more self-reliant". This new market citizen recognizes and takes responsibility for her own risk and that of her family. (2002, 16)

In this new polity, the actual costs of social reproduction are being shifted. Through the simultaneous emphasis on self-reliance and family obligation (Fudge and Cossman 2002, 28), 'once public goods, responsibilities and services are being reconstituted as naturally located within the family and its individual members' (ibid., 171) and families are being called upon to address the economic needs of dependants, primarily women and children, at precisely the time when the welfare state is being dismantled (Cossman 2002, 169) and the other concurrent structural conditions (for example, job security and child care) required to enable them to do so are lagging far behind. Clearly, these observations are of more than merely passing interest in the British context.

Michael Freeman highlighted in 1997 the euphemistically termed 'community care' policy as an example of a policy which increased the family's responsibility for the 'inept', in this case the elderly. He said rightly that community care is actually 'care by the family, which means disproportionately care by women' (1997, 326). Familial care of the elderly raises questions, he said (many of which remain unanswered) about the status that might come with this additional responsibility, the employment and pension implications that are attached to it and the general level of support provided to it (1997, 326). Yet, care for the elderly, for children and for the chronically ill or disabled is increasingly a gendered, familial responsibility that affects one's relationship not only with other family members, but with the state.

> New deal or other family-friendly work practices, not to mention providing so-called equal opportunities for carers to enter work or training programmes, present parents and carers as partners with the state and with the market in new ways. In this new partnership, private self reliance becomes one's social responsibility and founds one's claim to citizenship, and economic dependence becomes an individual failing that demands individualised solutions rather than social or structural ones. The new private partners also have the responsibility of "ensuring that their children behave responsibly and are sufficiently informed and educated to become citizen workers themselves" … while it is framed in gender neutral terms, this new partnership … frequently and profoundly affects women and the children in their care because structural conditions and the norms of family living encourage their continued and mutual economic dependencies. (Diduck 2005, 252, references omitted)

And so, the cultural, social and economic norms of privatisation and responsibility by which families must live provide a clear incentive for law to expand and to reorder relationships and to recognise them as family. Incentive is also provided by the demands of those previously excluded from family to be included, and these demands also increase the 'favour' (Fineman 2004) or the status of family and family law. Family law then, whether by design or accident, privatises more and more dependencies.

The second aspect of responsibility which I want to examine is linked to the first, but invokes a broader concept of social responsibility that is only foreshadowed by privatising/familialising (the costs of) dependency and care. The language of responsibility has become almost a mantra in government policy documents. And interestingly, one's responsibility to society, usually called the taxpayer, and even one's responsibility to self is increasingly framed within the discourse of family. Within this frame responsibility is not only construed in financial terms, but in terms also of providing solutions to all manner of social problems. We all are, were at one time or will be one or more of someone's mother, father, child or partner and that familial identity is increasingly seen to be the primary source of or foundation for the responsibility we owe to society. The political, social and economic problem of child poverty, for example, could be solved *by families* if non-resident parents acted responsibly and paid child support and resident parents earned income from employment outside the home. The problems of youth crime and disaffected youth generally similarly can be solved *by families* if all parents are employed outside the home and also take responsibility for their children's criminal, anti-social and truanting behaviour (see Keating in this book). The problems of an underfunded legal aid system and even the personal emotional difficulties of relationship breakdown can be solved *by families* if divorcing partners and their children take responsibility for arranging their own post-divorce families. Myriad social problems, it seems, can be solved by people simply taking their *family* responsibilities seriously. It seems to me therefore, that the trend toward expanding legal families has important political and social implications beyond those mentioned earlier: it facilitates the privatisation of responsibility for many social ills.

Expanding the scope and nature of the family's responsibility therefore means that one's family identity, as mother, father, son, daughter or grandparent, becomes one's principal identity in the eyes of the state and the law. One's legal, social or personal responsibilities will be cast as family responsibilities and understood and enforced only or primarily on those always gendered terms. One's social responsibility then becomes the responsibility to look after one's self and family and the state's responsibility is no longer to individuals as citizens, but is to individual men, women and children only insofar as they are members of families. The state's responsibilities to groups or to other collectivities such as unions is marginalised, if not abandoned entirely, unless those collectivities can be defined as families; the state's primary goal becomes supporting families.

I must be clear at this point that I don't think family members have no responsibility for each other's well-being and for the well-being of others. Care and support, intimacy and belonging are important personally and socially, and many of us wish to experience them in a 'family' however it is organised.[7] For others, though, new forms of intimacy and care relationships fit increasingly uneasily in the category of family (Budgeon and Roseneil 2004). My point is that the term 'family' evokes an ideal in which some of us want to live and which some of us want to avoid, but it is one in which few of us actually live. Yet it predicates not only the way in which responsibility is allocated to our intimates, but also the way in which much of our *social* living and *social* responsibility is regulated by law. There is, in my view, therefore, more normative and conceptual coherence in family law than Dewar's perspective reveals and it is about allocating responsibility for responsibility.

Roseneil and Budgeon (2004) say that in order to understand the meaning and effects for people of their 'new' intimate practices we should de-centre family in the sociological imagination. I am fascinated by this idea, as it seems to me to offer an interesting point of departure from which to understand the way law negotiates its discontents. I want to explore in the next section the degree to which the idea of family is or is not central to the legal imagination and the degree to which its positioning influences or limits that imagination. I am interested both in the degree to which 'family law' as an academic discipline is implicated in the privatisation of responsibility and in whether 'the family' has legal and political resonance outside of the 'black box' that is family law.

De-familialising Families and Family Law

In positivist terms family law can be defined as a collection of statutes and cases regulating the family. In 1957 Lord Evershed called it 'a convenient means of reference to so much of our Law, whether statutory or found among the rules of the Common Law or of Equity, as directly affects that essential unit of English social structure, the Family' (Evershed, MR 1957, vii-viii). The collection of these laws into a discrete discipline is only of recent vintage, however. And as Müller-Freienfels offered, knowledge of its long and specific historical development is 'a precondition for understanding it. ... Only when [family laws] are regarded as part of our history and social evolution do they emerge ... as the framework for our present way of life' (2003, 32).

Many scholars date the birth of 'family law' as the modern concept we know today in Britain at some time after the Second World War (Freeman 1997; Müller-Freienfels 2003; Probert 2004). Before that, the law regulating the family was fragmented into disparate parts and in addition to the law of property and testamentary law, included topics such as the law of husband and wife and the law relating to infants. Blackstone's direct legacy is perceptible here as is the legacy of the common law tradition in which the 'development of the concepts, categories and divisions of the common law is bound with the concrete problems that arise in individual cases' (Müller-Freienfels 2003, 39). The law, in other words, was made by the judges, and the 'family law' cases that came before them traditionally were indeed cases

7 Weeks (2002) describes how the term is being claimed and at the same time transformed and given alternative meaning by non-heterosexual communities.

about marriage and divorce, about settlement of property and about the liability for contracts and criminal actions of children. And so, despite the broad range of laws that might be seen to 'directly affect' the family, those fragments that were deemed to be family law and that eventually were gathered together under that heading reflected the concerns of those who were able to bring their causes before the courts: the propertied and middle class (usually men) for whom validity of marriage and divorce was profoundly important for establishing the legitimacy of their line and the legitimate passage of property along it. Laws that 'directly affected' the poor were simply not seen as family law at all. These laws were administered by the magistrates or were contained within and administered as part of the Poor Law and reflected a class-based division which arguably has left its mark on family law today (ten Broek 1964). Few family law textbooks even today contain chapters on income support, jobseekers' allowance, tax, employment or public housing.[8]

Probert suggests that a fragmented and segregated body of family law makes sense however, in the context of segregated (middle class) family living historically, in which children and servants were allocated to separate quarters within the household (2004, 902). The Victorian family just did not look like or live like families do now, so Victorian family law should not be expected to look like today's family law. She makes the reasonable point to which I shall return below, that 'the fact that earlier concepts of family law do not always resemble our own should not obscure the fact that they may have been better suited to the law and the families of their own time' (2004, 903). She reminds us that there was in fact a textbook published in 1885 entitled *The Law of Domestic Relations* which included a chapter on 'Master and Servant'.

Eventually, around the 1950s, however, a coherent body of law became conceptualised specifically as 'family law'. It was first taught at the London School of Economics by Professor Otto Kahn-Freund whose continental background may have influenced his pursuit of family law as a separate doctrinal discipline. The first textbook with family law in its title was published in 1957[9] and brought together the black letter law concerning the parties' status as husband and wife and the property entitlements that came with it (Lowe and Douglas 2007, v). There was neither discussion of children's welfare nor of the public law relating to children (Lowe and Douglas 2007, ibid.), nor indeed of many of the public consequences of marriage and divorce. This state of affairs changed over the years, however, until Cretney could say that by the year 2000 'there was in place a system [of family law] constructed on rational principles' (2003, 773).

Among the many reasons for the gathering together in the immediate post-war period of a body of case law under the heading family law may be that the subject of the law – a particular form of family – became politically important at that time, at least ideologically, in a formal, conceptually clear way. There are other factors also which may have influenced the subsequent development of family law from a collection of cases relating to that patriarchal family to a 'system constructed

8 But see Diduck, A. and Kaganas, F. (2006), *Family Law, Gender, and the State* (Oxford: Hart Publishing Ltd).

9 Bromley (1957).

on rational principles' such as welfare and equality. I wish to draw them out by highlighting some aspects of family law's development into a 'real' or legitimate sub-discipline of law.

Müller-Freienfels highlights the influence in Europe but not Britain upon the later treatise writers of the early Enlightenment philosophers, those 'cosmopolitan, rational legal scientists of natural law' (2003, 32) who sought methodically and systematically to construe the legal order as a coherent system. Pufendorf, for example, believed that family law should exist as an autonomous part of the law, conceptually constructed and containing an inner coherence (Müller-Freienfels 2003) and this belief informed the early French and German systems as it does today. The influence of the continental theorists was not, of course, felt in the common law system until much later. In the area of contract law, for example, Cornish and Clarke (1989) observe that by the time of Blackstone the academic exposition of a general or 'whole' view of contract was well established on the continent (1989, 200), but it took until the 19th century for its influence to be felt in Britain. They and other legal historians suggest however, that once begun, the search for a general law of contract, for an autonomous body of law with its own conceptual integrity, reached its high water mark in the 19th century when the 'classical' law of contract became expressed in terms of will theory.[10]

Cornish and Clarke contend that the desire of the judges for general principles, the rivalry between the common law and Chancery courts, the introduction of systematic teaching and examination for entry into the legal professions and the values which were embodied in the general and categorical doctrine of contract law all contributed to its appeal (1989, 201). Collins goes so far as to assert that those values, in this case, will theory as expressed through the principle of freedom of contract, helped to shape and structure not only the market order but our thoughts and conceptions of it (2003, Ch. 1). Without attempting to assess the merits of these particular histories of contract law, I am interested in their acknowledgement of the mutuality of the interaction between statements of law and the organisation of social relations and in particular in the appeal of the statements of law themselves. Legal statements that issue from a principled and autonomous 'system' of law have a legitimacy and authority that are lacking in statements issued from a law based on discretion rather than rules and empirical facts rather than abstract principles. Lack of legal authority means that a discipline, if it is recognised as such at all, has low status in the profession, among academics (Dewar 1998, 469) and among the general population and may affect the degree of influence it has in each of these spheres. Family law has suffered in the past, and still suffers, to some degree, from such a perceived low status.

> Close scrutiny of the family law reports, so the argument goes, will not yield an elegant and abstract doctrinal system, but little more than specific and unanalysable instances of the exercise of a discretion, far too enmired in the factual specifics of each case to yield

10 There are, of course, different schools of thought about the development of modern contract law. While they may differ on why 'classical' contract law developed the way it did, there is some agreement on its dominance in the 19th century. See for example, Atiyah (1979), Collins (2003), Gordley (1991), Hamburger (1989), Horwitz (1977), Simpson (1975).

> anything approaching a principle or *ratio*. As such it is not real law, just a poor relation of the harder disciplines of the common law, a falling away from the proud legal tradition. (Dewar 1998, 469-70)

Family law is in a difficult position, therefore. It must retain a wide discretion and be interested in the irrational as well as the rational interests of its constituency – families – while at the same time protect its status as 'real' law.

Let me illustrate my point with the example offered above of the changing definition of 'family' in law. Judges over the years have declined to define 'family' for all purposes, and instead have relied upon the view of the ordinary person in the street and changing social conditions to do so on a case by case basis. This process leaves family law a wide discretion to decide whether or not to assume jurisdiction over a particular personal relationship and appears to rely, inappropriately for 'real' lawyers, upon judicial discretion and public opinion. But the courts' discretion is not now and never has been exercised on an unprincipled basis. The set of principles on which adult relationships are defined as familial or not familial is 'thin but wide reaching' (Collins 2003, 5, writing of contract law principles) precisely in order to allow family law both to encompass and to exclude relationships from time to time. That set of principles is derived from law's 'original' family relationship of husband and wife. And so, laws regulating the interdependencies of cohabitants were not considered 'family law' for many years, for example, in part because lack of formalisation of their relationship rendered cohabitants too distantly related to their progenitor marital family to permit them to be called families at all. Unmarried cohabitants were not considered to be families until the 1970s.[11] The fact that their affairs are still governed by property law, trust law and contract law has been the subject of academic and professional criticism since then. Today, as family law's emphasis has switched from formality to conjugality as a relevant inherited characteristic from the progenitor marital family, so family law has become interested in conjugal cohabitants; they are sufficiently like their familial ancestors husband and wife to have been legitimised as a 'new family form'. This means, however, that the interdependencies of non-conjugal homesharers are still not governed by family law. Unlike conjugal cohabitants, the families that comprise them are not sufficiently like the descendants of 'marital' families which in turn are descended from the interest the law had in the affairs of 'Husband and Wife'.[12] The principled basis of family and therefore of family law can expand, in this example from formalisation to conjugality, but cannot be stretched beyond what is perceived from time to time to be a breaking point, otherwise it would appear to lose its coherence and therefore its legitimacy as 'real' law.

In the way that it has evolved since its initial claim to be an 'elegant and abstract doctrinal system' (Dewar 1998), family law has undergone a Darwinian-type mutation in concert with changing social and personal practices and changing policies and politics, as Dewar's observations about its contradictions, even antinomies, illustrate. But its ideal family – even though fewer and fewer of us experience it – remains the

11 *Dyson Holdings v Fox* [1976] QB 503.

12 Law Commission (2002); *Burden and Burden v UK* [2007] 1 FCR 69 (ECtHR).

classic exemplar of the organisation of life in the realm of the private. Textbooks are organised around it and expositions of the law begin from it before they then go on to explain the law in terms of interventions into it or derogations from it. Other ways of living are presented as alternatives to it. This pseudo-marital family and the law about it still structure our thoughts about the nature of 'proper' personal relationships and the 'proper' relationship between families and the societies in which they live,[13] including the 'proper' balance between the two of responsibility for responsibility.

Even as it 'stumbles forward', therefore, expanding or contracting its scope, or shifting its primary principles (between welfare and rights, for example), family law can claim for itself conceptual integrity. It is the body of law that defines and regulates the family, family relationships and family responsibilities. It thus can distance itself with a flourish from criticisms that it is at best a recent discipline and at worst a fraudulent one. By uniting only certain laws as being about the family, and at the same time keeping open the concept of the family, family law can claim a degree of conceptual purity which allows it to manage, in a holistic way, diverse social practices and values and regulate their personal and social consequences.

The timing of the origins of a 'whole' view of family law is important also. The post-war period was a period of retrenchment of traditional family roles. It was at that time, when the family itself became more entrenched in its post-war form and its responsibilities became more a matter for policy and regulation by the newly emerging welfare state, that a coherent body of family law began to develop. This timing may have influenced the result: what emerged as family law 'in the eyes of most family lawyers, academics, and practitioners, was a narrow and distorted image both of the subject of the discipline (the family) and of the processes which regulate the family' (Freeman 1997, 319). Of course family law has evolved from the 1950s, but arguably it has remained within its original framework for understanding social relations in a particular way and for the legitimate exercise of state power upon them.

Controlling admission into the category of family requires family law to engage with both family practices and state policy. Expanding the category of family so that more of us will fit into it may be evidence of the expansion of the realm of the private and the consequent colonisation of more and more 'familial' responsibility. Maintaining some degree of exclusivity too ensures that only certain kinds of dependencies are deemed appropriate from time to time in society. Family law thus presents a particular view of society and social relations. It may be, as Day Sclater and Piper said in 2000, a view that is concerned about remoralising the family in order to ease a perceived crisis in it, but it may also be, as I have said elsewhere (Diduck 2005), about remoralising society in order to ease a perceived crisis there.

> [Contemporary family law] engages with individualism's valuing of personal choice and its focus upon the subjective quality of individual life and relationships, but succeeds in reshaping those values within the contours of the traditional family, with all of the consequences this has for decisions about the responsibilities one bears or does not bear for self, family, community and "others". (Diduck 2005, 253)

---

13 See Collins on this in the context of contract law (2003, 3).

And so, while many suggest that family law's most recent stage of evolution is its shift in emphasis from the adult relationship to the adult/child link (e.g. Williams 2004), it seems to me that it doesn't matter, the links perform the same disciplinary role. In a society where responsibility is familialised, both, through family law, attach people to others to make a new family which can then legitimately be ascribed responsibility for at least part of that which was formerly a social or state responsibility: the general welfare of society and its individual citizens.

If family law is about the regulation of what it means to be, and the public or social, as well as the personal consequences of being, a mother, father, son, daughter, carer, sex partner or homesharer, then family law is also employment law,[14] criminal law,[15] youth justice,[16] tax law,[17] immigration law,[18] public and constitutional law,[19] property law,[20] social security law[21] and EU law,[22] and each of these is also family law. Yet, family law as a concept would suffer were it to open itself so wide. It would be almost a regression to the bad old days of fragmentation and would devalue family law's hard fought development from (ironically) 'pretended' to 'real' status as law. Family law thus tends to remain within its 'classical' boundaries, in no small part because of the flexible boundaries of its subject. Lawyers appear to have been unable or unwilling to de-centre family in the legal imagination the way that Roseneil and Budgeon say it must be de-centred in the sociological imagination (2004).

But what if we did? What would laws about relationships and responsibility look like? There are a number of possible alternatives. The first is to renounce entirely the concept of family law by abandoning the legal concept of family. Rather than saying that family law must march or stumble forward by expanding its remit, including, in the pursuit of inclusivity and equality, defining more and more affiliations as family, we say that nothing should be family, at least until family has shed its ideological baggage. This approach would require the law and the state to promote and support any number of different stable, caring, relationships and promote fairness in the assumption of physical, emotional and financial responsibilities within those relationships without forcing them into a category of 'family' which is laden with historical and ideological baggage that is peculiarly receptive to, actually almost designed to, bear ever increasing degrees and types of responsibility. For this I would venture not only that we do not *need* family law, but that using family law to do this, however it is reformed, may be antithetical to these objectives, or at least that it may inhibit the range of possibilities. It would keep us in the discourse of family.

---

14 See, e.g., Employment Act 2002; Work and Families Act 2006.

15 See, e.g., Domestic Violence, Crime and Victims Act 2004, section 5; *A v UK* [1998] 2 FLR 959.

16 Piper (2006).

17 Mumford (2006); Boyd and Young (2004).

18 Immigration Rules; and see, for a discussion of the concept of family life under Article 8 ECHR, *Singh v Entry Clearance Officer New Delhi* [2004] EWCA Civ 1075.

19 See, e.g., *I v UK* [2002] 2 FLR 518; *Goodwin v UK* [2002] 2 FLR 487.

20 Bottomley and Wong (2006).

21 See, e.g., Jobseeker's Act 1995; New Deal for Lone Parents; New Deal for Partners.

22 See, e.g., *Grant v Southwest Trains* [1998] 1 FLR 839; *Webb v EMO Air Cargo* [1994] ECR 1-03567.

If we step outside 'family' and family law we see that regulation of the consequences of intimacy and interdependence already takes place in medical law, social services law, immigration law, housing/property law, employment law, criminal law, tort law, tax law, and equity. One answer may be, therefore, to leave the consequences of relationships solely to these private law remedies. Just as they have had an effect on 'family law', human rights norms such as non-discrimination, substantive equality and protection of the dignity and integrity of the individual may also affect these areas of law and be fruitful areas for law and policy makers to explore in distributing fairly the functions and consequences of intimate living without the need to define or categorise the relationship. Similarly, values such as welfare and care that are deemed only to have their place in the private family may begin to inform these more 'public' areas of law. We would see a cross-fertilisation of norms and values and a more porous public/private boundary that may more realistically engage with everyday family practices. A version, perhaps, of the ECtHR's 'reality test', by which it looks for evidence of close personal links, including a relationship of emotional (as opposed to merely economic) dependency between the parties before it creates any responsibilities between them, in each situation or legal context in which the question arises, may be envisioned here.

There is, however, a problem with this approach. While it concedes some power to language in constructing legal and conceptual frameworks, it may not concede enough to the power of longstanding norms, both social and legal. We may refuse to use the terms 'family' or 'family law' but we are less likely to forgo entirely all the normative content of those terms, even while we adopt and adapt social roles 'to engage in activities not contemplated or even … beyond the boundaries set by law' (Minow 1985, 895). After the Revolution in France, for example, '"Family Relationships" had fallen into disrepute for emotional and ideological reasons, and thus the drafters of the Code Civil did not have the possibility to consider the family as a unified element within the larger communities' (Müller-Freienfels 2003, 34). They thus adopted 'the simplest and most radical solution: not to let the word *family* appear in the legal text at all' (ibid., 34), while still protecting social and personal relations through the traditional divisions of law of *personae*, *res* and *actionnes*.

The Law Commission of Canada proposed a similar approach in its review of how the state might promote and support the great variety of caring personal adult relationships in Canada and at the same time remain neutral in regard to the roles that people assume in them (2002). Instead of arguing that some relationships currently excluded should be included in legal recognition, it proposed that the law begin from scratch and examine the way governments have relied upon relational status in allocating rights and responsibilities, and try to design a legislative regime that accomplishes its goals by relying less on whether people are living in certain kinds of relationships. Sometimes some characteristics of the relationship will be important, other times they would not be, but, interestingly, conjugality would never be important. The danger of this approach, however, like the French revolutionary one, is the power of the family ideal. These approaches may lead to old family norms being extended to greater numbers of people, as Carol Smart (1984) said, of the regulatory net of family – more precisely, of a particular idea of family – spreading wider to capture more and more people, and normative familialisation continuing apace without its expression in or protection by 'real' law.

Another approach might be to transform family law rather than to discard it. Eekelaar, for example, also questions whether we need to bring increasing types of relationships under some concept of 'family', but does not wish to abandon a separate category of law to govern those relationships. He proposes the phrase personal law to encompass the 'role of law in relation to what is usually referred to as people's personal or private lives' (2006, 31). He describes the values that he believes ought to inform that law as friendship, truth, respect, responsibility and rights. In this, he rejects the principled doctrinal legacy of family law's history and appeals, like the enlightenment theorists, to norms beyond the positive law to inform his idea of a just personal law.[23] He believes that by considering them seriously, personal law can engage justly with a wider range of personal relationships and take seriously also communities of identity and broader structural and institutional conditions within which personal life is lived and with which it is connected.

As a final example, Probert also queries the nature of family law as it has developed over the years and agrees that it has defined itself too narrowly. She agrees that more attention to tax law, social security law and employment law would enrich our understanding of family law (2004, 905) and thus she advocates some crossing of the public/private boundary and opening up of family law's black box. Alternatively, she suggests 're-adopting the term "the law of domestic relations" to refocus attention on the household and the partners, relations and others who may share it' (2004, 905). It is interesting that both she and Eekelaar recall previous legal forms to guide their suggestions for family law's transformation.

I have no title for a new way of thinking about laws regulating our intimate and personal living and its public consequences. I wish merely to highlight and raise questions about the ways in which family law might do this work, the implications of its doing so and whether it can continue to do so. My observations lead me to conclude that family law exhibits both coherence and incoherence and the thread of coherence is found in its role as shaper of responsibility for care. Family law may indeed be in a period of discontent but a particular idea of family responsibility remains at its base as a result of a complex relationship between family practices, legal and social norms, legal forms and political imperatives. We may not, therefore, see in the next year a defamilialised family law 'framing work–life balance policies in terms of the range of important personal relationships and commitments within which people live their lives, rather than narrowly with reference to family responsibilities' (Roseneil 2004, 415), but we must also remember that the history of family law is not over. Each of what Minow calls the 'key elements of the story – social role, law and family' still provide 'terrains for struggle' rather than 'concepts with certain meanings' (1985, 895-6).

My observations about the rise (and fall?) of family law, therefore, are meant only to offer one perspective on the complicated relationship between family living, family law and social responsibility. In the context of changing family living, they raise questions like the one Martha Fineman posed in 2004: 'If the existence of a

23 See also Eekelaar (2003) on this.

certain type of family is a prerequisite for the coherent development of our concepts of the "public" market and the state, what happens when we are forced to concede that there have been widespread and not easily reversible changes in the way we think about and practice family ... ?' (2004, 28), and by implication about the way we think about family law. They raise questions about the traditional conferral of the social, legal and economic benefits and detriments that derive from intimate living, about 'the family's' institutional status and its relationship to the state, about the distribution of resources and responsibilities in society generally and consequently the material underpinnings both of the private family and the form of society based upon it. If just as changes in the social world – the entrenching of a particular family form at a particular historic time as the subject of family law – were a part of the creation of a coherent notion of 'family law', perhaps contemporary social changes may signal a time now for a challenge to that coherent notion.

Finally, my observations are intended to raise questions about care and the value and costs of care, questions about allocating responsibility for that care and for its consequences, and questions about allocating responsibility for the welfare, financial security, dignity and well-being of society and all its members, not only of 'families'. Civil society is more than just families. These questions are an attempt to seek a middle way between two revolutionary battle cries, one in France circa 1789: '*Il n'y a que l'individu et l'Etat*' and the other in England two hundred years later: 'There is no such thing as society. There are individual men and women, and there are families'.

References

Adam, B.D. (2004), 'Care, Intimacy and Same-Sex Partnership in the 21st Century' *Current Sociology* 52, 265.

Atiyah, P.S. (1979), *The Rise and Fall of Freedom of Contract* (Oxford: Clarendon Press).

Bottomley, A. and Wong, S. (2006), 'Shared Households: A New Paradigm for Thinking about the Reform of Domestic Property Relations' in Diduck, A. and O'Donovan, K. (eds), *Feminist Perspectives on Family Law* (London: Routledge Cavendish).

Boyd, S. (1999), 'Family, Law and Sexuality: Feminist Engagements', *Social and Legal Studies* 8, 369.

Boyd, S. and Young, C. (2004), 'Feminism, Law, and Public Policy: Family Feuds and Taxing Times', *Osgoode Hall L J* 42, 545.

Brodie, J. (1996), 'Restructuring and the New Citizenship' in Bakkes, I. (ed.), *Rethinking Restructuring: Gender and Change in Canada* (Toronto: University of Toronto Press).

Broek, J. (1964), 'California's Dual System of Family Law: Its Origin, Development and Present Status', *Stanford Law Review* 16, 257, 900.

Bromley, P.M. (1957), *Family Law* (London: Butterworths).

Budgeon, S. and Roseneil, S. (2004), 'Editors' Introduction: Beyond the Conventional Family', *Current Sociology* 52, 127.

Carling, A., Duncan, S. and Edwards, R. (eds) (2002), *Analysing Families. Morality and Rationality in Policy and Practice* (London: Routledge).

Carling, A. (2002), 'Family Policy, Social Theory and the State' in Carling, A., Duncan, S. and Edwards, R. (eds) (2002), *Analysing Families. Morality and Rationality in Policy and Practice* (London: Routledge).

Collins, H. (2003), *The Law of Contract* (4th edition) (London: LexisNexis).

Cornish, W.R. and Clark, G. de N. (1989), *Law and Society in England 1750–1950* (London: Sweet and Maxwell).

Cossman, B. (2002), 'Family Feuds: Neo-Liberal and Neo-Conservative Visions of the Reprivatization Project' in Fudge, J. and Cossman, B. (eds) (2002), *Privatization, Law and the Challenge to Feminism* (Toronto: University of Toronto Press).

Cretney, S. (2003), *Family Law in the Twentieth Century: A History* (Oxford: Oxford University Press).

Day Sclater, S. and Piper, C. (2000), 'Re-moralising the Family? Family Policy, Family Law and Youth Justice', *Child and Family Law Quarterly* 12:3, 135-51.

Dewar, J. (1998), 'The Normal Chaos of Family Law', *Modern Law Review* 61:4, 467-85.

Dewar, J. (2000), 'Family Law and its Discontents', *International Journal of Law, Policy and the Family* 14, 59-85.

Diduck, A. (2001), 'A Family by Any Other Name ... Or Starbucks Comes to England', *Journal of Law and Society* 28, 290-310.

Diduck, A. (2003), *Law's Families* (London: LexisNexis).

Diduck, A. (2005), 'Shifting Familiarity', *Current Legal Problems* 58, 235-54.

Diduck, A. (2007), '"If Only We Can Find the Appropriate Terms to Use the Issue Will be Solved": Law, Identity and Parenthood', *Child and Family Law Quarterly* 19, 458.

Diduck, A. (ed.) (2008, forthcoming), *Marriage and Cohabitation: Regulating Intimacy, Affection and Care* (London: Ashgate).

Diduck, A. and O'Donovan, K. (eds) (2006), *Feminist Perspectives on Family Law* (London: Routledge Cavendish).

Eekelaar, J. (2003), 'The End of an Era?' *Journal of Family History* 28, 108-22.

Eekelaar, J. (2006), *Family Law and Personal Life* (Oxford: Oxford University Press).

Evershed, Lord, MR (1957), 'Forword' in Graveson, R.H. and Crane, F.R. (eds), *A Century of Family Law 1857–1957* (London: Sweet and Maxwell).

Fineman, M.A. (2004), *The Autonomy Myth: A Theory of Dependency* (New York: The New Press).

Freeman, M. (1997), 'Family Values and Family Justice' *Current Legal Problems* 50, 315-59.

Fudge, J. and Cossman, B. (eds) (2002), *Privatization, Law and the Challenge to Feminism* (Toronto: University of Toronto Press).

Fudge, J. and Cossman, B. (2002), 'Introduction: Privatization, Law and the Challenge to Feminism' in Fudge, J. and Cossman, B. (eds) (2002), *Privatization, Law and the Challenge to Feminism* (Toronto: University of Toronto Press).

Goode, W. (2003), 'Family Changes over the Long Term: A Sociological Commentary', *Journal of Family History* 28:1, 15-30.

Gordley, J. (1991), *The Philosophical Origins of Modern Contract Doctrine* (Oxford: Clarendon Press).

Hamburger, P. (1989), 'The Development of the Nineteenth Century Consensus Theory of Contract', *Law and History Review* 7, 241.

Horwitz, M. (1977), *The Transformation of American Law, 1780–1860* (Cambridge, MA: Harvard University Press).

Law Commission (2002), *No. 278, Sharing Homes: A Discussion Paper*, Cm 3345 (London: The Stationery Office).

Law Commission (2006), *Cohabitation: The Financial Consequences of Relationship Breakdown*, Consultation Paper No. 179 (London: Law Commission).

Law Commission of Canada (2002), *Beyond Conjugality: Recognizing and Supporting Close Personal Adult Relationships* (Ottawa: Law Commission of Canada).

Lowe, N. and Douglas, G. (2007), *Bromley's Family Law* (Oxford: Oxford University Press).

Minow, M. (1985), '"Forming Underneath Everything that Grows": Toward a History of Family Law', *Wisconsin Law Review* 819.

Müller-Freienfels, W. (2003), 'The Emergence of *Droit de Famille* and *Familienrecht* in Continental Europe and the Introduction of Family Law in England', *Journal of Family History* 28:1, 31-51.

Mumford, A. (2006), 'Working Towards Credit for Parenting: A Consideration of Tax Credits as a Feminist Enterprise' in Diduck, A. and O'Donovan, K. (eds), (2006), *Feminist Perspectives on Family Law* (London: Routledge Cavendish).

Piper, C. (2006), 'Feminist Perspectives on Youth Justice' in Diduck, A. and O'Donovan, K. (eds) (2006), *Feminist Perspectives on Family Law* (London: Routledge Cavendish).

Probert, R. (2004), 'Family Law – A Modern Concept?', *Fam Law* 34, 901.

Roseneil, S. (2004), 'Why We Should Care about Friends: An Argument for Queering the Care Imaginary in Social Policy', *Social Policy and Society* 3:4, 409.

Roseneil, S. and Budgeon, S. (2004), 'Cultures of Intimacy and Care Beyond "The Family": Personal Life and Social Change in the Early 21st Century', *Current Sociology* 52, 135.

Simpson, A.W.B. (1975), 'Innovation in Nineteenth Century Contract Law', *Law Quarterly Review* 91, 247.

Smart, C. (1984), *The Ties that Bind* (London: Routledge and Keegan Paul).

Weeks, J. (2002), 'Elective Families: Lesbian and Gay Life Experiments' in Carling, A., Duncan, S. and Edwards, R. (eds), *Analysing Families. Morality and Rationality in Policy and Practice* (London: Routledge).

Williams, F. (2004), *Rethinking Families* (London: Calouste Gulbenkian Foundation).

Chapter 14

Conclusion: Regulating for Responsibility in an Age of Complex Families

Craig Lind

Introduction: Rights and Responsibilities

In the United Kingdom we have spent the last decade refining a rights discourse brought to legal prominence by the incorporation of the European Convention on Human Rights in the Human Rights Act 1998. This discourse has led to a surge of positive creativity in the debates and arguments that have populated the legal landscape, both in family law and in other legal terrains. But that discourse has diverted our attention away from the concept of responsibility.

This distraction has been doubly problematic; firstly, the concept of responsibility was never particularly well theorised in family law before the advent of the human rights era. That work remained to be done. Most serious work on responsibility had focused on criminal and tort law and some had gone on to reflect on the attributes of public law (see Bridgeman and Keating's Introduction to this book). Secondly, responsibility became important in family legal doctrine when parental responsibility rose to prominence in the Children Act 1989. But the concept had never been fully explored in the context of the enactment of that legislation. And early critical writing on the idea was just developing when rights discourse seemed to overshadow it.

While the advent of human (and also children's) rights is to be welcomed, the problems that the advent of legal responsibility in family law had heralded have not diminished. The continuing fragmentation and complication of modern family life and the growing state interest in regulating family relationships (particularly, but by no means exclusively, after family failure) have joined other social developments to create a new sense of urgency in the quest for a careful consideration of the idea of responsibility in the context of family relationships. Describing responsibility in conceptual terms that are useful to criminal and public law scholars has provided us with only the most rudimentary tools for the analysis of responsibility in family relationships. The concept seems incomplete when brought to an analysis of the way in which working and fragmented families relate to legal structures.

In this book we have brought together commentators to begin to address the problems we have identified in distilling a role for law in framing family responsibilities. These commentators span disciplinary divides. The chapters presented here have sought to set out a variety of understandings of responsibility in family life and of the relationship between law and the responsibilities which family members have, and ought to have, for one another. The tension between legal and actual responsibility is never far below the surface; its underlying conditions remain unresolved. Yet we believe that these chapters will foster debate on the way in which responsibility works (and ought to work) in the family relationships that people create and in the legal rules that do (and ought to) govern those relationships.

In an ideal world we might be able to resolve the tensions that lie at the heart of the ambitions of this book. But we did not imagine we inhabited that world. Instead I wish to bring this book to a conclusion with a number of observations about the families we experience, the responsibility we bear, and the law that governs us. I hope these thoughts will serve as points of departure for an ongoing debate on the conceptual uses to which 'responsibility' might be put when dealing with family relationships.

The Tension between Legal and Moral Responsibility

In any discussion of responsibility a clear tension always emerges between the legal and moral dimensions of the subject. What *some* (even most) people do, and should do, is not always what the law can compel *all* people to do. Furthermore, the extent to which law can (or, indeed, should) involve itself in compelling compliance with moral responsibility is always debatable. This tension is particularly pointed in the context of discussions about the family. Our history and our underlying ideological adherence to individual freedom and individual autonomy make it clear that we continue to be sceptical about the uses to which law can be put in the regulation of personal relationships (see, for example, Article 8 of the ECHR). The idea that law can be used to compel family responsibility is approached with some caution (unlike the view that law can be used to compel responsibility in criminal law or in public law, for example). Yet we have arrived in an era in which the law is (arguably) more intimately involved in the regulation of family life than at any other point in our history. Every day judges resolve tensions between parents by settling the detailed features of the day to day care that they bring to their children's lives. Similarly the courts are routinely involved in settling the material responsibilities of adult family members whose family relationship is ending. The question we are called upon to address, therefore, is not whether or not law should be involved in regulating family responsibility, but how that role should be conceptualised and framed; it is the age-old question of the extent to which law should direct the responsibilities which arise in family relationships. What, in short, is the relationship between legal regulation and the moral responsibilities to which family relationships give rise?

Social Engineering and Legal Responsibility

In trying to resolve this question we must acknowledge the limitations of law when working as a device of social engineering. The relationship between law and morality has long been a contentious issue in legal philosophy. Most have written about it in the context, once again, of criminal law. But where injury (criminal and tort law) and even civil duty (public law) are in issue it is submitted that the need for directive law to give effect to moral principle (responsibility) is less difficult to justify than in the context of family life. In those circumstances it seems right that the moral responsibilities of individuals (not to injure others, or to represent the public interest so that citizens can trust their representatives) should bear some significant resemblance to their legal obligations. Responsibility can be theorised as directive and related to the purposes of law in those contexts.

But family relationships – and, therefore, family law – are different. The rights and obligations that arise out of family relationships have, for the better part of the history of sophisticated legal regulation, been devoid of legal 'teeth'. Law, the legal system and legal institutions have not been the preferred mechanisms for the framing or the enforcement of family responsibilities. Families were left to fulfil their responsibilities without legal intervention. Thus, the responsibilities of financial and other material support between married couples and in relation to their children; of consortium in the marital relationship; and of care and fidelity were not enforceable as legal rights. Or, at least, not enforceable in the way that a contractual obligation of financial support might have been. The personal element of the relationship, and our concern to allow human relationships to develop and flourish in their own inexplicable ways, demanded a legal interest that seemed disinterested. A different conception of legal duty or responsibility was at play.

That is not to say that the law has no role to play in relation to family responsibility. It is clearly engaged in setting some parameters to those responsibilities by creating particular rights that vest in some family members against others. These rights do, to some (limited) extent, reflect a social view of the responsibilities that family members have for one another. But this legal view of family responsibility can never be anything more than incomplete. The law cannot comprehensively set out the family responsibilities of family members. It can only express the positive obligations to which some kinds of family responsibility give rise. In her writing on children's rights O'Neill (1992)[1] has challenged this limited role for law in the framing of responsibility. In identifying what she calls 'imperfect obligations' O'Neill reminds us that our concerns in family life are to encourage a much wider array of responsible behaviours than the law is capable of establishing if it were to resort only to a doctrine of rights observance. A society can, she argues, use its laws, its legal system and its legal institutions (as well as other institutions of the state) to create a framework in which appropriate family responsibilities are encouraged. It is beyond dispute that some of our institutional arrangements do already attempt to achieve these ends (Part III of the CA 1989, for example). But what some of the chapters in this book have reminded us, is that the relationship between the state (and policy makers) and families needs to be more carefully and more honestly arranged if legal regulation of this kind is to work effectively (see Churchill in this book).

Where family responsibility is conceived in real families, and where the best practices of responsibility are adopted from those families by policy makers, their encouragement in the institutions of the state stands some chance of working. But

1 O'Neill, O. (1992), 'Children's Rights and Children's Lives' in Alston, P., Parker, S. and Seymour, J. (eds), *Children, Rights and the Law* (Oxford: Clarendon Press).

where the state feels itself able to attempt to define responsibility without recourse to the responsibilities that people in families feel, and without a sense of what responsibility means, it is clear that state policy is destined to failure. The kind of responsibility that will be fostered is not family responsibility at all.

Gender and Family Responsibility

One of the features of any study of family responsibility remains – even in this era in which the equality of women and men is universally (in policy terms) admired and pursued – that family labour (like labour market work) is deeply gendered. This feature of family responsibility remains problematic for anyone concerned with the way in which law and responsibility in the family should be structured. Any legal regime that acknowledges the gendered roles of those bearing family responsibility appears to create a trap which keeps people in their gendered role. And any attempt to undermine the gendered imperatives that operate in family work has the consequence of prejudicing those who actually do that work. Structuring law in this (gender neutral) way has the consequence of fostering social inequalities that are profoundly gendered.

This trap, it is submitted, remains one of the most intractable problems for law as it relates to the responsibilities that are borne in family work and because its impacts are so personal, so deeply felt, and so endemic, it impacts on all other realms of social life.

Status and Family Responsibility

Family responsibilities have, traditionally, vested in those who fulfil certain status requirements in relation to one another. Family, that has been, and still is, in our legal tradition, linked to status. Married people have responsibilities to one another, and parents have responsibility for their children (Lind in this book). Perhaps adult children even have responsibilities for their parents. In an era in which our adherence to status-based understandings of the family has been considerably weakened, our understandings of the consequences for family responsibility have become more uncertain. But the problem is even more confused than that. Family relationships have, in the past, suffered from problems of status; the absence of formal marriage, or difficulties of establishing paternity are not new, and that did cause problems for the law of an earlier era in the allocation of family responsibilities. But in that earlier era status could be rekindled by reliance on other social conventions. Unmarried relationships could be regarded as marriage, parents could be identified by circumstantial evidence and compliance with norms of responsibility flowed from those (status-based) relationships.

Fragmenting and Shifting Family Patterns and Family Responsibility

The current era is much less certain. Families and family membership are not just uncertain in terms of their status; they are also flexible. We no longer concern ourselves if people decide to change their spouses (or their long-standing, unmarried partners). We do not even mind children moving from one home to another. The move away from status-based relationships and the introduction of much greater flexibility into our family relationships (not to mention the social movement towards gender equality) have altered the way in which we think family life should be lived. They have clouded our understandings of family responsibilities (Diduck in this book).

If families are more complicated the responsibilities to which they give rise have also grown in complexity. What responsibilities do people have for one another in these new floating families? How do we know what they are? Can the law create and enforce responsibilities which were not there before? These are some of the questions which our authors have addressed and attempted to answer. But they will remain contested and their answers will remain unclear for as long as flexible norms of family life are embraced (see Wade in this book). Law's role in this confusion is not easily settled. Is family responsibility limited to the existing family – what happens when it ends? Are some family relationships perpetual – never capable of being ended? Should the law foster a more inevitable family? Or does the 'clean' break still work in family responsibility?

Of course, the shifting of the parameters of families has also meant that the law has had to become more intimately involved in the ordering of family responsibilities. Moving children from home to home raises disputes which the courts have been called upon to settle. Divorcing (and separating unmarried) couples also have recourse to law to resolve the disputes in which they find themselves. Law has found a new role in policing at least some of the 'responsibilities' of the family. The responsibilities that the law would not consider enforcing during a relationship, it is now routinely called upon to resolve when the relationship flounders. This vigorous role for law has created the space in which law can conceive of a framing role for family responsibilities. It can dictate the kinds of responsibilities that it will demand should be met after the relationship ends, giving us a sense of what sorts of family responsibilities are to be met during the currency of a family relationship. Once again, however, questions arise as to how the law should resolve to settle these more easily defined responsibilities which it seeks to enforce. Should we look to family practices to distil responsibility (Wade and Morrow in this book), or is there some ideological context which we should draw on to frame our attributions of responsibility?

The Variety of Family Relationships and Family Responsibility

Finally, in the context of any discussion of family responsibility, 'family' is of central importance. We have acknowledged the fragmented nature of the modern family and our ideological embrace of diversity in family relationships. But there are still some noticeable features of family life that serve as the focus for our attempts to frame ideas of family responsibility. Perhaps it is in noting the distinctive features of different types of family relationships that we will be better able to reduce responsibility in the family to terms that are more easily digested. I will, therefore, end this chapter with some observations on the different types of family relationships that preoccupy us. I will try to outline the particular problems, for ideas of responsibility, to which each kind of family relationship gives rise.

Adult responsibilities for children

Our most commonly accepted conception of family responsibility is in relation to the care that parents (or adults) owe to (their) children (see Freeman in this book). This intergenerational dimension of family responsibility posits vulnerability and age as the central features of the responsibility relationship. But responsibility does not simply revolve around vulnerability and dependence (see James in this book). If it did, all those who were not vulnerable would have responsibility for all those who were (potentially collectively, and not simply individually). The responsibilities which adults have for children in family relationships also revolve around a status relationship; parents are presumed to provide care and support for their children (see Collier in this book). If they fail to do so the law finds people to substitute as parents and to fulfil those responsibilities. These people are given something akin to status in the legal recognition that is accorded to them. But what about the many others – who are never 'sanctioned' by law to bear responsibility – who do from time to time conduct themselves with a proper sense of responsibility for children? What is their place in the legal framework that we establish to frame responsibility? We know that many are involved in the care of children (Morrow in this book). How is the law to acknowledge their role? The problem for law is not how to create a status for these people but how to encourage an appropriate exercise of responsibility by all those who come into contact with children without having to accord status to them. Family responsibility and social responsibility are inevitably linked, but the terms of that connection remain unclear (Diduck in this book). Determining a better description for responsibility might assist in achieving a better idea of that connection.

Adult responsibility for vulnerable adult family members

There is a similarity between the vulnerability which frames family responsibility in relation to children and the responsibility which many adults take upon themselves for their aging relatives (most often, but not always, their parents) (see Herring and Williams in this book). It is, again, intergenerational responsibility. But, because the vulnerability does not occur at a time and in consequence of an immediate relationship of dependence, our legal prescriptions for responsibility follow a more difficult trajectory. We have to find a basis for responsibility which seems more difficult in these circumstances than is the case where responsibility for children is in issue. Our justifications for requiring responsibility seem to be less firmly established. And the nature of the responsibility which we feel to be appropriate remains unresolved.

Adult responsibility for similarly situated adults

The responsibilities which independent, capable adults have for one another is, perhaps, one of the most difficult to resolve. We know that people do undertake these responsibilities and we do, in many circumstances, expect those responsibilities to be borne – as a matter of morality – by those involved (often because there are children whose care is also at stake). But we are less adept at finding ways of using the law to frame and resolve these legal dilemmas. Who should have responsibility for whom? Should we wait for formal relationships before responsibility arises? And what is the content of the responsibilities borne in these adult relationships? Can the law be a participant in framing and enforcing these responsibilities? Or can responsibility only be imputed to relationships which are defined by reference to discernible responsibilities (contract or marriage, for example). Again these questions remain open and unresolved.

The state's responsibility for family members

The final relationship that requires consideration is not a family relationship at all, but one which has risen in prominence in the last century. Family responsibility may have been left beyond the ambit of a proper analysis of the moral foundations of responsibility because it was beyond the gaze of society. Family relationships were the business of those in them, and not the business of the state. The state's only role seemed to be to protect that privacy. That is clearly no longer the case. When we talk of family responsibility today we are also talking about the responsibility that the state bears both for the family as an idea (as a social institution) and for the members of the family in relation to each other. The state polices the family and it fills any void left by inadequate family practices. But what are the parameters of state involvement? Does the state only become involved as a last resort or is earlier intervention in settling family responsibility necessary? That too has been a pressing concern of this book (see, in particular, Keating, Churchill and Bridgeman in this book).

Conclusion

Family, responsibility and the law are, it is clear, inextricably linked. What we have tried to do in this volume is to discuss the ways in which they are linked. We have not set out to resolve a role for each in relation to the other. But we have explored what roles there might be for each in relation to the other. Each is of some conceptual importance in this society and in the way in which this society progresses. A more critical approach to each is, therefore, of considerable importance. This book represents a contribution to the development of a critical understanding of the responsibilities which family members have for one another and the legal rules that frame that responsibility.

Index

For Product Safety Concerns and Information please contact our EU representative GPSR@taylorandfrancis.com
Taylor & Francis Verlag GmbH, Kaufingerstraße 24, 80331 München, Germany

www.ingramcontent.com/pod-product-compliance
Ingram Content Group UK Ltd.
Pitfield, Milton Keynes, MK11 3LW, UK
UKHW020015200926
475702UK00014B/1901
9781138270527